Quantitative Economics and Development

Essays in Memory of Ta-Chung Liu

This is a Volume in
ECONOMIC THEORY, ECONOMETRICS, AND MATHEMATICAL ECONOMICS

A series of Monographs and Textbooks

Consulting Editor: KARL SHELL

A complete list of titles in this series appears at the end of this volume.

Quantitative Economics and Development

Essays in Memory of Ta-Chung Liu

Edited by

L. R. KLEIN

Department of Economics
University of Pennsylvania
Philadelphia, Pennsylvania

M. NERLOVE

Department of Economics
Northwestern University
Evanston, Illinois

S. C. TSIANG

Department of Economics
Cornell University
Ithaca, New York

 1980

ACADEMIC PRESS
A Subsidiary of Harcourt Brace Jovanovich, Publishers
New York   London   Toronto   Sydney   San Francisco

COPYRIGHT © 1980, BY ACADEMIC PRESS, INC.
ALL RIGHTS RESERVED.
NO PART OF THIS PUBLICATION MAY BE REPRODUCED OR
TRANSMITTED IN ANY FORM OR BY ANY MEANS, ELECTRONIC
OR MECHANICAL, INCLUDING PHOTOCOPY, RECORDING, OR ANY
INFORMATION STORAGE AND RETRIEVAL SYSTEM, WITHOUT
PERMISSION IN WRITING FROM THE PUBLISHER.

ACADEMIC PRESS, INC.
111 Fifth Avenue, New York, New York 10003

United Kingdom Edition published by
ACADEMIC PRESS, INC. (LONDON) LTD.
24/28 Oval Road, London NW1 7DX

Library of Congress Cataloging in Publication Data
Main entry under title:

Quantitative economics and development.

(Economic theory, econometrics, and mathematical economics)
Includes index.
1. Economics, Mathematical--Addresses, essays, lectures. 2. Econometrics--Addresses, essays, lectures. 3. Economic development--Mathematical models--Addresses, essays, lectures. 4. Taiwan--Economic conditions--Addresses, essays, lectures. 5. Liu, Ta–Chung.
I. Liu, Ta–Chung. II. Klein, Lawrence Robert.
III. Nerlove, Marc, Date. IV. Tsiang, Sho–chieh.
HB135.Q34   330'.01'51   79–8855
ISBN 0–12–413350–9

PRINTED IN THE UNITED STATES OF AMERICA

80 81 82 83   9 8 7 6 5 4 3 2 1

Contents

List of Contributors	ix
Preface	xi
Ta-Chung Liu, 1914–1975	xiii
Publications of Ta-Chung Liu	xvii

Society, Politics, and Economic Development Revisited
I. ADELMAN, CYNTHIA TAFT MORRIS, AND SVANTE WOLD

Disjoint Principal-Components Method	2
Statistical Results	5
Principal-Components Analysis within Groups	7
Conclusion	17
References	17

On Global Stability of Some Stochastic Economic Processes: A Synthesis
R. N. BHATTACHARYA AND M. K. MAJUMDAR

I. Introduction	19
II. Basic Definitions	20
III. Some Economic Examples	24
IV. Invariant Measures for Diffusions	27
V. Stability Results for the Economic Models	38
References	42

The Design of Mechanisms for Efficient Allocation of Public Goods
WILLIAM A. BROCK

I. Introduction	45
II. A Simple Method	48
III. The Design Problem under Coalition Formation	51
IV. Examples of Quadratic Incentive Design Using (3.3) and (3.4)	58

V.	Externalities in Consumption	61
VI.	The Design of Individually Incentive Compatible Mechanisms in an Abstract Setting	66
VII.	The Design of Mechanisms for Efficient Accumulation of Public Capital	73
VIII.	Suggestions for Further Research and Summary	78
	References	79

Critical Observations on the Labor Theory of Value and Sraffa's Standard Commodity

EDWIN BURMEISTER

I.	Introduction	81
II.	A Single Leontief–Sraffa Technique of Production	82
III.	A Pure Labor Theory of Value at Positive Profit Rates	83
IV.	Necessary and Sufficient Conditions for a Pure Labor Theory of Value in a Leonteif–Sraffa Technology	84
V.	Sraffa's Standard Commodity	88
VI.	Sraffa's "Real Wage" Measure and the Constant-Returns-to-Scale Assumption	92
VII.	A Pure Labor Theory of Neoclassical Production Functions	94
VIII.	Simultaneous Validity of the Pure Labor Theory and the Neoclassical Parable	96
IX.	A Few Fundamental Objections	100
	References	102

The Selection of Variables for Use in Prediction

GREGORY C. CHOW

I.	The Problem	105
II.	Hotelling's Solution	106
III.	A Geometric Interpretation of Hotelling's Solution	106
IV.	Solution for Two Sets of Fixed Variates	108
V.	Solution for Many Sets of Fixed Variates	112
VI.	The Multivariate Case	112
VII.	Concluding Remarks	113
	References	114

Regression When Each of Two Variables Is Dependent Some of the Time

CARL F. CHRIST

I.	Introduction and Summary	115
II.	The Estimating Equation for $\hat{\beta}$ in a Simple Regression	117
III.	The Estimating Equation for $\hat{\beta}$ in a Multiple Regression	119
IV.	The Estimator of $\hat{\beta}$	120
V.	Generalization to a Simultaneous Equation Model	121

An Exploratory Policy-Oriented Econometric Model of a Metropolitan Area: Boston
ROBERT F. ENGLE

I. Introduction	123
II. Distinctive Features of the Model	124
III. Individual Sectoral Models	129
IV. Simulations	146
V. Conclusion	154
Appendix: Variable Names	154
References	156

The Effect of Simple Specification Error on the Coefficients of "Unaffected" Variables 157
FRANKLIN M. FISHER

References	163

Temporal Aggregation and Econometric Models
GARY FROMM AND E. C. HWA

I. Introduction	165
II. Time Aggregation and Structural Specification	167
III. Time Aggregation of Forecasting Errors	169
IV. Time Aggregation and Linear Regression	171
V. Effects of Measurement Errors	174
VI. Empirical Tests	176
VII. Error Analysis	191
VIII. Policy Responsiveness	195
IX. Conclusion	221
Appendix	222
References	223

Recent Economic Fluctuations and Stabilization Policies: An Optimal Control Approach
LAWRENCE R. KLEIN AND VINCENT SU

I. Introduction and Summary	225
II. Experimental Design	229
III. Dynamic Multiplier	233
IV. The Optimal Control Solutions	239
V. A Final Correction	245
VI. An Algorithmic Variation	252
References	254

Notes on Income Distribution in Taiwan
SIMON KUZNETS

I. Introduction	255
II. Changes to Income Distribution, 1964–1975	258
III. Distribution among Groups by Occupation of Household Head, 1964–1975	264
IV. Differences in Per Worker Product between A and Non-A Sectors, and Disparities in Per Person Income between Farmer and Nonfarmer Households	273
V. Concluding Comments	278
References	280

On the Uniqueness of the Representation of Commodity-Augmenting Technical Change
LAWRENCE J. LAU

I. Introduction	281
II. Statement of the Problem	283
III. The Main Theorem	284
IV. Conclusion	288
References	289

Technological Change and Growth Performance in Taiwan Agriculture, 1946–1975
ERIK THORBECKE AND JACKSON KARUNASEKERA

I. Introduction	291
II. Growth Performance of the Agricultural Sector	292
III. Choice of Techniques in Taiwan's Agriculture	297
IV. Relative Income Shares and Technological Change in the Agricultural Sector	304
V. Conclusions	306
References	307

Exchange Rate, Interest Rate, and Economic Development
S. C. TSIANG

I. Introduction	309
II. Objections to Our Proposals and the Invalidity or Irrelevance of Their Arguments	314
III. The Effects of Our Proposals on the Economic Development of Taiwan	329
References	345

List of Contributors

Numbers in parentheses indicate the pages on which the authors' contributions begin.

I. ADELMAN (1), Department of Agriculture and Resource Economics, University of California, Berkeley, California 94720

R. N. BHATTACHARYA (19), Department of Mathematics, The University of Tucson, Tucson, Arizona 85724

WILLIAM A. BROCK (45), Department of Economics, The University of Chicago, Chicago, Illinois 60637

EDWIN BURMEISTER (81), Department of Economics, University of Virginia, Charlottesville, Virginia 22901

GREGORY C. CHOW (105), Princeton University, Princeton, New Jersey 08540

CARL F. CHRIST (115), Department of Political Economy, Johns Hopkins University, Baltimore, Maryland 21218

ROBERT F. ENGLE (123), Department of Economics, University of California, San Diego, La Jolla, California 92093

FRANKLIN M. FISHER (157), Department of Economics, Massachusetts Institute of Technology, Cambridge, Massachusetts 02139

GARY FROMM (165), SRI International, Arlington, Virginia 22209

E. C. HWA* (165), SRI International, Springfield, Virginia 22152

JACKSON KARUNASEKERA† (291), Commonwealth Secretariat, London, England

LAWRENCE R. KLEIN (225), Department of Economics, University of Pennsylvania, Philadelphia, Pennsylvania 19104

SIMON KUZNETS (255), Department of Economics, Harvard University, Cambridge, Massachusetts 02138

*Present address: International Monetary Fund, Washington, D.C.
†Present address: Department of Economics, Cornell University, Ithaca, New York 14853.

LAWRENCE J. LAU (281), Department of Economics, Stanford University, Stanford, California 94305

M. K. MAJUMDAR (19), Department of Economics, Cornell University, Ithaca, New York 14853

CYNTHIA TAFT MORRIS (1), Department of Economics, The American University, Washington, D.C. 20016

VINCENT SU (225), Baruch College, City University of New York, New York, New York 10010

ERIK THORBECKE (291), Department of Economics, Cornell University, Ithaca, New York 14853

S. C. TSIANG (309), Department of Economics, Cornell University, Ithaca, New York 14853

SVANTE WOLD (1), Department of Chemistry, Umeå University, Umeå, Sweden

Preface

Ta-Chung Liu suffered an untimely death in 1975, just prior to the third World Congress of the Econometric Society in Toronto. We recognized his parting at that congress, but many of us felt that a more lasting tribute would be more fitting to his honor and our memory of him.

Ta-Chung's professional career was centered at Cornell University, but he also spent considerable time at the International Monetary Fund, as Visiting Professor at Johns Hopkins, and as a consultant to the government of Taiwan. Some of those who knew him and were influenced by him at those places or in other professional encounters were brought together by their mutual respect and desire to honor him in order to put together this volume in his memory.

Some of the contributors are former students of Ta-Chung Liu, and he was truly an inspirational teacher with fruitful issue. Others are colleagues and economists who interacted with him over the years of his active career.

We believe, dear Ta-Chung, that we have produced a volume that is worthy of your high standards for scholarship.

LAWRENCE KLEIN
MARC NERLOVE
S. C. TSIANG

Ta-Chung Liu, 1914–1975 *

Ta-Chung was always a prodigious worker. His enormous energy and productivity astounded all of us who knew him and was, we suspect, due in no small part to the great support and help which his wife, Ya-Chao, gave him throughout his career. Although Ta-Chung first studied engineering in China, and later in the United States at Cornell University, it was as a student at Cornell that he enountered Professor Fritz Machlup, whose influence, Ta-Chung once said, was responsible for his conversion to economics. Ta-Chung mastered his chosen field with extraordinary rapidity, and received his Ph.D. in Economics from Cornell in 1940. Much of his dissertation was later published by the Brookings Institution in 1946 and dealt with China's national income from 1931 to 1936. It was, as far as we know, the first attempt to construct national accounts for China. Concern with the statistical data of China and construction of national accounts for that country were themes which were to occupy him throughout his professional career. In 1959, he reported preliminary estimates of the national income of China from 1952 to 1959, and these were later amplified and incorporated together with his earlier work, in his massive study with K. C. Yeh, *The Economy of the Chinese Mainland: National Income and Economic Development, 1933-59*, published by Princeton in 1965. His work on the Chinese economy and concern with the basic data resulted in many other publications and statements before the Joint Economic Committee of the Congress of the United States in 1967 and 1972. Few econometricians of his stature and high level of technical competence have been as concerned as Ta-Chung was with the basic data, which are the raw material of econometric models, and to which he was often to apply the most sophisticated of econometric methods.

As econometric modeling spreads from the United States to other developed market economies and to those of developing and socialist nations,

*Reprinted with permission from *Econometrica* **45**, No. 2, 529–530 (March 1977).

it is clear that we know very little about the economy of China. Eventually, we can expect to have input–output and macroeconometric models for China that are the equal of those now being prepared for the USSR and other socialist countries, and it is certain that researchers who achieve success in this endeavor will build significantly on the deep work already done by Ta-Chung.

Although much of Ta-Chung's later work dealt with econometric models and methods, he had more general interests in national economic policy and in problems of international trade and international monetary affairs. He not only wrote several important scholarly papers in these areas, but also had considerable practical experience during the Second World War as Assistant Commercial Counselor in the Chinese Embassy and as the Secretary of the Chinese delegation to Bretton Woods, and he was, for ten years, an economist with the International Monetary Fund in Washington, D.C., before taking a professorship at Cornell.

Beginning in 1954, Ta-Chung began a series of visits to Taiwan, which were to prove of the greatest significance to the development of that economy and which culminated in his Chairmanship of the Commission on Tax Reform (1968–1970) and the award of the Order of Bright Star with Grand Cordon, Second Class, by the Republic of China. His first trip in 1954 was with Tsiang to study the problems of the balance of payments and foreign exchange reserves. As a result of their advice, Taiwan abolished an extremely complicated system of multiexchange rates and effectively adopted a floating rate. The expansion of Tawian's exports and the accelerated growth of the economy were due in no small part to this reform.

In 1964, Ta-Chung once again journeyed to Taiwan, this time to assist in economic planning. As a good econometrician, he was quick to point out that sound policy must be based on an accurate aggregate econometric model of the economy, and, typically, when he found the basic data were not sufficient or reliable enough for this purpose, he set to work to improve them and to construct for important variables series which had not existed heretofore. In the course of his work he not only built an econometric model for Taiwan, but he developed an interindustry input–output table for the economy and improved the national income statistics.

Beginning in 1968, as Chairman of the Commission on Tax Reform, Ta-Chung took a more active role in policy formulation and implementation. He was able to check widespread tax evasion by computerizing the collection process and through a series of reforms which also reduced the burden of low-income taxpayers and increased the progressivity of the tax structure. Other reforms were also suggested to encourage more investment in capital-intensive industries and to substitute a value-added tax for the previous haphazard system of specific commodity taxes.

Finally, in 1973, he led a team of experts which made a number of proposals for monetary reform and for freeing money and exchange markets from artificial constraints. Few econometricians have been so actively engaged in the formulation of economic policy or so influential in the course of economic development of any country.

Beginning quite early in his career, perhaps stemming from his interest in the construction of national income accounts, Ta-Chung worked on a series of models of the U.S. economy and successively refined these models to apply to shorter and shorter time periods. In these efforts he was concerned, as always, with the development of the basic data, and he published estimates of national product components by month as early as 1951. His first annual model of the U.S. economy was published in 1955, and in 1963 he published an exploratory quarterly econometric model for the U.S. postwar economy. By 1969 he had published his first monthly econometric model of the United States, and in 1974 a more refined and elaborate version of his monthly model was published in the *International Economic Review*. He was able to construct not only a national monthly model but one for New York State as well! His national model and data were entered in the calculations of the Seminar on Comparisons of Econometric Models and came out very well in the final tabulations. In particular, Ta-Chung's monthly simulations compared favorably with those from the best of the quarterly models and looked especially promising when averaged into quarterly value. A significant breakthrough could yet be achieved in the use of monthly models constructed along the lines pioneered by Ta-Chung.

Besides his concern with macroeconometric models, we should not fail to mention Ta-Chung's important book, with George Hildebrand, on manufacturing production functions, using cross-section data for the United States. This study led to a great deal of debate and deepened our understanding of the problems of estimating economic relations from cross-sectional data.

Ta-Chung's interests in econometrics extended well beyond the problems of model construction into the more esoteric realms of methodology. But, as always, he drew inspiration from practical problems, and his papers on underidentification, structural estimation and forecasting, the effects of aggregation over time, and testing for identifiability, concern problems which he encountered in his more practical work.

In connection with the identification problem, he noted, quite correctly, that, in the spirit of the true Walrasian system, everything depends on everything else; therefore, the a priori constraints in the form of nil effects attributed to several variables in each individual equation of a complete model are, at best, suspect. These a priori zero restrictions are the principal means by which we identify our equations in econometric systems. If we reject these dubious restrictions, the structure of the economy is basically under-identified and the best that we can hope for is to estimate reduced form equations. These ideas set forth by Ta-Chung led Franklin Fisher to generalize the concept of identification to encompass "near identification," where coefficients may not be zero but have only small effects on other variables in a given relationship.

Ta-Chung's career, cut short by his untimely death, was a remarkable one which blended an interest in basic data and sophisticated econometric theory with the practical concerns of national income accounting and econometric modeling and, above all, with policy formulation and implementation. He was, and is, an inspiration to all of us who knew him and his work.

LAWRENCE R. KLEIN
MARC NERLOVE
S. C. TSIANG

Publications of Ta-Chung Liu *

I. General

A. Book

Manufacturing Production Functions in the United States, 1957: An Inter-Industry and Interstate Comparison of Productivity. Ithaca, New York: School of Industrial and Labor Relations, Cornell University, 1965 (with George H. Hildebrand).

B. Articles

A monthly econometric model of the U.S. economy, *International Economic Review*, June, 1974 (with E. C. Hwa).

Effects of aggregation over time on dynamic characteristics of an econometric model, in *Econometric Models of Cyclical Behavior*, B. G. Hickman, editor. New York: National Bureau of Economic Research, 1972 (with R. F. Engle).

The covariance matrix of the limited information estimator and identification test, *Econometrica*, April, 1969 (with William Breen).

Reply to Comments by A. R. Bergstrom, F. M. Fisher, and J. B. Kadane, on the preceding article in *Econometrica*, September, 1972.

A monthly recursive econometric model of United States: A test of feasibility, *The Review of Economics and Statistics*, February, 1969.

An exploratory quarterly econometric model of effective demand in the postwar U.S. economy, *Econometrica*, July, 1963.

Structural estimation and forecasting: A critique of the Cowles Commission method, *Tsing-Hua Journal* (in English), June, 1963. (Issue in honor of Professor Franklin Ho.)

Underidentification, structural estimation and forecasting, *Econometrica*, October, 1960. Reprinted in *Selected Readings in Econometrics from Econometrica*, J. W. Hooper and M. Nerlove, editors. Cambridge, Massachusetts: MIT Press, 1970.

A simple forecasting model of the U.S. economy, *International Monetary Fund Staff Papers*, August, 1955.

Stability of the exchange rate mechanism in a multi-country system, *Econometrica*, July, 1954 (with J. J. Polak).

*Reprinted with permission from *Econometrica* **45**, No. 2, 529–530 (March 1977).

The elasticity of U.S. import demand: A theoretical and empirical reappraisal, *International Monetary Fund Staff Papers*, February, 1954.

Employment, production and national security programs in the United States, *International Monetary Fund Staff Papers*, April, 1952.

Monthly estimates of certain national product components, 1946–49, *The Review of Economics and Statistics*, August, 1951 (with C. G. Chang).

U. S. consumption and investment propensities: Prewar and postwar, *American Economic Review*, September, 1950 (with C. G. Chang).

Rejoinder to Comments by F. M. Bator, T. Mayer, and G. C. Means on the preceding article, *American Economic Review*, March, 1953.

The construction of national income tables and international comparisons of national incomes, Part 4 in *Studies in Income and Wealth*, Volume 8. New York: National Bureau of Economic Research, 1946.

C. Notes and Comments

Discussion of "Survey of U.S. models," in *The Brookings Model: Perspectives and Recent Development*, G. Fromm and L. R. Klein, editors. Amsterdam: North-Holland Pub. Co., 1974.

Comment on What is output? Problems of concept and measurement, by A. B. Treadway, in *Production and Productivity in the Service Industries*, Victor R. Fuchs, editor, *Studies in Income and Wealth*, Volume 34, New York: National Bureau of Economic Research, 1969.

Comment on Changing factor shares by industry: Factor prices and factor substitutions, by A. C. Egbert, in *The Industrial Composition of Income and Product*, John W. Kendrick, editor. New York: National Bureau of Economic Research, 1968.

Comment on Asset identities in economic models, by Kenneth Boulding, *Studies in Income and Wealth*. New York: National Bureau of Economic Research, New York, 1952.

II. Quantitative Studies of the Chinese Economy

A. Books

The Economy of the Chinese Mainland: National Income and Economic Development, 1933–59. Princteon, New Jersey: Princeton University Press, 1965 (with K. C. Yeh).

Co-editor, *Economic Trends in Communist China*. Chicago, Illinois: Aldine, 1968. (Other editors: Walter Galenson and Alexander Eckstein.) Author of Chapter 3, Quantitative trends, in this volume.

China's National Income, 1931–36. The Brookings Institution, Washington, D.C.: 1946.

B. Articles and Other

Chinese and other Asian economies: A quantitative evaluation, *The American Economic Review (Papers and Proceedings)*, May, 1973 (with K. C. Yeh).

Statement prepared for the Joint Economic Committee, in *Economic Development in Mainland China: Hearings Before the Joint Economic Committee*. Washington, D.C.: Congress of the United States, June, 1972.

PUBLICATIONS OF TA-CHUNG LIU

The tempo of economic development of the Chinese Mainland, 1949–65, in *An Economic Profile of Mainland China*. Washington, D.C.: Joint Economic Committee, Congress of the United States, 1967.

Statement prepared for the Joint Economic Committee, in *Mainland China in the World Economy: Hearings Before the Joint Economic Committee*. Washington, D.C.: Congress of the United States, April, 1967.

Chinese economic statistics, in *International Encyclopedia of the Social Sciences*, 1968.

Preliminary estimates of the national income of the Chinese Mainland, 1952–59, *The American Economic Review*, May, 1959.

China's foreign exchange problems: A proposed solution, *American Economic Review*, June, 1941.

Society, Politics, and Economic Development Revisited

A Disjoint Principal-Components Analysis

I. ADELMAN, CYNTHIA TAFT MORRIS,
and
SVANTE WOLD

The present paper compares results obtained with two different statistical techniques applied to the same body of data. The data describe the economic, social, and political traits of 74 developing nations during 1955–1963 (Adelman and Morris, 1967). The purpose is to see whether the implications concerning the modernization processes involved in economic development draw on the basis of previous analyses are confirmed or not (Adelman and Morris, 1967, 1968, 1969, 1973a,b; Adelman et al., 1969).

A new method of analysis, that of disjoint principal-components models, is applied to the Adelman–Morris data. The method is a method of pattern recognition developed for applications in the chemical and biological sciences by S. Wold.[1] It simultaneously classifies observations into groups and derives models of variable interactions within each of the groups. The criterion used for classification is both the homogeneity of model fit within

---

[1] Wold, S. (1976). We are indebted to H. Wold for calling this method to our attention. The results discussed here were first presented at the Third World Congress of the Econometric Society in the Group Report by Wold (1975).

groups and the degree of difference between models among groups. The method is therefore theoretically appealing for those interested in classification for subsequent theory construction. Unlike other classification techniques, the criterion used is not primarily the degree of separation *between* group boundaries; it is rather the similarity in response patterns, or processes of change, or interaction *within* groups. The groups are constructed so as to "behave" in a homogeneous fashion.

The method achieves in a single step what was done in two steps in the earlier Adelman–Morris analysis (1967). The Adelman–Morris analysis first classified countries into three groups, then fit factor analyses within each group. But, to achieve theoretically satisfying models within groups much iteration between classification and modeling was necessary to determine where to draw group boundaries. The present analysis is both more economical of effort and likely to yield better results, since it performs classification and model fitting simultaneously, thereby in essence optimizing the classification with respect to model fit.

The results of the two analyses compare quite closely, both with respect to country classifications and with respect to their characterizations of development processes.

Disjoint Principal-Components Method

This method offers a transitional procedure for the modeling of complex phenomena with soft data.[2] The method starts with the principle that the observations in each of several classes are in some way similar. In the present application the classes are defined by the broad similarity in levels and patterns of economic development. Given data describing traits of the observations which are presumed a priori to be relevant to the phenomenon studied, principal-components analysis is applied to derive for each class a model summarizing the patterns of behavior of the observations within that class. One fits to each class the principal-components model

$$(1) \qquad Y_{ij} = \alpha_1 + \sum_{k}^{\kappa} \beta_{ik} P_{kj} + \varepsilon_{ij},$$

where the Y_{ij} is an element of the matrix of observations on variable i and object j, there are κ principal components, P_{kj}, and a set of residuals ε_{ij}.

---

[2] For a discussion of the implications for the philosophy of science of such approaches to modeling, see Wold (1975). Wold uses causal models with blocks of latent variables. See Wold (1976a, b).

[For simplicity of notation, the class index is omitted from all the parameters of (1).] Once the set of disjoint models is obtained, one for each class, further observations for which the correct classification is in doubt can be fitted to each class model and assigned to that model to which the fit is closest.[3] Degrees of similarity between classes can be computed and measures of the importance of each variable in accounting for both within-class and between-class variations can be evaluated.

Once the principal-components model has been estimated for each reference class, the method is then used to calculate the distance of each unclassified observation from the model for each class in order to determine in which class it should be placed. This is done for each class model separately by treating the variable values for the unclassified observation (less the mean for each variable) as the dependent variable in a linear regression in which the independent variables are the estimated coefficients β_{ik} relating variables to components. One calculates, for each observation in each class,

$$(2) \qquad Y_{ij} - \alpha_i = \sum_{k=1}^{K} b_k \beta_{ik} + \varepsilon_{ij},$$

where, again, the class index is omitted for notational simplicity. The result yields a set of coefficients b_k relating the variable values for the observation to the variable loadings of the components, together with a set of residuals ε_{ij} indicating the deviations of the variable values for the observation from the estimated line of relationship. The variance of these residuals

$$(3) \qquad S_j^2 = \sum_{i=1}^{I} \varepsilon_{ij/(I-K)}^2$$

standardized for degrees of freedom, indicates the distance of the observation from the model for the class. The calculation is made separately for each class model treating the observation as the dependent variable in regressions involving the principal-components model for each class. The observation is then assigned to the class for which its distance from the class model is the least provided it is also less than, say, two standard deviations away from the class model.

A matrix of the degree of similarity between all pairs of classes is obtained by fitting the observations for a given class to the models for all other classes. The variance of the observations when fitted to each other class model is

---

[3] The possibility that the observation belongs to an unidentified class is kept in mind. Observations were assigned to a class only if their distance from the class model is less than a prespecified multiple of the standard deviation of objects already in the class.

then compared to their variance when fitted to their own class model. If we let

$$S_{rq}^2 = \sum_{j=1}^{Jr} S_{jq/Jr}^2 \qquad (4)$$

denote the value of the variance for objects in class r (Jr in number) fitted to the model of class q, then the ratio

$$R = S_{rq}^2/S_{rr}^2 \qquad (5)$$

is the ratio of their variance, when fitted to a given alternative class, to their variance when fitted to their own class. The larger R the greater the distance between the two classes. That is, the greater the extent to which a given "correct" class model produces smaller residuals than do other class models for a given set of observations, the greater is the degree of separation between that class and other classes.

If there are three or more variables, one can obtain a measure of the explanatory power of each variable. The combined variance of the residuals from all the class models for a given variable is compared with its total variance for the original data. The combined variance of the class residuals over all Q classes

$$\sigma_{\varepsilon i}^2 = \sum_{q=1}^{Q} \sum_{j=1}^{J_q} \varepsilon_{ij}^2/(J_q - K_q - 1) \qquad (6)$$

represents the portion of the total sample variance for the given variable which is not explained by the class models. The explained portion is simply the difference between the total variance σ_i^2 and the variance of the class residuals. The proportion of total variance of a given variable that is explained by the class models

$$\sigma_{\varepsilon i/\sigma_i^2}^2 \qquad (7)$$

is thus a measure of its relevance to within-class variations.

One can also compute the importance of each variable in discriminating between classes. For a given variable one compares the variance of the class residuals when all observations are fitted to the classes to which they "belong" with the variance of the class residuals when all observations are fitted successively to those classes to which they do not "belong." It should be noted that the variances being compared cover different populations of observations. The variance with observations correctly classified counts each observation only once. The variance with observations incorrectly classified includes for each observation as many residuals as there are classes other than its own class. The ratio of the variance with "incorrect" assignments divided by $(Q - 1)$ to the variance with "correct" assignments gives a measure of the discriminatory power of the variable. The higher the ratio, the greater is the contribution of the variable to the correct assignment of individual observations.

The method of disjoint principal-components models has the great advantage that it enables one simultaneously to derive models summarizing the behavior of observations within each of a set of classes and to assign unclassified observations on the basis of the structure and processes most characteristic of each class. This procedure contrasts with other procedures that assign unclassified observations on the basis of estimated boundaries between classes. The advantage of the method over more conventional analysis-of-variance techniques is similar to the advantage of estimation procedures that make use of knowledge of the structural relationships among a set of interacting variables rather than relying on reduced form or single equation approaches. The method is extremely flexible in permitting exploration of a phenomenon where a priori knowledge is rather limited with minimal specification of the relationships among the variables. It can be used either for study of the nature of the structure and processes characteristic of each class; or it can be used for the purpose of classifying observations of uncertain classification; or it can be used for both.

Statistical Results

County Classification

In the original Adelman–Morris (A–M) study, 74 noncommunist developing nations were classified into three level-of-development groups: Low, Intermediate, and High. The classification was based on factor scores on the first factor in a factor analysis including 41 variables describing salient aspects of each country's economic, sociocultural, and political traits. After the split into subgroups a separate factor analytic model was fit to each group, and the results used to infer the nature of the development process at various stages of modernization.

We shall first compare the original A–M country classification with that obtained using disjoint principal components. In the next section, we shall compare the within-class models obtained with the two techniques.

To start the classification process by disjoint principal components we require a reference (or learning) set. Using the previous A–M classification of 74 nations, two reference sets were formed by selecting eight nations in the Low class, seven in the Intermediate, and nine in the High. In reference set one (S_1), in each class, the nations were selected so as to lie in the center of the

TABLE 1
Residual Mean Squares (rms) for Reference Sets (2 Principal Components)

Class	S_1			S_2		
	Low	Intermediate	High	Low	Intermediate	High
Class						
Low	0.063	0.112	0.156	0.051	0.129	0.210
Intermediate	0.118	0.076	0.113	0.126	0.077	0.153
High	0.168	0.128	0.066	0.198	0.162	0.065

class. In reference set two (S_2), the nations were selected so that the distance between classes is largest: near the lower extreme for the Low group, near the center for the Intermediate group, and at the upper end of the High group.

The principal–components models fitted to each reference set using Eq. (1) and two components gave the residual mean squares within and between the reference sets in Table 1. The diagonal entries in the table are the within-class residual mean squares. The nondiagonal entries represent the residual mean squares evaluated on the basis of the principal-components model of the class indicated in the leftmost column. They thus provide a measure of the differences between classes. For example, the residual mean square obtained for the Intermediate class of reference set S_1 using the principal-components model of the Low class is 0.112. The table suggests that: (1) The reference classes are well defined. (The within-class mean squares are considerably smaller than the between). (2) The reference set S_2 provides a better starting point than S_1. (The between-class mean squares are larger for S_2 than for S_1, and the within class are no larger.) (3) There is a natural ordering to the process described in the reference classification. (The distance from the class model increases the further away one moves from the class. For example, for S_2 the High sample fitted to the Low model has a rms of 0.210, to the Intermediate of 0.153, and to its own of 0.065. Similarly, the Low sample fitted to the High model has a rms of 0.198, the Intermediate fitted to the High model of 0.162, and the High fitted to the High of 0.065.) (4) The Intermediate process is the most diffuse (highest within rms) and development patterns within that group are closer to those of the Low countries than to the High ones (rms with the model of the Low countries is smaller than with the model of the High ones). These latter conclusions are in agreement with the previous A–M findings; once a nation approaches the take-off stage in economic modernization (i.e., enters the High sample), it pulls away relatively fast from the nations in the Intermediate class.

With respect to individual countries, with both training sets, all countries in the reference set were classified correctly, as indicated by their distances from their own class models as compared to their distance from other class

TABLE 2
Country Assignment

	A–M (1)	Disjoint Principal Components (2)	Ratio of rms $rms_{(2)}/rms_{(1)}$
South Africa	Intermediate	High	1.4
Sudan	Low	Intermediate	1.3
U.A.R.	High	Intermediate	1.3

models. Starting with the S_2 reference set, the set was successively expanded—by adding all those unassigned countries to the class for which the S_j^2 is smallest provided that it is still smaller than twice the within class variance and provided its rms is significantly less than that for the next best class. This procedure first permitted enlarging the reference set to 35 countries. The disjoint principal-components analysis was then repeated. But before the repetition five variables were omitted. These were of minor relevance with regard to the residual mean-square error within the class and also had minor discriminatory power with regard to the F ratio between classes.[4] The enlarged analysis confirmed the classification of the 35 countries within the reference set, and permitted classification of another 14 countries. Repetition of the disjoint principal-components analysis for 49 countries indicated that, while the rest could, of course, be classified to a subsample by using minimum rms criterion—for most the minimum rms was not much different from that obtained using the next-best class model. Of the remaining 25 countries, 14 had a minimum rms when assigned to the A–M category; for another eight, the rms with the A–M classification was within 0.015 (or 15%) of the minimum rms. For only three countries, South Africa, Sudan, and the U.A.R., was the difference in rms between the A–M and the disjoint principal-components assignment more significant (see Table 2). All three had been borderline cases in the A–M classification. In addition, for none of the three unclassified countries was the rms with the A–M classification more than twice the standard deviation of the class. We therefore conclude that the agreement with respect to country classification is extremely close.

Principal-Components Analysis within Groups

This section is devoted to a description of the principal-components analysis within groups. The results, reproduced in Tables 3, 5, and 7, compare

---

[4] The omitted variables were: social tension, national integration, cultural and ethnic homogeneity, level of effectiveness of the tax system and the degree of improvement of social overhead capital.

TABLE 3

DISJOINT PRINCIPAL-COMPONENTS ANALYSIS FOR 16 LOW COUNTRIES[a]

Economic, Social, and Political Indicators	Variable Loadings		
	P_1	P_2	P_3
Rate of Growth of Real per Capita GNP	0.114	[b]	0.196
Character of Basic Social Organization	**−0.127**	[b]	−0.054
Extent of Social Mobility	**−0.110**	0.085	[b]
Extent of Urbanization	**−0.114**	[b]	[b]
Extent of Mass Communication	**−0.134**	0.117	0.131
Extent of Literacy	**−0.120**	0.073	[b]
Improvement in Human Resources	**−0.133**	[b]	0.056
Degree of Modernization of Outlook	**−0.117**	[b]	0.054
Crude Fertility Rate	**0.072**	0.061	−0.065
Per Capita GNP	**−0.094**	0.072	0.074
Size of Traditional Agricultural Sector	**0.143**	[b]	[b]
Adequacy of Physical Overhead Capital	**−0.133**	0.073	[b]
Effectiveness of Financial Institutions	**−0.126**	0.086	0.095
Change in Degree of Industrialization	**−0.121**	[b]	[b]
Importance of Indigenous Middle Class	−0.116	**0.181**	[b]
Degree of Administrative Efficiency	−0.064	**0.351**	0.189
Strength of Democratic Institutions	−0.062	**0.239**	[b]
Degree of Freedom of Opposition and Press	[b]	**0.383**	−0.114
Basis of Political Party System	−0.060	**0.207**	−0.157
Competitiveness of Political Parties	−0.060	**0.309**	−0.183
Strength of Labor Movement	−0.061	**0.260**	0.072
Leadership Commitment for Economic Development	[b]	**0.129**	0.092
Modernization of Techniques in Agriculture	−0.119	**0.138**	0.071
Improvement in Agricultural Productivity	−0.078	**0.136**	0.106
Improvement in the Tax System	−0.087	**0.142**	0.066
Level of Modernization of Industry	−0.117	[b]	**0.130**
Structure of Foreign Trade	[b]	[b]	**0.257**
Abundance of National Resources	−0.068	0.068	**0.416**
Extent of Dualism	−0.144	0.137	**0.206**
Character of Agricultural Organization	−0.107	0.123	**0.105**
Improvement in Financial Institutions	−0.112	0.005	**0.211**
Gross Investment Rate	−0.101	[b]	**0.186**
Extent of Political Stability	[b]	[b]	**0.388**
Extent of Centralization of Political Power	[b]	−0.249	**0.449**
Strength of the Traditional Elite	[b]	[b]	**0.146**
Political Strength of the Military	−0.056	[b]	**−0.065**

[a] Bold figures indicate the factor to which each variable is assigned.
[b] Loading less than 0.05.

closely with those of A–M. In assessing the degree of agreement, it should be noted that the present results are based upon the reference sets only, and thus include a much smaller number of countries in each group than in the A–M study. Also, the number of components is less (three, rather than four or five), and no rotation is performed.

Results for the Low Sample

Table 3 gives the variables and their loadings in the three first components of the present analysis. Table 4 reproduces the results of the previous A–M study of Adelman and Morris (1967). Naturally, in view of the rotation, the loadings obtained with the present method are all lower. Also, in view of the smaller number of components extracted, some of the components are combined. But the grouping of variables into components, and the signs of the loadings are quite similar.

As in the previous results, the first component combines the social processes necessary to the transformation of the traditional subsistence sector into a commercialized exchange economy, with some of the induced changes involved in the spread of the market system. It includes most of the variables with high loadings in F_1 and F_3 in the A–M analysis of Table 4.[5]

The second component includes the political variables of F_2 describing the degree of democracy, together with the extent of leadership commitment to economic development and some of its economic concomittants: more modern agriculture, higher rate of improvement in agricultural productivity, and improvements in the tax system.

The third component combines the variables responsible for economic dynamism at this level of development with their associated political influences. We find more rapid rates of economic growth, characterized by natural-resource-based, dualistic, primary-export-oriented development patterns, associated with higher investment rates, more developed financial systems, more modern industrial structures, and economically more viable forms of agrarian tenure. Combined with these is more political stability, achieved by more centralization, based on stronger traditional elites and with politically weaker military. This component suggests "that there is a weak but positive relationship between more autocratic, less representative forms of government and more rapid growth rate within this group of countries" (Adelman and Morris, 1967, p. 197).

---

[5] It will be recalled that the present analysis excluded five variables: national integration, cultural and ethnic homogeneity, social tension, level of effectiveness of the tax system, and degree of improvement in physical overhead capital.

TABLE 4

ROTATED FACTOR MATRIX FOR CHANGE IN PER CAPITA GNP (1950/51–1963/64) TOGETHER WITH 35 POLITICAL, SOCIAL, AND ECONOMICAL VARIABLES[a] (LOW SAMPLE)

Political, Social, and Economic Indicators	F_1	F_2	F_3	F_4	F_5	h^2 (R^2)
Rate of Growth of Real Per Capita GNP: 1950/51–1963/64	0.41	−0.27	0.18	−0.03	−0.65	0.699
Importance of the Indigenous Middle Class	**0.76**	0.36	−0.10	−0.03	−0.15	0.744
Extent of Social Mobility	**0.57**	0.50	−0.03	−0.04	−0.28	0.662
Level of Effectiveness of Financial Institutions	**0.71**	0.12	0.23	−0.28	−0.31	0.744
Level of Effectiveness of the Tax System	**0.71**	0.33	0.24	0.01	−0.12	0.691
Level of Modernization of Techniques in Agriculture	**0.46**	0.44	0.35	−0.21	0.02	0.568
Character of Agricultural Organization	**0.51**	0.11	0.10	−0.04	−0.25	0.347
Degree of Improvement in Financial Institutions since 1950	**0.73**	−0.28	0.33	0.11	−0.16	0.764
Degree of Improvement in the Tax System since 1950	**0.68**	0.15	0.43	0.33	0.03	0.777
Change in Degree of Industrialization since 1950	**0.67**	−0.01	0.27	0.04	−0.06	0.532
Degree of Improvement in Agricultural Productivity since 1950	**0.89**	−0.03	−0.07	−0.04	−0.08	0.809
Strength of Democratic Institutions	0.21	**0.83**	0.11	−0.06	−0.08	0.758
Degree of Freedom of Political Opposition and Press	0.10	**0.87**	0.07	0.10	−0.04	0.791
Predominant Basis of the Political Party System	−0.03	**0.76**	0.17	−0.16	0.12	0.654
Degree of Competitiveness of Political Parties	0.10	**0.82**	0.04	−0.43	−0.12	0.889
Strength of the Labor Movement	0.13	**0.77**	0.12	−0.04	−0.33	0.730
Political Strength of the Traditional Elite	−0.25	**−0.57**	0.33	−0.24	−0.10	0.561
Political Strength of the Military	0.11	**−0.67**	0.07	−0.42	0.28	0.732
Degree of Administrative Efficiency	0.42	**0.54**	−0.06	−0.18	−0.42	0.682
Degree of National Integration and Sense of National Unity	0.04	−0.21	**0.68**	−0.03	0.48	0.740
Degree of Cultural and Ethnic Homogeneity	−0.12	−0.26	**0.56**	−0.02	0.41	0.564
Extent of Urbanization	0.11	0.02	**0.70**	−0.29	−0.14	0.603
Extent of Mass Communication	0.08	0.27	**0.75**	0.18	−0.26	0.739
Rate of Improvement in Human Resources	0.26	0.01	**0.85**	0.14	0.03	0.818
Level of Modernization of Industry	0.27	0.28	**0.59**	−0.03	−0.46	0.710
Level of Adequacy of Physical Overhead Capital	0.31	0.29	**0.68**	−0.13	−0.33	0.768
Extent of Political Stability	0.12	−0.04	0.02	**0.87**	−0.19	0.816
Degree of Social Tension	0.05	0.06	−0.11	**−0.80**	−0.12	0.678

TABLE 4 (*continued*)

Political, Social, and Economic Indicators	Rotated Factor Loadings					h^2 (R^2)
	F_1	F_2	F_3	F_4	F_5	
Extent of Leadership Commitment to Economic Development	0.56	0.16	−0.33	**0.47**[b]	0.09	0.672
Extent of Literacy	0.19	0.30	0.37	**−0.45**	−0.19	0.502
Character of Basic Social Organization	0.22	0.07	0.45	**−0.49**	0.40	0.659
Extent of Dualism	0.59	0.17	0.34	−0.04	**−0.60**	0.866
Structure of Foreign Trade	0.12	0.22	0.06	0.00	**−0.55**	0.371
Abundance of Natural Resources	0.03	0.23	0.47	0.30	**−0.61**	0.738
Gross Investment Rate	0.15	−0.02	−0.05	0.03	**−0.71**	0.532
Degree of Modernization of Outlook	0.55	0.24	−0.08	−0.23	**−0.57**	0.743

[a] Bold figures indicate the factor to which each variable is assigned. Variable omitted because of insignificant correlations: extent of centralization of political power. Variables omitted because of low high loadings: size of the traditional agricultural sector, degree of improvement in physical overhead capital since 1950, and crude fertility rate. Percentage of over-all variance explained by factors: 68.5. Percentage of variance explained by last factor included: 6.5.

[b] A variable having loadings on two factors which are not significantly different is assigned to that factor to which it is judged to have the closest affinity.

RESULTS FOR THE INTERMEDIATE SAMPLE

The results for this sample (Table 5) agree least well with the A–M results of Table 6. This is not surprising, in view of the diversity of development patterns represented in this group of transitional countries. Rapid transformations with diverse patterns of change and with a variety of unbalanced paths of modernization mark this group of countries. Hence, in their previous analysis Adelman and Morris stressed that

> [the] results of the factor analyses for nations at the intermediate level of development are not as clear-cut and unithematic as are the results for countries at the lowest and highest levels of socioeconomic development. The lack of a well-defined pattern for the intermediate countries is evidenced by a lower degree of explanatory power in the factor analyses than is found in the results for the other two groups and by a lesser degree of consistency among the several factor analyses (Adelman and Morris, 1967, p. 209).

The first component groups contain dynamic aspects of economic development, with more centralized, authoritarian, less pluralistic political structures. This association was also evident in the A–M studies.

TABLE 5

DISJOINT PRINCIPAL-COMPONENTS ANALYSIS FOR INTERMEDIATE COUNTRIES[a]

Economic, Social, and Political Variables	Variable Loadings		
	P_1	P_2	P_3
Rate of Growth of Real per capita GNP	0.184	0.187	0.079
Extent of Dualism	**0.052**	[b]	[b]
Improvement in Agricultural Productivity	**0.223**	[b]	−0.183
Effectiveness of Financial Institutions	**0.125**	−0.081	[b]
Improvement in Tax System	**0.250**	−0.157	−0.236
Improvement in Human Resources	**0.149**	[b]	−0.128
Extent of Mass Communication	**−0.127**	[b]	[b]
Basis of Political Party System	**−0.384**	−0.193	−0.116
Competitiveness of Political Parties	**−0.402**	−0.389	[b]
Degree of Freedom of Opposition and Press	**−0.285**	−0.142	−0.206
Strength of Democratic Institutions	−0.149	**−0.219**	−0.069
Extent of Centralization of Political Power	0.134	**0.222**	0.261
Strength of Traditional Elite	−0.150	**0.294**	−0.195
Strength of Labor Movement	−0.231	**−0.281**	[b]
Political Strength of Military	0.050	**0.323**	[b]
Extent of Political Stability	0.252	**−0.321**	[b]
Leadership Commitment to Economic Development	0.247	**−0.317**	0.163
Degree of Administrative Efficiency	0.068	**−0.356**	0.110
Degree of Modernization of Outlook	−0.119	**−0.270**	0.096
Structure of Trade	0.070	**−0.233**	0.139
Abundance of Natural Resources	−0.206	0.107	**0.347**
Level of Modernization of Industry	−0.056	[b]	**0.148**
Per Capita GNP	−0.060	0.083	**0.080**[c]
Adequacy of Physical Overhead Capital	[b]	[b]	**0.064**
Gross Investment Rate	[b]	−0.084	**0.134**
Size of Traditional Agricultural Sector	[b]	[b]	**0.115**
Modernization of Techniques in Agriculture	[b]	[b]	**−0.084**
Character of Agricultural Organization	[b]	[b]	**0.132**
Character of Basic Social Organization	−0.120	[b]	**−0.224**
Importance of Indigenous Middle Class	0.141	−0.063	**−0.253**
Extent of Social Mobility	[b]	[b]	**−0.109**
Extent of Literacy	−0.050	[b]	**−0.188**
Extent of Urbanization	−0.089	[b]	**0.107**
Crude Fertility Rate	[b]	0.080	**0.131**
Change in Degree of Industrialization	0.171	[b]	**−0.373**
Improvement in Financial Institutions	[b]	[b]	**−0.316**

[a] Bold figures indicate the factor to which each variable is assigned.

[b] Loading less than 0.05.

[c] Variable having loadings which are not significantly different is assigned to that component to which it has closest affinity.

SOCIETY, POLITICS, AND ECONOMIC DEVELOPMENT REVISITED 13

TABLE 6

Rotated Factor Matrix for Change in Per Capita GNP (1950/51–1963/64) together with 36 Political, Social, and Economic Variables[a] (Intermediate Sample)

Political, Social, and Economic Indicators	Rotated Factor Loadings					h^2 (R^2)
	F_1	F_2	F_3	F_4	F_5	
Rate of Growth of Real Per Capita GNP: 1950/51–1963/64	0.21	0.26	0.15	−0.05	0.59	0.484
Size of the Tranditional Agricultural Sector	−0.61	0.30	0.25	−0.06	−0.26	0.597
Extent of Dualism	0.67	−0.02	−0.24	−0.32	0.41	0.785
Extent of Mass Communication	0.60	−0.36	0.07	0.08	−0.42	0.668
Gross Investment Rate	0.53	0.02	0.06	−0.05	−0.07	0.287
Level of Modernization of Industry	0.58	−0.05	0.44	−0.28	0.30	0.695
Level of Modernization of Techniques in Agriculture	0.81	−0.25	−0.22	0.12	0.13	0.789
Character of Agricultural Organization	0.70	0.13	−0.07	−0.26	−0.06	0.588
Level of Effectiveness of the Tax System	0.71	−0.19	−0.01	0.03	0.08	0.550
Level of Adequacy of Physical Overhead Capital	0.82	0.03	0.05	−0.18	0.23	0.754
Strength of Democratic Institutions	0.12	−0.75	−0.09	−0.49	0.06	0.826
Degree of Freedom of Political Opposition and Press	0.22	−0.79	−0.15	0.05	−0.08	0.702
Predominant Basis of the Political Party System	0.02	−0.85	0.24	−0.01	−0.11	0.794
Degree of Competitiveness of Political Parties	0.31	−0.85	0.19	0.08	−0.15	0.890
Strength of the Labor Movement	0.09	−0.47[b]	0.06	−0.29	−0.51	0.578
Extent of Centralization of Political Power	0.12	0.74	0.15	0.11	−0.02	0.601
Extent of Literacy	0.17	−0.56	−0.51	0.05	−0.01	0.609
Character of Basic Social Organization	−0.57	−0.58	−0.22	0.30	−0.14	0.828
Degree of Social Tension	0.12	0.06	0.64	0.30	0.21	0.562
Importance of the Indigenous Middle Class	0.04	0.04	−0.70	0.04	0.22	0.549
Extent of Social Mobility	0.33	−0.03	−0.80	0.02	−0.08	0.762
Rate of Improvement in Human Resources	0.26	0.00	−0.68	−0.22	0.43	0.765
Abundance of Natural Resources	0.29	0.02	0.78	0.05	−0.14	0.717
Extent of Political Stability	0.07	−0.01	−0.56	−0.77	0.00	0.908
Extent of Leadership Commitment to Economic Development	0.05	0.21	−0.09	−0.83	0.03	0.743
Degree of Modernization of Outlook	0.39	−0.47	0.09	−0.66	−0.05	0.814
Degree of Administrative Efficiency	0.52	−0.12	−0.17	−0.68	0.12	0.794
Political Strength of the Military	−0.14	0.31	0.26	0.52	0.36	0.586
Degree of National Integration and Sense of National Unity	0.14	0.38	−0.47	0.55	−0.22	0.738
Degree of Cultural and Ethnic Homogeneity	0.10	0.54	−0.17	0.58	0.04	0.668

(*continued*)

TABLE 6 (*continued*)

Political, Social, and Economic Indicators	Rotated Factor Loadings					h^2 (R^2)
	F_1	F_2	F_3	F_4	F_5	
Structure of Foreign Trade	0.29	0.13	0.22	**−0.49**	0.39	0.544
Change in Degree of Industrialization since 1950	0.01	−0.18	−0.50	0.10	**0.71**	0.797
Level of Effectiveness of Financial Institutions	0.57	0.04	−0.12	−0.40	**0.61**	0.872
Degree of Improvement in Financial Institutions since 1950	0.04	−0.22	−0.08	0.08	**0.81**	0.713
Degree of Improvement in Physical Overhead Capital since 1950	0.13	0.17	0.27	−0.15	**0.65**	0.566
Degree of Improvement in Agricultural Productivity since 1950	0.31	0.11	−0.44	−0.18	**0.64**	0.747
Degree of Improvement in the Tax System since 1950	−0.06	0.16	−0.43	0.03	**0.60**	0.580

^a Bold figures indicate the factor to which each variable is assigned. Variables omitted because of insignificant correlations: crude fertility rate and political strength of the traditional elite. Variable omitted because of low/high loadings: extent of urbanization. Percentage of over-all variance explained by factors: 68.8. Percentage of variance explained by last factor included: 7.7.

^b A variable having loadings on two factors which are not significantly different is assigned to that factor to which it is judged to have the closest affinity.

The second component is one describing primarily political structure. In it we again find an association of more rapid growth with less democratic, more traditional political systems, and stronger military.

The final component combines a wide variety of economic and social processes. In it we find a generally negative association between levels of economic development and rates of economic change and degrees of social modernization. The more rapidly modernizing countries are those with less modern industrial structures, less natural resources, characterized by more export-oriented urban-enclave development, with smaller traditional sectors, and less viable agrarian structures. On the other hand, the more rapidly modernizing countries economically are generally more developed socially, with lower fertility, higher literacy, more social mobility, more nuclear family structures and larger indigenous middle classes.

RESULTS FOR THE HIGH SAMPLE

The first component obtained with the current method (Table 7) is quite similar to F_1 of the A–M analysis (Table 8). It includes most of the indices of levels of economic development and of levels of social modernization. As in the A–M analysis, these are negligibly related to rates of economic growth.

TABLE 7

Disjoint Principal-Components Analysis for High Countries[a]

Economic, Social, and Political Indicators	Variable Loadings P_1	P_2	P_3
Rate of Growth of Real per Capita GNP	0.093	0.088	0.336
Modernization of Techniques in Agriculture	**0.163**	0.163	[b]
Adequacy of Physical Overhead Capital	**0.158**	0.148	[b]
Modernization of Industry	**0.157**	0.107	[b]
Structure of Trade	**0.077**	[b]	[b]
Character of Basic Social Organization	**0.133**	0.050	−0.057
Importance of Indigenous Middle Class	**0.142**	0.104	[b]
Extent of Social Mobility	**0.161**	0.094	[b]
Improvement in Human Resources	**0.122**	0.120	−0.051
Extent of Mass Communication	**0.142**	0.118	−0.102
Extent of Urbanization	**0.121**	0.080	[b]
Degree of Modernization of Outlook	**0.151**	0.097	[b]
Basis of Political Party System	**0.101**	[b]	0.055
Competitiveness of Political Parties	**0.071**[c]	−0.066	−0.077
Extent of Centralization of Political Power	[b]	**−0.139**	0.123
Strength of Democratic Institutions	0.118	**0.296**	−0.126
Strength of Labor Movement	0.106	**0.273**	−0.155
Political Strength of Military	[b]	**−0.288**	[b]
Extent of Political Stability	0.058	**0.172**	0.105
Degree of Administrative Efficiency	0.102	**0.181**	0.079
Extent of Literacy	0.131	**0.181**	−0.085
Crude Fertility Rate	−0.120	**−0.308**	0.237
Size of Traditional Agricultural Sector	−0.142	**−0.168**	0.089
Extent of Dualism	0.141	**0.186**	−0.058
Per Capita GNP	0.153	**0.387**	[b]
Effectiveness of Financial Institutions	0.141	**0.173**	0.140
Abundance of Natural Resources	0.054	**−0.164**	−0.115
Leadership Commitment to Economic Development	0.079	0.222	**0.349**
Strength of Traditional Elite	−0.065	−0.109	**−0.149**
Degree of Freedom of Opposition and Press	0.096	0.135	**−0.154**
Gross Investment Rate	0.123	0.165	**0.210**
Improvement in the Tax System	0.073	−0.051	**0.226**
Change in Degree of Industrialization	0.087	−0.074	**0.170**
Improvement in Financial Institutions	0.073	0.026	**0.353**
Improvement in Agricultural Productivity	0.066	0.073	**0.457**
Character of Agricultural Organization	0.151	0.123	**0.192**

[a] Bold figures indicate the factor to which each variable is assigned.
[b] Loading less than 0.05.
[c] Variable having loadings which are not significantly different is assigned to that component to which it has closest affinity.

TABLE 8

Rotated Factor Matrix for Change in Per Capita GNP (1950/51–1963/64) Together with 36 Political, Social, and Economic Variables[a] (High Sample)

Political, Social, and Economic Indicators	F_1	F_2	F_3	F_4	h^2 (R^2)
Rate of Growth of Real Per Capita GNP: 1950/51–1963/64	−0.15	**0.88**	0.03	0.04	0.791
Size of Traditional Agricultural Sector	**0.86**	0.09	−0.12	−0.21	0.812
Extent of Dualism	**0.90**	0.04	0.11	−0.18	0.857
Importance of the Indigenous Middle Class	**−0.80**	0.20	0.22	−0.01	0.732
Extent of Social Mobility	**−0.70**	0.27	0.27	0.23	0.689
Extent of Literacy	**−0.62**	−0.16	0.06	0.35	0.528
Extent of Mass Communication	**−0.72**	0.03	−0.23	0.33	0.681
Degree of Modernization of Outlook	**−0.68**	−0.20	0.47	0.09	0.738
Crude Fertility Rate	**0.82**	0.13	0.02	0.03	0.692
Strength of Democratic Institutions	**−0.76**	−0.01	0.13	0.47	0.820
Strength of the Labor Movement	**−0.70**	0.01	0.22	0.55	0.837
Political Strength of the Military	**0.67**	−0.09	−0.07	−0.36	0.587
Political Strength of the Traditional Elite	**0.51**	−0.35	−0.30	0.27	0.543
Degree of Administrative Efficiency	**−0.59**	0.44	0.53	0.18	0.843
Level of Modernization of Techniques in Agriculture	**−0.84**	0.27	0.10	0.04	0.781
Character of Agricultural Organization	**−0.53**	0.40	0.48	0.17	0.698
Level of Modernization of Industry	**−0.61**	0.36	0.26	0.35	0.687
Level of Adequacy of Physical Overhead Capital	**−0.83**	0.23	0.12	0.11	0.770
Rate of Improvement in Human Resources	**−0.59**	0.19	0.08	−0.07	0.399
Extent of Leadership Commitment to Economic Development	−0.31	**0.66**	0.34	0.17	0.672
Gross Investment Rate	−0.43	**0.59**	0.03	0.35	0.661
Level of Effectiveness of the Tax System	−0.46	**0.60**	−0.15	0.20	0.625
Level of Effectiveness of Financial Institutions	−0.56	**0.59**	0.21	0.36	0.835
Degree of Improvement in Agricultural Productivity since 1950	0.06	**0.75**	0.25	0.14	0.643
Change in Degree of Industrialization since 1950	0.21	**0.70**	0.27	0.00	0.604
Degree of Improvement in the Tax System since 1950	−0.12	**0.64**	−0.30	−0.23	0.562
Degree of Improvement in Financial Institutions since 1950	−0.03	**0.81**	−0.16	−0.16	0.717
Degree of National Integration and Sense of National Unity	−0.26	0.09	**0.74**	0.01	0.632
Degree of Cultural and Ethnic Homogeneity	−0.07	−0.33	**0.54**	−0.33	0.512
Degree of Social Tension	−0.01	0.00	**−0.83**	0.01	0.696
Extent of Political Stability	−0.31	0.22	**0.71**	0.11	0.659
Degree of Freedom of Political Opposition and Press	−0.59	0.03	−0.29	**0.68**	0.885
Predominant Basis of the Political Party System	−0.21	0.40	0.25	**0.67**	0.709
Degree of Competitiveness of Political Parties	−0.17	0.13	−0.41	**0.56**	0.528
Extent of Centralization of Political Power	0.65	−0.08	0.03	**−0.67**	0.881
Character of Basic Social Organization	−0.27	−0.34	0.05	**0.70**	0.672
Abundance of Natural Resources	0.18	0.07	0.04	**0.70**	0.533

[a] Bold figures indicate the factor to which each variable is assigned. Variables omitted because of insignificant correlations: structure of foreign trade and improvement in physical overhead capital since 1950. Variable omitted because of low high loading: extent of urbanization. Percentage of over-all variance explained by factors: 68.9. Percentage of variance explained by last factor included: 6.7.

The second component combines the political variables of F_1 and F_4, with some of their close economic correlates. More democratic institutions, greater political stability, more administrative efficiency are associated with less dualism, smaller subsistence sectors, less natural resources, higher GNP and more developed financial systems. This component, too, is not significantly associated with more rapid growth.

The final component is quite like F_2. It combines greater leadership commitment to economic development with all the indices of dynamic economic growth. As in F_2, the quality of political leadership emerges in the results as the significant political force in short-run economic performance for countries at this level.

Conclusion

The results of applications of the disjoint principal-components analysis to the A-M data are quite encouraging. The results make sense both theoretically and empirically and are consistent with previous analyses of the same data with conventional techniques of multivariate analysis. This consistency serves to confirm both the usefulness of the new techniques and the validity of the previous findings.

REFERENCES

Adelman, I., and Morris, C. T. (1967). *Society, Politics, and Economic Development: A Quantitative Approach.* Baltimore, Maryland: Johns Hopkins Press. Rev. ed. 1971.

Adelman, I., and Morris, C. T. (1968). An econometric model of socio-economic and political change in underdeveloped countries. *American Economic Review* **58**, 1184–1218.

Adelman, I., and Morris, C. T. (1973a). *Economic Growth and Social Equity in Developing Countries*, Stanford, California: Stanford University Press.

Adelman, I. and Morris, C. T. (1973b). The derivation of cardinal scales from ordinal data: An application of multidimensional scaling to measure levels of national development. *Economic Development and Planning* (W. Sellekaerts, ed.), pp. 1–39. London: Macmillan.

Adelman, I., Geier, M., and Morris, C. T. (1969). Instruments and goals in economic development: A quantitative approach. *American Economic Association, Papers and Proceedings* **59**, 409–426.

Wold, H. (1975). Modelling in complex situations with soft information, Research Report 1975: 5. Department of Statistics, University of Göteborg. Group report presented to the Third World Congress of the Econometric Society.

Wold, H. (1976a). On the transition from pattern recognition to model building. The NIPALS approach, Research Report 1976:3. Department of Statistics, University of Göteborg. Presented at the European Meetings of the Econometric Society.

Wold, H. (1976b). On the transition from pattern cognition to model building. The NIPALS approach, Part I. Prepublication Paper, Department of Statistics, Upsala University.

Wold, S. (1976). Pattern recognition by means of disjoint principal components models. *Pattern Recognition*, 127–137.

I. Adelman
DEPARTMENT OF AGRICULTURE
AND RESOURCE ECONOMICS
UNIVERSITY OF CALIFORNIA
BERKELEY, CALIFORNIA

Cynthia Taft Morris
DEPARTMENT OF ECONOMICS
AMERICAN UNIVERSITY
WASHINGTON, D.C.

Svante Wold
DEPARTMENT OF CHEMISTRY
UMEÅ UNIVERSITY
UMEÅ, SWEDEN

On Global Stability of Some Stochastic Economic Processes: A Synthesis

R. N. BHATTACHARYA

and

M. K. MAJUMDAR

I. Introduction

Some of the more important questions in dynamic economics have to deal with the existence, uniqueness, and stability properties of a steady state of the process under consideration. This is true irrespective of whether one is studying an aggregative macroeconomic model or a more disaggregate micro model, or whether the model is primarily descriptive or has normative implications. In an analysis of the long-run behavior of a dynamic process a deterministic framework might be quite inadequate, since the underlying parameters are likely to be exposed to exogenous shocks with the passage of time. For this reason, a large number of recent papers are aimed at extending many of the well-known deterministic results to a stochastic context.[1] The purpose of this paper is to present a systematic and unified exposition of those continuous-time dynamic processes that can be formally described by *diffusion processes*. Such processes are Markovian with *continuous* sample paths (with probability one) and are of interest for a number of reasons. First, continuous-time Markov processes have richer structures (not every discrete-time Markov process can be imbedded in a continuous-time process), and it

---

[1] See the survey by Radner (1976) and the references cited there.

is possible to exploit such structures effectively to derive powerful stability results circumventing the awkward cycling problems that arise in discrete-time versions and are often quite nonintuitive. Second, it is also possible to obtain analytical characteristics of steady states that are relevant in comparative statics and dynamics. Since the densities of probability distributions representing the steady states can often be explicitly calculated, one can throw light on methodological questions like whether—and to what extent—a deterministic model is a "reasonable" approximation to a more complete stochastic system. Usually, this is *not* the case for any simple notion of approximation (like the expected values of the random variables in the steady state agreeing with the steady-state values of the corresponding nonrandom model). There are significant qualitative differences in the nature of steady states and in the global dynamic behavior even in relatively simple aggregative models.[2] Third, the stability property that we establish [see, e.g., Eqs. (4.5), (4.8), and (4.26)] is even stronger than the variables converging weakly (or in distribution) to the invariant distribution.

While the motivation behind a careful study of the stability properties of diffusions is suggested by the reasons just indicated, global stability questions are quite complex for a diffusion with a multidimensional state space, and are unavoidably technical. This is in contrast with one-dimensional diffusions that are understood well, and have already been studied exhaustively. Since the mathematical results needed are not readily available in the desired form, Section IV provides a self-contained, precise statement (and some proofs) of conditions guaranteeing the existence of an invariant measure for a multidimensional diffusion and its global stability. It is our hope that such conditions will be of interest whenever diffusion processes arise in other economic models. In Section II we summarize the basic definitions, and in Section III we present some examples of stochastic dynamic processes. No attempt is made to give a complete list of deterministic dynamic models involving many variables, or to compare in detail our stability conditions with those suggested for deterministic tatonnement or nontatonnement processes.

II. Basic Definitions

Let $\{X(t) : t \geq 0\}$ be a Markov process whose state space is either an open subset G of R^k or the closure $\bar{G}$ of an open subset G.[3] Let $P(t, x, dy)$ denote

---

[2] For a class of one sector growth models, the expected values of the stochastic steady states were computed by Merton (1975) [and by Bourguignon (1974)] and were shown to be different from "certainty" estimates. Moreover, the "bias" did not reveal any directional pattern.

[3] Just to avoid any misunderstanding, we allow for $G = R^k$.

its *transition probability function*, i.e., (a) for all $t \geq 0$, $x \in G$ (or $\bar{G}$), $B \to P(t, x, B)$ is a probability measure on $\mathcal{B}(G)$, the Borel sigma-field of G (or $\bar{G}$),[4] (b) for all $t \geq 0$ and B in $\mathcal{B}(G)$, $x \to P(t, x, B)$ is a Borel measurable function on G (or $\bar{G}$), and (c) the following (Chapman–Kolmogorov) equation holds:

$$(2.1) \quad \int P(t, y, B) P(s, x, dy) = P(t + s, x, B) \quad (t, s \geq 0, \quad x \in G \text{ (or } \bar{G})),$$

where the integral is over the state space G (or $\bar{G}$). The quantity $P(t, x, B)$ is the probability that the process will be in set B at time t if it is initially (i.e., at time zero) at x. Assume that the transition probability function satisfies the following regularity conditions:

$$(A.1) \quad \lim_{t \downarrow 0} \frac{1}{t} [1 - P(t, x, U_\varepsilon(x))] = 0$$

for each $x \in G$ and each $\varepsilon > 0$; here $U_\varepsilon(x) = \{y : |y - x| < \varepsilon\}$, (we use $|x|$ to denote the *Euclidean norm* of the vector x).

$$(A.2) \quad \lim_{t \downarrow 0} \int_{U_\varepsilon(x)} (y_i - x_i) P(t, x, dy) = b_i(x) \quad (1 \leq i \leq k)$$

for every $x = (x_1, \ldots, x_k) \in G$ and each $\varepsilon > 0$; here $b_i(\cdot)$ are Lipschitzian on compact subsets of G.

$$(A.3) \quad \lim_{t \downarrow 0} \frac{1}{t} \int_{U_\varepsilon(x)} (y_i - x_i)(y_j - x_j) P(t, x, dy) = a_{ij}(x) \quad (1 \leq i, \ j \leq k)$$

for every $x \in G$ and each $\varepsilon > 0$; here $((a_{ij}(\cdot)))$ is a $k \times k$ symmetric positive-definite matrix and the functions $a_{ij}(\cdot)$ are Lipschitzian on compacts.

A Markov process $\{X(t) : t \geq 0\}$ whose sample paths (or trajectories) are continuous (with probability one) and whose transition probability function satisfies (A.1)–(A.3) is called a *diffusion*. The vector $(b_1(\cdot), \ldots, b_k(\cdot))$ is called the *drift coefficient* and the matrix $(a_{ij}(\cdot))$ is called the *diffusion matrix* of the Markov process $\{X(t) : t \geq 0\}$. They are also referred to as the infinitesimal mean and dispersion of the diffusion, respectively, for reasons discussed in the following paragraph. Condition (A.1) excludes the possibility of violent discontinuities of the trajectories.

The most well-known example of a diffusion is the *standard Brownian motion*. In this case $G = R^k$, $b_i(\cdot) = 0$ for $1 \leq i \leq k$, and $((a_{ij}))$ is the $k \times k$ identity matrix I. The transition probability function admits a density p (with respect to Lebesgue measure) given by

$$(2.2) \quad p(t, x, y) = (\sqrt{2\pi t})^{-k} \exp\{-\tfrac{1}{2}|y - x|^2\} \quad (t > 0; \ x, y \in R^k).$$

---

[4] For a metric space S, the Borel σ field $\mathcal{B}(S)$ is the smallest σ field containing the open sets. See Billingsley (1968).

Let $B(t) \equiv (B_1(t), \ldots, B_k(t))'$ be a standard Brownian motion with $B(0) = 0$ (with probability one). Then (i) $B(t)$ is Gaussian with mean (vector) zero and dispersion matrix tI, and (ii) the diffusion $B(t)$ has independent increments. Next consider a constant vector $b = (b_1, \ldots, b_k)$ and a constant positive definite symmetric matrix $A = ((a_{ij}))$. Define the stochastic process

(2.3) $$X(t) = x_0 + bt + \Sigma B(t) \qquad (t \geq 0),$$

where Σ is the symmetric positive definite square root of A ($\Sigma^2 = A$) and x_0 is a fixed vector in R^k. It is easy to check that $\{X(t): t \geq 0\}$ is a diffusion and that, for each $\Delta t > 0$

(2.4) $$\Delta X(t) \equiv X(t + \Delta t) - X(t) = b \Delta t + \Sigma \Delta B(t) \qquad (t \geq 0),$$

which may also be written symbolically

(2.5) $$dX(t) = b \, dt + \Sigma \, dB(t) \qquad (t \geq 0).$$

The increments of this diffusion $\{X(t): t \geq 0\}$ on disjoint intervals are independent, and $\Delta X(t)$ is Gaussian with mean $b \Delta t$ and dispersion matrix $A \Delta t$. To pass from constant coefficients to nonconstant coefficients $b(\cdot)$, $A(\cdot) = ((a_{ij}(\cdot)))$, set up the formal equation

(2.6) $$dX(t) = b(X(t)) \, dt + \Sigma(X(t)) \, dB(t) \qquad (t \geq 0),$$

where $\Sigma(\cdot)$ is the symmetric positive definite matrix satisfying $\Sigma^2(\cdot) = A(\cdot)$; one may try to solve (2.6) in some sense for each given initial state x_0. That is, one would like to construct a diffusion $\{X(t): t \geq 0\}$ such that given $X(t) = x$, the displacement $\Delta X(t) = X(t + \Delta t) - X(t)$ in a small time interval $(t, t + \Delta t)$ is approximately Gaussian with mean $b(x) \Delta t$ and dispersion matrix $A(x) \Delta t$. Since the Brownian trajectories are nowhere differentiable [see McKean (1969, p. 9)], (2.6) is not a (system of k) differential equations in the usual sense. Its integral form

(2.7) $$X(t) = x_0 + \int_0^t b(X(s)) \, ds + \int_0^t \Sigma(X(s)) \, dB(s) \qquad (t \geq 0),$$

cannot be interpreted as an ordinary integral equation, since the Brownian trajectories are (with probability one) of unbounded variation over every nondegenerate interval [and, therefore, the second integral in (2.7) cannot be treated as a Lebesgue–Stieltjes integral]. Note that the ith coordinate of $\Sigma(X(s)) \, dB(s)$ is $\sum_{j=1}^{k} \sigma_{ij}(X(s)) \, dB_j(s)$, where $\Sigma(\cdot) = ((\sigma_{ij}))$. The appropriate definition of the second integral in (2.7), called a *stochastic integral*, was given by K. Itô (1951), who also proved that if $b(\cdot)$ and $\Sigma(\cdot)$ are Lipschitzian (on all of R^k), then there exists a unique solution of (2.7) which is a diffusion [see Friedman (1975, p. 115, Theorem 4.2)]. If $b(\cdot)$ and $\Sigma(\cdot)$ are merely assumed to be Lipschitzian on compacts, then also a unique solution of (2.7) exists for $t < \zeta$, where ζ is a random time, called the *explosion time*. The resulting stochastic process is a Markov process (with continuous trajectories up to time ζ), which is also referred to as a diffusion. In case of explosion, $|X(t)| \to \infty$ at $t \uparrow \zeta$. General conditions under which the diffusion is nonexplosive or *conservative* (i.e., $\zeta = \infty$ with probability one) are given in McKean (1969, pp. 102–104). Itô's construction extends to arbitrary open G; in this case $|X(t)| \to \infty$ or the boundary ∂G of G at $t \uparrow \zeta$, if $\zeta < \infty$. If the state space is $\bar{G} = G \cup \partial G$, then diffusions on $\bar{G}$ are defined by first constructing the diffusion on G (as above) up to time ζ and, then imposing appropriate boundary conditions (absorption, reflection, etc.) on the diffusion when it reaches ∂G.

In (2.7) one may take x_0 to be an arbitrary random vector independent of $\{B(t): t \geq 0\}$. If m is the distribution of x_0, called the *initial distribution* of the diffusion, and $P(t, x, dy)$ is the transition probability function of the diffusion, then the distribution of $X(t)$ is given by

$$(2.8) \qquad \text{Prob}(X(t) \in B) = \int P(t, x, B) m(dx),$$

where B is an arbitrary Borel subset of the state space (G or $\bar{G}$) and the integral is over the entire state space. If there exists an m such that the right side of (2.8) is independent of t, i.e.,

$$(2.9) \qquad \int P(t, x, B) m(dx) = m(B)$$

for all B in $\mathscr{B}(G)$ and $t > 0$, then the probability measure m is called an *invariant measure* for the diffusion. Whether or not an invariant probability measure exists (on an open state space G or a noncompact state space $\bar{G}$ with reflecting boundary) depends solely on the functions $b(\cdot)$ and $A(\cdot) = \Sigma^2(\cdot)$. If there exists an invariant probability measure m, then the diffusion $\{X(t), t \geq 0\}$ constructed with m as the initial distribution is a stationary stochastic process which is metrically transitive and one has the steady state relation

$$(2.10) \qquad \lim_{t \to \infty} \text{Prob}(X(t) \in B) = m(B)$$

for all B in $\mathscr{B}(G)$, no matter what the distribution of $X(0)$ is [see Khasminskii (1960)]. We prove a stronger convergence than (2.10), however, in what follows.

If $\{X(t): t \geq 0\}$ is an explosive one-dimensional diffusion on the state space (r_1, r_2) such that $X(t)$ tends to r_i as t tends to infinity with positive probability, then r_i is called an *accessible boundary*.

Finally, an n vector $x = (x_i)$ is *nonnegative* (written $x \geq 0$) if $x_i \geq 0$ for all i; x is *semipositive* (written $x > 0$) if $x \geq 0$ and $x_i > 0$ for some i; x is *positive* (written $x \gg 0$) if $x_i > 0$ for all i. R^n_+ (resp. R^n_{++}) denotes the set of all nonnegative (resp. positive) vectors in R^n; Δ denotes the set of all positive vectors the sum of whose coordinates is one, i.e.,

$$\Delta = \left\{ x = (x_i) : x \gg 0, \sum_{i=1}^{n} x_i = 1 \right\}.$$

III. Some Economic Examples

We shall now consider a number of economic models in which the relevant dynamic processes are described by diffusions.

A. Price Adjustment in a Two-Commodity Model

Models with two commodities have been studied extensively, particularly in the literature on international trade. To some extent the popularity of such models is surely due to the fact that sharp qualitative results can be obtained even in a general equilibrium framework, results that cannot be established easily in a system with three or more commodities. We shall only sketch the model, since it is a special case of the standard model discussed, e.g., in Arrow and Hahn (1971, Chapter II).

The *excess demand* function $z(x) = (z_1(x), z_2(x))$ is a continuous function from Δ into R^2 (where $\Delta = \{x = (x_1, x_2) : x \gg 0, x_1 + x_2 = 1\}$) such that for each x in Δ

(3.1) $$\langle x, z(x) \rangle = x_1 z_1(x) + x_2 z_2(x) = 0.$$

With two commodities, (3.1) ("Walras's law") enables us to concentrate on the behavior of just one excess demand, say $z_1(x)$. A Walrasian equilibrium price vector $x^* = (x_1^*, x_2^*)$ in Δ has the property that

(3.2) $$z_1(x^*) = z_2(x^*) = 0.$$

Even in a static model one can consider the excess demand function as a function not just of prices (x_1, x_2) but also of a random parameter ω. In this case, the market clearing prices [satisfying $z_1(x^*, \omega) = 0$] are in general functions of ω. Models of this type where randomness is due to stochastic preferences were analyzed by Hildenbrand (1971) and Bhattacharya and Majumdar (1973). There is, of course, no reason that the system will be in equilibrium over a significant period of time even if it "starts" in equilibrium.

Price adjustments in a market are usually linked to the excess demands generated. In this spirit, we consider the stochastic process

(3.3) $\qquad dX_1(t) = z_1[X_1(t), 1 - X_1(t)] \, dt + \sigma(X_1(t)) \, dB(t),$

where $X_1(t)$ varies in the open interval $(0, 1)$ and $\sigma : (0, 1) \to R_{++}$ is a given function. In this case over a small interval $(t, t + \Delta t)$, $\Delta X_1(t)$—the change in price—is a random variable whose expected value [conditional on $X_1(t)$] is given approximately by $z_1[X_1(t), 1 - X_1(t)] \Delta t$, maintaining the link between price change and excess demand. A steady state of the price process $\{X_1(t) : t \geq 0\}$ is an invariant distribution m [satisfying (2.9)] such that if $X_1(t)$ happens to have the distribution m, so does $X_1(t')$, $t' > t$. We shall spell out the technical conditions on the functions z_1 and σ that guarantee the existence of a unique steady state and its global stability in Section V.

B. STOCHASTIC CHANGES IN THE SIZE OF THE INDUSTRY

Consider a competitive industry of "size" or "productive capacity" x (assumed to be any positive real number). The size of the industry responds stochastically to the profit level p_t in excess of the "normal" level $\bar{p}$. When profits fall below the "normal" level, "firms" tend to drop out, leading to a reduction in the size of the industry. On the other hand, if profits are high relative to the normal level, productive capacity is increased as new firms enter. If the demand condition for the product is taken as exogeneously given, the current profit level p_t is itself a function of the size of the industry. It is assumed to be a monotonically decreasing function

(3.4) $\qquad\qquad\qquad p_t = f(x_t)$

where $f : R_{++} \to R_{++}$ is a continuously differentiable function with $f' < 0$.

The stochastic process of changing industry size can be formally described as

(3.5) $\qquad dX(t) = b[p(t) - \bar{p}] \, dt + \sigma(X(t)) \, dB(t)$

where $f(\infty) < \bar{p} < f(0)$ and b is a continuously differentiable function on $(f(\infty) - \bar{p}, f(0) - \bar{p})$. By using (3.4) one rewrites (3.3)

(3.6) $\qquad dX(t) = b[f(X(t)) - \bar{p}] \, dt + \sigma(X(t)) \, dB(t).$

We should mention here the interesting paper by Inaba (1976), who considered a more complete and elaborately specified model of this type for a discrete-time case. His analytical results were obtained, however, with assumptions like the relevant functions being linear or quadratic ones. In Section V.B we shall derive stability under what may be described as an asymptotic sign-preserving property of b.

C. Miscellaneous Examples with One-Dimensional Diffusions

Stochastic one-sector models of descriptive and optimal growth have been studied in Bourguignon (1974) and Merton (1975). An informal discussion of several examples can be found in Bismut (1975). To test his understanding, the interested reader is invited to develop a stochastic version of the well-known "classical dynamic model" of Baumol (1970, pp. 266-8) and to examine the long-run behavior of the population size by using our discussion of the examples A and B. We now turn to diffusions with many variables.

D. Dynamic Models with Many Variables

Dynamic models involving many variables arise unavoidably as soon as one goes beyond partial equilibrium analysis or a "two-sector" framework. In describing how a Walrasian equilibrium might be attained or in analyzing the long-run evolution of an economy with multiple capital goods ("turnpike properties"), one is led to examine systems of differential equations. A further motivation has come from Samuelson's "correspondence principle": Local or global stability conditions often contain information helpful for deriving comparative static results. Of particular interest has been systems of *linear* differential equations which have been used not only in linear economic models (e.g., dynamic Leontief systems) but also as approximations to a nonlinear system in a neighborhood of steady states. Since the relevant economic literature is much too voluminuous,[5] we shall concentrate on the mathematical systems, and make some general remarks on the application of our results to special models.

The general nonlinear system is [to recall (2.6)]

$$(3.7) \qquad dX(t) = b[X(t)]\,dt + \sum (X(t))\,dB(t),$$

whereas the general linear system with a constant diffusion matrix that we shall study, for the sake of simplicity, is

$$(3.8) \qquad dX(t) = [D(X(t))X(t)]\,dt + (\sigma I)\,dB(t),$$

where $\sigma > 0$ is a constant, I is the $k \times k$ identity matrix and D is a function from R^k with values in the space of all square matrices of order k.

In (3.7) and (3.8) we have not imposed any nonnegativity requirements on the variables $X(t)$. Such additional restrictions may be handled at the

---

[5] References to earlier works of Samuelson and others are given in Baumol (1970). The turnpike literature has recently been surveyed by McKenzie (1976). See also the definitive paper by Cass and Shell (1976) and the references there.

cost of some technical complications. The standard technique of treating a diffusion in a state space diffemorphic to R^k is indicated in Section III. A simple example of a diffusion $X(t)$ in $(0, \infty)^k$ will also be considered.

One can interpret $X(t)$ as k vectors of prices at time t and consider (3.7) as a generalization of the two-commodity system (3.3). We shall refer to this interpretation later on. One can also consider simultaneous adjustment of prices and stocks (negative stocks being interpreted as "pent up" demand—accepted but unfulfilled orders). In this context the discrete-time model of price and stock adjustment studied by Radner and Hildenbrand (1975) should be mentioned. In their model conditions were directly imposed that played the role of reflecting boundaries. They were able to show that their Markov chain (with a countable state space) was ergodic. Since they were unable to rule out cycling, their "stability" notion was considerably weaker than what we establish [see Eqs. (4.5), (4.8), and (4.26)]. We shall prove that for *any* Borel set B in the state space, $\text{Prob}(X(t) \in B)$ converges to $m(B)$, where m is the invariant measure, uniformly over all Borel sets B as t goes to infinity. This *implies* (but is *not* implied by) the weak convergence of the distribution of $X(t)$ to m [see Billingsley (1968)]. Thus, the stability result is stronger than the one in the discrete time price adjustment model of Green and Majumdar (1975) where stability in the sense of weak convergence of $X(t)$ was obtained under quite artificial restrictions on the adjustment rule. The convergence we assert is in (variation) norm.

IV. Invariant Measures for Diffusions

A. THE ONE-DIMENSIONAL STATE SPACE

We begin with diffusions whose state space is the interval (r_1, r_2), where r_1 may be finite or $-\infty$ and r_2 may be finite or ∞. In this case, the stochastic differential equation (2.6) may be written

(4.1) $\qquad dX(t) = b(X(t))\,dt + \sigma(X(t))\,dt \qquad (t \geq 0).$

Fix r_0 in (r_1, r_2) and define

(4.2) $\qquad a(x) = \sigma^2(x),$

$$m(x) = \int_{r_0}^{x} \frac{2}{a(u)} \exp\left\{ \int_{r_0}^{u} \frac{2b(y)}{a(y)}\,dt \right\} du \qquad \text{if} \quad x \geq r_0$$

$$= \int_{x}^{r_0} \frac{2}{a(u)} \exp\left\{ -\int_{u}^{r_0} \frac{2b(y)}{a(y)}\,dy \right\} du \qquad \text{if} \quad x < r_0.$$

The following result is proved in Mandl (1968, p. 90). The assertion (4.5) follows from m-recurrence of the diffusion. Indeed, from the general theory of (m-recurrent) Markov chains (see Orey, 1971, Theorem 7.1), the assertion holds for the discrete-time Markov process $X(0), X(1), \ldots$; to get the result in continuous time, one uses the fact that the map that transforms a finite signed measure μ to the finite signed measure $\mu_t(B) = \int p(t, x, B)\mu(dx)$ ($B \in B((r_1, r_2))$) is a contraction on the Banach space of finite signed measures.

Theorem 4.1 *Assume that $b(\cdot)$ and $\sigma^2(\cdot)$ are Lipschitzian on compact subsets of (r_1, r_2) and $\sigma(\cdot) > 0$. Then an invariant probability measure for $\{X(t): t \geq 0\}$ satisfying (4.1) exists if and only if*

(4.3)   (i) $\int_{r_1}^{r_2} m(x)\exp\left\{-\int_{r_0}^{x} \frac{2b(y)}{a(y)} dy\right\} dx = \infty,$

(ii) $\int_{r_1}^{r_0} m(x)\exp\left\{\int_{x}^{r_0} \frac{2b(y)}{a(y)} dy\right\} dx = \infty,$

(iii) $\lim_{r \uparrow r_2} m(r) < \infty,$

(iv) $\lim_{r \downarrow r_1} m(r) < \infty.$

In case (4.3) holds, the invariant probability measure is unique and has a density (with respect to Lebesgue measure), which is a constant multiple of the density of m:

(4.4) $g(x) = \frac{c}{a(x)} \exp\left\{2\int_{r_0}^{x} \frac{b(r)}{a(r)} dr\right\} \quad (r_2 \geq x \geq r_0)$

$= \frac{c}{a(x)} \exp\left\{-2\int_{x}^{r_0} \frac{b(r)}{a(r)} dr\right\} \quad (r_1 \leq x \leq r_0).$

Also, in this case,

(4.5) $\lim_{t \uparrow \infty} \operatorname{Prob}(X(t) \in B) = \int_B g(x) \, dx$

uniformly for all Borel subsets B of (r_1, r_2).

Thus, for the one-dimensional state space, we have a complete set of conditions guaranteeing the existence, uniqueness, and global stability of the stochastic steady state of the diffusion. The formula (4.4) can be used to get insight into the nature of the steady state.

B. Multidimensional Diffusions

We now turn to the multidimensional case, considering R^k to be the state space in the first place. Let us introduce the notation

(4.6) $\quad x' = x - z,$

$$A_z(x) = \sum_{i,j=1}^{k} a_{ij}(x' + z) x'_i x'_j / |x'|^2, \qquad B(x) = \sum_{i=1}^{k} a_{ii}(x' + z),$$

$$C_z(x) = 2 \sum_{i=1}^{k} x'_i b_i(x' + z), \qquad \bar{\beta}_z(r) = \sup_{|x'|=r} \frac{B(x) - A_z(x) + C_z(x)}{A_z(x)},$$

$$\underline{\beta}_z(x) = \inf_{|x'|=r} \frac{B(x) - A_z(x) + C_z(x)}{A_z(x)}, \qquad \bar{\alpha}_z(r) = \sup_{|x'|=r} A_z(x),$$

$$\underline{\alpha}_z(r) = \inf_{|x'|=r} A_z(x), \qquad \bar{I}_z(r) = \int_{r_0}^{r} [\bar{\beta}_z(u)/u] \, du,$$

$$\underline{I}_z(r) = \int_{r_0}^{r} [\underline{\beta}_z(u)/u] \, du \qquad (x \in R^k, \ z \in R^k, \ 0 < r_0 < \infty).$$

Parts (a) and (b) of the next theorem are proved in Bhattacharya (1977). Analogous results under additional smoothness assumptions were announced earlier without proof by Khas'minskii (1960, Theorem III of Supplement). Part (c) may be proved by the general argument indicated before the statement of Theorem 4.1.

Theorem 4.2 *Let $k \geq 2$. Assume that $A(\cdot)$ is positive definite and $b(\cdot)$ and $A(\cdot)$ are Lipschitzian on compact subsets of R^k.*

(a) *The diffusion [satisfying (2.6)] admits a unique invariant probability measure if there exist z in R^k and $r_0 > 0$ such that*

(4.7) $\quad \displaystyle\int_{r_0}^{\infty} \exp\{-\bar{I}_z(u)\} \, du = \infty, \qquad \int_{r_0}^{\infty} \frac{1}{\underline{\alpha}_z(u)} \exp\{\underline{I}_z(u)\} \, du < \infty.$

(b) *If there exists z in R^k and $r_0 > 0$ such that*

$$\lim_{N \to \infty} \frac{\int_{r_0}^{N} \exp\{-\bar{I}_z(s)\} \left(\int_{r_0}^{s} [\exp\{\bar{I}_z(u)\}/\bar{\alpha}_z(u)] \, du \right) ds}{\int_{r_0}^{N} \exp\{-\underline{I}_z(u)\} \, du} = \infty$$

then there does not exist an invariant measure for the diffusion.

(c) *In case (4.7) holds, one also has*

(4.8) $\quad \displaystyle\lim_{t \to \infty} \sup_{B \in \mathcal{B}(R^k)} |\mathrm{Prob}(X(t) \in B) - m(B)| = 0,$

for all B in $(\mathcal{B}(R^k)$ independent of the initial distribution of $X(0)$, where m is the unique invariant probability measure.

Remark In some important cases, (a) and (b) are actually necessary *and* sufficient conditions for the existence of an invariant probability measure [see Bhattacharya (1977)].

The problem of computing the invariant measure for diffusions on R^k is taken up later on in the section. Our next task is to consider diffusions on certain open subsets G of R^k and the corresponding invariant measures. Since all nondegenerate open intervals (of R^1) are C^∞ diffeomorphic to R^1, any Markov process with state space R^1 may be viewed as a Markov process with state space $(0, 1)$ [or, $(0, \infty)$, or, (c, d), say] or vice versa. More significantly, a transformation law of K. Itô's, known as Itô's lemma [see McKean (1969)], allows one to compute the drift and diffusion coefficients of one process in terms of those of the other. In general one has the following result.

Proposition 4.3 (a) *There exists a one–one correspondence between the class of all diffusions (with coefficients which are Lipschitzian on compacts) on R^k and the class of all diffusions (with coefficients which are Lipschitzian on compacts) on an open set G (of R^k) which is C^2 diffeomorphic to R^k.*

(b) *Let $h = (h_1, \ldots, h_k)$ denote this diffeomorphism (on G onto R^k), and let $\tilde{b}(\cdot)$ and $\tilde{A}(\cdot)$ be the drift coefficient and the diffusion matrix, respectively, for the diffusion on G. Then the drift coefficient $b(\cdot)$ of the corresponding diffusion on R^k is given by*

$$(4.9) \quad b_i(x) = \sum_{j=1}^k \tilde{b}_j(h^{-1}(x))D_j h_i)(h^{-1}(x))$$

$$+ \left[\frac{1}{2} \sum_{j,j'=1}^k \tilde{a}_{jj'}(h^{-1}(x)) \cdot (D_j D_{j'} h_i)(h^{-1}(x))\right] \quad (1 \leq i \leq k).$$

The diffusion matrix $A(\cdot)$ is given by

$$(4.10) \quad a_{ij}(x) = \sum_{j',j''=1}^k (D_{j'} h_i)(h^{-1}(x)) \cdot D_{j''} h_j(h^{-1}(x))\tilde{a}_{j',j''}$$

$$= \langle \operatorname{grad} h_i, \tilde{A} \operatorname{grad} h_j \rangle_{h^{-1}(x)},$$

where $\langle \, , \, \rangle$ denotes Euclidean inner product.

We now turn to diffusions whose state spaces are of the form $\bar{G} = G \cup \partial G$, where G is a connected open subset of R^k and ∂G its topological boundary. In case $k = 1$ one needs to consider either $G = (0, 1)$, $\bar{G} = [0, 1]$ or $G = (0, \infty)$, $\bar{G} = [0, \infty)$, because all other cases may be reduced to one of these two by diffeomorphism. In general to define (or construct) a diffusion on $\bar{G}$ it is not enough to specify the coefficients $b(\cdot)$ and $A(\cdot)$. One must also prescribe (consistently with the Markov property) the behavior of the stochastic process at (or, on reaching) the boundary ∂G. The two most important types of boundary conditions are (i) absorption and (ii) instantaneous reflection. In the first case (i) once the Markov process hits the boundary it stays there for ever; in the second case (ii) the process gets instantaneously reflected to the interior when it hits the boundary. To keep the exposition simple we consider as our G a connected open subset of R^k given by

$$(4.11) \qquad G = \{x : \phi(x) > 0\}, \qquad \partial G = \{x : \phi(x) = 0\},$$

where ϕ is a real-valued function on R^k whose partial derivatives of order three exist and are continuous. Also, assume that

$$(4.12) \qquad \sum_{i=1}^{k} \left(\frac{\partial \phi(x)}{\partial x_i}\right)^2 > d \quad \text{for} \quad x \in \partial G,$$

d being a positive constant. Let now a drift $b(\cdot)$ and a diffusion matrix $A(\cdot)$ be specified on G. Assume that these coefficients may be extended to all of R^k such that (i) the extended $b(\cdot)$ and $A(\cdot)$ are Lipschitzian on compact subsets of R^k, (ii) the extended $A(\cdot)$ is positive definite, (iii) the resulting diffusion (whatever be the initial state) is nonexplosive. For some specified initial distribution μ on $\bar{G}$, let $\{X(t) : t \geq 0\}$ be the diffusion so defined. Let

$$(4.13) \qquad \zeta = \inf\{t > 0 : X(t) \in \partial G\},$$

taking $\zeta = \infty$ in case the trajectory never hits ∂G. Let

$$(4.14) \qquad \tilde{X}(t) = \begin{cases} X(t) & \text{if } t < \zeta \\ X(\zeta) & \text{if } t \geq \zeta. \end{cases}$$

Then $\{\tilde{X}(t) : t \geq 0\}$ is the diffusion process (having initial distribution μ) with absorption at ∂G. In this case every probability measure whose support is contained in ∂G is invariant. However, there does not exist a unique limiting distribution of $\tilde{X}(t)$ (as $t \to \infty$) that is independent of the initial state (or distribution). From our point of view, therefore, the process $\{\tilde{X}(t) : t \geq 0\}$ is not very important. For a precise construction of a diffusion with instantaneous reflection we refer to Stroock and Varadhan (1971). We restrict ourselves to the case in which the reflection takes place in the direction of the inward *conormal* $n(x) = (n_1(x), \ldots, n_k(x))$ defined by

$$(4.15) \qquad n_j(x) = \sum_{i=1}^{k} a_{ij} \frac{\partial \phi(x)}{\partial x_i} \qquad (i \leq j \leq k).$$

Recall that ϕ and G are related by (4.11). Denote by $\mathscr{D}$, $\mathscr{D}^*$ the differential operators

(4.16)
$$(\mathscr{D}f)(x) = \frac{1}{2}\sum_{i,j=1}^{k} a_{ij}(x)\frac{\partial^2 f(x)}{\partial x_i \partial x_j} + \sum_{i=1}^{k} b_i(x)\frac{\partial f(x)}{\partial x_i},$$

$$(\mathscr{D}^*f)(x) = \frac{1}{2}\sum_{i,j=1}^{k} \frac{\partial^2}{\partial x_i \partial x_j}(a_{ij}(x)f(x))$$

$$- \sum_{i=1}^{k} \frac{\partial}{\partial x_i}(b_i(x)f(x)).$$

Then if f and g are twice continuously differentiable functions defined on a neighborhood of $\bar{G} = G \cup \partial G$, then one has

(4.17)
$$\int_{G \cup \partial G} [g(x)(\mathscr{D}f)(x) - f(x)(\mathscr{D}^*g)(x)]\, dx$$

$$= \frac{1}{2}\int_{G \cup \partial G} \sum_{i=1}^{k} \frac{\partial}{\partial x_i}\left\{\left[\sum_{j=1}^{k} a_{ij}(x)\left(g(x)\frac{\partial f(x)}{\partial x_j} - f(x)\frac{\partial g(x)}{\partial x_j}\right)\right.\right.$$

$$\left.\left. - f(x)g(x)\frac{\partial a_{ij}(x)}{\partial x_j}\right] + 2f(x)g(x)b_i(x)\right\}dx.$$

It follows from the divergence theorem [see Smirnov (1964, p. 431)] that

(4.18)
$$\int_{G \cup \partial G} [g(x)(\mathscr{D}f)(x) - f(x)(\mathscr{D}^*g)(x)]\, dx$$

$$= \int_{\partial G} [g(x)(\mathscr{L}f)(x) - f(x)(\mathscr{L}g)(x) + f(x)g(x)Q(x)]\, ds$$

where ds is the surface area measure on ∂G, and

(4.19)
$$(\mathscr{L}f)(x) = \frac{1}{2}\sum_{i,j=1}^{k} a_{ij}(x)\frac{\partial f(x)}{\partial x_j}\frac{\partial \phi(x)}{\partial x_i}\bigg/|\operatorname{grad}\phi(x)|,$$

$$Q(x) = \sum_{i=1}^{k}\left(b_i(x) - \frac{1}{2}\sum_{j=1}^{k}\frac{\partial a_{ij}(x)}{\partial x_j}\right)\frac{\partial \phi(x)}{\partial x_i}\bigg/|\operatorname{grad}\phi(x)|,$$

where $\operatorname{grad} \phi(x) = (\partial \phi(x)/\partial x_1, \ldots, \partial \phi(x)/\partial x_k)$. If f satisfies the boundary condition

(4.20)
$$\sum_{i,j=1}^{k} a_{ij}(x)\frac{\partial f(x)}{\partial x_j}\frac{\partial \phi(x)}{\partial x_i} = 0 \qquad (x \in \partial G),$$

and g satisfies the boundary condition

(4.21) $$\sum_{i,j=1}^{k} a_{ij}(x) \frac{\partial g(x)}{\partial x_j} \frac{\partial \phi(x)}{\partial x_i}$$
$$+ g(x) \sum_{i=1}^{k} \left(-2b_i(x) + \sum_{j=1}^{k} \frac{\partial a_{ij}(x)}{\partial x_j} \right) \frac{\partial \phi(x)}{\partial x_i} = 0 \quad (x \in \partial G),$$

then (4.18) reduces to

(4.22) $$\int_{G \cup \partial G} g(x)(\mathcal{D}f)(x)\, dx = \int_{G \cup \partial G} f(x)(\mathcal{D}^*g)(x)\, dx,$$

and $\mathcal{D}$ and $\mathcal{D}^*$ become formal adjoints of each other. The role of $\mathcal{D}^*$ in computation of invariant measures is brought out in the following theorem. Parts (b) and (c) of this theorem deal with diffusions reflected at the boundary in the direction of the inward conormal. We shall write $\mathcal{D}_y^*$ instead of $\mathcal{D}^*$ to indicate that the differentiation is with respect to y, in case of possible ambiguity.

Theorem 4.4 (a) *Let G be an open connected subset of R^k. Let $b(\cdot)$ be a thrice continuously differentiable function on G into R^k and let $A(\cdot)$ be a thrice continuously differentiable matrix ($k \times k$) valued function on G. Assume also that $A(\cdot)$ is symmetric and positive definite. If there exists an invariant probability measure m for the diffusion on G with drift coefficient $b(\cdot)$ and diffusion matrix $A(\cdot)$, then m is absolutely continuous with respect to Lebesgue measure and the density g of m satisfies*

(4.23) $$\mathcal{D}^*g(x) = 0 \quad (x \in G).$$

(b) *Let G be an open connected subset of R^k such that G, ∂G admit the representation (4.11), where ϕ is thrice continuously differentiable and satisfies (4.12). Let $b(\cdot)$ and $A(\cdot)$ be as in (a). Assume further that $b(\cdot)$ and $A(\cdot)$ may be extended to all of R^k to satisfy the same differentiability and positive definiteness. If the diffusion on R^k with the extended coefficients $b(\cdot)$ and $A(\cdot)$ is nonexplosive, then for each initial distribution on G there exists a unique diffusion $\{\bar{X}(t): t \geq 0\}$ on $\bar{G}$ whose transition probability function $P(t, x, dy)$ admits a density $p(t, x, y)$ satisfying*

(4.24) $$\frac{\partial p(t, x, y)}{\partial y} = \mathcal{D}_y^* p(t, x, y) \quad (x \in \bar{G}, \quad y \in G, \quad t > 0),$$
$$\mathcal{M}_y p(t, x, y) = 0 \quad (x \in \bar{G}, \quad y \in \partial G, \quad t > 0),$$

where $\mathscr{M}_y$ is the differential operator

(4.25) $$\mathscr{M}_y p = \sum_{i,j=1}^{k} a_{ij}(y) \frac{\partial \phi(y)}{\partial y_i} \frac{\partial p}{\partial y_j}$$
$$+ p \sum_{i=1}^{k} \left[-2b_i(y) + \sum_{j=1}^{k} \frac{\partial a_{ij}(y)}{\partial y_i} \right] \frac{\partial \phi(y)}{\partial y_i}.$$

If this diffusion admits an invariant probability measure (necessarily unique), then it has a density g satisfying

(4.26) $\quad \mathscr{D}_y^* g(y) = 0 \quad (y \in G), \quad \mathscr{M}_y g(y) = 0 \quad (y \in \partial G).$

In case such an invariant measure exists one has

(4.27) $$\lim_{t \to \infty} \text{Prob}(\bar{X}(t) \in B) = \int_B g(y)\, dy$$

uniformly for all Borel sets B of $\bar{G}$.

(c) *In* (b) *if one assumes that G is bounded* (i.e., $\bar{G}$ *compact*), *then there exists a unique invariant probability measure and the convergence* (4.27) *is exponentially fast uniformly over all Borel subsets of $\bar{G}$.*

Proof It follows from Theorem 1 of Itô (1958) that the diffusion on G under the hypothesis of (a) as well as the diffusion on $\bar{G}$ under the hypothesis (b) admit a transition density $p(t, x, y)$ ($t > 0$, x, y in the state space) such that (4.24) hold [only the first relation in case (a)]. In view of (2.9) this implies that the invariant probability measure (when it exists) has a density g, say. By modifying g on a set of Lebesgue measure zero, if necessary, one has

(4.28) $$g(y) = \int p(t, x, y) g(x)\, dx \quad (y \in G \text{ or } \bar{G}),$$

where the integral is over the state space. By Theorem 9 in Itô (1958) the right-hand side of (4.28) satisfies (4.24) (with p replaced by this integral). This proves Eqs. (4.23) and (4.26). Relation (4.27) follows from the general argument indicated before the statement of Theorem 4.1. It remains to prove that the convergence (4.27) is exponentially fast uniformly over all Borel subsets of $\bar{G}$ under the hypothesis of (c). For this it is enough to check Doeblin's condition [see Doob (1953, Theorem 2.1, p. 256)]. (D): *there exist $\varepsilon > 0$, $t > 0$, and a finite measure λ on $\bar{G}$ such that for all $x \in \bar{G}$ and all Borel sets B of $\bar{G}$ the inequality $\lambda(B) \leq \varepsilon$ implies $P(t, x, B) \leq 1 - \varepsilon$.* Fix $t > 0$ and take λ to be Lebesgue measure restricted to $\bar{G}$. Suppose (D) does not hold. Then there exist sequences $\{x_n\}_{n \geq 1}$ in $\bar{G}$ and $\{B_n\}_{n \geq 1}$ such that $\lambda(B_n) \leq 1/2^n$, $P(t, x_n, B_n) \geq 1 - 1/2^n$. Since $\bar{G}$ is compact, assume, without loss of generality, that $x_n \to x_\infty \in \bar{G}$ as $t \to \infty$. In view of the continuity of $p(t, x, y)$ as a function of x, it follows from Scheffé's theorem [see Billingsley (1968)] that $P(t, x_n, B) \to P(t, x_\infty, B)$ uniformly over all Borel subsets B of $\bar{G}$. Hence, given $\delta > 0$, $P(t, x_\infty, B_n) \geq 1 - 1/2^n - \delta$ for all sufficiently large n. Letting $B_\infty = \limsup B_n$ one then has $P(t, x_\infty, B_\infty) \geq 1 - \delta$, $\lambda(B_\infty) = 0$. Therefore, $P(t, x_\infty, B_\infty) = 1$, $\lambda(B_\infty) = 0$. But this is not possible, since $P(t, x_\infty, dy)$ is absolutely continuous with respect to Lebesgue measure. Thus Doeblin's condition holds. Q.E.D.

C. Computation of Invariant Measures

1. One-Dimentional Diffusions

Since (4.4) gives the density of the invariant probability measure when the diffusion is on an open interval, we need to consider only the state spaces $[0, \infty)$, and $[0, 1]$. Write $a(x) = \sigma^2(x)$. If there exists a finite invariant measure with density g, then g satisfies the equation $\mathscr{D}^*g = 0$ [see (4.25)], i.e.,

$$\frac{1}{2}\frac{d^2}{dx^2}(a(x)g(x)) - \frac{d}{dx}(b(x)g(x)) = 0$$

for all x in the interior of the state space. This leads to

$$\frac{d}{dx}(a(x)g(x)) = 2b(x)g(x) + C_1$$

or

$$a(x)\frac{dg(x)}{dx} = \left[2b(x) - \frac{da(x)}{dx}\right]g(x) + C_1.$$

If the interval (state space) has a boundary point (or two boundary points) then the boundary condition at the boundary is precisely (4.28) with $C_1 = 0$ [see Eq. (4.25); use $\phi(x) = x$ if state space is $[0, \infty)$, and $\phi(x) = x(1-x)$ in case it is $[0, 1]$]. Thus in all cases g is given by

$$\frac{d \log g(x)}{dx} = \frac{2b(x)}{a(x)} - \frac{d \log a(x)}{dx},$$

or

$$\frac{d}{dx}\log[a(x)g(x)] = \frac{2b(x)}{a(x)},$$

or

(4.29) $$g(x) = \frac{C}{a(x)}\exp\left\{2\int_0^x [b(y)/a(y)]\,dy\right\}.$$

If the diffusion is on $[0, \infty)$, $b(\cdot)$ and $\sigma^2(\cdot)$ are locally Lipschitzian, and (4.3) (ii), (iv) hold, then one can show [see Mandl (1968)], that there exists a unique invariant probability measure whose density is given by (4.29) for $0 \le x < \infty$. Note that (4.29) is of the same form as (4.4) with $r_0 = 0$.

1. Multidimensional Diffusions

Example 1 (Symmetric diffusions on R^k) If the relations

$$(4.30) \qquad b_i(x) = \frac{1}{2} \sum_{j=1}^{k} \frac{\partial a_{ij}(x)}{\partial x_j} \qquad (1 \le i \le k),$$

hold on a k-dimensional state space R^k or $\bar{G}$ and if reflection (in case ∂G is nonempty) is in the direction of the inward conormal, then the corresponding diffusion is said to be *symmetric*. The reason for this nomenclature is that under standard assumptions the transition density p then satisfies

$$(4.31) \qquad p(t, x, y) = p(t, y, x).$$

This follows from the fact that in this case $\mathscr{D} = \mathscr{D}^*$, so that the backward equation of Kolmogorov $\partial p/\partial t = \mathscr{D}_x p$ is of the same form as the forward equation $\partial p/\partial t = \mathscr{D}_y^* p$, and the boundary condition (4.20) (satisfied by p as a function of x) coincides with the boundary condition (4.21) (satisfied by p as a function of y). If the state space is $G \cup \partial G$ and G is bounded (we assume, or course, that ∂G is smooth), then the unique invariant probability measure is the *uniform distribution* on $G \cup \partial G$. As a very special case, the standard Brownian motion on $[0, 1]$ reflected at $\{0, 1\}$ has as its invariant probability measure the uniform distribution on $[0, 1]$. Note that the function $g(x) \equiv 1$ solves $(\mathscr{D}^* g)(x) = 0$ along with the boundary condition (4.21).

Example 2 Consider a diffusion on an open set G admitting an invariant probability measure or a reflecting diffusion on $G \cup \partial G$ (for a smooth bounded G) with diffusion matrix $\sigma^2 I$ (I is the identity matrix) and drift vector $b(\cdot)$ as the gradient of a ("potential") function ψ. Then

$$(4.32) \qquad g(x) = c \exp\left\{\frac{2}{\sigma^2} \psi(x)\right\}$$

satisfies $(\mathscr{D}^* g)(x) = 0$ as well as the boundary condition (4.21). Hence g is the density of the unique invariant probability measure (if

$$c = \left[\int_{G \cup \partial G} \exp\left\{\frac{2}{\sigma^2} \psi(x)\right\} dx\right]^{-1}).$$

More generally, suppose that the diffusion matrix $A(\cdot)$ and the drift vector $b(\cdot)$ are such that

(4.33) $$A(x)^{-1} \begin{Bmatrix} 2b_1(x) - \sum_{j=1}^{k} \dfrac{\partial a_{ij}(x)}{\partial x_j} \\ \cdots\cdots\cdots\cdots\cdots\cdots \\ 2b_k(x) - \sum_{j=1}^{k} \dfrac{\partial a_{kj}(x)}{\partial x_j} \end{Bmatrix} = (\operatorname{grad} \tilde{\psi})(x)$$

(x belonging to a neighborhood of $G \cup \partial G$) for a ("potential") function $\tilde{\psi}$, then the invariant density is given by

(4.34) $$g(x) = c \exp[\tilde{\psi}(x)\}$$

where $c = [\int_{G \cup \partial G} \exp\{\tilde{\psi}(x)\} \, dx]^{-1}$. To see this note that [see (4.16)]

$$(\mathscr{D}^*g)(x) = \frac{1}{2} \sum_{j=1}^{k} \frac{\partial}{\partial x_i} \left[\sum_{j=1}^{k} a_{ij}(x) \frac{\partial g(x)}{\partial x_i} - 2b_i(x)g(x) + g(x) \sum_{j=1}^{k} \frac{\partial a_{ij}(x)}{\partial x_j} \right]$$

vanishes on G if

(4.35) $$\sum_{j=1}^{k} a_{ij}(x) \frac{\partial g(x)}{\partial x_i} - g(x)\left[2b_i(x) - \sum_{j=1}^{k} \frac{\partial a_{ij}(x)}{\partial x_i}\right] = 0 \quad (1 \leq i \leq k),$$

or

$$\sum_{j=1}^{k} a_{ij}(x) \frac{\partial \log g(x)}{\partial x_j} = 2b_i(x) - \sum_{j=1}^{k} \frac{\partial a_{ij}(x)}{\partial x_j}, \quad (1 \leq i \leq k),$$

or grad log g is equal to the left-hand side of (4.33).

Hence, if there exists $\tilde{\psi}$ satisfying (4.38), then one can solve the equation $\mathscr{D}^*g = 0$ by using (4.34). Note that the boundary condition (4.21) is automatically satisfied since (4.35) holds in a neighborhood of $G \cup \partial G$. It is also well known [see Allendoerfer (1974, pp. 39–40)] that if G is simply connected (e.g., if G is a convex open set) and $\bar{b}(\cdot)$ is a vector-valued continuously differentiable function on G (into R^k), then $\bar{b}(\cdot)$ is the gradient of a real-valued function $\tilde{\psi}$ on G if and only if $\partial \bar{b}_i(x)/\partial x_j = \partial \bar{b}_j(x)/\partial x_i$ for all i, j ($1 \leq i, j \leq k$); the function $\tilde{\psi}(x)$ may then be obtained as the line integral along a smooth curve joining x to a fixed point $x_0 \in G$. The value $\tilde{\psi}$ is unique up to the addition of a constant. Note that if (4.33) holds for a diffusion on an unbounded domain and there exists a finite invariant measure, then its density is still given by (4.34). It is also clear that Example 1 is a special case of Example 2.

We now make a few concluding remarks.

Remark 1 An invariant probability measure (when it exists) describes the limiting (as $t \to \infty$) *steady-state* behavior of the Markov process; when such measures do not exist, under suitable conditions, other types of asymptotic behavior may be deduced. For example as $t \to \infty$, $X(t)/\sqrt{t}$ may have a limiting Gaussian distribution [see Friedman (1975, Theorem 4.1, p. 185)].

Remark 2 Some of the theory outlined in this paper can be extended to the case of time dependent (drift and diffusion) coefficients. The corresponding diffusions are called (time) *nonhomogeneous*. It is one of the beauties of the theory of K. Itô that the construction of such diffusions poses no additional problem. Physically, nonhomogeniety corresponds to a change (in time) in the law of evolution of the process. In order that a nonhomogeneous process may reach a steady state (as $t \to \infty$) the coefficients will have to converge in some manner to those of a homogeneous diffusion admitting such a steady state [see, e.g., Bhattacharya and Subramanian (1980)].

Remark 3 In this article we have not considered diffusions that are reflected at the boundary in directions other than the inward conormal direction. Under suitable conditions existence of unique invariant probability measures may be proved when the reflection is in other (oblique) directions [see, e.g., Freidlin, (1963)].

V. Stability Results for the Economic Models

We now go back to the particular examples of Section III and try to see the implications of the mathematical results of Section IV. The examples III.A and III.B give rise to one-dimensional diffusions and are handled first by Theorems 4.1 and 4.4.

A. THE PRICE ADJUSTMENT PROCESS IN THE TWO-COMMODITY WORLD

For the two-commodity world in which the price adjustment was specified by (3.3), our main smoothness assumptions are

Assumption 5.1 $z_1(x_1, x_2)$ *is continuously differentiable on* Δ.

Assumption 5.2 $\sigma(x_1)$ *is continuously differentiable on* $(0, 1)$ *and* $\sigma(x_1) > 0$ *for all x in* $(0, 1)$.

Going back to Theorem 4.1, let us take $r_1 = 0$ and $r_2 = 1$. The necessary and sufficient condition for the existence of a stochastic steady state follows from (4.3), and (4.5) is the global stability property of the steady state [it implies that $x(t)$ converges weakly to m, which obtains if (4.5) holds for sets B whose boundaries are of m measure 0]. It may be possible to get some idea of the restrictions involved in (4.3). Take, for example, $\sigma(x_1) = \sigma > 0$, a positive constant (independent of x_1). Then (4.3) is satisfied if $z_1(x_1, 1 - x_1)$ goes to plus infinity at least at the rate of $1/x_1$ as x_1 goes to zero, and $z_1(x_1, 1 - x_1)$ goes to minus infinity at least as fast as $1/(1 - x_1)$ as x_1 goes to one. Next, note that the condition is quite unrelated to the nature or number of points x_1^* in $(0, 1)$ satisfying $z_1(x_1^*, 1 - x_1^*) = 0$. Suppose now that $\partial z_1/\partial x_1$ and $\partial z_1/\partial x_2$ are both continuous and bounded on Δ and $\sigma^2(\cdot)$ is bounded away from zero and plus infinity. Then the boundary points for x_1, namely, 0 and 1, are accessible for the process $\{X_1(t), t \geq 0\}$ satisfying (3.3). If, now, it is assumed that the process is reflected instantaneously upon hitting the boundary as discussed in Section IV, the existence of an invariant measure, and exponential convergence to it are now obtained by appealing to Theorem 4.4.

The density of the unique invariant measure is given by (4.29). It follows that when the process is in stochastic equilibrium, neither the expected price system EX_1 will in general satisfy $z_1(EX_1, 1 - EX_1) = 0$, nor will it be true that $Ez_1 = 0$. It will be of some interest to characterize the largest class of excess demand functions for which such properties can be obtained.

B. Stochastic Steady State of the Industry Size

Since the analysis in this case is very similar to our previous example, we shall omit the details. Make the assumptions

Assumption 5.3 $\sigma(\cdot) = \sigma > 0$ *is a constant.*

Assumption 5.4 $\lim \sup_{x \to \infty} b[f(x) - \bar{p}] < 0.$

Assumption 5.5 $b[f(x) - \bar{p}]$ *goes to plus infinity as x goes to zero at least as fast as $1/x$.*

Under these assumptions there exists a unique globally stable stochastic steady state.

C. Stability Results for Multidimensional Diffusions

We shall now discuss global stability conditions for diffusions in R^k. The principal mathematical result here is Theorem 4.2, and we shall try to interpret the condition (4.3) for some simpler cases.

It is convenient to recall a well-known sufficient condition for global stability of a deterministic price adjustment process. Recall that if one is studying the system

(5.1) $$dx_i/dt = z_i(x_1(t), \ldots, x_k(t)) \qquad (i = 1, \ldots, k),$$

where x_i is the price of commodity i and z_i is the excess demand, global stability can be proved [see Arrow and Hahn (1971, Chapter 11) for the appropriate differentiability and other technical conditions] if

(5.2) there is some x^* such that $\sum_{i=1}^{k}(x_i - x_i^*)z_i(x) < 0 \qquad$ for all $\quad x \neq x^*$.

Since $\sum_{i=1}^{k} x_i z_i(x) = 0$ by Walras's law, (5.2) is equivalent to $\sum_{i=1}^{k} x_i^* z_i(x) > 0$ for all $x \neq x^*$. The property (5.2), often referred to as the weak axiom of revealed preference, holds in a number of cases (e.g., when commodities are gross substitutes).

Needless to say, the general stochastic system is considerably more complicated. But let us investigate the following special case where the "error term" does not depend on the state variable, i.e., let us assume

Assumption 5.6 $\sum(x) = \sigma I$ where $\sigma > 0$ and I is the $k \times k$ identity matrix.

We can now state the

Basic Stability Condition *There are positive numbers $d > 0$, $M > 0$ and a vector x^* in R^k such that for all x in R^k with $|x| \geq M$ one has*

(5.3) $$\sum_{i=1}^{k}(x_i - x_i^*)b_i(x)/|x - x^*| < -d < 0.$$

Going back to (4.6) and using Assumption 5.5, we can compute the following (taking $z = x^*$, and dropping the subscript to simplify notation):

(5.4) $$A(x) = \sigma^2, \qquad B(x) = k\sigma^2$$

$$C(x) = 2\sum_{i=1}^{k}(x_i - x_i^*)b_i(x), \qquad \alpha(r) - \bar{\alpha}(r) = \sigma^2.$$

To apply Theorem 4.2 one can simply choose any r_0 satisfying

(5.5) $$r_0^2 \geq M + |x^*|.$$

The convergence and divergence of the integrals involved in (4.7) can be easily verified. Thus, with a $\sum(x) = \sigma I$, our basic stability condition (5.3) is enough to ensure the existence of a stochastic steady state and its global stability.

For the linear system

(5.6) $$dX(t) = [D(X(t))X(t)]\,dt + (\sigma I)\,dB(t)$$

the stability conditions can be simplified further. Let D' be the transpose of the matrix D. Our first assumption for the linear system is

Assumption 5.7 $[D(x) + D'(x)]/2$ *is negative definite.*

Let $-\lambda(x)$ be the largest eigenvalue of $[D(x) + D'(x)]/2$. In addition to the negative definiteness condition just mentioned we require

Assumption 5.8 *There are $\varepsilon > 0$ and $r_0 > 0$ such that $|x| \geq r_0$ implies*

(5.7) $$\lambda(x) > (k + \varepsilon)\sigma^2/2|x|^2.$$

Two important cases in which (5.7) can be verified are (a) $\inf_{x \in R^k} \lambda(x) > 0$ or (b) when $D(x)$ does not depend on x and is a constant $k \times k$ matrix satisfying Assumption 5.6. In the last case, $\lambda > 0$ and (5.7) can be met by choosing r_0 large enough. With such a constant D, let

$$\psi(x) = \frac{1}{\sigma^2} \sum_{i,j=1}^{k} x_i x_j D_{ij}.$$

Then $b(x) = \operatorname{grad} \psi(x)$. From (4.32), the density $g(x)$ of the invariant measure is

(5.8) $$g(x) = c \exp[2\psi(x)/\sigma^2],$$

which is a Gaussian density.

D. Diffusions in $(0, \infty)^k$

Since nonnegativity requirements are quite common in economics, it is useful to consider an interesting example of a diffusion in $(0, \infty)^k$ that has a steady state given by a log normal distribution.

Let h be the C^∞ diffeomorphism on $(0, \infty)^k$ onto R^k defined by

(5.9) $$h(x) = (\log x_1, \ldots, \log x_k) \qquad x = (x_1, \ldots, x_k) \in (0, \infty)^k.$$

Suppose that we have the following diffusion on $(0, \infty)^k$:

(5.10) $$dX(t) = \tilde{b}(X(t))\, dt + \tilde{\Sigma}(X(t))\, dB(t) \qquad t \geq 0,$$

where there exist a matrix valued function $\tilde{D}(\cdot)$ and a positive constant σ such that, writing $\tilde{A}(\cdot) = \tilde{\Sigma}(\cdot)^2$,

$$\tilde{b}_i(x) = x_i \sum_{j=1}^{n} \tilde{D}_{ij}(x)\log x_j + \frac{1}{2}\sigma^2 x_i \qquad (1 \leq i \leq k).$$

(5.11) $$\tilde{a}_{ij}(x) = 0 \qquad \text{if } i \neq j$$

$$\tilde{a}_{ii}(x) = \sigma^2 x_i^2 \qquad (1 \leq i, j \leq k).$$

Applying Proposition 4.3, the diffusion $\{Y(t) = h(X(t)) : t \geq 0\}$ on R^k has a drift coefficient $b(\cdot)$ and a diffusion matrix $A(\cdot)$ given by

(5.12) $\qquad b_i(y) = \sum_{j=1}^{k} D_{ij}(y) y_j \qquad (1 \leq i \leq k)$

$$a_{ij}(y) = 0 \text{ if } i \neq j, \qquad a_{ii}(y) = \sigma^2 \qquad (i \leq i, j \leq k).$$

Here we have written

(5.13) $\qquad D_{ij}(y) = \tilde{D}_{ij}(e^{y_1}, \ldots, e^{y_k}) \qquad (y \in R^k).$

From (5.12) the reader should be able to recognize that we are really back to our "linear" example of the last section. When the diffusion $\{Y(t) : t \geq 0\}$ on R admits a unique invariant measure m with a density g, the diffusion $\{X(t) : t \geq 0\}$ we started with admits a unique invariant measure $\tilde{m}$ with a density $\tilde{g}$ given (by a change of variables) by

(5.14) $\qquad \tilde{g}(x) = (x_1 \cdots x_k)^{-1} g(\log x_1, \ldots, \log x_k) \qquad x \in (0, \infty)^k,$

In the special case where $\tilde{D}(\cdot) = \tilde{D}$, a constant matrix with $[\tilde{D} + \tilde{D}']/2$ being negative definite, $\tilde{g}$ becomes a (*multivariate*) *log normal density*

(5.15) $\qquad g(x) = c(x_1 \cdots x_k)^{-1} \exp\left[\frac{1}{\sigma^2} \sum_{i,j=1}^{k} D_{ij}(\log x_i)(\log x_j) \right].$

The diffusion $\{Y(t) : t \geq 0\}$ in this case is (the multidimensional analog of) the *Ornstein–Uhlenbeck* process.

ACKNOWLEDGMENTS

The research reported in this paper was supported by N.S.F. Grants MCS-76-06118 and SOC-76-14342 and a fellowship from the John Simon Guggenheim Foundation for Mukul Majumdar.

REFERENCES

Allendoerfer, C. B. (1974). *Functions of Several Variables and Calculus on Manifolds*. New York: Macmillan.
Arrow, K. J., and Hahn, F. (1971). *General Competitive Analysis*. San Francisco, California: Holden Day.
Baumol, W. J. (1970). *Economic Dynamics*. New York: Macmillan.
Bhattacharya, R. N. (1977). Criteria for recurrence and existence of invariant measures for multidimensional diffusions. *Annals of Probability* **6**, 541–553.
Bhattacharya, R. N., and Majumdar, M. (1973). Random exchange economies. *Journal of Economic Theory* **6**, 37–67.

Bhattacharya, R. N., and Ramasubramanian, S. (1980). Recurrence and ergodicity of diffusions (to appear)
Billingsley, P. (1968). *Convergence of Probability Measures.* New York: Wiley.
Bismut, J. (1975). Growth and optimal intertemporal allocation of risks. *Journal of Economic Theory* **10**, 239-257.
Bourguignon, F. (1974). A particular class of continuous time stochastic growth models. *Journal of Economic Theory* **9**, 141-158.
Cass, D., and Shell, K. (1976). The structure and stability of competitive dynamical systems. *Journal of Economic Theory* (*Symposium on Hamiltonian Dynamics in Economics*) **12**, 31-70.
Dobb, J. L. (1953). *Stochastic Processes.* New York: Wiley.
Freidlin, M. (1963). Diffusion processes with reflection and the directional derivative problem on a manifold with boundary. *Theory of Probability and Its Applications* **8**, 80-88.
Friedman, A. (1975). *Stochastic Differential Equations and Applications*, Vol. 1. New York: Academic Press.
Green, J., and Majumdar, M. (1975). The nature of stochastic equilibria. *Econometrica* **43**, 647-660.
Hildenbrand, W. (1971). Random preferences in equilibrium analysis. *Journal of Economic Theory* **3**, 414-429.
Inaba, F. (1976). Stochastic entry and exit without expectations. *The Review of Economic Studies* **45**, 535-545.
Itô, K. (1951). On stochastic differential equations. *Memoirs of the American Mathematical Society* **4**.
Itô, S. (1958). Fundamental solutions of parabolic differential equations and boundary value problems. *Journal of the Mathematical Society of Japan* **27**, 55-102.
Khas'minskii, R. Z. (1960). Engodic properties of recurrent diffusion processes and stabilization of the solution to the Cauchy problem for parabolic equations. *Theory of Probability and Applications* **5**, 179-196.
Mandl, P. (1968). *Analytical Treatment of One Dimensional Markov Processes.* Berlin and New York: Springer-Verlag.
McKean, H. (1969). *Stochastic Differential Equations*, Vol. 44, pp. 841-866. New York: Academic Press.
McKenzie, L. (1976). Turnpike theory. *Econometrica* **44**, 841-865.
Merton, R. (1975). An asymptotic theory of growth under uncertainty. *Review of Economic Studies* **42**, 375-394.
Radner, R. (1976). Market equilibrium and uncertainty: Concepts and problems. *Frontiers of Quantitative Economics* (M. Intrilligator and D. Kendrick, eds.), Vol. 2, pp. 43-91. Amsterdam: North-Holland Publ.
Radner, R., and Hildenbrand, W. (1976). *Market Adjustment in Disequilibrium with Random Disturbances* (mimeographed).
Stroock, D. W., and Varadhan, S. R. S. (1971). Diffusion processes with boundary conditions. *Communications on Pure and Applied Mathematics* **24**, 147-225.
Smirnov, V. I. (1964). *A Course in Higher Mathematics*, Vol. 4. Oxford: Pergamon.

R. N. Bhattacharya
DEPARTMENT OF MATHEMATICS
THE UNIVERSITY OF ARIZONA
TUCSON, ARIZONA

M. K. Majumdar
DEPARTMENT OF ECONOMICS
CORNELL UNIVERSITY
ITHACA, NEW YORK

The Design of Mechanisms for Efficient Allocation of Public Goods

WILLIAM A. BROCK

I. Introduction

The purpose of this paper is to present a systematic method for constructing and classifying individually incentive-compatible mechanisms that lead to Pareto-optimal allocations of public and private goods at each Nash noncooperative equilibrium in messages and furthermore balance the budget at each such allocation. The equilibrium concept and setup that we use is the same as that used by Groves and Ledyard (1977).

Our paper is motivated by the desire to have a systematic method of constructing "Groves–Ledyard-type" mechanisms. The papers by Groves and Ledyard present a very clever set of quadratic tax functions that turn out to be individually incentive compatible and to balance the budget. But how Groves and Ledyard came upon these particular functions is not spelled out in their papers. It is hoped that the treatment presented here will enable the reader routinely to construct individually incentive-compatible mechanisms that balance the budget in a variety of different situations and, furthermore, tailor the mechanisms to achieve different objectives that are specific to the particular situation at hand.

The paper is organized as follows. Section I contains the introduction. Section II derives two conditions on tax functions that must be satisfied if the tax functions are to lead to a Pareto-optimal provision of pure public goods and if the budget is to be balanced in the sense that the amount allocated to the construction of each public good is equal to the amount spent on the construction of each public good under these tax functions. The efficiency condition amounts to the requirement that the sum of marginal taxes across individuals must add up to the pure public-good price for each public good where all prices are denominated in terms of some pure private good as numeraire. Neither the efficiency condition nor the budget balance condition involves subjective information such as utility functions or individual incomes. Of course, the conditions only guarantee Pareto optimality. They do not say any thing about the desirability of the resulting distribution of utility income. The Groves–Ledyard quadratic tax functions are shown to satisfy the two conditions.

In Section III the method is applied to designing tax functions on individuals that belong to a fixed exogenously given coalition structure that lead to Pareto-optimal balanced budget allocations in equilibrium even though members of each coalition collude in sending their messages to the government. The coalition structure is assumed fixed, however, and the problem is treated only to illustrate a use of the design method and it is not intended as a serious treatment of the "coalition problem."

Section IV derives conditions on the matrices of the tax functions that lead to Pareto optimality and budget balance. For example, in the case of N agents, one pure private good with price p, one pure public good with price q, consider tax functions of the form

$$C_h(q, m) = \alpha_h q \cdot \left(\sum_{j=1}^{N} m_j\right) + m^t A_m^h m$$

where $\sum_{h=1}^{N} \alpha_h = 1$, m_h denotes a real number that is the proposed increment by h to the total quantity of public good, and $m \equiv (m_1, \ldots, m_n)$. Here $m^t A_m^h m$ denotes the quadratic form with $N \times N$ matrix A^h. It is shown that if

(*) $$\sum_{h=1}^{N} A_{hj}^h = 0, \quad j = 1, 2, \ldots, N,$$

then the first-order conditions for Pareto-optimal allocation obtain at any equilibrium solution $\{\bar{x}_h\}_{h=1}^{N}, \bar{m}$ to the noncooperative game defined by

(1.1) $$\underset{x_h, m_h}{\text{maximize}} \; U_h\left(x_h, \sum_{j=1}^{N} m_j\right),$$

(1.2) $$\text{s.t.} \quad px_h + C_h(q, m) \leq w_h,$$

where x_h denotes private good consumption by h and w_h denotes the income of h.

Furthermore, if

(**) $$\sum_{h=1}^{N} A_{ij}^h = 0, \quad i,j = 1, 2, \ldots, N,$$

then budget balance obtains. Also if

(***) $$A_{hh}^h > 0, \quad h = 1, 2, \ldots, N$$

holds, then convexity of C_h in m_h holds and each $\bar{x}_h, \bar{m}_h$ that solves the first-order conditions of optimality will, indeed, be a maximum of utility subject to the budget constraint (1.2) for each $h = 1, 2, \ldots, N$.

It is straightforward to show that the Groves–Ledyard tax functions

$$C_h(q, m) \equiv \alpha_h q \cdot \left(\sum_{j=1}^{N} m_j\right) + \frac{\gamma}{2}\left\{\frac{N-1}{N}(m_h - \hat{\mu}_h)^2 - \hat{\sigma}_h^2\right\},$$

$$\hat{\mu}_h \equiv \frac{1}{N-1}\sum_{i \neq h} m_i, \quad \hat{\sigma}_h^2 \equiv \frac{1}{N-2}\sum_{j \neq h}(m_j - \hat{\mu}_h)^2$$

satisfy (*)–(***).

In Section V we attack the general problem of constructing consumption allocation functions and tax functions on consumption externalities that lead to Pareto optimality and budget balance. The problem is solved by the usual (to students of public goods) device of creating an artificial pure public good "the consumption of good r by agent h," and putting the allocation function $f_{hr}(m) = \sum_{i=1}^{N} \sum_{j=1}^{N} m_{jr}^i$, where m_{jr}^i denotes the proposed increment by agent i to the consumption of r by agent j. Thus, we are back to the pure public goods case. The necessary conditions for this case are rearranged into a useful form for incentive design in Section V.

In Section 6 an abstract theory of optimal incentive design is presented that includes all of the examples contained in the other sections of the paper. It is based upon some work of Smale (1974a, b), which presents first-order conditions for Pareto optima with constraints on the state space in an abstract framework. In this section we present a rather abstract condition on gradients of tax functions that guarantee that Smale's first-order conditions for Pareto optima are satisfied at all noncooperative equilibria.

Finally, in Section VII we briefly discuss optimal incentive design when public capital goods are introduced and capital markets are imperfect in the sense that individuals cannot borrow against their future incomes.

II. A Simple Method

In order to see the ideas more clearly, we shall consider the simplest imaginable model. Let there be N individuals, where individual h chooses his private goods bundle $x_h \in R^L_+$ and his "message" $m_h \in R^K$ to solve

(2.1)
$$\text{maximize } U_h\left(x_h, \sum_{j=1}^{N} m_j\right)$$

$$\text{s.t.} \quad p \cdot x_h + C_h(q, m_1, \ldots, m_N) \leq w_h$$

where U_h, C_h, p, q, w_h denote utility function, tax function, private goods price vector, public goods price vector, and income, respectively.

Note that $G \equiv \sum_{j=1}^{N} m_j$ enters the utility function of each h. G is the amount of public goods provided if the message vector is $(m_1, \ldots, m_N)$. Thus, for this model, think of m_h as the incremental amount of public good proposed by h.

Groves and Ledyard, operating in a much more general context than (2.1), must solve two problems. First, they must design, given their equilibrium concept, which is noncooperative equilibrium in $(m_1, \ldots, m_N)$, a set of C_h so that the equilibrium demands generated by (2.1) for each p, q, w_h satisfy the Samuelson–Lindahl first-order conditions for a Pareto-optimal allocation:

(2.2)
$$\sum_{h=1}^{N} (U_{hk}/U_{hl}) = q_k/p_l$$

(equality holds because m_{hk} is allowed to be negative, $h = 1, 2, \ldots, N$) where U_{hk}, U_{hl} are short for marginal utility of h, with respect to public good k and private good l.[1] Here q_k, p_l denote price of public good k and private good l. A set of C_h that satisfy (2.2) will ensure that demanders will not "under-reveal" their preferences for public goods.

Second, Groves and Ledyard must further restrict the C_h, the utility functions, the initial endowments, and the production sets, so that a general equilibrium exists.

In this section, we are interested only in the design of the C_h so that the Samuelson–Lindahl condition (2.2) and budget balance (to be defined below) holds for each p, q, w_h. Nothing will be done on the existence of general equilibrium in this paper.

---

[1] If negative m_{hk} is allowed for each h, k, then (2.2) will hold with equality. Negative m_{hk} allows public bads and/or allows individual h to communicate desires to reduce the amount of k produced.

Definition 1.1 Given $p, q; w_1, \ldots, w_N; C_1, \ldots, C_N$ a *demand* vector $(\bar{x}_1, \ldots, \bar{x}_N; \bar{m}_1, \ldots, \bar{m}_N)$ is any vector $z \equiv (x_1, \ldots, x_N; m_1, \ldots, m_N)$ that satisfies: For each $h = 1, 2, \ldots, N$

$$(2.3) \qquad U_h\left(\bar{x}_h, \sum_{j \neq h}^{N} \bar{m}_j + \bar{m}_h\right) \geq U_h\left(x_h, \sum_{j \neq h}^{N} \bar{m}_j + m_h\right)$$

for all x_h, m_h that satisfy the budget constraint

$$p \cdot x_h + C_h(q, m_h, \hat{\bar{m}}_h) \leq w_h, \quad x_h \geq 0.$$

Here $(m_h, \hat{\bar{m}}_h)$ denotes $(\bar{m}_1, \ldots, \bar{m}_{h-1}, m_h, \bar{m}_{h+1}, \ldots, \bar{m}_N)$.

The equilibrium concept is just a standard noncooperative equilibrium a la Cournot–Nash. Groves and Ledyard also need the C_h to satisfy the

Budget Balance Condition For each $p, q, w_1, \ldots, w_N$

$$(2.4) \qquad q \cdot \left(\sum_{j=1}^{N} \bar{m}_j\right) = \sum_{j=1}^{N} C_j(q, \bar{m}),$$

i.e., the taxes C_h collected must sum up to the expenditure $q \cdot (\sum_{j=1}^{N} \bar{m}_j)$ upon goods in order that the government budget be balanced.

We may now state the

Basic Problem Design the C_h so that for each $p, q, w_1, \ldots, w_N$ equations (2.2) and (2.4) are satisfied.

The Basic Problem is important because, at the very least, the tax structure designed to provide public goods should generate an efficient allocation. The tax structure may be further manipulated to achieve desirable social objectives such as income redistribution, but certainly efficiency is a basic property.

Theorem 2.1 Assume that $\bar{x}_h \gg 0$ for each h, for each $p, q, w_1, \ldots, w_N$. In order that the C_h solve the Basic Problem, it is sufficient that for each demand vector $(\bar{x}_1, \ldots, \bar{x}_N; \bar{m}_1, \ldots, \bar{m}_N)$

$$(2.5) \qquad \sum_{h=1}^{N} C_{hk} = q_k, \quad k = 1, 2, \ldots, K,$$

$$(2.6) \qquad \sum_{h=1}^{N} C_h = q, \quad \left(\sum_{j=1}^{N} \bar{m}_j\right).$$

Here $C_{hk} = \partial C_h / \partial m_{hk}$.

Proof Write down the necessary conditions for a solution to (2.3):

(2.7) $$U_{hl} \leq \lambda_h p_l \quad (= \lambda_h p_l, \text{ if } x_{hl} > 0),$$

(2.8) $$U_{hk} = \lambda_h C_{hk},$$

where λ_h is the marginal utility of income to h, $C_{hk} = \partial C_h/\partial m_{hk}$, and m_{hk} is the kth component of the message vector m_h. Since m_{hk} is allowed to vary over all of R, therefore (2.8) holds with equality. Take the quotient of (2.8) to (2.7), use the assumption that $\bar{x}_h \gg 0$, and sum over h to get

(2.9) $$\sum_{h=1}^{N} U_{hk}/U_{hl} = \sum_{h=1}^{N} C_{hk}/p_l.$$

From (2.9), we see that if we require

(2.10) $$\sum_{h=1}^{N} C_{hk} = q_k$$

for each q, $(m_1, \ldots, m_N)$, then the Samuelson–Lindahl condition (2.2) will be satisfied. But (2.10) is just (2.5). Equation (2.6) is just the budget balance condition. This ends the proof.

Theorem 1 gives a useful method of search for tax functions C_h that generate Pareto-optimal allocations. Note especially that (2.9) and (2.10) do not depend on *utility functions*.

Let us show how (2.5) and (2.6) lead naturally to the Groves–Ledyard tax functions. Consider tax functions of the form

(2.11) $$C_h = \alpha_h q \cdot \left(\sum_{j=1}^{N} m_j\right) + D_h(m_1, \ldots, m_N),$$

where $\alpha_h > 0$, $\sum_{h=1}^{N} \alpha_h = 1$. One might think of α_h as the fraction of the total government budget imputed to h. Obviously, if we put $D_h \equiv 0$ for all h, then (2.5) and (2.6) will be satisfied. But Groves–Ledyard point out that $D_h = 0$ leads to nonexistence problems for general equilibrium (Bennett and Conn, 1977, p. 36). Therefore, we must look for nontrivial D_h.

From (2.11), (2.5), and (2.6), the D_h must satisfy

(2.12) $$\sum_{h=1}^{N} D_{hk} = 0, \quad k = 1, 2, \ldots, K,$$

(2.13) $$\sum_{h=1}^{N} D_h = 0.$$

Here D_{hk} denotes $\partial D_h/\partial m_{hk}$. Groves and Ledyard choose, e.g.,

(2.14) $$D_h = \frac{\gamma}{2}\left[\frac{N-1}{N}(m_h - \hat{\mu}_h)^2 - \hat{\sigma}_h^2\right],$$

where $(x - y)^2 \equiv \sum_{i=1}^{K} (x_i - y_i)^2$ for x, y in R^K, where $\gamma > 0$ is arbitrary, and

$$(2.15) \quad \hat{\mu}_h = \frac{1}{N-1} \sum_{i \neq h} m_i, \quad \hat{\sigma}_h^2 = \frac{1}{2(N-1)(N-2)} \sum_{i \neq j} \sum_{j \neq h} (m_i - m_j)^2$$

$$= \frac{1}{N-2} \sum_{j \neq h} (m_j - \hat{\mu}_h)^2.$$

It is straightforward to verify by computation that the Groves–Ledyard D_h satisfy (2.12) and (2.13). Equations (2.12) and (2.13) generate the Groves–Ledyard tax rules in a "natural" way, viz, positing D_h of quadratic form and proceeding to find the coefficients implied by (2.12) and (2.13). If one further adds the "equity" requirement that h and j be treated equally in some sense, the coefficients of D_h are restricted even further. Note that the Groves–Ledyard D_h have an equal treatment character, i.e., D_h is the *same function* of $m_h, \hat{\mu}_h, \hat{\sigma}_h^2$ independent of h.

What happens if a group of individuals form a coalition and collaborate in sending their messages? Quite clearly such a coalition can make itself better off if the other players play noncooperatively.[2] This is so because each member of the coalition would internalize the external effect of his message on the utilities and on the tax bills of his fellows. This suggests

Design Problem with Coalitions Design tax functions on coalitions as well as on individuals, so that a Pareto–optimal allocation of public and private goods results.

Since for Pareto-optimality to obtain, the Samuelson–Lindahl first-order necessary condition (2.2) and budget balance condition (2.4) must hold; therefore, we must consider the problem of designing tax functions on coalitions and on individuals so that (2.2) and (2.4) hold. Obviously, this design problem will depend upon the game theoretic equilibrium concept used.

III. The Design Problem under Coalition Formation

There are many ways to formulate this problem. Since my main interest is in the lobbying problem, as discussed in Brock and Magee (1978), we shall

---

[2] Bennett and Cohn (1977) have established that coalitions can cheat Groves (1970, 1973)–Clarke (1971)-type mechanisms. However, the same logic applies to the Groves–Ledyard mechanism (2.14) as well. Bennett and Cohn call a mechanism "group incentive compatible" if no *group* of agents can make themselves better off by misrepresenting their preferences. Bennett and Cohn use a result of Green and Laffont (1977) to show that no revelation mechanism that is satisfactory (a weak requirement) and group incentive compatible exists.

look at equilibrium concepts that have a mixed cooperative and nonco-operative nature. Let us first look at a situation where the coalitions that are able to police their members are exogenously given.

Let $S_1, \ldots, S_I, S_{I+1}$ be a partition of $\{1, 2, \ldots, N\}$ into nonoverlapping subsets such that

$$\bigcup_{i=1}^{I+1} S_i = \{1, 2, \ldots, N\}.$$

Here $\bigcup_{i=1}^{I+1} S_i$ denotes the set theoretic union of the sets S_i. The players in set S_i, $|S_i| \geq 2$, $i = 1, 2, \ldots, I$, are assumed to collaborate in sending their messages and deciding on their private-goods consumption, whereas the players in the last set, S_{I+1}, do not cooperate at all. Call $S_1, \ldots, S_I, S_{I+1}$ a coalition structure.

We have to say something about how the members of S_i cooperate. Intuitively, we want each player in S_i to internalize his impact on the other players into his own decision when he chooses his m_h. Given the messages of the players outside of S_i, the players of S_i can make themselves better off if they cooperate in sending the m_i. Coalition S_i chooses $\{x_h\}_{h \in S_j}$, $\{m_h\}_{h \in S_j}$ to solve

(3.1) $$\text{``Pareto Optimize''} \left\{ U_s\left(x_s, \sum_{j=1}^{N} m_j\right) \right\}_{s \in S_i}$$

s.t. $$\sum_{s \in S_i} \left[p \cdot x_s + \alpha_s q \cdot \left(\sum_{j=1}^{N} m_j\right) + D_s \right] \leq \sum_{s \in S_i} w_s.$$

Definition 3.1 Given $p, q, w_1, \ldots, w_N$, a noncooperative equilibrium relative to the coalition structure $S_1, S_2, \ldots, S_I, S_{I+1}$ is a vector $\bar{x}_1, \ldots, \bar{x}_N$, $\bar{m}_1, \ldots, \bar{m}_N$ such that for each coalition S_i, $i = 1, 2, \ldots, I$, $\{\bar{x}_s\}_{s \in S}$, $\{\bar{m}_s\}_{s \in S_i}$ solves (3.1) for $s \in S_i$, with $x_j = \bar{x}_j$, $m_j = \bar{m}_j$, $j \notin S_i$ for each i.[3]

[3] This definition may be reformulated by making use of the old trick that gives Pareto-optimum allocation, a set of weights may be found so that the Pareto Optimum may be realized as the solution to the first order condition gotten by maximizing the weighted sum of utilities over the set of feasible allocations. We want our equilibrium concept to be: $(\bar{x}_1, \ldots, \bar{x}_N, \bar{m}_1, \ldots, \bar{m}_N)$ is an equilibrium relative to $S_1, S_2, \ldots, S_I : S_{I+1}$ if $\{\bar{m}_s\}_{s \in S_i}$, $\{\bar{x}_s\}_{s \in S_i}$ is Pareto optimum over the members of S_i given $\{\bar{m}_s\}_{s \in S_i}$, $\{\bar{x}_s\}_{s \in S_i}$ for each i, and $\{\bar{m}_j\}_{j \in S_{I+1}}$ is a noncooperative equilibrium given $\{\bar{m}_j\}_{j \in S_{I+1}}$, $\{\bar{x}_j\}_{j \in S_{I+1}}$. But if $\{\bar{m}_s\}_{s \in S_i}$, $\{\bar{x}_s\}_{s \in S_i}$ is a Pareto optimum given $\{\bar{m}_s\}_{s \in S_i}$, $\{\bar{x}_s\}_{s \in S_i}$, then there must exist a nontrivial set of nonnegative weights $\{\lambda_t\}_{t \in S_i}$ such that $\{\bar{x}_s\}_{s \in S_i}$, $\{\bar{m}_s\}_{s \in S_i}$ satisfies the first order necessary conditions to the problem

(*) $$\text{maximize} \sum_{t \in S_i} \lambda_t U_t$$

s.t. $$\sum_{t \in S_i} p x_t + \sum_{t \in S_i} C_t \leq \sum_{t \in S_i} w_t$$

given $\{\bar{x}_s\}_{s \in S_i}$, $\{\bar{m}_s\}_{s \in S_i}$. Hence we may reformulate Definition 3.1 in terms of (*).

For $h \in S_{I+1}$, $\bar{x}_h$, $\bar{m}_h$

(3.2) $$\text{maximize } U_h\left(x_h, \sum_{j \neq h} \bar{m}_j + m_h\right)$$

$$\text{s.t. } p \cdot x_h + \alpha_h q \cdot \left(\sum_{j \neq h} \bar{m}_j + m_h\right) + D_h(m_h, \hat{\bar{m}}_h) \leq w_h.$$

The idea of the definition is that given the strategies of the other players, the players of S_i pick their strategies to componentwise maximize the set of utility functions of the players of S_i. Coalitions S_i, S_j are not allowed to cooperate and each player of S_{I+1} plays noncooperatively. We hasten to add that the coalition structure is *fixed* in this definition.

Think of $S_1, \ldots, S_I$ as "lobbies" that for some exogenously given reason are able to "police" their members well enough so that each S_i member takes into account, in some way, the impact of his message on his S_i-fellows' utility levels. Such "pressure groups" are cited as a cause of inefficiency of the economic system. This is so because they are "concentrated," whereas the rest of the economy is "diffuse." For the rather special concept of pressure-group equilibrium outlined above, we will show that $\{D_h\}_{h=1}^N$ may be constructed so that a noncooperative equilibrium of Definition 3.1 (D.3.1) type will satisfy the Samuelson–Lindahl condition (2.2) and the budget balance condition (2.4).

Theorem 3.1 *Assume $x_h \gg 0$ for all h and $U_{sl} \neq 0$ for all s, l. In order that a noncooperative equilibrium of type D.3.1 satisfy (2.2) and (2.4), it is sufficient that for each $(m_1, m_2, \ldots, m_N)$ the following hold:*

(3.3) $$\sum_{i=1}^{I} |S_i|^{-1} \left(\sum_{s \in S_i} \sum_{s_0 \in S_i} D_{sm_{s_0k}}\right) + \sum_{h \in S_{I+1}} D_{hm_{hk}} = 0, \quad k = 1, 2, \ldots, K,$$

(3.4) $$\sum_{h=1}^{N} D_h = 0.$$

Here $D_{sm_{s_0k}}$ denotes $\partial D_s / \partial m_{s_0k}$ and $|S_i|$ denotes the number of elements in S_i.

Proof Write out the necessary conditions for an equilibrium of type D.3.1. It is well known and is discussed in more detail in Section VI below that one may generate Pareto optima by finding the solutions to the first-order conditions gotten by maximizing a weighted sum of utilities where each U_h receives nonnegative weight λ_n. In this spirit consider the following problem for each coalition S_i. Choose $\{x_h\}_{h \in S_i}$, $\{m_h\}_{h \in S_i}$ to solve the first-order necessary conditions for

(3.1') $$\text{maximize} \sum_{s \in S_i} \lambda_s U_s\left(x_s, \sum_{j=1}^{N} m_j\right)$$

$$\text{s.t.} \sum_{s \in S_i} \left[p \cdot x_s + \alpha_s q \cdot \left(\sum_{j=1}^{N} m_j\right) + D_s\right] \leq \sum_{s \in S_i} w_s.$$

The reason we always have to add the qualifying phrase "solve the first-order necessary conditions" instead of just "maximize" is because the U_h are not necessarily concave and, as is pointed out in Section VI below, under weak sufficient conditions may be found so that any solution to the first-order conditions of the above problem are Pareto optima. However, some of these Pareto optima may not maximize the above weighted sum of utilities. With the above qualifications in mind let us solve (3.1)' and continue on with the proof. Let Λ_{S_i} denote the "marginal utility of income" to S_i. From (3.1)', for each $l, k, s_0 \in S_i$

(3.5) $$\lambda_{s_0} U_{s_0 l} \leq \Lambda_{S_i} p_l \, (= \Lambda_{S_i} p_l \quad \text{if} \quad x_{s_0 l} > 0),$$

(3.6) $$\sum_{s \in S_i} \lambda_s U_{sm_{s_0 k}} = \Lambda_{S_i}\left[\sum_{s \in S_i} \alpha_s q_k + \sum_{s \in S_i} D_{sm_{s_0 k}}\right].$$

Substitute (3.5) into (3.6) to get (when $x_{sl} > 0$)

(3.7) $$\sum_{s \in S_i} [\Lambda_{S_i} p_l U_{sl}^{-1}] U_{sm_{s_0 k}} = \Lambda_{S_i}\left[\sum_{s \in S_i} \alpha_s q_k + \sum_{s \in S_i} D_{sm_{s_0 k}}\right].$$

But, if $\Lambda_{S_i} > 0$, which we assume (a very mild requirement!), this is equivalent to

(3.8) $$\sum_{s \in S_i} [U_{sm_{s_0 k}} / U_{sl}] = \left\{\sum_{s \in S_i} \alpha_s q_k + \sum_{s \in S_i} D_{sm_{s_0 k}}\right\} p_l^{-1}.$$

Here $D_{sm_{s_0 k}}$ denotes $\partial D_s / \partial m_{s_0 k}$. For $h \in S_{I+1}$, we get as in Section II,

(3.9) $$U_{hk} / U_{hl} = \alpha_h q_k + D_{hm_{hk}}.$$

Sum (3.8) over $s_0 \in S_i$ and use $U_{sm_{s_0 k}} = U_{sG_k}$, where $G_k \equiv \sum_{j=1}^{I} m_{jk}$ to get (3.10) and (3.11).

(3.10) $$\sum_{s_0 \in S_i} \sum_{s \in S_i} [U_{sm_{s_0 k}} / U_{sl}] = \left\{|S_i|\left(\sum_{s \in S_i} \alpha_s q_k\right) + \sum_{s_0 \in S_i} \sum_{s \in S_i} D_{sm_{s_0 k}}\right\} p_l^{-1}.$$

MECHANISMS FOR EFFICIENT ALLOCATION OF PUBLIC GOODS 55

Here $|S_i|$ denotes the number of elements of S_i.

(3.11) $\quad$ L.H.S. (3.10) $= \sum_{s \in S_i} |S_i|(U_{sG_k}/U_{sl})$.

Substitute (3.11) into (3.10) and simplify to get

(3.12) $\quad \sum_{s \in S_i} (U_{sG_k}/U_{sl}) = \left\{ \sum_{s \in S_i} \alpha_s q_k + |S_i|^{-1} \sum_{s, s_0 \in S_i} \sum D_{sm_{s_0}k} \right\} \bigg/ p_l$.

Note that (3.12) is "part" of the Samuelson–Lindahl condition (2.2). Note also that (3.12) is independent of the weights λ_t. Now, sum (3.12) over $i = 1, 2, \ldots, I$ and add the result to the sum of (3.9) over $h \in S_{I+1}$ to get

(3.13) $\quad \sum_{j=1}^{N} (U_{jG_k}/U_{jl}) = q_k/p_l$

$+ \left\{ \sum_{i=1}^{I} |S_i|^{-1} \left(\sum_{s, s_0 \in S_i} \sum D_{sm_{s_0}k} \right) + \sum_{h \in S_{I+1}} D_{hm_hk} \right\} \bigg/ p_l$.

Thus for (2.2) to hold, we need

(3.14) $\quad 0 = \sum_{i=1}^{I} |S_i|^{-1} \left(\sum_{s, s_0 \in S_i} \sum D_{sm_{s_0}k} \right) + \sum_{h \in S_{I+1}} D_{hm_hk}$.

But (3.14) is just (3.3). Equation (3.4) is just the budget balance condition. This ends the proof.

It is important to notice that both conditions (3.3) and (3.4) are independent of "subjective" information, such as utility functions and "welfare weights" λ_t. Let us use conditions (3.3) and (3.4) to work up an example of Groves–Ledyard tax functions for coalitions.

Theorem 3.2 *Let $C = I + |S_{I+1}|$ equal the number of coalitions, where unit coalitions, $\{j\}, j \in S_{I+1}$ are counted as one coalition. Let*

(3.15) $\quad \mu_i = \dfrac{1}{|S_i|} \sum_{h \in S_i} m_h, \quad \text{for } i = 1, 2, \ldots, I,$

$\mu_i = m_i, \quad i \in S_{I+1},$

(3.16) $\quad \hat{\mu}_i = \dfrac{1}{C-1} \sum_{\substack{j \neq i}}^{C} \mu_j,$

(3.17) $\quad \hat{\sigma}_i^2 = \dfrac{1}{C-2} \sum_{\substack{j \neq i}}^{C} (\mu_j - \hat{\mu}_i)^2$

Let $C > 2$, $\gamma > 0$, $\{\alpha_h\}_{h=1}^N$ be given. Put

$$C_i = \alpha_i q \cdot \left(\sum_{h=1}^N m_h\right) + D_i, \qquad i = 1, 2, \ldots, N,$$

where

(3.18) $$D_i = \frac{\gamma}{2}\left\{\frac{C-1}{C}(\mu_i - \hat{\mu}_i)^2 - \hat{\sigma}_i^2\right\}.$$

Then $\{D_i\}_{i=1}^N$ is a set of functions that satisfy (3.3) and (3.4) for all vectors $(m_1, \ldots, m_N)$.

Proof Let $(z)_k$ denote the kth component of vector z. Calculate

(3.19) $$D_{sm_{s_0}k} = \gamma\left(\frac{C-1}{C}\right)(\mu_i - \hat{\mu}_i)_k |S_i|^{-1}, \qquad s \in S_i.$$

Here $(x)_h$ denotes the kth component of vector x. Sum (3.19) over s, s_0 to get

$$\gamma\left(\frac{C-1}{C}\right)(\mu_i - \hat{\mu}_i)_k |S_i| = \sum_{s \in S_i}\sum_{s_0 \in S_i} D_{sm_{s_0}k}$$

In calculating L.H.S. (3.3), use the fact that $|S_j| = 1$ for $j \in S_{I+1}$ to get

(3.20) $$\gamma\left(\frac{C-1}{C}\right)\sum_{i=1}^C (\mu_i - \hat{\mu}_i)_k = \text{L.H.S. (3.3)}.$$

Our problem reduces to: Show that for any sequence of vectors in R^K, denoted by $\mu_1, \mu_2, \ldots, \mu_C$, that

(3.21) $$\sum_{i=1}^C (\mu_i - \hat{\mu}_i)_k = 0.$$

But (3.21) is obvious from the definition

$$\hat{\mu}_{ik} = \frac{1}{C-1}\sum_{h \neq i} \mu_{hk}$$

of $\hat{\mu}_{ik}$.

It remains to check (3.4). We must show

(3.22) $$\frac{C-1}{C}\sum_{i=1}^C (\mu_i - \hat{\mu}_i)^2 - \sum_{i=1}^C \hat{\sigma}_i^2 = 0.$$

But that problem is just equivalent to: Given C numbers $\mu_1, \ldots, \mu_C$, form $\hat{\mu}_i$, $\hat{\sigma}_i^2$; then show that (3.22) holds. This is exactly what Groves and Ledyard (1977, p. 28) prove. In fact, if we think of each coalition as being an individual, then proving that (3.21) and (3.22) hold is identical to the Groves and Ledyard proof. This ends the proof of Theorem 3.2.

The above treatment of coalitions is not very interesting for the following reason. It will not necessarily be in the interest for each s to remain in his *exogenously given* S_i. In other words, some other coalition may be able to improve upon the allocation supplied by a noncooperative equilibrium of type D.3.1. What is really needed for a satisfactory resolution of the "coalition problem" is a set of tax functions $\{C_h\}$ so that allocations that "are equilibrium" (in some interesting sense of that much-used word) are Pareto optimal.

One way out would be to impose huge taxes on any coalition that attempted to form. Thus, no coalition would ever find it in its self interest to form. Thus, the problem would collapse to the no-coalition case and we have already solved that one. But this sort of thing is not very interesting from a practical point of view. Bennett and Cohn show, in a related context, that there is *no* mechanism that is immune to manipulation by colluding agents.

It is worth mentioning that coalitional agreements are not costless to enforce in the "real world." Hence, each coalition has a "free rider" problem of its own to solve. There is not always some government agency to enforce the agreement.[4] So, a "Groves–Ledyard" mechanism cannot be enforced by the coalition against its own members.

---

[4] Even when there is no regulatory body to enforce the agreement the force of the state may be used anyway under certain conditions. For suppose a group wanted to form a coalition C of size N and wanted to prevent the formation of subcoalitions of C as well as entry and exit of individuals from C. Labor unions are of this character.

One way to enforce C might be to lean on the law of contract which is enforced by the state free to C, i.e., suppose that for C to be effective some number, say $Y\%$ of a particular group, A, of individuals must join C. The C organizer goes around to each member of A with a contract that reads as follows:

> We should like to form C to bargain for our rights. In the past we've been done in by free riders who chisel on the organization. This contract is designed to police free riders and provide for a viable C.
>
> The undersigned agrees to put up X dollars in escrow to be deposited in the account of Coalition C at bank _____, which will be forfeited if the undersigned is found guilty of violating the bylaws of C. A copy of the bylaws of C is attached to this contract.
>
> This contract becomes legally binding if and only if $Y\%$ of the members of A sign. If $Y\%$ of the members of A have not signed by date Z, the X dollars will be returned immediately to the undersigned.
>
> The amount X, percent Y, and date Z may be varied to suit the particular needs of C. X is chosen large enough to deter strikebreakers if C calls a walkout of the members of A. Furthermore, Y must be large enough so that a walkout is effective. Also, the data Z may be set further into the future the more time consuming the task of obtaining $Y\%$ of A as signatories. The indenture on the contract may include dues, provisions for meetings, organizer's salaries, mechanisms of trial for violators of the C bylaws, etc.

In theory, the harnessing of the power of the state (which is free to C) in enforcing the law of contract may be a useful way to voluntarily provide A-specific public goods but in practice legal hassles and court entanglements may prove to be fatal to this scheme.

If the scheme could be made to work it could be used to police the type of coalition structure studied above and thus the solution concept treated above may become more interesting than it is at present.

Hence, the question of coalitions is unsettled. We offer our exercise in constructing mechanisms for a fixed coalition structure only as an application of our general method of constructing mechanisms. Analysis of such a subproblem may be useful to someone in their attempt to present a solution to the coalition problem.

IV. Examples of Quadratic Incentive Design Using (3.3) and (3.4)

Let us show how to use (3.3) and (3.4) to systematically search for quadratic D_h that assure Pareto-optimal allocation of public goods. Return to the case $I = N$, and $|S_i| = 1$ of an equilibrium of type 3.1. This is just the Groves–Ledyard case of where each coalition contains just one member. For the sake of simplicity, let us design quadratic D_h for one public good only. Put

$$(4.1) \quad D_h(m_1, \ldots, m_N) = m^T A^h m \equiv \sum_{i=1}^{N} \sum_{j=1}^{N} A_{ij}^h m_i m_j$$

where m^T denotes the transpose of the column vector m, and A^h is the matrix $[A_{ij}^h]$. Equation (4.1) just states that D_h is quadratic. The linear terms are already embodied in $\alpha_h q(\sum_{j=1}^{N} m_j)$, the share of the budget imputed to h. We want to use (3.3) and (3.4) in order to classify the matrices $\{A^h\}_{h=1}^{N}$ that correspond to Pareto-optimal quadratix tax structures.

In the case $I = N$ and $|S_i| = 1$, $i = 1, 2, \ldots, N$, record (3.3) and (3.4) for convenience. Equations (3.3) and (3.4) become, for this case,

$$(4.2) \quad \sum_{h=1}^{N} D_{hk} = 0 \quad \text{for all} \quad (m_1, \ldots, m_N),$$

$$(4.3) \quad \sum_{h=1}^{N} D_h = 0 \quad \text{for all} \quad (m_1, \ldots, m_N).[5]$$

Here, as usual, $D_{hk} = \partial D_h / \partial m_{hk}$. Apply (4.2) and (4.3) to (4.1) in the case of one public good to get

$$(4.4) \quad \sum_{h=1}^{N} D_{hk} = \sum_{h=1}^{N} \frac{\partial}{\partial m_h}(m^T A^h m) = 0,$$

$$(4.5) \quad \sum_{h} D_h = \sum_{h} m^T A^h m = m^T \left(\sum_{h} A^h \right) m = 0.$$

---

[5] Actually these are only required to hold for *demand* vectors $(\bar{m}_1, \ldots, \bar{m}_N)$ but in many applications it will be useful to construct $\{D_h\}_{h=1}^{N}$ such that (4.2), (4.3) hold for *all* $(m_1, \ldots, m_N)$.

MECHANISMS FOR EFFICIENT ALLOCATION OF PUBLIC GOODS   59

Since (4.4) and (4.5) must hold for all vectors m; therefore it immediately follows that

(4.6) $$\sum_{h=1}^{N} A_{hj}^{h} = 0, \quad j = 1, 2, \ldots, N,$$

(4.7) $$\sum_{h=1}^{N} A^{h} = 0$$

must hold.[6]

If, in addition, differential convexity of $m^T A^h m$ in m is desired [so that the constraint set defined by the budget constraint and the tax function $C_h = \alpha_h q \cdot (\sum_{j=1}^{N} m_j) + D_h$ is a convex set], then

(4.8) $$A_{hh}^{h} > 0, \quad h = 1, 2, \ldots, N$$

must hold.

The quadratic incentive design problem is to classify the solutions of (4.6), (4.7) and (4.8).

Theorem 4.1 *For $N = 2$, there is no solution to (4.6)–(4.8). For $N > 2$, there are solutions.*

Proof Equation (4.7) implies

(4.9) $$A^1 = -A^2, \quad \text{i.e.,} \quad \text{(a)} \quad A_{11}^1 = -A_{11}^2$$
$$\text{(b)} \quad A_{12}^1 = -A_{12}^2$$
$$\text{(c)} \quad A_{21}^1 = -A_{21}^2$$
$$\text{(d)} \quad A_{22}^1 = -A_{22}^2$$

for $N = 2$. But (4.6) implies

(4.10) (a) $A_{11}^1 = -A_{21}^2$, (b) $A_{12}^1 = -A_{22}^2$.

Now symmetry requires

$$A_{ij}^h = A_{ji}^h \quad \text{for all} \quad i, j.$$

---

[6] In detail

$$\frac{\partial}{\partial m_h}\left(\sum_{i=1}^{N}\sum_{j=1}^{N} A_{ij}^h m_i m_j\right) = \frac{\partial}{\partial m_h}\left(\sum_{j=1}^{N} A_{hj}^h m_h m_j\right) + \frac{\partial}{\partial m_h}\left(\sum_{i \neq h}\sum_{j=1}^{N} A_{ij}^h m_i m_j\right)$$

$$= 2A_{hh}^h m_h + \sum_{j \neq h} A_{hj}^h m_j + \sum_{i \neq h} A_{ih}^h m_i = 2\sum_{j=1}^{N} A_{hj}^h m_j.$$

If $\sum_{h=1}^{N}\sum_{j=1}^{N} A_{hj}^h m_j = 0$ for all $(m_1, \ldots, m_N)$, then $\sum_{h=1}^{N}\sum_{j=1}^{N} A_{hj}^h m_j = \sum_{j=1}^{N}\left(\sum_{h=1}^{N} A_{hj}^h\right) m_j = 0$ implies $\sum_{h=1}^{N} A_{hj}^h = 0, j = 1, 2, \ldots, N.$

Use (4.10)(a), (4.9)(b), and (4.10)(b) in turn to get

(4.11) $$A^1_{11} = A^1_{12} = -A^2_{22}.$$

But (4.11) is an immediate contradiction to (4.8).[7]

Turn now to the case $N > 2$. The Groves–Ledyard solution is one solution to (4.6)–(4.8). We show how to generate others. From (4.7)

(4.12) $$A^1 = -(A^2 + \cdots + A^N).$$

Equation (4.6) requires

(4.13) $$-(A^2_{1j} + \cdots + A^N_{1j}) + A^2_{2j} + \cdots + A^N_{Nj} = 0, \quad j = 1, 2, \ldots, N.$$

Apply (4.8) to get

(4.14) $$-(A^2_{11} + \cdots + A^N_{11}) > 0, \quad A^2_{22} > 0, \ldots, A^N_{NN} > 0$$

for the restriction implied by convexity of D_h in m_h.

Obviously, any selection of matrices $A^2, \ldots, A^N$ that satisfy (4.13) and (4.14) will satisfy (4.6)–(4.8), with A^1 defined by (4.12). To give an example of a solution to (4.13) and (4.14) for $N = 3$, let $x \in \dot{R}$, $x > 0$. Put

(4.15) $$A^2 = \begin{bmatrix} -x & -x & x \\ & x & -x \\ & & y \end{bmatrix}, \quad A^3 = \begin{bmatrix} -x & x & -x \\ & y & -x \\ & & x \end{bmatrix}.$$

Here y is arbitrary and the lower half of each matrix is defined by symmetry. It is obvious that (4.15) is a solution to (4.12) and (4.13) for $N = 3$.

We leave to the reader the straightforward job of proving that solutions to (4.13) and (4.14) exist for $N > 3$, and extending the above analysis to K public goods.

It is instructive to see how the restrictions on the $\{D_h\}$ needed to insure the Samuelson–Lindahl conditions under the fixed coalition structure $\{S_1, S_2, \ldots, S_I; S_{I+1}\}$ translate into requirements on the sequence of matrices $\{A^h\}^N_{h=1}$. The relevant equations are (3.3) and (3.4). Obviously, (3.4) is just

(4.16) $$\sum_{h=1}^{N} A^h = 0,$$

so this is the same as the noncooperative case. This is to be expected since (4.16) is just the budget balance condition, and that has nothing to do with coalitions.

---

[7] The same proof shows that there are no twice continuously differentiable tax functions C_1, C_2 that solve (4.6)–(4.8) either. To see it replace each A^h_{ij} by $\partial C_h/\partial m_{ij}$ and follow the same steps.

Equation (3.3) is a different matter. It is a straightforward exercise to verify the fact that

$$(4.17) \qquad \sum_{i=1}^{I} |S_i|^{-1} \left(\sum_{s \in S_i} \sum_{s_0 \in S_i} A^s_{s_0 j} \right) + \sum_{h \in S_{I+1}} A^h_{hj} = 0$$

is necessary and sufficient for (3.3) to hold.

V. Externalities in Consumption

The design of Groves–Ledyard type mechanisms to achieve an efficient allocation in the face of consumption externalities may be facilitated by our methods. Furthermore, the minimum dimension of the message space required for efficient allocation may be systematically explored as a function of the externality pattern among individuals. This is especially important in designing mechanisms to internalize "local" externalities such as lawnmower noise when only a neighboring set of people are affected by the emitter. We illustrate these ideas by means of an example.

Consider man h's problem: Choose $x_h \in R^J_+$ to

$$(5.1) \qquad \text{maximize } U_h(x_1, \ldots, x_N) \quad \text{s.t.} \quad P \cdot x_h \leq w_h,$$

where each $x_i \in R^J_+$. Here everyone else's consumption affects h, $h = 1, 2, \ldots, N$. First we find necessary conditions for Pareto optimality by solving the first-order conditions to

$$(5.2) \qquad \text{maximize } \sum_{h=1}^{N} \lambda_h U_h(x_1, \ldots, x_n),$$

$$\text{s.t.} \quad \sum_{h=1}^{N} P \cdot x_h \leq \sum_{h=1}^{N} w_h.[8]$$

Here $\lambda_1 \geq 0, \ldots, \lambda_N \geq 0$ is a set of nonnegative utility weights. Form the Lagrangian

$$(5.3) \qquad L = \sum_{h=1}^{N} \lambda_h U_h(x_1, \ldots, x_N) + \Lambda \left(\sum_{h=1}^{N} w_h - \sum_{h=1}^{N} P \cdot x_h \right).$$

---

[8] The procedure of finding Pareto optima by maximizing a nonnegative weighted sum of utilities should be viewed as a "deus ex machina" type of procedure for remembering the correct [Smale (1974b, pp. 213–222)] first order necessary conditions which are: there exists $\{\lambda_h\}_{h=1}^{N}$, Λ all nonnegative, $(\lambda_1, \ldots, \lambda_N, \Lambda) \neq 0$ such that (5.4) is satisfied. The problem of deriving first order conditions for a Pareto Optimum is dismissed in more detail below in Section VI.

First-order necessary conditions for an interior maximum are

(5.4) $$\frac{\partial L}{\partial x_{ir}} = 0 = \sum_{h=1}^{N} \lambda_h U_{hx_{ir}} - P_r \Lambda = 0,$$
$$i = 1, 2, \ldots, N, \quad r = 1, 2, \ldots, J.$$

Let us eliminate the multipliers $\{\lambda_h\}_{h=1}^{N}$, and Λ from (5.4) and write it in a form analogous to (2.2), which we derived for the case of L pure private goods and K pure public goods. Put $r = s$ and solve (5.4) for $\{\lambda_h\}_{h=1}^{N}$ in terms of Λ, P_s, and the matrix $[U_{hx_{is}}]$. We get, writing matters in matrix notation

(5.5) $$\lambda^t [U_{hx_{is}}] = P_s \Lambda e^t,$$

where t denotes transpose and e denotes the column vector with $e_i = 1$, $i = 1, 2, \ldots, N$, and $\lambda^t \equiv (\lambda_1, \lambda_2, \ldots, \lambda N)$.

Solving (5.5) (assuming $[U_{hx_{is}}]^{-1}$ exists) for the column vector λ gives us

(5.6) $$\lambda = [U_{hx_{is}}^t]^{-1} P_s \Lambda e.$$

Inserting the solution for λ from (5.6) into (5.4) gives us

(5.7) $$e^t P_s \Lambda [U_{hx_{is}}^t]^{-1} [U_{hx_{ir}}] = P_r \Lambda e^t, \quad r = 1, 2, \ldots, J.$$

Rewrite this

(5.8) $$e^t [U_{hx_{is}}^t]^{-1} [U_{hx_{ir}}] = P_r P_s^{-1} e^t, \quad r = 1, 2, \ldots, J.$$

Notice that in the case where 1 is a pure private good and 2 is a pure public good then
$$U_{hx_{i1}} = U_{hx_{h1}} \delta_{hi}, \quad h = 1, 2, \ldots, N, i = 1, 2, \ldots, N,$$
where $\delta_{hi} \equiv 1$, $h = i$, $\delta_{hi} \equiv 0$, $h \neq i$, and $[U_{hx_{i1}}]$ is a diagonal matrix. Also, in this case, we must have

(5.9) $$U_{hx_{i2}} = U_{hx_{j2}}, \quad i, j = 1, 2, \ldots, N$$

since
$$U_h(x_1, x_2, \ldots, x_N) = U_h\left(x_{h1}, \sum_{j=1}^{N} x_{j2}, x_3, \ldots, x_N\right)$$

in the case when 1 is a pure private good and 2 is a pure public good. Hence, in this case, (5.8) collapses to

(5.10) $$\{e^t [U_{hx_{h1}}^t \delta_{hi}]^{-1} [U_{hx_{i2}}]\}_j = \{P_2 P_1^{-1} e^t\}_j = \sum_{h=1}^{N} U_{hx_{h1}}^{-1} U_{hx_{j2}}$$
$$= \sum_{h=1}^{N} U_{hx_{h1}}^{-1} U_{hx_{h2}}.$$

Here $\{a\}_j$ denotes jth component of row vector a. Notice that (5.9) was used in obtaining the right-hand side of (5.10). But (5.10) is just (2.2) for the case when 1 is a pure private good and 2 is a pure public good. It should be clear now that (2.2) is a special case of the general efficiency condition (5.8).

It should be mentioned that the assumption that $[U_{hx_{is}}]^{-1}$ exists as a severe restriction for good s. For example if good s is a pure public good then $[U_{hx_{is}}]^{-1}$ will not exist. This is so because

$$U_{hx_{is}} = U_{hx_{js}}, \quad i, j = 1, 2, \ldots, N.$$

Hence, all the columns of $[U_{hx_{is}}]$ are identical when s is a pure public good.

In fact, when all of the goods are pure public goods it is not possible to reduce the Pareto-optimum necessary conditions (5.4) to a form like (5.8), because $[U_{hx_{is}}]^{-1}$ does not exist for any s. It is desirable to reduce the Pareto-optimum necessary conditions to such a form in order to use the simple design procedure for informationally decentralized tax functions that will be discussed later in this section.

If there is at least one pure private good s that everyone desires, then (5.4) may be expressed in the form (5.8). This is so because $U_{hx_{is}} = U_{hx_{hs}} \delta_{hi}$ reduces to a diagonal matrix with diagonal element $U_{hx_{hs}} > 0, h = 1, 2, \ldots, N$ in this case.

Even if the matrices $[U_{hx_{is}}]$ are all singular there may still be informationally decentralized individually incentive compatible procedures. For example, if there are only two pure public goods and three individuals, then (5.4) becomes, putting $U_{hx_{is}} = U_{hG_s}$,

$$\lambda_1 U_{1G_1} + \lambda_2 U_{2G_1} + \lambda_3 U_{3G_1} = P_1 \Lambda,$$
$$\lambda_1 U_{1G_2} + \lambda_2 U_{2G_2} + \lambda_3 U_{3G_2} = P_2 \Lambda.$$

It may be possible to create allocation functions f_{is} and message spaces M_i to achieve the above relationship but that will require different methods which are developed in Section VI of this paper.

Can we achieve (5.8) with an informationally decentralized incentive mechanism like that presented in Section II? To attack this question we set up an N player noncooperative game as in Section II.

Consider h's problem: Choose $m_h \in M_h$ to

(5.11)
$$\text{maximize } U_h(y_1, \ldots, y_r)$$
$$\text{s.t. } C_h(P; m_1, \ldots, m_N) \leq w_h.$$
$$y_i = f_i(m_1, \ldots, m_N), \quad i = 1, 2, \ldots, N.$$

Here C_h is not the same function as in previous sections. The functions f_i are called allocation functions by Groves and Ledyard. The function f_{ir}

gives for example, the amount of commodity r allocated by the "Government" to consumption by i as a function of the message vector $(m_1, \ldots, m_N)$. Equilibrium is just a standard noncooperative equilibrium to the N player game defined by (5.11).

At first, motivated by Groves and Ledyard's treatment of pure private goods and pure public goods, I tried to get by with

$$(5.12) \qquad f_{ir}(m_1, \ldots, m_N) \equiv \sum_{h=1}^{N} m_{ir}^h,$$

where

$$(5.13) \quad m_{ir}^h \equiv m_r^h, \quad i = 1, 2, \ldots, N, \quad r = 1, 2, \ldots, J, \quad h = 1, 2, \ldots, N.$$

In other words (5.13) means the incremental amount proposed to the government by h that i be allowed to consume of r should be independent of i. By hindsight it is obvious that the NJ dimensional message space implied by (5.13) is not "large enough" to attain the necessary condition for Pareto-optimal allocation, viz equation (5.8). We will become more specific below.

Our task is to design the allocation functions f, construct message spaces M_h, and design C_h so that a noncooperative equilibrium to the N player game defined by (5.11) satisfies the necessary condition for Pareto-optimal allocation, viz. (5.8) above.

To do this, write down the necessary conditions for a noncooperative equilibrium: for each h, $m_{ir}^h \in R^1$ solves

$$(5.14) \qquad 0 = \frac{\partial L_h}{\partial m_{ir}^h} = \frac{\partial U_h}{\partial f_{ir}} \frac{\partial f_{ir}}{\partial m_{ir}^h} - \Lambda_h \frac{\partial C_h}{\partial m_{ir}^h}.$$

Note that (5.14) is not an inequality since negative messages m_{ir}^h are allowed as well as positive ones. Here we are taking M_h to be the space of all NJ dimensional matrices $[m_{ir}^h]$, $h = 1, 2, \ldots, N$. Let us put $f_{ir}(m_1, \ldots, m_N) \equiv \sum_{h=1}^{N} m_{ir}^h$ and see how far we can go with this specification of f. Hence, (5.14) becomes

$$(5.15) \qquad 0 = U_{hx_{ir}} - \Lambda_h C_{hm_{ir}^h},$$

where subscripts denote the obvious partial derivations. Put $r = s$ in (5.15) and solve for the diagonal matrix $[\Lambda_h]$:

$$(5.16) \qquad [U_{hx_{is}}^t][C_{hm_{is}^h}^t]^{-1} = [\Lambda_h].$$

(Construct the C_h so that the required inverse matrix exists for each s.) From (5.16) and (5.15) we get

$$(5.17) \qquad [U_{hx_{is}}^t]^{-1}[U_{hx_{ir}}] = [C_{hm_{is}^h}^t]^{-1}[C_{hm_{ir}^h}].$$

MECHANISMS FOR EFFICIENT ALLOCATION OF PUBLIC GOODS

Premultiply (5.17) by e^t,

(5.18) $e^t [U^t_{hx_{is}}]^{-1} [U_{hx_{ir}}] = e^t [C^t_{hm^h_{is}}]^{-1} [C_{hm^h_{ir}}].$

Comparing (5.8) with the necessary condition (5.18) for Pareto optimality allows us to uncover

Design Rule for Pareto Optimality

(5.19) $e^t [C^t_{hm^h_{is}}]^{-1} [C_{hm^h_{ir}}] = P_r P_s^{-1} e^t,$ $r = 1, 2, \ldots, N, \ s = 1, 2, \ldots, N.$

Remark (5.19) is assumed to hold only for s such that $[U^t_{hx_{is}}]^{-1}$ exists. This inverse exists if s is a pure private good provided that each $U_{hx_{hs}} \neq 0$. Notice that (5.19) does not guarantee budget balance.

In order to derive a condition for budget balance, we need to isolate the expenditure on good r. Specialize each C_h to the form

(5.20) $C_h(P, m) = \sum_{r=1}^{J} C_{hr}(P_r, m^1_{\cdot r}, \ldots, m^N_{\cdot r}).$

Here $m^h_{\cdot r}$ denotes the N dimensional vector with ith component m^h_{ir}. The amount budgeted by h for good r is C_{hr}. The total amount X_r allocated by the government to the production of r with the allocation functions

$$f_{ir} \equiv \sum_{h=1}^{N} m^h_{ir}$$

is

(5.21) $X_r = \sum_{i=1}^{N} P_r \cdot f_{ir} = \sum_{i=1}^{N} P_r \left(\sum_{h=1}^{N} m^h_{ir} \right).$

The total amount T_r allocated by consumers $h = 1, 2, \ldots, N$ to the consumption of r is given by

$$T_r = \sum_{h=1}^{N} C_{hr}.$$

Thus budget balance requires the

Budget Balance Condition

(5.22) $P_r \cdot \left(\sum_{i=1}^{N} \sum_{h=1}^{N} m^h_{ir} \right) = \sum_{h=1}^{N} C_{hr}(P_r, m^1_{\cdot r}, \ldots, m^N_{\cdot r})$

for all $r = 1, 2, \ldots, J$; for all noncooperative equilibrium messages m.

Conditions (5.19) and (5.22) constitute a fairly concrete design procedure for constructing $\{C_{hr}\}_{h,r}$ that are individually incentive compatible and balance the budget at a Nash noncooperative equilibrium in messages. The reader may use (5.19) and (5.22) to design quadratic $\{C_{hr}\}$ corresponding to our analysis of Section IV. Furthermore, if the externality network, i.e., the sets $E(r) = \{(h, i) | (\partial U_h/\partial X_{ir}) \neq 0\}$ are known to the designer then the dimensions of the message spaces required can be economized upon. In the above analysis we assumed $E(r) = \{(h, i) | h = 1, 2, \ldots, N, i = 1, 2, \ldots, N\}$, $r = 1, 2, \ldots, J$. In many practical applications $E(r)$ will be a much smaller set of "externality pairs" and the dimensions of the corresponding message spaces may be reduced.

This is a good place to point out that we have not solved the problem of finding if optimal incentive mechanisms are to be designed for the Arrow–Hahn–McKenzie (AHM) model with *production* externalities as well as consumption externalities such that a general equilibrium is Pareto optimal. This is a subject that is important but beyond the scope of this article. It is hoped that the methods presented here will prove useful in attacking this more general and more interesting problem. We turn now to an abstract formulation of the incentive design problem.

VI. The Design of Individually Incentive Compatible Mechanisms in an Abstract Setting

It is worthwhile to look at an abstract formulation that contains all of the examples considered in this paper in order that the common unifying structure be exposed. This section will build on Smale (1974b). First, we shall outline Smale's setup and state his first-order necessary and sufficient condition that a local Pareto point must satisfy. Second, we shall define the incentive design problem in this setup, and then we shall derive a sufficient condition on individual tax functions so that Smale's first-order conditions for a local Pareto point obtain at a Nash noncooperative equilibrium in message space. Notation used will be Smale's where possible.

Consider the following problem: Pareto-optimize real C^2 functions $U_1, \ldots, U_N$ defined on an open set $W \subseteq R^l$ subject to constraints given by contributions of the form $g_\beta(x) \geq 0$, $\beta = 1, 2, \ldots, n$. We say that $x \in \theta$ if there is no admissible curve passing through x. By an *admissible* curve we mean a C^1 curve $\rho:(a, b) \to W$ such that: (1) $U_i'(\rho(t)) > 0$ for $t \in (a, b)$; (2) if $g_\beta(\rho(t_0)) = 0$ for some $t_0 \varepsilon(a, b)$, then there is a neighborhood J of t_0 such that $g_\beta(\rho(t))$ is nondecreasing in J. θ is the set of local Pareto optima. Smale shows that $x \in \theta$ implies there exist nonnegative multipliers $\{\lambda_i\}_{i=1}^{N}$, $\{\mu_\beta\}_{\beta \in B_x}$

not all zero such that

(*) $$\sum_{i=1}^{N} \lambda_i DU_i(x) + \sum_{\beta \in B_x} \mu_\beta Dg_\beta(x) = 0,$$

where $B_x = \{\beta | g_\beta(x) = 0\}$. Also he shows that if $\{Dg_\beta(x)\}_{\beta \in B_x}$ is a linearly independent family of gradients, for all x in W and if a nonnegative, not all zero, set of multipliers $\{\lambda_i\}_{i=1}^{N}$ $\{\mu_\beta\}_{\beta \in B_x}$ exists such that (*) holds, then $x \in \theta$. Hence, speaking very loosely, (*) is necessary and sufficient for $x \in \theta$. Interpret (*) as: There is no open half-space that contains all of the gradients $\{DU_i(x)\}_{i=1}^{N}$, $\{Dg_\beta(x)\}_{\beta \in B_x}$.

Smale's theorem may be applied to obtain first order necessary and sufficient conditions for a local Pareto optimum in the general AHM model presented in Arrow and Hahn (1971, Chapter 6).

The general Nash noncooperative equilibrium incentive design problem (NEIDP) for the AHM model may now be defined as: Characterize tax functions $\{C_j\}_{j=1}^{N}$ on consumers and firms and design message spaces for consumers and firms together with allocation functions that allocate consumption vectors to consumption and production vectors to producers such that a Nash noncooperative equilibrium in messages is Pareto optimal. We put the words "Nash noncooperative equilibrium" in the definition in order to emphasize that the same problem may be studied with a different game theoretic solution concept. It is important to realize, as Roberts (1979) points out, that under some game-theoretic setups, no individually incentive compatible mechanisms will exist. We shall not attack the problem in its full generality here. Rather, we shall consider a subproblem described below.

In Smale's setup let

$$x \equiv (x_{11}, x_{12}, \ldots, x_{1J}, x_{21}, \ldots, x_{2J}, \ldots, x_{N1}, \ldots, x_{NJ})$$

denote the state vector of the system where x_{ir} denotes the consumption of good r by person i. Let the income of person i be w_i, and let the price of good r be P_r. Then consider the problem, "Pareto-optimize" $(U_1(x), \ldots, U_N(x))$

(6.1) $$\text{s.t.} \quad g(x) \geq 0 : \sum_{i=1}^{N} w_i - \sum_{i=1}^{N} P \cdot x_i \geq 0.$$

Problem (6.1) describes Pareto-optimal "demand vectors." Notice that the whole state vector enters each utility function as an argument. Thus, general *consumption* externalities are covered by Eq. (6.1). Smale's (*) becomes, for this special case: $x \in \theta$ if there exist a nonzero vector $(\lambda_1, \ldots, \lambda_N, \mu) \geq 0$ such that

(6.2) $$\sum_{i=1}^{N} \lambda_i DU_i(x) + \mu Q = 0,$$

where $Q = Dg(x)$,
$$Q_{ir} = -P_r, i = 1, 2, \ldots, N, \quad r = 1, 2, \ldots, J.$$

To move toward a precise definition of the NEIDP, let consumer h solve

(6.3) $$\underset{m^h \in M_h}{\text{maximize}} \ U_h(f(m)) \quad \text{s.t.} \quad C_h(P, m) \le w_h,$$

where $m \equiv (m^1, \ldots, m^N) \in M_1 x \cdots x M_N$, and $f_{ir}(m)$ is the amount of good r allocated by the "government" to consumption by i as a function of the message vector as received by the government, and $C_h(P, m)$ denotes the tax levied on h as a function of the price vector P and the community message vector m. The first order part of the NEIDP is to find f, $\{M_h\}_{h=1}^N$, $\{C_h\}_{h=1}^N$ such that at each Nash noncooperative equilibrium $\bar{x} = f(\bar{m})$, in messages for the N player game defined by (6.3), we have (6.2) satisfied at $\bar{x}$ for some nonzero $(\lambda_1, \ldots, \lambda_N, \mu) \ge 0$.

The budget balance part of the NEIDP requires that the amount spent on each good r equal the amount allocated to r at each Nash noncooperative equilibrium $\bar{x} = f(\bar{m})$. In order to pose this nicely and to say something more specific about characterizing $\{C_h\}$ that solve the NEIDP, we specialize still further. Put $M_h = R^{NJ}$,

$$f(m) = \sum_{h=1}^N m_{ir}^h, \quad m_{ir}^h \in R, \ C_h(P, m) = \sum_h C_{hr}(P, m_{\cdot r}),$$

where the (h, i) component of the N^2 vector $m_{\cdot r}$ is m_{ir}^h.

First-order necessary conditions for a Nash noncooperative equilibrium $\bar{x} = f(\bar{m})$ are: There are numbers $\Lambda_h \ge 0$, $h = 1, 2, \ldots, N$ such that at $\bar{x}$, $\bar{m}$ we have

(6.4) $$D_h U_h = \Lambda_h D_h C_h, \quad h = 1, 2, \ldots, N.$$

Here the (i, r) component of the symbol $D_h C_h$ is $\partial C_h / \partial m_{ir}^h$, and Λ_h is the marginal utility of income to h. Equations (6.4) were derived on the assumption that equilibrium $x_{ir} > 0$ for all i, r. If inequalities $x_{ir} \ge 0$ are effective at Nash equilibrium then an extra multiplier will appear in (6.4). We cavalierly assume such boundary problems away. It is beyond the scope of this article to extend the theory to the case of boundary equilibria. However, the presence of the extra multipliers at boundaries should make the generalization interesting and nontrivial. Plug (6.4) into (6.2) to get

(6.5) $$\sum_{i=1}^N \lambda_i(\Lambda_i D_i C_i) + \mu Q = 0.$$

Now if we assume all $\Lambda_i > 0$ at Nash equilibrium (a weak restriction) then we may state

Proposition 1 *Assume $\Lambda_h > 0$ for all h, at all Nash equilibria. If $\{C_h\}_{h=1}^N$ are such that each Nash equilibrium $\bar{x} = f(\bar{m})$ of the noncooperative game (6.3)*

is Pareto optimal then it is necessary that there exist $(\lambda_1(\bar{m}), \ldots, \lambda_N(\bar{m}), \mu(\bar{m})) \geq 0$ such that

(6.6) $$\sum_{i=1}^{N} \lambda_i(\bar{m}) D_i C_i(P, \bar{m}) + \mu(\bar{m}) Q = 0.$$

Proof Let $\bar{m}$ be a Nash equilibrium. Then (6.4) must hold for some $(\Lambda_1, \ldots, \Lambda_N) \geq 0$. Now $\bar{x} = f(\bar{m})$ is a Pareto optimum. Therefore, there is $(\lambda'_1, \ldots, \lambda'_N, \mu') \geq 0$ such that (6.2) holds at $\bar{x}$. Insert (6.4) into (6.2). Q.E.D.

Condition (6.6) says, geometrically, that for noncooperative equilibrium to be Pareto optimal, it is necessary to design the $\{C_h\}_{h=1}$ so that at each Nash equilibrium to (6.3) the vectors

$$D_1 C_1(P, \bar{m}), D_2 C_2(P, \bar{m}), \ldots, D_N C_N(P, \bar{m}), Q$$

do not lie in the same open half space.

Remark It should be noted that additional restrictions need to be added to the cost functions in the case

$$\partial U_h / \partial x_{jr} = 0 \quad \text{for some} \quad h, j, r,$$

i.e., in case $\partial U_h / \partial x_{jr} = 0$ the cost function C_h must be restricted so that $\partial C_h / \partial m^h_{jr} = 0$ in order that it be possible for $\partial U_h / \partial m^h_{jr} = \Lambda_h \partial C_h / \partial m^h_{jr}$ to hold. All of the examples that we have treated in the previous sections of this paper are special cases of (6.6).

The budget balance (BB) condition is: For each good r, for each Nash equilibrium $\bar{x} = f(\bar{m})$,

(6.7) $$\sum_{h=1}^{N} C_{hr}(P, \bar{m}_{\cdot r}) = P_r \cdot \sum_{h=1}^{N} \sum_{i=1}^{N} \bar{m}^h_{ir}.$$

Conditions (6.6) and (6.7) constitute first-order necessary conditions for a solution to the NEIDP for the sub problem (6.1). The words "first order" are to be emphasized since Smale develops second-order conditions for $x \in \theta$ as well and these are quite different from the first-order conditions. Development of second-order solutions to the NEIDP is beyond the scope of this paper.

Conditions (6.6) and (6.7), while general, are not very useful in their present form since it is difficult to tell, a priori, what $\bar{x}, \bar{m}$ are Nash equilibrium. Thus we turn to the

Basic Problem Classify the $\{C_h\}_{h=1}^N$ that satisfy (6.6) and (6.7) for all m and all $P \geq 0$.

Since we want the $\{C_h\}$ to generate Pareto optima at Nash equilibria generated by a wide class of utility functions, goods prices, and income distributions, it is natural to study the Basic Problem defined above. In order that local constrained *maxima* and not other types of critical points are generated by the $\{C_h\}$ we will also require: for all h

(6.8) $$[\partial C_h/\partial m_{ir}^h]$$

is a positive definite matrix for each m, P. Notice that (6.6) just says that for all $P \geq 0$, and all m we have

(6.9) $$C^+(D_1 C_1(P, m), \ldots, D_N C_N(P, m)) \subseteq C^+(-Q).$$

Here

(6.10)
$$C^+(a_1, \ldots, a_N) = \left\{ z \,\middle|\, \text{there is } \lambda_1 \geq 0, \ldots, \lambda_N \geq 0 \text{ such that } z = \sum_{i=1}^N \lambda_i a_i \right\}$$

denotes the convex cone generated by the vectors $a_1, \ldots, a_N$. We now have a geometric criterion that must be satisfied by the $\{C_h\}_{h=1}^N$ in order that Pareto optimality obtain at Nash equilibrium.

Criterion (6.9) is still not very useful from the practical point of view in the case that the Center knows the externality pattern among individuals. In order to see why, consider the case where all goods are pure private goods and assume that the Center *knows* that all goods are pure private goods. Here, in order to minimize bureaucratic cost, the Center orders each h to send messages m_{hr}^h and to send no m_{ir}^h, $i \neq h$. The cost functions and budget balance condition, for the pure private goods case become

(6.11) $$C_{hr}(P, m) = C_{hr}(P_r, m_{hr}^h)$$

and

(6.12) $$\sum_{h=1}^N C_{hr}(P_r, m_{hr}^h) = P_r \left(\sum_{h=1}^N m_{hr}^h \right).$$

The allocation functions are

(6.13) $$f_{hr}(m) = m_{hr}^h$$

and the utility functions are of the form

(6.14) $$U_h(x) = U_h(f(m)) = U_h(f_{h1}(m), \ldots, f_{hJ}(m)).$$

Criterion (6.9) is not practically useful in this case since it does not take into account the natural implicit restriction on the functional form of each C_h due to the character of pure private goods. Of course, (6.11)–(6.13) is not the only mechanism for efficiently allocating pure private goods, but it seems unreasonable to bear the extra bureaucratic cost of communicating and

MECHANISMS FOR EFFICIENT ALLOCATION OF PUBLIC GOODS

processing messages of the form m_{ir}^h, $i \neq h$ and using the allocation mechanism

$$f_{hr}(m) = \sum_{j=1}^{N} m_{hr}^j$$

when the utility functions are of the form (6.14), i.e., there are no external effects.

Analogous remarks are pertinent to the case when each good is either a pure public good or a pure private good, and the Center knows this. For pure public goods it is natural to impose the requirement

(6.15) $\qquad m_{hr}^j = m_{h'r}^j,\qquad$ for all h, h',

for all j and for all pure public goods r. Equation (6.15) captures the anonymity of a *pure* public good—the external effect on j caused by the consumption of h is independent of who h is. A natural allocation rule for pure public good r is

(6.16) $\qquad f_{hr}(m) = \sum_{j=1}^{N} m_{hr}^j = \sum_{j=1}^{N} m_{jr}^j$

since $m_{jr}^j = m_{hr}^j$ by (6.15).

Natural implicit restrictions such as (6.15) are not taken into account by (6.9). Notice, however, that (6.4) implies

(6.17) $\qquad \Lambda_h \dfrac{\partial C_h}{\partial m_{ir}^h} = \dfrac{\partial U_h}{\partial m_{ir}^h} = \dfrac{\partial U_h}{\partial f_{ir}} \dfrac{\partial f_{ir}}{\partial m_{ir}^h} = 0,\qquad$ for $i \neq h$, r pure private

and

(6.18) $\qquad \Lambda_h \dfrac{\partial C_h}{\partial m_{ir}^h} = \dfrac{\partial U_h}{\partial m_{ir}^h} = \dfrac{\partial U_h}{\partial f_{ir}} \dfrac{\partial f_{ir}}{\partial m_{ir}^h} = \dfrac{\partial U_h}{\partial y_r}\qquad$ for r pure public,

where for each pure public good r,

(6.19) $\qquad y_r \equiv f_{ir}(m),\qquad i = 1, 2, \ldots, N.$

Hence, if $\Lambda_h > 0$ then

(6.20) $\qquad \dfrac{\partial C_h}{\partial m_{ir}^h} = 0,\qquad$ for $i \neq h$, r pure private

(6.21) $\qquad \dfrac{\partial C_h}{\partial m_{ir}^h} = \dfrac{\partial C_h}{\partial m_{hr}^h},\qquad$ for all i, r pure public.

The restrictions (6.20), (6.21) are not captured by (6.9). The criterion (6.9) is most appropriate for cases when the "Office of Efficient Allocation" does not know the externality pattern among the agents of the economy.

Notice that in all events (6.9) is only necessary for efficient allocation. We have *not* proved that it is sufficient in any sense of that word.

Let us show that for pure public good k when there is at least one pure private good n and all goods are either pure private or pure public, the condition

(6.22a) $$\sum_{h=1}^{N} \frac{\partial C_{hk}}{\partial m_{hk}^{h}}(P_k, m) = P_k$$

derived in Section II of this paper is a special case of requirement (6.9) when (6.20) and (6.21) are assumed to be satisfied and $C_{hn}(P, m) = P_n m_{hn}^h$ for pure private goods n.

Put

$$P \equiv (p_1, \ldots, p_L, q_1, \ldots, q_k), \quad K + L = J.$$

Assume that the first L goods are private goods, the last K goods are public goods so that

$$U_h(x) \equiv U_h(x_{11}, x_{12}, \ldots, x_{1J}, x_{1J}, x_{21}, \ldots, x_{2J}, \ldots, x_{N1}, \ldots, x_{NJ})$$

is of the form

$$U_h(x) = U_h\left(x_{j1}, \ldots, x_{hL}, \sum_{i=1}^{N} x_{i,L+1}, \ldots, \sum_{i=1}^{N} x_{iJ}\right), \quad h = 1, 2, \ldots, N.$$

Consider for private good n the necessary condition (6.9): For all m, P there exists nonzero $(\lambda_1, \ldots, \lambda_N, \mu) \geq 0$ such that

(6.22b) $$\sum_{h=1}^{N} \lambda_h D_h C_h = \mu Q.$$

We get for the (i, n) component of (6.22b), using (6.20),

(6.23) $$\sum_{h=1}^{N} \lambda_h \frac{\partial C_{h1}}{\partial m_{i1}^h} = \mu P_n = \lambda_i \frac{\partial C_{in}}{\partial m_{in}^i}, \quad i = 1, 2, \ldots, N.$$

For k pure public we get from (6.22b) using (6.21)

(6.24) $$\sum_{h=1}^{N} \lambda_h \frac{\partial C_h}{\partial m_{ik}^h} = \mu P_k = \sum_{h=1}^{N} \lambda_h \frac{\partial C_{hk}}{\partial m_{hk}^h}, \quad i = 1, 2, \ldots, N.$$

Notice that if the Center uses the natural specification,

(6.25) $$C_{in}(P, m) = P_n m_{in}^i$$

for private goods n, then

(6.26) $$\frac{\partial C_{in}}{\partial m_{in}^i} = P_n$$

MECHANISMS FOR EFFICIENT ALLOCATION OF PUBLIC GOODS

and (6.23) implies for $P_n > 0$

(6.27) $$\mu = \lambda_i, \quad i = 1, 2, \ldots, N.$$

Insert (6.27) into (6.24) to get

(6.28) $$\mu P_k = \sum_{h=1}^{N} \mu \frac{\partial C_{hk}}{\partial m_{hk}^h}.$$

Now $\mu > 0$ since for all i, $\mu = \lambda_i$ and $(\lambda_1, \ldots, \lambda_N, \mu) \neq 0$. Hence, canceling μ from (6.27) we get

(6.29) $$P_k = \sum_{h=1}^{N} \frac{\partial C_{hk}}{\partial m_{hk}^h},$$

which is (6.22a)

We leave it to the reader to explore the meaning of (6.9) for more general externality patterns than pure public and pure private goods. Notice that the results are much more specific if the Center is assumed to know the externality pattern because then it is reasonable to impose additional restrictions on the C_{hr} such as (6.20), (6.21), and (6.25). These restrictions together with (6.8), (6.9) and budget balance are useful tools for narrowing down the close of C_{hr} that lead to Pareto-optimal allocation at Nash equilibrium for arbitrary utility functions $U_1, \ldots, U_N$, goods prices $P_1, \ldots, P_J$, and income distributions $w_1, \ldots, w_N$.

VII. The Design of Mechanisms for Efficient Accumulation of Public Capital

The methods outlined above may be used to design tax functions over time that will lead to efficient allocation of public capital. When capital is introduced into the model, we must specify how time is to be introduced. At the abstract level, if capital markets are perfect so that individuals may borrow against their future income, then by the usual procedure we may reduce an intertemporal model of capital accumulation and current consumption to a static model by dating the goods where the "new budget constraint" is just that the present value of the expenditure stream must not be larger than the present value of the income stream. The static methods developed above may be applied directly, and the only interesting question that remains is the *intertemporal structure* of the class of C_h that generate Pareto optima in Nash equilibrium.

In the case that capital markets are not perfect, a second-best concept of Pareto optimality, i.e., a component-wise maximum of the vector of utility functions subject to institutional constraints must be formulated and tax functions must be designed (if possible) in such a way to attain a second-best Pareto optimum. Such an approach is needed for problems where, to take a well-known example, institutional restraints prevent perfect capitalization of future wage income. We believe that a fruitful way to approach this problem is to use Smale's work on characterizing Pareto optima with constraints and to follow the analysis outlined in Section VI above. Due to space limitations, we must refer this problem to future research and move on.

Let us quickly illustrate the designs of $\{C_h\}$ for public capital allocation under perfect capital markets by working through an example in continuous time. Let there be one public capital good and one private good, and revert back to the notation of Sections II–IV. Assume each individual lives T periods and gets utility from $x_h(t)$, $f(m(t)) \equiv \sum_{j=1}^{N} m_j(t)$, $F(M(t)) \equiv \sum_{j=1}^{N} M_{j0} + \sum_{j=1}^{N} \int_0^t m_j(s)\,ds$, where $x_h(t)$ denotes consumption of the private good at time t, $f(m(t))$ denotes the allocation of investment in the public capital good at time t as a function of the sum of the proposed increments to public *investment* by each agent j, and $F(M(t))$ denotes the allocation of the *stock* of public capital at time t, which is assumed to be the sum of capital held by the agents at time 0, $\sum_{j=1}^{N} M_{j0}$, plus the sum of past proposed investments by the members of the community up to time t.

Put

$$g(t) \equiv \sum_{j=1}^{N} m_j(t), \qquad G(t) \equiv \sum_{j=1}^{N} M_j(0) + \sum_{j=1}^{N} \int_0^t m_j(s)\,ds.$$

Note that

(7.1a) $\qquad \dot{M}_j(t) = m_j(t), \qquad j = 1, 2, \ldots, N$

(7.1b) $\qquad M_j(0) = M_{j0},$

where an overdot denotes time derivative.

Consider the problem of finding first order conditions to

(7.2)
$$\text{maximize} \sum_{h=1}^{N} \lambda_h \int_0^T U_h\left(x_h(t), \sum_{j=1}^{N} m_j(t), \sum_{j=1}^{N} M_j(t), t\right) dt + \sum_{h=1}^{N} \lambda_h B_h(G(T)),$$

(7.3) s.t. $\quad \sum_{h=1}^{N} [p(t) \cdot x_h(t) + \dot{A}_h(t) + q(t) m_h(t)] \leq \sum_{h=1}^{N} [w_h(t) + r(t) A_h(t)],$

(7.4) $\quad A_h(0) = A_{h0}, \quad A_h(T) \geq 0, \quad x_h(t) \geq 0, \quad m_h(t) \in R,$

(7.5) $\quad \dot{M}_h(t) = m_h(t), \quad M_h(0) = M_{h0}, \quad h = 1, 2, \ldots, N,$

where $B_h(G(T))$ is the terminal value placed upon "left-over" public capital $G(T)$. Problem (7.2) says that each consumer gets a sum of instantaneous utility over his lifetime [0, T] when the instantaneous utility function U_h depends on private consumption flow, public investment flow, and the stock of public capital. The budget constraint for agent h is

$$p(t)x_h(t) + \dot{A}_h(t) + q(t)m_h(t) \leq w_h(t) + r(t)A_h(t)$$

when $A_h(t)$ denotes assets at time t. Finding necessary conditions for a Pareto optimum is done by finding first-order conditions for the optimal control problem (7.2) subject to constraints (7.3)–(7.5). The controls are $\dot{A}_h(\cdot)$, $m_h(\cdot)$ and the states are $A_h(\cdot)$, $M_h(\cdot)$. The controls are assumed to be drawn from the set of piecewise continuous controls.

It is straightforward to show, by multiplying both sides of (7.3) by $\exp[-\int_0^t r(s)\,ds]$, integrating, and using the fact that $\sum A_h(T) = 0$ at any optimum, that the set of optima to (7.2) subject to the constraints (7.3)–(7.5) is the same as the set of optima to (7.2) under the constraints (7.3′), (7.4), and (7.5), where (7.3′) is given by

(7.3′) $\quad \displaystyle\int_0^T \sum_{h=1}^N [(p(t)x_h(t) + q(t)m_h(t))] \exp\left[-\int_0^t r(s)\,ds\right] dt$

$$\leq \sum_{h=1}^N A_{h0} + \int_0^T \left[\sum_{h=1}^N w_h(t)\right]\exp\left[-\int_0^t r(s)\,ds\right] dt.^9$$

This familiar reduction requires some sort of nonsatiation, e.g., $\partial U_h/\partial x_h > 0$, $h = 1, 2, \ldots, N$ so that (7.3), (7.3′) will hold with equality at optimum for each t. More will be said about this reduction technique later. Let $\mu_h(t)$ denote the costate variable for $M_h(t)$ and let Λ denote the shadow price of constraint (7.5). Then assuming that optimal $x_h(t) > 0$ for all t standard optimal control theory given us the necessary conditions for an optimum of

---

[9] In order to see it write $C(t) \equiv \sum_{h=1}^N (p(t) \cdot x_h(t) + q(t)m_h(t))$, $A(t) \equiv \sum_{h=1}^N A_h(t)$, $Y(t) \equiv \sum_{h=1}^N w_h(t)$. Then (7.3) becomes upon multiplication by $\exp[-\int_0^t r(s)\,ds]$, $\{C(t) + \dot{A}(t) \leq r(t)A(t) + Y(t)\}\exp[-\int_0^t r(s)\,ds]$. Now integrate from 0 to T: $\int_0^T C(t)\exp[-\int_0^t r(s)\,ds]\,dt \leq A_0 + \int_0^T Y(t)\exp[-\int_0^t r(s)\,ds] - A(T)\exp[-\int_0^T r(s)\,ds]$. But $A_h(T) = 0$ for all h at any optimum if nonsatiation obtains.

In order to prove that the set of optima under (7.3)–(7.5) is the same as the set of optima to (7.3′), (7.4), (7.5) use concavity of each U_h plus standard sufficiency theory for isoperimetric problems.

(7.2) subject to (7.3'), (7.4), and (7.5) which are listed below. Put $r(s) \equiv r$ to ease notation. For all h, all t,

(7.6) $$\lambda_h U_{hx_h}(t) - p(t)e^{-rt}\Lambda = 0,$$

(7.7) $$\sum_{j=1}^{N} \lambda_j U_{jg}(t) + \mu_h(t) - q(t)e^{-rt}\Lambda = 0,$$

(7.8) $$\dot{\mu}_h(t) = -\sum_{j=1}^{N} \lambda_j U_{jG}(t),$$

(7.9) $$\mu_h(T) = B_{hG}(G(t)),$$

where subscripted symbols denote the obvious partial derivatives evaluated along the optimum path at time t. Equations (7.6)–(7.9) may be rearranged by integrating (7.8) backwards, using (7.9), then using (7.6) and (7.7) to obtain

(7.10) $$\sum_{j=1}^{N}\left(\frac{U_{jg}(t)}{U_{jx_j}(t)}\right) + \sum_{j=1}^{N}\int_{t}^{T} p(s)\left(\frac{U_{jG}(s)}{U_{jx_j}(s)}\right)\left(\frac{1}{p(t)}\right)e^{r(t-s)}\,ds$$
$$= \frac{q(t)}{p(t)} - \frac{\mu_h(T)e^{rt}}{p(t)\cdot\Lambda}$$

must hold. Equation (7.10) is intuitive because when there is no utility from stocks of public capital, $U_{jG} \equiv 0$, $B_{jG} = 0$, for all j, then (7.10) collapses, as expected, to the static or "flow utility" case analyzed in Sections II–IV. Hence, the difference between stocks and flows is highlighted by (7.10). Turn now to the formulation of the incentive design problem; it will follow that given in the previous sections of this paper.

Write down the obvious problem facing agent h:

(7.11) $$\underset{m_h(\cdot),\,A_h(\cdot)}{\text{maximize}} \int_0^T U_h\!\left(x_h(t),\,\sum_{j=1}^{N} m_j(t),\,\sum_{j=1}^{N} M_{j0} + \sum_{j=1}^{N} M_j(t),\,t\right)dt$$
$$+ B_h\!\left(\sum_{j=1}^{N} M_{j0} + \sum_{j=1}^{N} M(t)\right),$$

(7.12) s.t. $p(t)x_h(t) + \dot{A}_h(t) + C_h(q(t), m(t), M(t), t) \le w_h(t) + r(t)A_h(t),$

(7.13) $\qquad\qquad A_h(0) = A_{h0}, \qquad A_h(T) \ge 0,$

(7.14) $\qquad\qquad \dot{M}_h(t) = m_h(t).$

Reduce (7.12) as was done to get (7.3')

(7.12') $$\int_0^T (p(t)x_h(t) + C_h(q(t), m(t), M(t), t))e^{-rt}\,dt \le \int_0^T w_h(t)e^{-rt}\,dt + A_{h0}.$$

The equilibrium concept will be intertemporal Nash noncooperative equilibrium, i.e., equilibrium $m_h(\cdot)$, $\dot{A}_h(\cdot)$ maximize (7.11) over the set of piecewise continuous functions of time subject to (7.13), (7.14) and (7.12′)—given the functions $\{m_j(\cdot), \dot{A}_j(\cdot)\}_{j \neq h}$ chosen by the other players. Such an equilibrium is called an open-loop equilibrium (OLE).

The OLE has been criticized by Kydland (1975) for not being the appropriate concept for economics. We shall analyze it here anyway and defer the fascinating problem of incentive design for Kydland's "feedback equilibrium" concept to future research.

Let $\gamma_h(t)$ denote the costate variable for $M_h(t)$ and Λ_h denote the shadow price of constraint (7.12′) along an OLE $\{m_h(\cdot), \dot{A}_h(\cdot)\}_{h=1}^N$. Since $m_h(\cdot)$, $\dot{A}_h(\cdot)$ must maximize (7.11) subject to (7.13), (7.14) and (7.12′) standard application of optimal control theory leads to the necessary conditions [assuming $x_h(t) > 0$, all t],

(7.15) $$U_{hx_h}(t) - p(t)e^{-rt}\Lambda_h = 0,$$

(7.16) $$U_{hg}(t) + \gamma_h(t) - C_{hm_h}(t)e^{-rt}\Lambda_h = 0,$$

(7.17) $$\dot{\gamma}_h(t) = -U_{hG}(t) + \Lambda_h C_{hM_h} e^{-rt},$$

(7.18) $$\gamma_h(T) = B_{hG}(G(T)).$$

We may integrate (7.17) as was done to get (7.10) and manipulate (7.15) and (7.16) in order to eliminate Λ_h and obtain, finally,

(7.19) $$\frac{U_{jg}(t)}{U_{jx_j}(t)} + \left\{\int_t^T \left(\frac{U_{jG}(s)}{U_{jx_j}(s)}\right) e^{r(t-s)} p(s)\, ds\right\} \bigg/ p(t)$$
$$= \frac{C_{hm_h}(t)}{p(t)} + \left(\int_t^T C_{hm_h}(s) e^{r(t-s)}\, ds\right) \bigg/ p(t) - \frac{\gamma_h(T)e^{rt}}{p(t)\Lambda_h}.$$

Obviously to attain (7.10) we need only require that the $C_h(\cdot)$ satisfy

(7.20) $$\sum_{h=1}^N C_{hm_h}(t) + \sum_{h=1}^N \int_t^T C_{hM_h}(t) e^{r(t-s)}\, ds = q(t)$$

for each t and $\mu_h(T) = \gamma_h(T) = B_{hG}(G(T))$. Quite clearly when each player is satiated in left-over public capital: $B_{hG}(G(T)) = 0$ (7.20) can be achieved by tax functions that are independent of M_h and are independent of time t. In other words, any member of the class of tax functions constructed in Sections II–IV will satisfy (7.20). It is somewhat surprising that taxes at time t need only be made a time *independent* function of proposed increments to public *investment* levels at time t and $q(t)$ even though utility functions are time *dependent* and depend upon *stocks* of the public good as well as investment levels and still (7.10) may be achieved.

Budget balance requires, for each t,

$$(7.21) \qquad \sum_{h=1}^{N} C_h(t) = q \cdot (\sum m_j(t)).$$

Equations (7.20) and (7.21) constitute the dynamic versions of the static formulae derived in Sections II–IV.

We must apologize for the sketchy treatment given above but, we hope, the objective of showing that our design technique can be easily extended to the case of public capital goods was achieved by the above few paragraphs at a minimal cost in space. A complete treatment requires another paper.

The problem of incentive design for efficiency becomes especially interesting when posed in the context of Samuelson–Diamond–Cass type of overlapping generations models where the economy goes on forever. For the open endedness of these models opens up new problems of characterizing efficient paths of public and private capital accumulation as well as the problem of incentive design. The well-known work of Cass (1972), Majumdar (1974), and others treats the characteristics of efficient paths for private goods.

VIII. Suggestions for Further Research and Summary

It remains to be seen whether our technique is useful for the construction of Smith-type mechanisms [Smith (1979)] when the price of the public good may depend upon the messages that each agent sends. It is reasonable to conjecture that the method of using the necessary conditions of Nash equilibrium together with the necessary conditions of Pareto optimality in order to find the partial differential equation (2.5) that the C_h must satisfy in order to generate Pareto optima that is espoused in this paper should be applicable to Smith's case as well.

Furthermore, it is of interest to see if the family of mechanisms that Green and Laffont (1977) call "Groves" mechanisms which were motivated by the well-known work of Groves (1970, 1973) in team theory can be usefully designed by use of our methods.

In this paper we derived two basic conditions that tax functions must satisfy in order to generate Pareto optimal allocations of public goods. In Section II we treated the case of all goods were either pure public goods or pure private goods and showed that the tax functions must satisfy for each public good k, using the notation of Section II:

$$(8.1) \qquad \sum_h C_{hk} = q_k \left(\sum_{j=1}^{N} m_{jk} \right), \quad k = 1, 2, \ldots, k$$

in order that Pareto optimality and budget balance obtain respectively. Groves and Ledyard's (1977) famous quadratic tax functions satisfy (8.1) and (8.2). Furthermore, (8.1) and (8.2) were derived following a natural and elementary chain of reasoning.

In Section III, in order to show the virtue of the method used to (8.1) and (8.2), we extend the analysis of Section II to the case of designing taxes on an exogenously fixed coalition structure that guarantee Pareto optima for a mixed cooperative–noncooperative equilibrium concept.

Section IV develops and characterizes a general class of quadratic tax functions that guarantee Pareto-optimal equilibrium allocations.

General consumption externalities are treated in Section V. A general abstract context for the design of individually incentive compatible mechanisms is presented in Section VI. Here recent work of Smale (1977) on the necessary conditions for Pareto optimality under constraints is used to give a characterization of such mechanisms in terms of convex cones generated by gradients of tax functions. The characterization is shown to contain those developed in the previous sections.

Finally, Section VII shows that our methods can be used to design mechanisms for the efficient accumulation of public capital and to investigate systematically and to simplify the structure of these mechanisms.

ACKNOWLEDGMENTS

This paper is a revised version of The Design of Mechanisms for Efficient Allocation of Public Goods. I am grateful to F. Chang for valuable help and for finding and correcting errors in this work. John Roberts, Richard Schuler and Steve Slutsky provided useful comments. This research was done at Cornell University and was partially supported by NSF grant #74-19692. None of the above are responsible for any errors or shortcomings that remain.

REFERENCES

Arrow, K. J., and Hahn, F. H. (1971). *General Competitive Analysis*. San Francisco, California: Holden-Day.

Bennett, E., and Conn, D. (1977). The group incentive properties of mechanisms for the provision of public goods. *Public Choice* **XXIX-2** (special supplement to Spring 1977 issue), 95–102.

Brock, W., and Magee, S. (1978). The economics of special interest politics: The case of the tariff. *American Economic Review* **68**, No. 2, 246–250.

Cass, D. (1972). On capital overaccumulation in the aggregative neoclassical model of economics growth: A complete characterization. *Journal of Economic Theory* **4**, 200–223.

Clarke, E. (1971). Multipart pricing of public goods. *Public Choice* **11**, 17–33.

Green, J., and Laffont, J. J. (1977). Characterization of satisfactory mechanisms for the revelation of preferences for public goods. *Econometrica* **45**, 427–438.

Groves, T. (1970). The Allocation of Resources Under Uncertainty: The Informational and Incentive Roles of Prices and Demands in a Team. T.R. #1, Center for Research in Management Science, University of California, Berkeley; also unpublished Ph.D. dissertation, University of California, Berkeley.

Groves, T. (1973). Incentives in teams. 617–631.

Groves, T., and Ledyard, J. (1977). Optimal allocation of public goods: A solution to the "free rider" problem. *Econometrica* **45**, No. 4, 783–810.

Kydland, F. (1975). Non cooperative and dominant player solutions in discrete dynamic games. *International Economic Review* **16**, 2, 321–335.

Majumdar, M. (1974). Efficient programs in infinite dimensional spaces: A complete characterization. *Journal of Economic Theory* **7**, 4, 335–369.

Roberts, J. (1979). Incentives in planning procedures for the provision of public goods. *Review of Economic Studies* **46** (2), No. 143, 283–292.

Smale, S. (1974a). Global analysis and economics III, pareto optimal and price equilibria. *Journal of Mathematical Economics* **1**, 107–118.

Smale, S. (1974b). Global analysis and economics V, pareto theory with constraints. *Journal of Mathematical Economics* **1**, 3, 213–223.

Smith, V. (1977). Mechanisms for the optimal provision of public goods. *In American Re-Evolution/Papers and Proceedings* (R. Auster and B. Sears, eds.). Tucson, Arizona: University of Arizona.

Smith, V. (1979). Incentive compatible experimental processes for the provision of public goods. *Research in Experimental Economics* (V. Smith, ed.). Greenwich, Connecticut: Jai Press.

DEPARTMENT OF ECONOMICS
THE UNIVERSITY OF CHICAGO
CHICAGO, ILLINOIS

Critical Observations on the Labor Theory of Value and Sraffa's Standard Commodity

EDWIN BURMEISTER

I. Introduction

The pure Ricardo–Marx labor theory of value asserts that the ratio of the "values" of any two commodities is equal to the ratio of their *total* labor costs, i.e., the sum of direct labor costs and indirect labor costs embodied in machines and other factors of production. Samuelson (1971) provides an exposition and critique of this labor theory of value and its relationship to the so-called "transformation problem" between Marxian values and competitive prices; when such values and prices differ, the door is open for a Marxian theory of "exploitation."

As a formal matter, such a labor theory of value can be stated in three equivalent forms, each having certain advantages. Moreover, a labor theory of value can be interpreted as a mark-up theory of pricing. These matters are discussed in Section IV, after preliminaries in Sections II and III. Section V contains a brief examination of the close relationship between the pure labor theory of value and Sraffa's Standard Commodity, and it is argued that "more general" labor theories of value based on Sraffa's results are economically insignificant. These conclusions are reinforced in Section VI where the assumption of constant returns to scale is discussed.

When substitution among factor inputs is possible, the labor theory of value must be modified since now labor and other input coefficients will depend upon factor prices. As demonstrated in Section VII a labor theory of value is possible in such circumstances, although the necessary and sufficient conditions for its validity are so severe that the case must be dismissed as a freak. Ironically, when this labor theory of value is valid for a technology with neoclassical production functions, then the model behaves qualitatively similar to the one-sector Solow–Swan model much criticized by Cambridge, U.K., economists! The latter assertion is proved in Section VIII and provides yet another objection to the pure labor theory of value.

Finally in Section IX we conclude with a brief discussion of some fundamental objections to the labor theory of value. In particular, it is argued that the labor theory is not valid when (i) joint production exists, (ii) there are several types of primary factors, or (iii) the economy is out of steady-state equilibrium.

II. A Single Leontief–Sraffa Technique of Production

Consider an economy in which n commodities are produced by themselves and labor under constant-returns-to-scale by n nonjoint production functions. In the simplest case these production functions define a single Leontief–Sraffa production technique

$$\begin{pmatrix} a_0 \\ \hline a \end{pmatrix} = \begin{bmatrix} a_{01} & \cdots & a_{0n} \\ \hline a_{11} & \cdots & a_{1n} \\ \vdots & & \vdots \\ a_{n1} & \cdots & a_{nn} \end{bmatrix},$$

where the a_{ij}s are fixed input coefficients indicating the quantity of factor i required to produce one unit of commodity j and where the subscript 0 denotes a labor input. It is well known that *total* embodied labor inputs are given by the vector

(1) $\quad a_0 + a_0 a + a_0 a^2 + \cdots = a_0[I - a]^{-1} \equiv (l_1, \ldots, l_n) = l;$

see, for example, Dorfman *et al.* (1958, pp. 253–254); Bruno *et al.* (1966, pp. 544–545) and Samuelson and von Weizsäcker (1971). It is also well known that these total embodied labor requirements are equal to prices at a zero interest or profit rate. To see this fact, write the "price = cost" conditions as

(2) $\quad P_j = a_{0j}W + (1 + r)\sum_{i=1}^{n} P_i a_{ij}, \quad j = 1, \ldots, n,$

where P_j is the price of commodity j, W is the nominal *post factum* wage rate, and r is the interest or profit rate, and where for simplicity we postulate a technology with circulating capital. Defining the price vector

$$p = (p_1, \ldots, p_n) = (P_1/W, \ldots, P_n/W),$$

we write (2) as

(3) $$p = a_0 + (1 + r)pa,$$

which has a solution

(4) $$p(r) = a_0[I - (1 + r)a]^{-1}, \quad 0 \le r < r^*.$$

The assumption that r^* is positive is equivalent to the condition that the economy is productive and capable of generating positive steady-state equilibrium p_is at a zero rate of profit. Substituting $r = 0$ in (4) gives the total embodied labor requirements (1), i.e.,

(5) $$p(0) = l.$$

III. A Pure Labor Theory of Value at Positive Profit Rates

For positive profit rates steady-state equilibrium prices given by (4) do not equal total embodied labor requirements, i.e.

(6) $$p(r) \ne l \quad \text{for} \quad r > 0.$$

However, it still may be true that *relative prices* reflect total labor embodied requirements in the sense that

(7) $$p_i(r)/p_j(r) = l_i/l_j, \quad 0 \le r < r^*.$$

To put the matter another way, if relative prices are independent of the profit rate, then they must equal relative prices at the particular profit rate $r = 0$, and hence they must equal relative total embodied labor requirements, i.e., *if relative prices are independent of r, we have*

(8) $$p_i(r)/p_j(r) = p_i(0)/p_j(0) = l_i/l_j.$$

Conversely the pure labor theory of value expressed by (7) or (8) cannot hold whenever relative prices change with the profit rate.

Thus if, and only if, relative prices do not change with the interest or profit rate r, price ratios are equal to the ratios of total embodied labor inputs, as asserted by equation (8) above.

IV. Necessary and Sufficient Conditions for a Pure Labor Theory of Value in a Leontief–Sraffa Technology[1]

We wish to derive necessary and sufficient conditions for a pure labor theory of value in a technology consisting of a single Leontief–Sraffa production technique. As we have seen, this is equivalent to deriving necessary and sufficient conditions for equation (8) to hold, in which case relative prices are independent of the interest or profit rate r.

Let us first suppose the single Leontief–Sraffa technique is

$$\begin{bmatrix} b_0 \\ \hline b \end{bmatrix}$$

with prices q_j in terms of the *post factum* wage given by

$$(9) \qquad q_j(r) = b_{0j} + (1 + r) \sum_{i=1}^{n} q_i(r) b_{ij}.$$

Define

$$(10) \qquad \gamma_j(r) \equiv \frac{(1 + r) \sum_{i=1}^{n} q_i(r) b_{ij}}{b_{0j}}, \qquad j = 1, \ldots, n.$$

Relative prices are constant for all feasible r if, and only if,

$$(11) \qquad q_j(r)/q_1(r) = b_{0j}[1 + \gamma_j(r)]/b_{01}[1 + \gamma_1(r)]$$

are constant, and this is possible if, and only if,

$$(12) \qquad [1 + \gamma_j(r)]/[1 + \gamma_1(r)] \equiv \alpha_j = \text{const}, \qquad j = 2, \ldots, n.$$

Consider new prices defined by

$$(13) \qquad p_i \equiv q_i/\alpha_i, \qquad \alpha_1 \equiv 1, \qquad i = 1, \ldots, n.$$

We have

$$(14) \qquad \frac{p_j(r)}{p_1(r)} = \frac{q_j(r)/\alpha_j}{q_1(r)/\alpha_1} = \frac{1}{\alpha_j} \frac{q_j(r)}{q_1(r)} = \frac{b_{0j}}{b_{01}} = \frac{a_j a_{0j}}{a_{01}},$$

where new Leontief–Sraffa input coefficients are defined by

$$(15) \qquad a_{0j} \equiv b_{0j}/\alpha_j, \qquad a_{ij} \equiv \alpha_i b_{ij}/\alpha_j, \qquad i, j = 1, \ldots, n.$$

---

[1] Many of the results in this section are familiar to Marxian economists, but we restate and prove them here to make this paper self-contained. Morishima (1973) is an excellent reference for a more complete exposition.

Now we see that

$$(16) \quad \gamma_j(r) \equiv \frac{(1+r)\sum_{i=1}^n q_i(r)b_{ij}}{b_{0j}} \equiv \frac{(1+r)\sum_{i=1}^n [q_i(r)/\alpha_i][\alpha_i b_{ij}/\alpha_j]}{b_{0j}/\alpha_j}$$

$$\equiv \frac{(1+r)\sum_{i=1}^n p_i(r)a_{ij}}{a_{0j}}, \quad j = 1, \ldots, n.$$

Thus the expressions $\gamma_j(r)$ are independent of the particular constants $\alpha_1 \equiv 1, \alpha_2, \ldots, \alpha_n$.

If relative prices are constant for *all* units of measurement, it is *necessary* that they be constant for the particular choice

$$\alpha_1 = \alpha_2 = \cdots = \alpha_n = 1.$$

Thus in view of (12) it is *necessary* that

$$(17) \quad \gamma_j(r) = \gamma_1(r) \equiv \gamma(r), \quad j = 2, \ldots, n.$$

On the other hand, suppose that (17) holds; from (10) we then see that $\alpha_i = 1$, and thus (14) implies that relative prices are constant with

$$(18) \quad p_j(r)/p_1(r) = a_{0j}/a_{01} = \text{const}, \quad j = 2, \ldots, n.$$

We summarize our conclusions as

Theorem 1 *Relative prices in any units of measurement are constant for all feasible r if, and only if, (17) holds. In view of (16), this means that the pure labor theory of value is valid if, and only if, there exists a scalar function $\gamma(r)$ such that*

$$(19) \quad a_{0j}\gamma(r) = (1+r)\sum_{i=1}^n p_i(r)a_{ij}, \quad j = 1, \ldots, n.$$

We shall now prove that this labor theory of value may be stated in three equivalent forms, namely,

(I) $\quad p(r) = \alpha(r)a_0,$

(II) $\quad (1+r)pa = \gamma(r)a_0, \quad \alpha(r) = \gamma(r) + 1,$

(III) $\quad (1+r)pa = \mu(r)p, \quad \mu(r) = \dfrac{\alpha(r) - 1}{\alpha(r)}.$

Note that (II) is simply (19) in vector-matrix notation.

Lemma *(I), (II), and (III) stated above are equivalent.*

Proof To prove (I) iff (II), observe that

$$p = \alpha a_0 = a_0 + (1 + r)pa$$

or

$$(1 + r)pa = (\alpha - 1)a_0 = \gamma a_0$$

with $\gamma = \alpha - 1$. To prove (II) iff (III), we write

$$a_0 = p - (1 + r)pa = (1 + r)pa/\gamma$$

or

$$p = (1 + 1/\gamma)(1 + r)pa$$

or

$$1 + r = \left(\frac{\gamma}{\gamma + 1}\right)p = \left(\frac{\alpha - 1}{\alpha}\right)p = \mu p$$

with $\mu = (\alpha - 1)/\alpha$. Q.E.D.

Thus (I), (II), and (III) are all necessary and sufficient for constant relative prices and hence for a pure labor theory of value in which price ratios always are equal to both total embodied and direct labor requirements. In particular, note that (I) implies that prices are simply a mark-up on direct labor cost since, as we shall see below, $\alpha(r) > 1$ for $r \geq 0$. Equivalently, we see that labor's relative share given by

$$(20) \qquad \frac{a_{0i}}{p_i(r)} = \frac{WL_i}{p_i(r)Q_i} = \frac{1}{\alpha(r)}, \qquad i = 1, \ldots, n,$$

is the *same* function of r alone, namely $1/\alpha(r)$, for every industry. This interpretation will become important when we generalize our results to neoclassical production functions in Section VII below.

We now prove that $1/\alpha(r)$ is a linear function of r:

Theorem 2 *The scalar function $\alpha(r)$ in condition* (II) *is given by*

$$(21) \qquad \alpha(r) = \frac{(1 + r^*)/r^*}{1 - r/r^*}$$

with $\alpha(0) = (1 + r^*)/r^*$ and $\alpha(r^*) = \infty$.

Proof Condition (I) may be written

$$\alpha a_0 = a_0 + (1 + r)\alpha a_0 a$$

or

$$(22) \qquad a_0[\lambda I - a] = 0 \qquad \text{where} \quad \lambda = (\alpha - 1)/\alpha(1 + r).$$

For simplicity we shall presume that the matrix a is indecomposable and that the direct labor vector a_0 is strictly positive; straightforward generalizations of the stated results are easily derived when these assumptions are relaxed.

It is well known that (22) has a solution with $a_0 > 0$ if, and only if, $\lambda = \lambda^*$ where λ^* is the Frobenius root of a. Thus, a_0 is a left-hand eigenvector associated with the Frobenius root λ^* of a; see, for example, Miyao (1976). But it also is well known that λ^* is related to the maximal interest or profit rate r^* by $r^* = 1/\lambda^* - 1$, and thus

$$(\alpha - 1)/\alpha(1 + r) = \lambda = \lambda^* = 1/(1 + r^*)$$

or

$$\alpha = \frac{(1 + r^*)/r^*}{1 - r/r^*}. \quad \text{Q.E.D.}$$

The economic interest in this case stems from the fact that the factor-price frontiers

(23) $$\omega_i(r) \equiv W/P_i(r), \quad i = 1, \ldots, n,$$

are *linear* functions of r:

(24) $$\omega_i(r) = \frac{1}{p_i(r)} = \frac{a_{0i}}{\alpha(r)} = \frac{a_{0i}(1 - r/r^*)}{(1 + r^*)/r^*}, \quad i = 1, \ldots, n.$$

Thus the real wage rate in terms of any commodity as *numéraire* is the linear function of r given by (24); these real wage rates decrease from their maxima

$$\omega_i(0) = a_{0i} r^*/(1 + r^*), \quad i = 1, \ldots, n,$$

at a zero profit or interest or profit rate ($r = 0$) to their minima $\omega_i(r^*) = 0$ at the maximal interest or profit rate ($r = r^*$).

Similarly, our necessary and sufficient condition (II) may be written

$$\frac{\sum_{i=1}^n P_i(r) K_{ij}}{W L_j} = \frac{\sum_{i=1}^n p_i(r) a_{ij}}{a_{0j}} = \frac{\gamma(r)}{1 + r} = \frac{\alpha(r) - 1}{1 + r}$$

$$= \frac{1}{r^* - r} \text{ [using (21)]}, \quad j = 1, \ldots, n.$$

Thus in this case of "equal organic composition of capital" each "labor/value of capital" ratio is the same function of r for every industry:

(25) $$\frac{W L_j}{\sum_{i=1}^n P_i(r) K_{ij}} = \frac{a_{0j}}{\sum_{i=1}^n p_i(r) a_{ij}} = r^* - r, \quad j = 1, \ldots, n.$$

The linearity in equations (24) and (25) is crucial for a proper evaluation of Sraffa's analysis [Sraffa (1960)] and of various interpretations of the labor theory of value [e.g., Meek (1967), pp. 175–178)]. It is also crucial for various notions of "exploitation" as, for example, in Eatwell (1975). Unfortunately, the linearity of (24) and (25) is a freak case that depends upon arbitrary and unrealistic assumptions, namely:

(i) This linearity is lost if the presumption of a *post factum* wage is replaced by a symmetric assumption regarding factor payments whereby labor, as well as capital services, are all paid for at the beginning of the production period.

(ii) If the circulating capital assumption, which means that the depreciation rates δ_i are all unity, is replaced by the more realistic case where in general $\delta_i \neq \delta_j$, then the linearity of (24) and (25) is destroyed.

We now turn to the "Standard Commodity" introduced by Sraffa (1960) and show how it is used to define a "real" wage which is a linear function of the interest or profit rate even when the pure labor theory of value is invalid and (24) does not hold.

V. Sraffa's Standard Commodity

Sraffa's "Standard Commodity" is constructed by finding unique weights that preserve the basic linear relationships in (24) between real wage rates and the profit rate; see Sraffa (1960). Sraffa's weights define a "Standard Commodity" that is used to construct his very special "real" wage rate. This construction rests on the following result:

Theorem 3 (Burmeister, 1968) *Assume the matrix a is indecomposable, and let x^* be the (right-hand) characteristic vector associated with the Frobenius root λ^*, normalized by the labor constraint $a_0 x^* = L \equiv 1$. Then*

$$(26) \qquad px^* = \frac{(1 + r^*)/r^*}{1 - r/r^*},$$

where $p = P/W$.

Proof

$$p = a_0 + (1 + r)pa,$$

and postmultiplying by x^* gives

$$(27) \qquad px^* = a_0 x^* + (1 + r)pax^*.$$

But x^* satisfies $ax^* = \lambda^* x^* = x^*/(1 + r^*)$ and $a_0 x^* = 1$; substituting the latter into (27) yields (26). Q.E.D.

Accordingly, by using Sraffa's "Standard Commodity" to measure a "real Standard Commodity wage," $\omega(r)$, we find that

$$(28) \qquad \omega(r) \equiv \frac{W}{\sum_{i=1}^{n} P_i x_i^*} = \frac{1 - r/r^*}{(1 + r^*)/r^*},$$

a linear relationship as in (24). Moreover, this "real wage" behaves exactly like the real wage rates defined by (24) when the pure labor theory of value is valid, i.e., $\omega(r)$ declines linearly in r from its maximum value $\omega(0) = r^*/(1 + r^*)$ at $r = 0$ to its minimum value $\omega(r^*) = 0$ at the maximal interest or profit rate $r = r^*$.

Some authors have attempted to use Sraffa's result to resurrect a "generalized labor theory of value" when our stringent necessary and sufficient conditions (I), (II), and (III) for a pure labor theory of value fail. To see the analogy, first assume that the pure labor theory of value is valid. Then for *any* consumption basket $(c_1, \ldots, c_n)$ we can define the real wage in terms of a market basket of goods by

$$(29) \qquad w \equiv W/Pc = 1/pc.$$

We have postulated circulating capital and $c = x - ax$ or $pc = px - pax$. Thus we may calculate

$$(30) \qquad 1 - w = 1 - 1/pc = 1 - 1/(px - pax).$$

Since we assume that the pure labor theory of value is valid, we can use (I) and (II) to calculate

$$(31) \qquad px = \alpha a_0 x$$

and

$$(32) \qquad pax = \frac{\gamma}{1 + r} a_0 x = \frac{\alpha - 1}{1 + r} a_0 x.$$

However, quantities are normalized by the labor constraint $a_0 x = L \equiv 1$, and combining this result with (30), (31), and (32) yields

$$1 - w = 1 - [\alpha - (\alpha - 1)/(1 + r)]^{-1}.$$

Then using

$$\alpha = (1 + r^*)/(r^* - r)$$

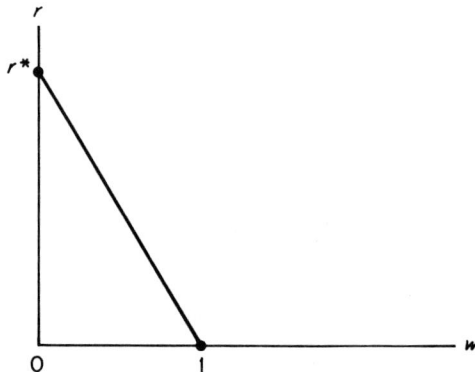

Figure 1 Linear relationship between the profit rate r and the real wage rate w for *any* consumption basket weights when the labor theory of value is valid.

from (21), by direct calculation we find that

$$1 - w = 1 - \left[\frac{1 + r^*}{r^* - r} - \frac{(1 + r^*)/(r - r^*) - (r^* - r)/(r^* - r)}{1 + r}\right]^{-1}$$

$$= 1 - (r^* - r)/r^* = r/r^*.$$

Thus for *any* consumption basket weights the interest or profit rate r is related to the real wage rate w by the linear function

(33) $$r = r^*(1 - w),$$

provided the pure labor theory of value is valid; see Fig. 1.

Now consider a very special consumption basket defined by Sraffa's weights:

(34) $$c^* \equiv x^* - ax^*,$$

where x^* is the vector in Theorem 3, namely, the right-hand characteristic vector associated with the Frobenius root of the matrix a. Sraffa's "real" wage in terms of this particular consumption basket is defined by

(35) $$w^S \equiv W/Pc^* = 1/pc^*.$$

Note that this "real" wage w^S differs by a constant proportionality factor from ω defined by (28) because w^S is constructed using the c^* weights given by (34), while ω is constructed using x^* weights. Since $ax^* = x^*/(1 + r^*)$ (see Theorem 3) and the labor constraint must be satisfied with $a_0 x^* = 1$,

(36) $$pc^* = px^* - pax^* = px^* - \frac{px^*}{1 + r^*} = px^*\left(\frac{r^*}{1 + r^*}\right).$$

THE LABOR THEORY OF VALUE AND SRAFFA'S STANDARD COMMODITY

Substituting (26) into (36) yields

$$pc^* = [1 - (r/r^*)]^{-1}$$

or, from the definition (35),

(37) $$w^S \equiv 1/pc^* = (r^* - r)/r^*.$$

Equivalently

(38) $$r = r^*(1 - w^S),$$

and this is analogous to (33) which holds when the pure labor theory of value is valid. Equation (38) is precisely the relationship asserted by Sraffa (1960, p. 22); also see Burmeister (1968) and Miyao (1976) who have provided a generalization and complete characterization of Sraffa's Standard Commodity.

There is no quarrel with the validity of (38); it is a logical conclusion that must hold given the stated assumptions. But how does this justify a "generalized labor theory of value"? The following passage from Meek (1967, pp. 177–178) illustrates one futile attempt:

> What both economists are trying to show, in effect, is that (*when wages are given*) [italics added] the average rate of profits, and therefore the deviations of price ratios from embodied labour ratios, are governed by the ratio of direct to indirect labour in the industry whose conditions of production represent a sort of "average" of those prevailing over the economy as a whole. Marx reached this result by postulating as his "average" industry one whose "organic composition of capital" was equal to the "social average." But his result could only be a provisional and approximate one, since in reaching it he had abstracted from the effect which a change in the wage would have on the prices of the means of production employed in the "average" industry. Sraffa shows that the same result can be achieved, without abstracting from this effect at all, if we substitute his "standard" industry for Marx's industry of "average organic composition of capital." Sraffa's "standard" industry, seen from this point of view, is essentially an attempt to *define* "average conditions of production" in such a way as to achieve the identical result which Marx was seeking.

This argument contains a fatal flaw. The phrase "when wages are given" must be understood to mean "when given wages are measured in terms of the very special weights defined through (34) by Sraffa's Standard Commodity." But this "real" wage rate w^S is not related in any way to human needs or preferences. *Sraffa's unique consumption basket weights are determined from* the technology alone; they are the weights derived from the right-hand characteristic vector associated with the Frobenius root of the production technique matrix a. There is absolutely no economic reason why these weights should be relevant for defining any "real" wage.

Thus, for example, Sraffa's Standard Commodity may require that we assign a relatively large weight in his consumption basket to a commodity such as pig iron which is *never* consumed by humans! To argue that "the deviations of price from embodied labor ratios" [Meek (1967, p. 177)] are "determined" when wages, assumed given, are calculated using these special weights is an absurd proposition because, except in completely freak cases, any consumption basket relevant for an actual economy will bear no resemblance to Sraffa's weights which define his "real" wage w^S: also see Burmeister (1968, 1975a) where I previously have called into question the economic significance of Sraffa's exercise. Moreover, once the economic *insignificance* of Sraffa's Standard Commodity is realized, attempts to base a notion of "exploitation" upon this foundation, such as in Eatwell (1975), are also doomed to failure.

VI. Sraffa's "Real Wage" Measure and the Constant-Returns-to-Scale Assumption

For a given Leontief–Sraffa technology, say economy I, Sraffa's unique consumption basket weights $c_1^*(I), \ldots, c_n^*(I)$ are determined by the technology alone. These weights are derived from the right-hand characteristic vector associated with the Frobenius root of the production technique matrix for technology I and are not related in *any* way to human needs or preferences. For an alternative Leontief–Sraffa technology, economy II, there will be consumption basket weights $c_1^*(II), \ldots, c_n^*(II)$ that in general are different from those in economy I.

These consumption basket weights are used to construct what I have called Sraffa's measure of the "real wage" which is denoted by $w^S(I)$ in economy I and $w^S(II)$ in economy II. Suppose for simplicity that workers receive only wage income, have identical preferences, and always desire to consume consumption baskets with fixed properties $(b_1, b_2, \ldots, b_n)$, $b_1 \equiv 1$; that is, workers always wish to consume the largest possible number of commodity bundles, each bundle containing one unit of commodity one, b_2 units of commodity two, ..., and b_n units of commodity n. Since these preferences bear no relationship to technological production conditions, in general

$$b_i \neq c_i^*(I) \neq c_i^*(II) \neq b_i, \qquad i = 1, \ldots, n.$$

Now, given the stated assumptions, assume we observe economies I and II with $w^S(I) > w^S(II)$. Can we conclude that workers are better off in economy I in the sense of being able to consume a larger number of their desired consumption baskets with weights $(b_1 \equiv 1, b_2, \ldots, b_n)$? *The answer is a definite, "No!"* (The reader may construct simple examples for $n = 2$.) Thus *simply by observing alternative values of Sraffa's w^S, one cannot conclude anything about the welfare of workers.*

If we confine ourselves to comparing situations within a single economy, there is a Leontief–Sraffa production technique defined for *each* configuration of commodity outputs. *If, and only if,* constant returns to scale is assumed, there will be one production technique matrix that is independent of outputs. Thus assuming constant returns, this single technique will possess unique Sraffa consumption basket weights $c_1^*, \ldots, c_n^*$ and a corresponding Sraffa wage measure w^S. If, on the other hand, constant returns do *not* prevail, two different output configurations, I and II, give rise to two *different* technique matrices. These two techniques give rise to the weights $c_1^*(I), \ldots, c_n^*(I)$ with an associated $w^S(I)$, and *different* weights $c_1^*(II), \ldots, c_n^*(II)$ with an associated $w^S(II)$. But this corresponds precisely to the case just discussed in which nothing can be concluded about workers' welfare from the observation that $w^S(I) > w^S(II)$.

Alternatively, suppose we do postulate constant returns and a single production technique so that the Sraffa wage measure w^S has unique weights. In these particular circumstances there exists a *single* relationship

$$r = r^*(1-w)^S,$$

which is independent of output configurations because constant returns to scale has been assumed. Consider two different equilibria positions in this economy, 1 and 2, with $w_1^S > w_2^S$; then necessarily $r_1 < r_2$. It now follows from Samuelson's nonsubstitution theorem that workers are better off in equilibrium 1 no matter what their preferences, for we know that (assuming indecomposability for convenience)

$$d\left[\frac{W}{P_i}(r)\right]\bigg/dr < 0, \quad i = 1, \ldots, n,$$

where W is the wage rate and P_i is the price of the ith commodity. It follows that a worker earning W will be able to purchase more units of *any* consumption basket at $r_1 < r_2$ because

$$\frac{W}{P_i}(r_1) > \frac{W}{P_i}(r_2), \quad r_1 < r_2, \quad i = 1, \ldots, n.$$

While the observation $w_1^S > w_2^S$ allowed us to conclude that $r_1 < r_2$, the conclusion about workers' welfare follows from the fact that the $W/P_i(r)$

curves are negatively sloped for every i. Thus Sraffa's measure w^S plays no crucial role, and one could just as well have observed that

$$\frac{W}{P_h}(r_1) > \frac{W}{P_h}(r_2)$$

for *any* commodity h, since obviously the latter also implies that $r_1 < r_2$.

In summary, under the circumstances just described it is true that one can reach conclusions about workers' welfare from the observation that $w_1^S > w_2^S$. But in general no such conclusion is possible simply from the observation that Sraffa's index w^S is higher in one situation than in another, and for this reason his measure is economically flawed and must be rejected as an appropriate measure of the "real wage." Should it not be obvious to any novice that, except under very special conditions, an index constructed without regard for preferences is incapable of correctly measuring economic welfare?

VII. A Pure Labor Theory of Neoclassical Production Functions

So far we have considered only one admissible Leontief–Sraffa production technique defined by a single set of fixed a_{ij} coefficients. In general, however, substitutability among factor inputs is possible, and all a_{ij}s on the unit isoquants

(39) $\qquad 1 = f^j(a_{0j}, a_{1j}, \ldots, a_{nj}), \qquad j = 1, \ldots, n$

are technically feasible. The cost-minimizing selection of a_{ij}s will depend on factor prices, i.e.,

(40) $\qquad a_{ij} = a_{ij}(1, q_1, \ldots, q_n)$

where q_i is the rental rate of the ith commodity in terms of the wage rate as numéraire.

For any fixed r (less than some maximal r^*, possibly infinite), Samuelson's nonsubstitution theorem guarantees that steady-state equilibrium prices are determined independently of demand; see, for example, Samuelson (1961), Burmeister and Kuga (1970a), Mirrlees (1969), and Morishima (1964). Since steady-state factor prices must equal

(41) $\qquad q_i = (1 + r)p_i,$

all a_{ij}s also are determined and we shall write

(42) $\qquad a_{ij} = a_{ij}(r), \qquad 0 \leq r < r^*.$

Thus we are back in the fixed coefficient case already analyzed, and total labor requirements are reflected in price ratios if, and only if,

$$(43) \qquad \frac{p_i(r)}{p_j(r)} = \frac{a_{0i}(r)}{a_{0j}(r)} = \frac{a_{0i}(0)}{a_{0j}(0)} = \frac{l_i}{l_j} \qquad \text{for all} \quad 0 \le r < r^*,$$

where the direct labor input coefficients depend on r via (22).

There is one special case in which (43) is valid, namely when labor's relative share is identical for all production processes, i.e., when there exists a scalar function of r, $\beta(r)$, such that

$$\beta(r)p_i(r) = a_{0i}(r)$$

or

$$(44) \quad \text{labor's relative share} \equiv \frac{WL_i}{P_iQ_i} = \frac{L_i/Q_i}{P_i/W} = \frac{a_{0i}}{p_i(r)} = \beta(r), \qquad i = 1, \ldots, n.$$

We now state and prove this result as

Theorem 4 *In a technology consisting of neoclassical production functions given by (39), a pure labor theory of value is valid [in the sense that (43) holds] if, and only if, (44) holds and labor's relative share is the same function of r alone for every industry.*

Proof Relative prices are constant if, and only if, (43) holds and

$$(44) \qquad p_i(r)/p_1(r) = l_i/l_1 = \text{const}, \qquad i = 2, \ldots, n.$$

Let primes denote total differentiation with respect to r. Equation (44) holds if, and only if,

$$(45) \qquad p_i'(r)/p_i(r) = p_1'(r)/p_1(r), \qquad i = 2, \ldots, n,$$

which is equivalent to the existence of some scalar function $\pi(r)$ such that

$$(46) \qquad p'(r) = \pi(r)p(r).$$

Differentiating

$$(47) \qquad p = a_0[I - (1+r)a]^{-1}$$

yields

$$(48) \quad \begin{aligned} p' &= a_0'[I - (1+r)a]^{-1} \\ &\quad + a_0[I - (1+r)a]^{-1}[(1+r)a' + a][I - (1+r)a]^{-1} \\ &= [a_0' + (1+r)pa'][I - (1+r)a]^{-1} + pa[I - (1+r)a]^{-1}. \end{aligned}$$

But $a_0' + (1 + r)pa' = 0$ by an envelope theorem; see Burmeister and Dobell (1970, Corollary 3.4, p. 278). Thus

(49) $$p' = pa[I - (1 + r)a]^{-1}$$

and the necessary and sufficient condition (46) becomes, using (47),

(50) $$p' = pa[I - (1 + r)a]^{-1} = \pi p = \pi a_0[I - (1 + r)a]^{-1}.$$

Postmultiplying by $[I - (1 + r)a]$ gives

(51) $$pa = \pi a_0.$$

Therefore

(52) $$p = a_0 + (1 + r)pa = a_0 + (1 + r)\pi a_0 = [I + (1 + r)\pi]a_0.$$

But (44) in vector-matrix notation is

(53) $$a_0 = \beta p,$$

and thus (52) and (53) are equivalent with

(54) $$\beta(r) = [1 + (1 + r)\pi(r)]^{-1} \quad \text{Q.E.D.}$$

Theorem 4 is illustrated by the very special Cobb–Douglas technology where the production functions (39) are

(55) $$1 = a_{0j}^{\alpha_{0j}} a_{1j}^{\alpha_{1j}} \cdots a_{nj}^{\alpha_{nj}}, \quad \alpha_{ij} > 0, \quad \sum_{i=0}^{n} \alpha_{ij} = 1, \quad j = 1, \ldots, n.$$

For this technology the pure labor theory of value is valid if, and only if

(56) $$\text{labor's relative share} = WL_i/PQ_i = \alpha_{0i} = \beta(r),$$

i.e., the technologically given elasticity parameters α_{0i} must be equal for every industry with

(57) $$\beta(r) = \alpha_{0i} \equiv \alpha_0 = \text{const}, \quad i = 1, \ldots, n.$$

Empirical evidence about the α_{0i}s cited in our concluding Section IX is inconsistent with (57), and thus a pure labor theory of value for this technology is refuted.

VIII. Simultaneous Validity of the Pure Labor Theory and the Neoclassical Parable

One fundamental aspect of the Cambridge controversy in capital theory concerns the comparisons of alternative steady-state equilibrium positions when the profit or interest rate is varied as an exogenous parameter. Thus, for example, if we confine our attention to interest rates above the Golden Rule value (the exogenous rate of labor force growth g) it is possible that a *fall* in the rate of interest results in a *fall* in steady-state per capita consumption (measured in the per capita number of fixed consumption baskets). In this case the economy is said to exhibit "paradoxical consumption behavior," the "paradox," of course, being that this consumption behavior contradicts the neoclassical parable. More precisely, the Solow–Swan one-sector model leads us to expect that any economy in a steady-state equilibrium with a lower interest rate (but still above g) will also have a higher value of steady-state per capita consumption. Furthermore, in the Solow–Swan model, where there is no problem of aggregating bolts and hammers into a single measure of "capital," a lower steady-state interest rate always implies a larger value in the stock of homogeneous machines (Swan's meccano sets or Joan Robinson's LEETS).

Accordingly, the existence of paradoxical consumption behavior destroys the validity of simple conclusions based on one-capital good models. Burmeister and Turnovsky (1972) studied this question and showed that if the price-weighted average of increments to capital stocks across steady-state equilibria is negative everywhere, then paradoxical behavior is excluded. That is, if

$$(58) \qquad pk' \equiv \sum_{i=1}^{n} p_i \frac{dk_i}{dr} < 0,$$

then it is valid to base qualitative conclusions about steady-state consumption behavior on a one-sector Solow–Swan model.

Ironically, pk' is always negative and paradoxical behavior is excluded when the pure labor theory of value holds! We now prove this assertion.

Theorem 5 *If the pure labor theory of value holds for neoclassical production functions* (39), *i.e., if equation* (43) *holds, then*

$$(59) \qquad pk' \equiv \sum_{i=1}^{n} p_i \frac{dk_i}{dr}$$

is always negative and hence paradoxical consumption behavior does not exist.

Proof[2] For (43) to hold for all r we must have

$$(60) \qquad p_i(r) = \alpha(r) a_{0i}(r), \quad i = 1, \ldots, n$$

---

[2] An alternative but very indirect proof of Theorem 5 follows from the fact that relative prices are all constant when the pure labor theory of value holds. Under these circumstances we may apply the Hicks composite commodity theorem to aggregate the heterogeneous capital goods into one well-behaved index; see Brown and Chang (1976), Brown (1976), and Burmeister (1976b). Since a one-capital-good model does not exhibit paradoxical consumption behavior, the theorem follows immediately; see Burmeister and Dobell (1970, p. 288–289).

where from (44) $\alpha(r) \equiv 1/\beta(r)$ and where $a(r) > 1$ for $0 \leq r < r^*$. [*Warning*: This $\alpha(r)$ function will not be given by (21) which we derived for the one-technique case because the matrix a and hence its Frobenius root both vary with r.]

We consider here a circulating-capital technology with a single consumption good, which we index by one. Denoting differentiation with respect to r across steady-state equilibria by primes, it can be proved that

(61) $$p_1 c' = (r - g)pk';$$

see Burmeister and Turnovsky (1972) and Burmeister and Dobell (1970, p. 286). [When there is more than one consumption good and a social utility function $u(c_1, \ldots, c_n)$ is maximized, analogous to (61) one has

(62) $$u' = (r - g)pk';$$

see Brock and Burmeister (1976).] Of course, $c' = 0$ at the Golden Rule point $r = g$. Moreover, since pk' is negative in a neighborhood of $r = g$, it suffices to prove that pk', which is a function of r, can never vanish for $r \neq g$.

Assume there exists an $\bar{r}, 0 \neq \bar{r} \neq g$, such that

(63) $$c'(\bar{r}) = 0, \quad pk' = 0 \quad \text{at} \quad 0 \neq \bar{r} \neq g.$$

We shall now prove that (58) and (63) imply a contradiction.

Full employment of capital and steady-state restrictions are

(64) $$k = ay$$

(where k is a column vector of per capita capital stocks and y is a column vector of per capita gross outputs) and

(65) $$y = (1 + g)k + c,$$

respectively, which may be solved for

(66) $$y = [I - (1 + g)a]^{-1} c, \quad 0 \leq r < r^*.$$

Thus at $r = \bar{r}$ where $c' = 0$, we have from (66)

(67) $$y' = [I - (1 + g)a]^{-1}(1 + g)a'y.$$

For neoclassical production functions

(68) $$q'a' < 0,$$

where q is a row vector of capital rental rates, and, since $y > 0$,

(69) $$q'a'y < 0.$$

This envelope result follows directly from the strict quasi-concavity of the production functions (39) and is proved in Burmeister (1976a). Using the steady-state condition

(70) $$q = (1 + r)p,$$

we have

(71) $$q' = p + (1 + r)p';$$

then combining (69) and (71) we conclude

(72) $$[p + (1 + r)p']a'y < 0.$$

By calculation

(73) $$p' = pa[I - (1 + r)a]^{-1},$$

see Eq. (49). Likewise, differentiation of (64) gives

(74) $$k' = ay' + a'y$$

or

$$pk' = pay' + pa'y.$$

Thus if (63) holds, from the latter we have

(75) $$-pay' = pa'y \quad \text{at} \quad \bar{r} \neq g;$$

combining (75) with (72) yields

(76) $$(1 + r)p'a'y + pa'y = (1 + r)p'a'y - pay' < 0.$$

Now substitute (67) and (73) into (76):

(77) $$\{(1 + r)pa[I - (1 + r)a]^{-1} - pa[I - (1 + g)a]^{-1}(1 + g)\}a'y < 0$$
$$\text{at} \quad 0 \neq \bar{r} \neq g.$$

Manipulation of the latter yields

(78) $$pa[I - (1 + r)a]^{-1}(r - g)[I - (1 + g)a]^{-1}a'y < 0$$
$$\text{at} \quad 0 \neq \bar{r} \neq g.$$

If (60) holds, then from (I) and (II) in Section IV we have

(79) $$(1 + r)pa = \gamma(r)a_0,$$

where

$$0 < \gamma(r) = \alpha(r) - 1 \quad \text{and} \quad \alpha(r) > 1 \quad \text{for} \quad 0 \leq r < r^*.$$

Thus since $\gamma(r) > 0$, (78) and (79) imply

(80) $\quad a_0[I - (1 + r)a]^{-1}[I - (1 + g)a]^{-1}a'y$
$\qquad = p[I - (1 + g)a]^{-1}a'y \neq 0 \quad$ at $\quad 0 \neq \bar{r} \neq g$.

But from (67) and (74)

(81) $\quad k' = a[I - (1 + g)a]^{-1}(1 + g)a'y + a'y = [I - (1 + g)a]^{-1}a'y$.

The combination of (70) and (81) implies that $pk' \neq 0$ at $0 \neq \bar{r} \neq g$, a contradiction. Q.E.D.

Theorem 5 proves that when the pure labor theory of value is valid for a technology consisting of neoclassical production functions, then the paradoxes in capital theory associated with the Cambridge controversy do not exist. Since these paradoxes are known to exist—indeed the economic significance of their existence has been stressed by Cambridge, U.K., authors such as Joan Robinson—our result provides additional damning evidence against the pure labor theory of value.

IX. A Few Fundamental Objections[3]

The labor theory of value expressed by (7) or (43) is not supported by any empirical evidence of which I am aware[4]; see, for example Ripley and Segal (1973), Sellekaerts and Lesage (1973), and especially the excellent survey by Weiss (1971). Aside from the question of empirical validity, one must question the theoretical relevance of a labor theory of value. Of course, the word "value" itself is misleading because in fact we have a *labor cost of production theory*. "Value" is at best dubious terminology since consumer preferences have been neglected completely!

---

[3] Morishima (1973, Chapter 14, pp. 179–196) has stated all the fundamental objections discussed in this section, although his treatment is explicitly sympathetic to the Marxist approach. The interested reader is referred to Morishima's excellent book for an opposite viewpoint to mine expressed in this paper.

[4] There is a simple direct test for the validity of the pure labor theory of value for a given Leontief–Sraffa technique. There exist units of measurement such that, in new units $\tilde{a}_{ij}$, prices in terms of the wage rate as *numéraire* are all (simultaneously) unity at a zero profit rate. The pure labor theory of value is valid if, and only if, in these new units the labor input coefficients are all equal with $\tilde{a}_{0i} = \tilde{a}_{02} = \cdots \tilde{a}_{0n}$. In such circumstances labor and other productive factors are used in the same proportions in various industries and there is "equal organic composition of capital," whence relative prices do not change with the rate of profit; see Burmeister (1968, pp. 84–86).

Alternatively, let A_j denote the jth column of the matrix a. The pure labor theory of value is valid if, and only if, the ratios $a_0 A_j/a_{0j}$ are equal for all $j = 1, \ldots, n$; see Parys (1976).

THE LABOR THEORY OF VALUE AND SRAFFA'S STANDARD COMMODITY 101

Once one realizes that it is the cost of production that is at issue, it is evident that all problems of joint production, such as wool-mutton examples, must be excluded if any labor theory is to hold up. When joint production exists, there may exist many steady-state equilibria price vectors at the same profit rate, depending upon the pattern of final demand for commodities; see Burmeister and Kuga (1970b).

But empirical and joint production issues aside, one must question the choice of *labor* as the unique factor of production used to measure "value." In general, the vector of labor input coefficients $(a_{01}, \ldots, a_{0n})$ must be replaced by the matrix

$$\begin{pmatrix} b_{11} & \cdots & b_{1n} \\ \vdots & & \\ b_{m1} & \cdots & b_{mn} \end{pmatrix}$$

where b_{ij} designates the quantity of the ith primary factor ($i = 1, \ldots, m$) required to produce one unit of commodity j ($j = 1, \ldots, n$). If $w = (w_1, \ldots, w_m)$ is a vector of primary factor prices, in place of (4) we have

(82) $\qquad p(w, r) = wb[I - (1 + r)a]^{-1}, \qquad 0 \leq r < r^*.$

In particular, note that this criticism includes the obviously realistic case in which there are many types of heterogeneous labor inputs since these different types of labor inputs may be included in the b matrix and their corresponding wage rates in the vector w.

In the neoclassical case (39) is replaced by

(83) $\qquad 1 = f^j(b_{1j}, \ldots, b_{mj}, a_{1j}, \ldots, a_{nj}), \qquad j = 1, \ldots, n,$

where now input coefficients depend on both primary factor prices and capital rental rates with

$$b_{ij} = b_{ij}(w, q) \qquad \text{and} \qquad a_{ij} = a_{ij}(w, q).$$

A complete analysis of such a model with many primary factors is given by Burmeister (1975b), but here we make one important observation. *Even at $r = 0$, at best one could have a valid "primary factor theory of cost," and even that would require knowledge of relative primary factor prices.* Since these primary factor prices are determined in general equilibrium and are *not* independent of demand, such a "primary factor theory of cost" must be rejected. This observation is absolutely fatal for all attempts to construct a theory of "value" based on labor alone, or a theory of "value" which is independent of the demands and preferences of economic agents. That realistic economies are simultaneous general equilibrium systems is a complicating fact we cannot deny.

Finally, in addition to all the objections discussed above, a "labor" or "primary factor" theory of "value" (or cost) is a statement *only* about steady-state equilibria positions. Out of steady-state equilibria prices will not be constants and commodity price changes are reflected in factor prices, so that $q_i = (1 + r)p_i$ holds only in steady-state equilibria. Thus rates of price change do influence costs of production, thereby destroying any labor theory of value out of steady states.

In closing we do warn the reader about what we have *not* said. Although we reject a Marxian labor theory of value, it does not necessarily follow that all Marxian conclusions about the capitalistic system are erroneous. Purely as a matter of logic, a theorem is not proved false because a step in its proof is shown to be wrong. On the other hand, when that step is apparently crucial and fundamental to the general argument, one cannot help but become very suspicious.

ACKNOWLEDGMENTS

I am grateful to G. C. Harcourt, Michio Morishima, and Paul Samuelson for critical comments on an earlier draft of this paper. Research support from the National Science Foundation and the Center for Advanced Studies at the University of Virginia is acknowledged with thanks.

REFERENCES

Brock, W. A., and Burmeister, E. (1976). Regular economies and conditions for uniqueness of steady states in optimal multi-sector economic models. *International Economic Review* 105–120.

Brown, M. (1976). The Measurement of Capital Aggregates—A Post Reswitching Problem. Paper presented at the NBER Conference on Research in Income and Wealth, Toronto, October 14–15.

Brown, M., and Chang, W. W. (1976). Capital aggregation in a general equilibrium model of production. *Econometrica* **44**, 1179–1200.

Bruno, M., Burmeister, E., and Sheshinski, E. (1966). The Nature and implications of the reswitching of techniques. *Quarterly Journal of Economics* **80**, 526–553.

Burmeister, E. (1968). On a theorem of Sraffa. *Economica* **35**, 83–87.

Burmeister, E. (1975a). Comment: This age of Leontief . . . and who? *Journal of Economic Literature* **13**.

Burmeister, E. (1975b). Many primary factors in non-joint production economies. *Economic Record*.

Burmeister, E. (1976a). Real Wicksell effects and regular economies. In *Essays in Modern Capital Theory* (M. Brown *et al.*, eds.). Amsterdam: North-Holland Publ.

Burmeister, E. (1976b). Comments on capital aggregation. Paper presented at the *NBER Conference on Research in Income and Wealth, Toronto, October 14–15*; reprinted in *The Measurement of Capital* (D. Usher, ed.). Chicago, Illinois: The University of Chicago Press (forthcoming).

Burmeister, E., and Dobell, A. R. (1970). *Mathematical Theories of Economic Growth*. New York: Macmillan.

REFERENCES

Burmeister, E., and Kuga K. (1970a). The factor-price frontier, duality and joint production. *The Review of Economic Studies* **37**, 11–19.
Burmeister, E., and Kuga K. (1970b). The factor-price frontier in a neo-classical multi-sector model. *International Economic Review* **11**, 162–174.
Burmeister, E., and Turnovsky, S. J. (1972). Capital deepening response in an economy with heterogeneous capital goods. *American Economic Review* **62**, 842–853.
Dorfman, R., Samuelson, P. A., and Solow, R. M. (1958). *Linear Programming and Economic Analysis.* New York: McGraw-Hill.
Eatwell, J. (1975). Mr. Sraffa's standard commodity and the rate of exploitation. *Quarterly Journal of Economics* 543–555.
Meek, R. L. (1967). *Economics and Ideology and Other Essays.* London: Chapman and Hall.
Mirrlees, J. (1969). The dynamic nonsubstitution theorem. *Review of Economic Studies* **26**, 67–76.
Miyao, T. (1977). A generalization of Sraffa's standard commodity and its complete characterization. *International Economic Review* **18**, 151–163.
Morishima, M. (1964). *Equilibrium, Stability, and Growth: A Multi-Sectoral Analysis.* London and New York: Oxford Univ. Press (Clarendon).
Morishima, M. (1973). *Marx's Economics.* London and New York: Cambridge Univ. Press.
Parys, W. (1976). A Simple Criterion for Equal Value Composition of Capital, Mimeograph.
Ricardo, D. (1911). *The Principles of Political Economy and Taxation.* London: Dent (reprinted 1962).
Ripley, F. C., and Segal, L. (1973). Price determination in 395 manufacturing industries. *Review of Economics and Statistics* **55**, 263–271.
Samuelson, P. A. (1961). A new theorem on nonsubstitution. *In Money, Growth and Methodology*, published in honor of Johan Akerman, Volume 20, pp. 1–30. Lund Social Science Studies. Lund, Sweden: CWK Gleerup. Reprinted *In The Collected Scientific Papers of Paul A. Samuelson* (J. E. Stiglitz, ed), Vol. I. Cambridge, Massachusetts: MIT Press, 1966.
Samuelson, P. A. (1971). Understanding the Marxian notion of exploitation: A summary of the so-called transformation problem between Marxian values and competitive prices. *Journal of Economic Literature* **9**, 399–431. Reprinted *In The Collected Scientific Papers of Paul A. Samuelson* (R. C. Merton, ed.), Volume III. Cambridge, Massachusetts: MIT Press, 1972.
Samuelson, P. A., and von Weizsäcker, C. C. (1971). A new labor theory of value for rational planning through use of the bourgeois profit rate. *Proceedings of the National Academy of Sciences, U.S.* **68**, 1192–1194. Reprinted *In The Collected Scientific Papers of Paul A. Samuelson* (R. C. Merton, ed.), Volume III. Cambridge, Massachusetts: MIT Press, 1972.
Sellekaerts, W., and Lesage, R. (1973). A reformulation and empirical verification of the administered prices inflation hypothesis: The Canadian case. *Southern Economic Journal* **39**, 345–360.
Sraffa, P. (1960). *Production of Commodities by Means of Commodities.* London and New York: Cambridge Univ. Press.
Weiss, L. (1971). Quantitative studies of industrial organization. *In Frontiers of Quantitative Economics* (M. D. Intriligator, ed.). Amsterdam: North-Holland Publ.

DEPARTMENT OF ECONOMICS
UNIVERSITY OF VIRGINIA
CHARLOTTESVILLE, VIRGINIA

The Selection of Variates for Use in Prediction

A Generalization of Hotelling's Solution

GREGORY C. CHOW

I. The Problem

In a 1940 issue of the *Annals of Mathematical Statistics,* Hotelling (1940) posed the following problem. Given a vector y whose n components are normally and independently distributed, and given the corresponding n observations on two sets of explanatory variables X and Z, test the null hypothesis that the standard errors in the regressions of y on X and y on Z are equal. Hotelling provided a solution for the case where X and Z are both univariate. We propose to generalize Hotelling's solution to the case where X and Z are sets of variates, and where there may be more than two sets. It will be assumed, up to Section V, that X and Z are *fixed* variates. In Section VI, our solution will be shown to apply also to random X and Z.

This problem first came to my attention while I was studying the factors affecting the demand for total stock and for annual purchase of automobiles in the United States (Chow, 1957, p. 65). In that study, the questions arose as to whether automobile stock y was better explained by liquid asset X or income Z, and whether annual purchase y was better explained by permanent income X or by another pair of variables Z consisting of current income and lagged stock of automobiles.

II. Hotelling's Solution

For the case where both X and Z are single vectors, there is no loss of generality to rescale them to make the elements of each sum to zero and their squares sum to one. Let the ith elements of these vectors be denoted by x_i and z_i, respectively. Hotelling further transformed these vectors to two orthogonal vectors X^* and Z^* where the ith element of X^* is

$$x_i^* = (x_i - z_i)/\sqrt{2(1 - r_{xz})} \qquad (i = 1, \ldots, n)$$

and the ith element of Z^* is

$$z_i^* = (x_i + z_i)/\sqrt{2(1 + r_{xz})} \qquad (i = 1, \ldots, n)$$

with r_{xz} denoting the correlation coefficient between X and Z. To test the hypothesis that the coefficient of X^* in the regression of y on both X^* and Z^* is zero, one can apply the standard t test. The t statistic is easily shown to be

$$\text{(1)} \qquad \frac{(r_{yx} - r_{yz})}{s} \sqrt{\frac{\sum (y_i - \bar{y})^2}{2(1 - r_{xz})}} = t(r - 3),$$

where s is standard error of the multiple regression. Since this statistic is a monotone transformation of the difference between the sample correlation coefficients r_{yx} and r_{yz}, Hotelling used it to test the null hypothesis that the population correlation coefficients ρ_{yx} and ρ_{yz} are equal.

The test statistic (1) can be derived in another way. We assume, after rescaling, that the vectors X and Z have unit length and that their elements sum to zero. The rescaling does not affect the predictive power of these explanatory variables. In the linear regression of y on both X and Z, we can test the null hypothesis that the difference between the two regression coefficients is zero by using a t statistic. This statistic is the same as the one given by (1).

Hotelling also pointed out that, when k other fixed variates are present, the equality between the partial correlation coefficients $\rho_{yx\cdot}$ and $\rho_{yz\cdot}$ can be tested by the analogous expression

$$\text{(2)} \qquad \frac{(r_{yx\cdot} - r_{yz\cdot})}{s} \sqrt{\frac{\sum (y_{i\cdot} - \bar{y}_\cdot)^2}{2(1 - r_{xz\cdot})}} = t(n - 3 - k),$$

where s stands for the standard error of the regression of y on all fixed variates.

III. A Geometric Interpretation of Hotelling's Solution

Interpreting Hotelling's solution from the geometric viewpoint will facilitate its generalization to the case of comparing two sets of fixed variates

X and Z. The problem will be formulated in the following way, which will be shown to be identical with the original problem. Consider the random vector y in an n-dimensional vector space. The alternative hypothesis is that $E(y)$ lies in the subspace spanned by X and Z, to be denoted by $\{X \quad Z\}$. The null hypothesis is that $E(y)$ is of equal distance from the space $\{X\}$ spanned by X and the space $\{Z\}$ spanned by Z. We shall now show that this null hypothesis is equivalent to the null hypothesis that the population standard errors of the regressions of y on X and y on Z are equal. Throughout the discussion, y is a column vector of n elements; each of X and Z is a matrix consisting of column vectors of n elements.

Theorem 1 *The population standard errors of the regressions of y on X and y on Z are equal if and only if $E(y)$ is of equal distance from $\{X\}$ and $\{Z\}$.*

Proof The population standard error of the regression of y on X is defined as the minimum of $\sqrt{(1/n)E\|y - X\alpha_1\|^2}$ with respect to α_1. Differentiating $E\|y - X\alpha_1\|^2$ with respect to α_1, we have $-2X'(Ey) + \alpha X'X\alpha_1$, which, when set equal to 0, gives the minimizing α_1, $\alpha_1 = (X'X)^{-1}X'(Ey)$. Thus $X\alpha_1$ is the orthogonal projection of $E(y)$ on the space $\{X\}$. Similarly, the population standard error of the regression of y on Z is defined as $\sqrt{(1/n)E\|y - Z\alpha_2\|^2}$, where $\alpha_2 = (Z'Z)^{-1}Z'(Ey)$ and $Z\alpha_2$ is the orthogonal projection of $E(y)$ on $\{Z\}$.

On substituting $(X'X)^{-1}X'(Ey)$ for α_1 in $(1/n)E\|y - X\alpha_1\|^2$ we find the square of the standard error in the regression of y on X to be

$$(1/n)[E(y'y) - (Ey)'X(X'X)^{-1}X'(Ey)].$$

Similarly the square of the standard error in the regression of y on Z is

$$(1/n)[E(y'y) - (Ey)'Z(Z'Z)^{-1}Z'(Ey)].$$

The expressions $(Ey)'X(X'X)^{-1}X'(Ey)$ and $(Ey)'Z(Z'Z)^{-1}Z'(Ey)$ are respectively the squared lengths $\|X\alpha_1\|^2$ and $\|Z\alpha_2\|^2$ of the orthogonal projections of $E(y)$ on $\{X\}$ and on $\{Z\}$. Therefore, the two standard errors are equal if and only if the lengths of the orthogonal projections are equal. But the orthogonal projections have the same length if and only if $E(y)$ is of equal distance from $\{X\}$ and $\{Z\}$. This completes the proof of Theorem 1.

In the case where X and Z are single vectors, the null space consists of the union of two lines bisecting the angles between X and Z. By comparing the distances of y from the null space and from the space $\{X \quad Z\}$, under the alternative hypothesis one can test the null hypothesis stated above using the theory of general linear hypotheses. Simple algebra will show that the resulting F test is identical with (1). Kruskal (1959) has pointed out that, since the null space is nonlinear even in this case, the F test is not exact but approximate, and that the assumption of equality between ρ_{yx} and ρ_{yz} is different from the assumption of equality between $E\|y - X\alpha_1\|^2$ and $E\|y - Z\alpha_2\|^2$ since the latter assumption includes $\rho_{yx} = -\rho_{yz}$. We have taken the equality between the standard errors as our null hypothesis.

IV. Solution For Two Sets of Fixed Variates

Once the problem has been formulated in Section III, we proceed to apply the well-known theory of general linear hypotheses and to show that the resulting test is an approximate test. Without loss of generality, we assume that $\{X\}$ and $\{Z\}$ are disjoint. If they are not, we can eliminate the vectors in common and deal with the residuals in the regressions of y and of the remaining two (disjoint) sets of fixed variates on these vectors. Hotelling's second test as given by (2) above is a special case of this procedure.

Let X be an n by p_1 matrix with rank p_1 and Z be an n by p_2 matrix with rank p_2. Let the rank of $[X \quad Z]$ be $p = p_1 + p_2$. Under the alternative hypothesis, we project y on $\{X \quad Z\}$, giving

(3) $$y = Y + e,$$

where Y is in the space $\{X \quad Z\}$ and e is orthogonal to Y. $\|e\|^2/\sigma^2$ is distributed as $x^2(n - p)$.

Under the null hypothesis, the mean of y, now denoted by β, is not only in $\{X \quad Z\}$ but is of equal distance from $\{X\}$ and $\{Z\}$. This means that β satisfies

(4) $$\beta = [X \quad Z]\alpha$$

for some vector α with p elements, and

(5) $$\beta'[I - X(X'X)^{-1}X']\beta = \beta'[I - Z(Z'Z)^{-1}Z']\beta.$$

From (4) and (5) follows

(6) $$\alpha'\begin{bmatrix}X' \\ Z'\end{bmatrix}[X(X'X)^{-1}X' - Z(Z'Z)^{-1}Z'][X \quad Z]\alpha = 0.$$

We now find α to minimize the squared distance $\|y - [X \quad Z]\alpha\|^2$ subject to the quadratic constraint (6). Since the least-squares estimator $\hat{\alpha}$ in our case is a maximum likelihood estimator subject to constraints, the recent work of Aitchison and Silvey (1958) applies—with modifications as will soon be discussed.

For ease of reference to Aitchison and Silvey (1958), we shall use the same notations for functions as theirs, while retaining our own symbols for the arguments in the functions. The log-likelihood function L in our case is

$$L(y; \alpha, X, Z) = -n \log(\sqrt{2\pi}\sigma) - 2\sigma^{-2}\|y - [X \quad Z]\alpha\|^2$$

and the set of constraints $h(\alpha) = 0$ consists only of (6). Following stepwise maximization and thus treating σ as a constant, we will simply rewrite our log-likelihood function, without using a new symbol,

(7) $$L(y; \alpha, X, Z) = -\tfrac{1}{2}\|y - [X \ Z]\alpha\|^2.$$

Introducing a Lagrange multiplier λ, we proceed to differentiate the expression $L + \lambda h$ with respect to α, and obtain the necessary condition for a constrained maximum

(8) $$\begin{bmatrix} X' \\ Z' \end{bmatrix} y - \begin{bmatrix} X' \\ Z' \end{bmatrix}[X \ Z]\hat{\alpha} + \hat{\lambda}H\hat{\alpha} = 0,$$

where H denotes the p by p matrix

$$\begin{bmatrix} X' \\ Z' \end{bmatrix}[X(X'X)^{-1}X' - Z(Z'Z)^{-1}Z'][X \ Z].$$

The product $H\alpha$ corresponds to the function H_α in Aitchison and Silvey (1958); the first two terms of (8) correspond to $1(y, \alpha)$ in Aitchison and Silvey (1958).

Equations (8) and (6) form a set of $p + 1$ equations for the unknowns $\hat{\alpha}$ and $\hat{\lambda}$. These equations are difficult to solve analytically. A method of numerical solution and a proof of the existence of a maximizing (the likelihood function) solution for the more general problem are given by Aitchison and Silvey (1958). The numerical method recommended by them amounts essentially to linearizing equations (8) and (6) about an initial guess $\alpha^{(1)}$ for $\hat{\alpha}$, solving the resulting linear equations in $(\hat{\alpha} - \alpha^{(1)})$ and $\hat{\lambda}$ to obtain a second guess for $\hat{\alpha}$, and continuing to iterate until convergence. They have also shown the consistency of the estimators. Since X and Z are regarded as fixed in our case, and thus a sequence of estimators is by no means well specified, we will define consistency for our problem and show that $\hat{\alpha}$ is consistent.

Let us expand (8) in a Taylor series about α_0 and divide by n:

(8a) $$\frac{1}{n}\left\{\begin{bmatrix} X' \\ Z' \end{bmatrix} y - \begin{bmatrix} X' \\ Z' \end{bmatrix}[X \ Z]\alpha_0\right\} - \frac{1}{n}\begin{bmatrix} X' \\ Z' \end{bmatrix}[X \ Z][\hat{\alpha} - \alpha_0]$$
$$+ \frac{1}{n}\hat{\lambda}[H\alpha_0 + H(\hat{\alpha} - \alpha_0)] = 0,$$

which in the notations of Aitchison and Silvey (1958) is

(8b) $$\frac{1}{n} 1(y, \alpha_0) - B[\hat{\alpha} - \alpha_0] + \frac{1}{n}\hat{\lambda}[H_{\alpha_0} + \hat{h}(y)] = 0.$$

Let us also expand (6) in a Taylor series about α_0:

(6a) $\qquad \alpha_0' H[\hat{\alpha} - \alpha_0] + \tfrac{1}{2}[\hat{\alpha}' - \alpha_0']H[\hat{\alpha} - \alpha_0] = 0,$

or

$$[\alpha_0' H + \tfrac{1}{2}(\hat{\alpha}' - \alpha_0')H][\hat{\alpha} - \alpha_0] = 0,$$

which in the notations of Aitchison and Silvey (1958) becomes

(6b) $\qquad [H'_{\alpha_0} + \hat{h}^*(y)][\hat{\alpha} - \alpha_0] = 0.$

Both $\hat{h}(y)$ in (8b) and $\hat{h}^*(y)$ in (6b) obviously satisfy the requirement stated in Aitchison and Silvey (1958) that they approach 0 as $\|\hat{\alpha} - \alpha_0\| \to 0$. In order to define consistency, something need be said about the fixed variates X and Z. We state that the elements in each of these vectors are "a sequence of constants fixed in advance but unknown to the statistician," using the definition of Wolfowitz (1953, p. 18). Each sequence can be arbitrary, and no probability distribution is ascribed to it. However, we do make the sufficient assumption that the covariance matrix

$$\frac{1}{n}\begin{bmatrix} X' \\ Z' \end{bmatrix}[X \ Z],$$

or B in the notation of Aitchison and Silvey (1958), converges to some limit as n increases.

With the conditions on $\hat{h}(y)$, $\hat{h}^*(y)$, and B as just stated, we rewrite (8b) and (6b) as equations in the unknowns $\hat{\alpha} - \alpha_0$ and $(1/n)\hat{\lambda}$:

(9) $\qquad \begin{bmatrix} B & -[H_{\alpha_0} + \hat{h}(y)] \\ -[H'_{\alpha_0} + \hat{h}^*(y)] & 0 \end{bmatrix} \begin{bmatrix} \hat{\alpha} - \alpha_0 \\ (1/n)\hat{\lambda} \end{bmatrix} = \begin{bmatrix} (1/n)1(y, \alpha_0) \\ 0 \end{bmatrix}.$

Remember that we have defined $1(y, \alpha_0)$ as

$$\begin{bmatrix} X' \\ Z' \end{bmatrix}[y - (X \ Z)\alpha_0],$$

which, under the null hypothesis, equals

$$\begin{bmatrix} X' \\ Z' \end{bmatrix}\varepsilon.$$

Simply by the law of large numbers, $(1/n)1(y, \alpha_0)$ must approach 0 stochastically as n increases. Hence, equation (9) implies, together with our conditions on $\hat{\lambda}(y)$, $\hat{h}^*(y)$, and B, that both $\hat{\alpha} - \alpha_0$ and $(1/n)\hat{\lambda}$ will approach 0 stochastically. This result is stated in the following theorem.

THE SELECTION OF VARIATES FOR USE IN PREDICTION   111

Theorem 2 *The sequence of maximum-likelihood estimators $\hat{\alpha}(n)$ is a consistent sequence of estimators for α_0, where the term consistency has been defined above.*

Having defined and proved the consistency of $\hat{\alpha}$, we can justify using the test of general linear hypothesis as an approximate solution to our problem. We will first show that $\|y - (X \ Z)\hat{\alpha}\|^2/\sigma^2$ or $\|y - \hat{\beta}\|^2/\sigma^2$ is approximately distributed as $x^2(n - p + 1)$ under the null hypothesis, as it may be expected.

Observe first that

(10) $$(y - \hat{\beta}) \perp \hat{\beta},$$

which can be easily demonstrated by premultiplying (8) by $\hat{\alpha}'$. Let α_0 and β_0 be the true values of α and β respectively. Consider the squared distance from y to β_0 and use (10):

(11) $$\|y - \beta_0\|^2 = \|y - \hat{\beta}\|^2 + \|\hat{\beta} - \beta_0\|^2 - 2\beta_0'(y - \hat{\beta}).$$

Premultiplying (8) by α_0', we can write the cross-product term

(12) $$\beta_0'(y - \hat{\beta}) = \lambda\beta_0'[X(X'X)^{-1}X' - Z(Z'Z)^{-1}Z']\hat{\beta}$$
$$= \lambda\alpha_0' H\hat{\alpha} = \lambda\alpha_0' H[\hat{\alpha} - \alpha_0].$$

The term $\lambda\alpha_0' H[\hat{\alpha} - \alpha_0]$ is approximately 0 in view of our expansion (6a) if the second derivative in (6a) is disregarded. Thus the vectors $y - \hat{\beta}$ and $\hat{\beta} - \beta_0$ in (11) can be treated approximately as orthogonal.

This approximation can be viewed in the following way. We are projecting y on the null space given by the quadratic (5). We also know that y is orthogonal to $\hat{\beta}$ in (5). But if β_0 is also in (5) and is near $\hat{\beta}$, that neighborhood of the null space can be regarded as linear. What we have done is to expand (5) in a Taylor series about β_0, or expand (6) in a Taylor series about α_0, and omit the second derivative. This would amount to treating the constraint, for the purpose of differentiation, as

(13) $$\beta_0'[X(X'X)^{-1}X' - Z(Z'Z)^{-1}Z']\beta = 0$$

or

$$\alpha_0' H\alpha = 0.$$

After replacing the constraint (5) by the constraint (13), we have reduced our problem to one of testing general linear hypotheses. Our null space becomes a vector space of dimension $p - 1$ since it is a subspace of $\{X \ Z\}$ subject to the linear restriction (13). In the identity

(14) $$y - \hat{\beta} = y - Y + Y - \hat{\beta} = e + Y - \hat{\beta},$$

where Y and e have been defined by (3), e is certainly orthogonal to $Y - \hat{\beta}$ since both Y and $\hat{\beta}$ are in $\{X \quad Z\}$. $y - \hat{\beta}$ has rank $n - p + 1$, and e has rank $n - p$. Applying the theory of linear hypotheses to our situation, we have the following theorem.

Theorem 3 *Under the null hypothesis as stated in Theorem 1, the ratio*

$$\text{(15)} \qquad \frac{\|y - \hat{\beta}\|^2}{\|e\|^2/(n - p)}$$

is approximately distributed as $F(1, n - p)$.

It can be proved that (15) reduces to Hotelling's test (1) when each of X and Z is a vector. Without exhibiting the simple algebra involved in the proof, we would like to point out that, in this special case, the quadratic constraint becomes the square of a linear constraint.

V. Solution for Many Sets of Fixed Variates

When there are more than two sets of fixed variates to compare, we observe that, for one additional set, there will be one additional quadratic constraint of the form (5) or (6). If the constraints are linearized as in (13), and if we have r sets of fixed vectors with total rank p, there will be $r - 1$ linear constraints. The vector space under the alternative hypothesis will have rank p, and the null space will have rank $p - (r - 1)$. To test the null hypothesis that Ey is of equal distance from all r sets of explanatory variables, we use the F ratio

$$\text{(16)} \qquad \frac{\|Y - \hat{\beta}\|^2/(r - 1)}{\|e\|^2/(n - p)} \simeq F(r - 1, n - p),$$

where, as before, the observed y is decomposed into Y (spanned by the r sets of fixed variates) and e (orthogonal to Y); and $\hat{\beta}$ is obtained by projecting y on the null space under the assumption that the mean of y is of equal distance from all sets of fixed variates.

VI. The Multivariate Case

Our solution to the case where all variates are random can be briefly stated.

Theorem 4 *When all the variates concerned satisfy a multivariate distribution, tests* (15) *and* (16) *remain valid provided that certain general assumptions as required by Aitchison and Silvey* (1958) *hold.*

Proof There are two views on the multivariate case. The first view is to consider the *conditional* distribution of y given the observed X and Z. If this view is taken, our former arguments concerning the case of fixed X and Z apply, except that the definition of consistency of $\hat{\alpha}$ has to be modified. But $\hat{\alpha}$ is known to be consistent (Aitchison and Silvey, 1958).

The second view is to consider the distribution of the ratio (15) or (16) when X and Z are random variables. It has been shown above that, as n increases, the cdf of this ratio approaches the cdf of the F ratio for any sequences of X and Z whose second moments converge. When X and Z are also random variables, the cdf of the ratio (15) or (16) can be obtained by taking the expectation of the previous cdf over X and Z. By Lebesque's convergence theorem, the resulting cdf approaches the cdf of the F ratio. We have required that the matrix of the second moments of X and Z converges to some limit with probability one, and that the assumptions stated in Aitchison and Silvey (1958) hold. The multivariate normal distribution for y, X and Z is certainly sufficient.

VII. Concluding Remarks

Starting from the problem of selecting a set of variates for predicting y, we have provided a new example of applying the theory of general linear hypotheses to a case of nonlinear hypotheses. The solution for the case when the predictors are fixed is extended to the multivariate case. As a conjecture, we shall point out that a comparison of (1) and (15) may yield a useful definition of a (scalar) correlation coefficient between two sets of variates X and Z.

ACKNOWLEDGMENTS

I should like to thank William H. Kruskal and John Pratt for providing a number of valuable suggestions.

This paper was presented before the Econometric Society Meetings held in Washington, D.C., in December 1959, with Lawrence Klein as the discussant. The author received several offers to publish this paper during the intervening years, but all failed to be carried out, because of unusual circumstances. The interest in the subject of selecting one of several competing hypotheses has grown in recent years, as witnessed by the papers of Cox (1961, 1962), Gaver and Geisel (1974), Quandt (1974), and Pesaran and Deaton (1978), just to cite a few examples. However, the solution given in this paper remains a useful one when compared with the alternative solutions proposed by others.

REFERENCES

Aitchison, J., and Silvey, S. D. (1958). Maximum-likelihood estimation of parameters subject to restraints. *Annals of Mathematical Statistics* **29**, 813–828.

Chow, G. C. (1957). *Demand for Automobiles in the United States.* Amsterdam: North-Holland Publ.

Cox, D. R. (1961). Tests of separate families of hypotheses. *Proceedings of the Fourth Berkeley Symposium of Mathematical Statistics and Probability* Vol. 1. Berkeley, California: University of California Press.

Cox, D. R. (1962). Further results on tests of separate families of hypotheses. *Journal of the Royal Statistical Society Series B* **24**, 406–424.

Gaver, K. M., and Geisel, M. S. (1974). Discriminating among alternative models: Bayesian and non-bayesian methods. In *Frontiers in Econometrics* (P. Zarembka, ed.), pp. 49–77. New York: Academic Press.

Hotelling, H. (1940). The selection of variates for use in prediction with some comments on the general problem of nuisance parameters. *Annals of Mathematical Statistics* **11**, 271–283.

Kruskal, W. H. (1959). Private communication.

Pesaran, M. H., and Deaton, A. S. (1979). Testing non-nested non-linear regression models. *Econometrica* **46**, 677–694.

Quandt, R. E. (1974). A comparison of methods for testing non-nested hypotheses. *Review of Economics and Statistics* **56**, 92–99.

Wolfowitz, J. (1953). Estimation by the minimum distance method. *Annals of the Institute of Statistical Mathematics* **5**, 9–23.

PRINCETON UNIVERSITY
PRINCETON, NEW JERSEY

Regression When Each of Two Variables Is Dependent Some of the Time

CARL F. CHRIST

I. Introduction and Summary

This paper deals with the problem of estimating the coefficients in a linear equation from a sample of T observations, when it is known that in a certain subset of the observations one of the variables (denoted by y) is dependent in the classical sense, and in the remaining subset of the observations another of the variables (denoted by x) is dependent instead.

This situation can arise as follows. Suppose that a policymaker is confronted with a linear relationship among several variables. Suppose that all but two of these variables are predetermined by some process that does not involve the linear equation; they may be under or outside the control of the policymaker. As to the remaining pair of variables, y and x, the policymaker either arbitrarily sets the value of x whereupon the linear relationship determines the value of y, or arbitrarily sets the value of y whereupon the linear relationship determines the value of x. He or she need not make the same decision for all points in the sample: x may be set in some cases, and y in others.

For example, the Federal Reserve can either fix the level of money-market interest rates and let the money stock be determined by the equation for the demand for money, or fix the money stock and let interest rates be determined by the demand-for-money equation.[1]

Let the equation be

$$(1) \qquad y_t = \beta x_t + \sum_{i=1}^{K} \gamma_i z_{it} + u_t \qquad t = 1, \ldots, T,$$

or in equivalent matrix form

$$(2) \qquad \mathbf{y} = \mathbf{x}\beta + \mathbf{Z}\gamma + \mathbf{u},$$

where y_t, x_t, and $z_{1t}, \ldots, z_{Kt}$ are observable variables, one of the z_k is a dummy equal to 1 if the equation has a nonzero intercept, u_t is an unobservable independent normal disturbance with mean zero and constant variance σ^2, and $\beta, \gamma_1, \ldots, \gamma_K$ are unknown coefficients to be estimated; $\mathbf{y}, \mathbf{x}$, and $\mathbf{u}$ are $T \times 1$, γ is $K \times 1$, and $\mathbf{Z}$ is $T \times K$ and has rank K.

It is assumed to be known that u_t is independent of z_{is} for all i, s, and $t \geq s$; hence the z_{it} are predetermined variables. Further, it is assumed to be known that u_t for all t is independent of x_s for all $s \leq t$ and belonging to a certain subset containing P of the T sample observations, where $P \leq T$; and that u_t for all t is independent of y_s for all $s \leq t$ and belonging to the remaining subset containing Q of the T sample observations (where $P + Q = T$). Then in the subset of P observations, y_t is dependent, while in the subset of Q observations, x_t is dependent.

The maximum likelihood estimator of β is obtained in Sections II–IV. It turns out to be a function of the two ordinary least-squares estimators of β, one obtained by regarding y_t as the dependent variable for the whole sample of T observations (denote this estimator by b_y), and the other obtained by regarding x_t as the dependent variable for the whole sample of T observations and inverting the resulting coefficient of y (denote this estimator by b_x). This maximum-likelihood estimator of β is given by the following expression provided that $Q < T$, that is, provided that there is at least one observation for which y_t is the dependent variable:[2]

$$(3) \qquad \hat{\beta} = \left(1 - \frac{1}{1+\theta}\right) b_y \pm \frac{1}{1+\theta} \sqrt{b_y[\theta^2 b_y + (1-\theta^2)b_x]},$$

---

[1] Of course the Federal Reserve example does not correspond exactly to the situation set forth in the text above. For one thing, some variables in the demand-for-money equation are endogenous in addition to interest rates or the money stock, e.g., income. The generalization to simultaneous-equations contexts, proposed below, is useful here.

[2] If $Q = T$ the maximum-likelihood estimator is obtained by solving (1) for x_t and forming the expression that is analogous to (3) for that case.

REGRESSION WHEN EACH OF TWO VARIABLES IS DEPENDENT

where θ is defined by

(4) $$\theta = 1 - 2Q/T \qquad (-1 \le \theta \le 1)$$

and where the positive square root is taken and the $\pm$ sign is replaced by the sign of b_y.

Note that $\hat{\beta}$ is a three-stage weighted average of b_y and b_x. First, form a weighted arithmetic mean of b_y and b_x, with weights θ^2 and $1 - \theta^2$. Second, form the unweighted geometric mean of b_y and that first weighted arithmetic mean. Third, form the weighted arithmetic mean of b_y and that geometric mean, with weights $1 - 1/(1 + \theta)$ and $1/(1 + \theta)$.

Note that if $P = T$, that is, if y_t is the dependent variable in every observation of the sample, then $Q = 0$ and $\theta = 1$ and $\hat{\beta}$ reduces to b_y as expected. If $Q = T$, that is, if x_t is the dependent variable in every observation of the sample, then $\theta = -1$ and it can be shown that $\hat{\beta}$ reduces to b_x as expected. If $P = Q = T/2$, that is, if half of the observations have y_t dependent and half have x_t dependent, then $\theta = 0$ and $\hat{\beta}$ reduces to $\pm\sqrt{b_y b_x}$ where the positive square root is taken and the $\pm$ sign is replaced by the sign of b_y.

Note further than $\hat{\beta}$ must lie in the closed interval whose end points are b_y and b_x. If $Q < T/2$, i.e., $\theta > 0$, this is obvious from the fact that $\hat{\beta}$ is a three-stage weighted average of b_y and b_x with all weights lying between 0 and 1 inclusive. If $Q > T/2$, it can be shown by observing that then $\partial\hat{\beta}/\partial Q$ has the same sign as b_y, and that when $Q = T/2$ we have $\hat{\beta} = \sqrt{b_y b_x}$ with the same sign as b_y [even though $1/(1 + \theta)$ is outside the interval from 0 to 1].

II. The Estimating Equation for $\hat{\beta}$ in a Simple Regression

In this section we consider the case of simple regression, obtained by setting $K = 1$ in Eq. (1):

(5) $$y_t = \gamma + \beta x_t + u_t.$$

Now for those observations where u_t is independent of x_t and the dependent variables is y_t, the conditional density function is

(6) $$\phi(y_t | x_t, \gamma, \beta, \sigma) = \frac{\exp[-(y_t - \gamma - \beta x_t)^2/2\sigma^2]}{\sqrt{2\pi}\sigma}.$$

And for the remaining observations where u_t is independent of y_t and the dependent variable is x_t, the conditional density function is

(7) $$\psi(x_t | y_t, \gamma, \beta, \sigma) = \frac{\exp[-(y_t - \gamma - \beta x_t)^2/2\sigma^2]}{\sqrt{2\pi}\sigma/|\beta|}.$$

Then the likelihood function for the whole sample is the product of P expressions like (6) and Q expressions like (7); thus

$$(8) \quad \frac{|\beta|^Q \exp[-\sum_1^T (y_t - \gamma - \beta x_t)^2 / 2\sigma^2]}{(\sqrt{2\pi})^T \sigma^T}$$

This can be easily seen by means of a transformation from the variables y_t and x_t to the new variables v_t and w_t, as follows: When y_t is dependent, let $v_t = y_t$ and $w_t = x_t$. Then Eq. (5) is as follows, where the disturbance u_t is independent of w_s for $s \leq t$ and has variance σ^2:

$$(9) \quad v_t = \gamma + \beta w_t + u_t.$$

When x_t is dependent, let $v_t = x_t$ and $w_t = y_t$. Then equation (5) is as follows, where the disturbance u_t/β is independent of w_s for $s \leq t$ and has variance σ^2/β^2:

$$(10) \quad v_t = -\gamma/\beta + w_t/\beta - u_t/\beta.$$

The conditional density functions of v_t given w_t and γ, β, and σ when y_t is dependent and when x_t is dependent are then, respectively,

$$(11) \quad \frac{\exp[-(v_t - \gamma - \beta w_t)^2 / 2\sigma^2]}{\sqrt{2\pi}\,\sigma}$$

and

$$(12) \quad \frac{\exp[-(v_t + \gamma/\beta - w_t/\beta)^2 \beta^2 / 2\sigma^2]}{\sqrt{2\pi}\,\sigma/|\beta|}.$$

The likelihood function of the whole sample of T observations is the product P expressions like (11) and Q expressions like (12), which after transforming back to y and x yields the above expression (8).

Taking the natural logarithm of the likelihood function (8), we obtain

$$(13) \quad -T \ln \sqrt{2\pi} - T \ln \sigma + Q \ln|\beta| - \sum_1^T \frac{(y_t - \gamma - \beta x_t)^2}{2\sigma^2}.$$

The following three estimating equations, analogous to the estimating equations for ordinary least squares, are obtained by setting equal to zero the partial derivatives of the logarithmic likelihood function (13) with respect to β, γ, and σ, respectively:

$$(14) \quad Q\hat{\sigma}^2/\hat{\beta} + \sum x_t y_t = \hat{\gamma} \sum x_t + \hat{\beta} \sum x_t^2,$$

$$(15) \quad \sum y_t = T\hat{\gamma} + \hat{\beta} \sum x_t,$$

$$(16) \quad \hat{\sigma}^2 = \sum (y_t - \hat{\gamma} - \hat{\beta} x_t)^2 / T.$$

The estimating equation for $\hat{\beta}$, obtained from (14)–(16), is

(17) $\quad (1 - Q/T)m_{xx}\hat{\beta}^2 + (2Q/T - 1)m_{xy}\hat{\beta} - (Q/T)m_{yy} = 0,$

where m_{xx}, m_{xy}, and m_{yy} are the sample second moments about the mean for the variables x_t and y_t, e.g., $m_{xy} = \sum(x - \bar{x})(y - \bar{y})$. Using the facts that $b_y = m_{xy}/m_{xx}$ and $b_x = m_{yy}/m_{xy}$, (17) can be expressed as

(18) $\quad (1 - Q/T)\hat{\beta}^2 + (2Q/T - 1)b_y\hat{\beta} - (Q/T)b_y b_x = 0.$

In the next section we obtain the analogous equation for the case of multiple regression.

III. The Estimating Equation for $\hat{\beta}$ in a Multiple Regression

Return to Eq. (2). For those observations where the dependent variable is y_t, the conditional density function is analogous to (6) except that the term $\sum_i \gamma_i z_{it}$ replaces γ in the exponential function. Similarly, for those observations where the dependent variable is x_t, the conditional density function is analogous to (7) with the same exception. Therefore the natural logarithm of the likelihood function of the whole sample of T observations is

(19) $\quad -T \ln \sqrt{2\pi} - T \ln \sigma + Q \ln |\beta| - \|\mathbf{y} - \mathbf{x}\beta - \mathbf{Z}\gamma\|^2/2\sigma^2.$

The following estimating equations, analogous to the least-squares estimating equations for ordinary multiple regression, are obtained by setting equal to zero the partial derivatives of the logarithmic likelihood function (19) with respect to β, γ, and σ, respectively:

(20) $\quad Q\hat{\sigma}^2/\hat{\beta} + \mathbf{x}'\mathbf{y} = \mathbf{x}'\mathbf{x}\hat{\beta} + \mathbf{x}'\mathbf{Z}\hat{\gamma},$

(21) $\quad \mathbf{Z}'\mathbf{y} = \mathbf{Z}'\mathbf{x}\hat{\beta} + \mathbf{Z}'\mathbf{Z}\hat{\gamma}$

(22) $\quad \hat{\sigma}^2 = \|\mathbf{y} - \mathbf{x}\hat{\beta} - \mathbf{Z}\hat{\gamma}\|^2/T.$

Note the similarity between these estimating equations and equations (14)–(16) for the two-variable case. For simplicity of notation, define the $T \times T$ matrix $\mathbf{D}$ thus:

(23) $\quad \mathbf{D} = \mathbf{Z}(\mathbf{Z}'\mathbf{Z})^{-1}\mathbf{Z}'.$

The estimating equation for $\hat{\beta}$, obtained from (20)–(23), is

(24) $\quad (1 - Q/T)\mathbf{x}'(\mathbf{I} - \mathbf{D})\mathbf{x}\hat{\beta}^2 + (2Q/T - 1)\mathbf{x}'(\mathbf{I} - \mathbf{D})\mathbf{y}\hat{\beta} - (Q/T)\mathbf{y}'(\mathbf{I} - \mathbf{D})\mathbf{y} = 0.$

This is strictly analogous to the quadratic equation (17) that was obtained for the case of simple regression. Using the facts that $b_y = \mathbf{x}'(\mathbf{I}-\mathbf{D})\mathbf{y}/\mathbf{x}'(\mathbf{I}-\mathbf{D})\mathbf{x}$ and $b_x = \mathbf{y}'(\mathbf{I}-\mathbf{D})\mathbf{y}/\mathbf{x}'(\mathbf{I}-\mathbf{D})\mathbf{y}$, the quadratic estimating equation for $\hat{\beta}$ can be expressed as

(25) $\qquad (1 - Q/T)\hat{\beta}^2 + (2Q/T - 1)b_y\hat{\beta} - (Q/T)b_yb_x = 0.$

This is identical in form to Eq. (18), which was obtained for the case of simple regression.

IV. The Estimator of $\hat{\beta}$

The solution of the estimating Eq. (18) or (25) for $\hat{\beta}$ is

(26) $\qquad \hat{\beta} = \dfrac{(1 - 2Q/T)b_y \pm \sqrt{(1 - 2Q/T)^2 b_y^2 + 4(1 - Q/T)(Q/T)b_yb_x}}{2(1 - Q/T)}.$

When θ is defined by $\theta = 1 - 2Q/T$ as in Eq. (4) above, the estimator $\hat{\beta}$ can be expressed in terms of θ and the two ordinary least-squares estimators b_y and b_x as in Eq. (3) above. The remarks following Eq. (3) may aid in interpreting the result.

Once β has been estimated from Eq. (3), then the other parameters can be estimated, γ from (21) and σ^2 from (22).

The maximum-likelihood estimator $\hat{\beta}$ obtained under the assumptions made in Section I depends of course on the sample size T and on the number Q of observations for which x_t is the dependent variable (the observations for which y_t is the dependent variable being the remainder of the sample, numbering $T - Q$, denoted above by P). $\hat{\beta}$ *does not* depend on how these Q observations, for which x_t is independent, are distributed among the T observations of the sample: they could be the first Q observations in the sample, or the last Q, or scattered through the sample in any manner. This independence would be lost if the assumptions of the model were made less restrictive, for example, by permitting the disturbance u_t to be serially dependent.

These estimators, being maximum likelihood, are consistent, asymptotically normal, and asymptotically efficient. Their approximate covariance matrix is obtained by inverting the negative of the matrix of second partials of the logarithmic likelihood function (19), and is as follows (taking the parameters in the order $\hat{\beta}$, $\hat{\gamma}$, and $\hat{\sigma}^2$):

(27) $\qquad \hat{\sigma}^2 \begin{bmatrix} \mathbf{x}'\mathbf{x} + \hat{\sigma}^2 Q/\hat{\beta} & \mathbf{x}'\mathbf{Z} & -2Q\hat{\sigma}/\hat{\beta} \\ \mathbf{Z}'\mathbf{x} & \mathbf{Z}'\mathbf{Z} & 0 \\ -2Q\hat{\sigma}/\hat{\beta} & 0 & 2T \end{bmatrix}^{-1},$

Observe that if $Q = 0$ so that y is the dependent variable throughout the entire sample, this covariance matrix reduces to the usual covariance matrix for ordinary least squares estimation in the classical case when y is dependent. A corresponding result holds when $Q = T$, i.e., when x is the dependent variable throughout the entire sample.

V. Generalization to a Simultaneous Equation Model

The foregoing estimation principle is readily generalized to a simultaneous-equations model in which there are two variables, y_1 and z_1, such that y_1 is endogenous and z_1 is exogenous in one subset of the observations, while z_1 is endogenous and y_1 is exogenous in the remaining subset of observations.

Suppose that the system of equations is

$$(28) \qquad \mathbf{B}\mathbf{y}_t + \mathbf{\Gamma}\mathbf{z}_t = \mathbf{u}_t, \qquad t = 1, \ldots, T$$

where $\mathbf{y}_t \equiv (y_{1t}, \ldots, y_{Gt})'$ and $\mathbf{z}_t \equiv (z_{1t}, \ldots, z_{Kt})'$ are observable variables, $\mathbf{u}_t \equiv (u_{1t}, \ldots, u_{Gt})'$ are unobservable normal disturbances with mean zero and nonsingular covariance matrix $\mathbf{\Sigma}$ of order $G \times G$, u_{it} is independent of u_{js} for all $s \leq t$, and $\mathbf{B}$ and $\mathbf{\Gamma}$ are matrices of coefficients to be estimated, $G \times G$ and $G \times K$, respectively.

If in the entire sample the ys are endogenous and the zs are predetermined (i.e., if u_{it} is independent of z_{ks} for all i, k, s, and $t \geq s$), then the logarithm of the likelihood function for estimating $\mathbf{B}, \mathbf{\Gamma}$, and $\mathbf{\Sigma}$ is well known to be

$$(29) \qquad L = -\frac{1}{2} \sum_{t=1}^{T} (\mathbf{y}_t' \mathbf{B}' + \mathbf{z}_t' \mathbf{\Gamma}') \mathbf{\Sigma}^{-1} (\mathbf{B}\mathbf{y}_t + \mathbf{\Gamma}\mathbf{z}_t)$$
$$- \tfrac{1}{2} TG \ln(2\pi) - \tfrac{1}{2} T \ln |\mathbf{\Sigma}| + T \ln |\mathbf{B}|.$$

Maximization of this logarithmic likelihood function, subject to identifying restrictions on the parameters, yields the familiar full information maximum likelihood estimators.

Now suppose, in the spirit of the present paper, that for one subset of P observations in the sample (where $P \leq T$), the ys are endogenous and the zs are predetermined, but that for the remaining Q observations of the sample (where $P + Q = T$), the endogenous variables are $z_1, y_2, \ldots, y_G$ and the predetermined variables are $y_1, z_2, \ldots, z_K$. Denote the vectors of endogenous and predetermined variables and the matrices of their coefficients as follows for the part of the sample where $y_1, z_2, \ldots, z_K$ are predetermined:

$\mathbf{y}_t^* = \mathbf{y}_t$ with its first element replaced by z_{1t};
$\mathbf{z}_t^* = \mathbf{z}_t$ with its first element replaced by y_{1t};
$\mathbf{B}^* = \mathbf{B}$ with its first column replaced by that of $\mathbf{\Gamma}$;
$\mathbf{\Gamma}^* = \mathbf{\Gamma}$ with its first column replaced by that of $\mathbf{B}$.

Therefore we have

(30) $$\mathbf{B}^*\mathbf{y}_t^* + \mathbf{\Gamma}^*\mathbf{z}_t^* = \mathbf{B}\mathbf{y}_t + \mathbf{\Gamma}\mathbf{z}_t = \mathbf{u}_t.$$

Then by an argument analogous to that of Section II above, the logarithm of the likelihood function for the whole sample, in which zs are predetermined during P of the observations, while $y_1, z_2, \ldots, z_K$ are predetermined during the remaining Q observations ($P + Q = T$), is

(31) $$L^* = -\frac{1}{2}\sum_{t=1}^{T}(\mathbf{y}_t'\mathbf{B}' + \mathbf{z}_t'\mathbf{\Gamma}')\mathbf{\Sigma}^{-1}(\mathbf{B}\mathbf{y}_t + \mathbf{\Gamma}\mathbf{z}_t)$$
$$-\tfrac{1}{2}TG\ln(2\pi) - \tfrac{1}{2}T\ln|\mathbf{\Sigma}| + P\ln|\mathbf{B}| + Q\ln|\mathbf{B}^*|.$$

Maximization of this function, subject to identifying restrictions, yields maximum likelihood estimators of the parameters for the present case. The computations are rather lengthy except in simple special cases.[3]

It is clear that this estimation principle applies just as well to situations in which more than two variables are involved in the switch between being endogenous in one part of the sample and predetermined in another part, and to situations in which there are more than two parts of the sample, each with a different set of endogenous variables.

ACKNOWLEDGMENTS

Based on research supported in part by an NSF grant to the Johns Hopkins University. Helpful comments were made by Dennis Aigner, David J. Reid, and Geoffrey S. Watson. The generalization to a simultaneous-equations model in Section V was suggested to me independently by Tsuneo Ishikawa and J. D. Sargan.

DEPARTMENT OF POLITICAL ECONOMY
THE JOHNS HOPKINS UNIVERSITY
BALTIMORE, MARYLAND

---

[3] Tsuneo Ishikawa in an unpublished paper has given the explicit estimators in a simple just-identified two-equation model.

An Exploratory Policy-Oriented Econometric Model of a Metropolitan Area: Boston

ROBERT F. ENGLE

I. Introduction

When I studied econometrics with T.-C. Liu, he opened his first class with a discussion of his quarterly model (Liu, 1963). He described the economics, the data, and the purposes of model building. The paper and his discussion concluded with several simulations of the model to show its behavior and to draw inferences about policy effectiveness. This was the ultimate goal of econometrics, the appropriate use of statistical tools to build useful models of the real world. He often said that as a young econometrician it was important to work on theoretical problems, but that eventually it would be time to tackle real problems and real data.

This paper is an attempt to follow that path by modeling a metropolitan economy and performing policy simulations. T.-C. Liu had plans to build models of New York State and New York City, and although they had a form rather different from the model to be presented in this paper, he grappled with many of the same issues discussed here. This paper presents the first complete description of an econometric model of the Boston metropolitan area, developed over a five year period at MIT.

This paper is a description of the "macro" model that treats the Boston area as a single region without any geographical distinction. A parallel and interconnected line of research, not discussed here examines the determinants of the spatial structure of the area. Bradbury *et al.* (1977) and Bradbury (1976) present a simultaneous equation approach, while Wheaton (1976) develops a bid-rent-based estimation technique.

Throughout all of these research efforts, the objective has been to obtain models that can estimate the effects of various policies available to the local administrators or the effects of external forces beyond their control. For a model to be useful for this type of policy analysis, it must be a reasonable approximation to the true structural relationships that govern the economy. It must also mirror historical behavior; but, unlike a forecasting model, this is not the main criterion for model adequacy. The paper makes a determined effort to ground each relationship in solid economic theory, and for this reason, the model looks rather different from some of the existing alternative econometric models of small areas. Because of the uncertainty surrounding some of the parameter estimates and the novel formulation, this is entitled an "exploratory" model.

Section II describes the distinctive features of the model and presents a list of equations. Section III derives the equations for each of the sectors and discusses the estimates. Section IV presents simulation results and Section V ventures some conclusions.

II. Distinctive Features of the Model

The main objective for the model is to evaluate the effectiveness of regional policies. Because these often enter only on the demand or supply side of a particular market, it is important to allow the data to estimate the importance of each component in determining the outcome. Thus, following Engle (1974a), demand and supply relationships are specified for each market insofar as possible. This approach leads to a variety of distinctive features of the model that are generally not present in other regional models, although some models have some of the features.

1. Output and employment in the export sectors are determined jointly by demand and supply for the product and therefore the local policymaker is able to influence the output of his export sector by shifting the supply schedule. This could be done by influencing wage rates, the availability of various skilled workers, or subsidies or taxes on the industries.

2. Several of the service sectors are allowed to export part of their product, thus recognizing the importance of financial, insurance, business consulting, and nonprofit industries in Boston's economic base.

3. Local government expenditures and tax rates are jointly determined by local demand. The level of deficit financing and revenue sharing formulas

are taken as exogenous. Deficit financing, however, leads to higher debt service costs in the future, which becomes a component of expenditures.

4. Wage rates faced by each industry may differ due to the different skill mixes required and the relative cost and availability of each type of labor.

5. Wage rates and consumer prices are determined in part by local conditions and in part by national inflation rates.

6. Labor migration responds to real wages and unemployment and in turn is allowed to influence wage rates and thus employment and income.

7. Capital is assumed to migrate in response to relative rates of return achievable in Boston and elsewhere. Some portion of this migration may be exogenous as a result of various nonpecuniary attractions or public relation campaigns.

8. The calculation of personal and disposable income recognizes a variety of federal and state as well as local taxes and estimates the share of profits which are distributed to local residents.

The strategy that was used to derive the relationships of the model and to generate the data was initially to formulate simple behavioral relationships that presumably govern the economy, even though some of the endogenous variables were not measurable. By successive substitutions, it was possible generally to formulate estimable relationships in terms of observable data series. Thus the data used in the estimates are as close as possible to the original observed series, and whatever corrections might be necessary are imposed directly in the structure of the equation or in separate identities.

For example, there are no data on output for most sectors, but from substitution in the relevant derived demand for labor schedule, it is possible to obtain a relation with employment as the dependent variable. This relationship is a partial reduced form, and in some cases it is possible to recover the structural parameters from this estimate. In any case, forecasts of measurable employment are of more interest than forecasts of unmeasurable output. The relation between employment, wages, and value added is introduced as an identity rather than generating artificial data to be used in the estimation.

Annual data from 1950 through 1971 are used in estimating almost all equations. Generalized least squares with first-order serial correlation correction is used in most cases. Simultaneous-equation estimation techniques were not used, partly because the small sample biases may be worse than for least squares, and partly because other models of regions have found little difference or in fact some deterioration from the use of simultaneous methods. See for example Adams *et al.* (1975). Furthermore, serial correlation correction in the context of simultaneous equations is computationally more demanding and has less well studied small sample properties.

The structure of the model is considerably more interrelated than other similar models. In order to focus on the basic structure, each equation is kept simple and there has been little optimization in terms of choosing lag structures or intersectoral relationships. This version of the model therefore may suffer somewhat in its dynamic response to policy variables and in its short run forecasting properties. However, these are not inherent in the structure, only in this implementation.

An overview of the general relations will be helpful in reading the balance of the paper. The most basic relations of the model are the employment equations. Upon these are built the superstructure of the regional accounts, so that an understanding of the model is best managed through an understanding of the employment equation. The total employment is divided into 14 sectors, four manufacturing, two government, and eight nonmanufacturing. In each case, employment depends in part upon the demand for the commodity being produced and in part on the costs of producing it. In many of the sectors, the primary demand is from consumers outside of the metropolitan area, while for others it is from consumers in the area. Some industries are very competitive so that an increase in factor costs or any other rise in the supply schedule will lead to a substantial decrease in output and employment, whereas others have strong monopoly positions so that an increase in supply prices can be passed on to the consumers.

Income received by the residents of the metropolitan area is closely related to the level of economic activity. The largest component of personal income comes from wages. Almost all the workers in Boston metropolitan area plants are residents of Boston, and therefore the payroll paid by these firms is the bulk of the income received. Income is also received from other sources such as transfers from the government sector and return to investment. The profit income in the Boston area is partly paid out to state and federal tax collectors, partly retained for future expansion, and partly paid out to owners of the plants (stockholders). Because some of the owners live in the area, increases in Boston profits will lead to some increase in income received. Similarly, some residents own businesses in other areas and thus some external profit income flows into the Boston area.

Of the total income received, a substantial portion is taken by tax collectors of all types. The federal collectors take a share, the state takes more, and finally the local government takes some through property taxes. Disposable income is total income received less the taxes paid. This income measure is influential in the demand for some of the commodities produced in Boston.

The cost of labor may be different to different industries, depending on the type of labor they require. The overall level of wages, however, depends upon the interaction between the demand for labor from all of these sectors, and the supply of labor. Through the familiar Phillips curve the wage varies with unemployment. In the long run, the supply of labor will also vary through labor migration. It is through this linkage that U.S. and metropolitan wages are related.

The cost of living in the Boston area depends upon the cost of commodities, housing, and services. Commodities are mostly imported and so are little affected by local conditions. Housing prices are difficult to explain in a metropolitan model. Since this is an important link with the location model, this cost will remain exogenous for now. The cost of services is directly related to wage rates.

In the long run, both labor and capital may migrate in or out of the metropolitan area in response to economic conditions. These responses happen relatively slowly, but can have important long-run consequences.

In Table 1 the equations of the model and the included variables are characterized for easy reference. The order of the equations follows the order in which the details and the economic theory are presented in the following section of the paper.

TABLE 1

EQUATIONS IN THE MODEL[a]

Dependent Variable(s)	Current and Lagged Endogenous	Current and Lagged Exogenous
A. EMPLOYMENT		
1. Manufacturing Employment (4)	Capital, industry wage, total investment	U.S. value added, U.S. industry price level, transport cost
2. Export Service Employment (2)	Capital, industry wage, disposable income	U.S. value added, U.S. price of services, nonprofit employment
3. Local Employment (5)	Disposable income, industry wage, consumer price index, total investment	U.S. unemployment
4. Local Government Employment	Tax rate, personal income, consumer price index	Nonpayroll government expenditures (mostly welfare and transfers), revenue sharing
Local Government Tax Rate*	Government industry wage, local government employment, debt service, personal income	Nonpayroll government expenditures, revenue sharing
Debt*	Previous debt	Deficit
Debt Service[b]	Debt	Municipal bond rate
5. Total Employment	Employment in sectors above	Nonprofit employment, state and federal employment

(*continued*)

TABLE 1 (*continued*)

Dependent Variable(s)	Current and Lagged Endogenous	Current and Lagged Exogenous
B. PRICES AND WAGES		
1. Production Worker Wage Rate	Unemployment rate, consumer price index	
2. Industry Wage Rate (12)	Production worker wage rate	Skill mix requirements and occupational relative wage
3. Service Component of CPI	Production worker wage	
4. Commodity Component of CPI		U.S. commodity component
5. Consumer Price Index[b]	Service component, commodity component	Housing component
C. INCOME ACCOUNTS		
1. Total Earned Income[b]	Industry wage, employment for all sectors	Industry adjustment from payroll to earnings
2. Metropolitan Value Added[b]	Earnings all sectors	Industry adjustments to value added
3. Corporate Taxes[b]	Values added all sectors	U.S. industry average tax rate
4. Property Income	Metro value added, total earned income, corporate taxes	U.S. profits
5. Personal Income[b]	Property income, earned income	Social security contribution rate, transfers
6. Income Taxes[b]	Personal income	Social security contribution rate, transfers, state income tax rate, federal income tax rate
7. Disposable Income[b]	Personal income, income taxes, local government tax rate	
D. FACTOR MIGRATION		
1. Labor Force[b]	Total employment, unemployment rate	
Unemployment Rate	Total employment, production worker wage rate, consumer price index	Natural population increase, U.S. wage rate, U.S. consumer price index
2. Capital (5)[b]	Investment, previous capital	Depreciation rate
Investment (5)	Value added, earnings, capital	U.S. rate of return, best state rate of return

[a] All variables are defined for the Boston SMSA unless otherwise stated.
[b] Equation is an identity.

III. Individual Sectoral Models

A. Employment

1. Manufacturing Employment

Manufacturing is divided into four sectors, each of which is modeled separately. For more details on the estimation, or data, the reader is referred to Engle (1979a).

The demand for the value added from a Boston manufacturing industry is the key structural relation. As the price of Boston products rises, the quantity demanded will decrease. This decrease will occur partly because consumers of this good will shift to some other products through the conventional income and substitution effects. However, the major effects should be through the shift to the same good that is produced in another region. For products that can be easily transported and for which there are many alternative sources of supply, the price elasticity of demand should be very large and negative, primarily because of this regional substitution effect.

A simple specification for the demand function is

$$(1) \quad q = b_0 + b_1 y^* + b_2(p^* - p),$$

where q is the logarithm of value added in constant dollars, p is the log of the price of goods produced in Boston, and p^* is the log of the price of this good in the national market less the cost of transportation from Boston to the national market. The variable y^* is the log of an income measure for the consumers of this good. In order to avoid estimating income elasticities for all goods, the total constant dollar output in the nation is taken as the measure of the size of the market. According to this specification, b_1 is the elasticity of Boston production relative to industry output, and b_2 is the price elasticity of demand for Boston goods. Notice that the demand function is homogenous with respect to prices and that if price elasticities are zero, a "pure demand" model is obtained. If on the other extreme b_2 approaches infinity, the model becomes the competitive model whereby Boston prices must be equal to national prices.

To derive a supply function for output, a production function is necessary. For simplicity and because of its long history, the Cobb–Douglas production function is chosen for a first approximation. Let

$$(2) \quad q = a_0 + a_1 k + a_2 l,$$

where k and l are the logs of capital stock and employment. While it is reasonable in the short run to take the level of capital stock as fixed, since investment plans take several years, it is not plausible to treat employment as

TABLE 2

Manufacturing Employment Equations[a]

$$\text{LOG(SEMND1)} = 0.169 \text{ LOG(CAPMND1/[IWMND1/PTMND1]}^{1.41})$$
$$(2.60)$$
$$+ 0.677 \text{ LOG(DUVAMND1)} + 1.96$$
$$(3.15) \qquad\qquad (0.36)$$
$$+ \text{LOG(PTMND1/IWMND1)}$$
$$\text{RHO} = 0.89, \quad R^2 = 0.68, \quad \text{SER} = 0.039$$

$$\text{LOG(SEMND2)} = -0.597 \text{ LOG(CAPMNd2/[IWMND2/PTMND2]}^{0.70})$$
$$(-2.92)$$
$$+0.304 \text{ LOG(DUVAMND2)} + 21.04$$
$$(4.36) \qquad\qquad (4.59)$$
$$+ \text{LOG(PTMND2/IWMND2)}$$
$$\text{RHO} = 0.51, \quad R^2 = 0.80, \quad \text{SER} = 0.020$$

$$\text{LOG(SEMD1)} = -0.600 \text{ LOG(CAPMD1/[IWMD1/PTMD1]}^{1.22})$$
$$(-1.11)$$
$$+ 0.147 \text{ LOG(DUVAMD1)} + 0.151 \text{ LOG(DINVTOT)}$$
$$(1.23) \qquad\qquad (2.82)$$
$$+ 0.588 \text{ LOG(SPMD1}(-1)) + \text{LOG(PTMD1/IWMD1)}$$
$$+ 7.65$$
$$(1.47)$$
$$\text{RHO} = -0.26, \quad R^2 = 0.79, \quad \text{SER} = 0.053$$

$$\text{LOG(SEMD2)} = -0.203 \text{ LOG(CAPMD2/[IWMD2/PTMD2]}^{1.14})$$
$$(2.08)$$
$$+0.306 \text{ LOG(DUVAMD2)} + 13.66 + \text{LOG(PTMD2/IWMD2)}$$
$$(3.70) \qquad\qquad (5.02)$$
$$\text{RHO} = 0.73, \quad R^2 = 0.68, \quad \text{SER} = 0.025$$

[a] Asymptotic t statistics are in parentheses. Variable names are defined in the Appendix.

fixed in the short run. Presumably firms hire more labor in good times and when the price of labor is low. The demand for labor is a derived demand for a variable factor of production. Assuming there are many firms in each industry, they will act as perfect competitors in both the factor and the product markets. Thus the derived demand for labor will be obtained by setting the marginal value product equal to the wage rate

$$(3) \qquad l = q - (w - p) + \log(a_2),$$

where w is the log of the wage rate specific to the industry in question. That is, it will depend upon the skill requirements of the labor force demanded by the firm and upon the wages of each type of worker. The variable w might also include the costs of other variable factors of production which are used in fixed proportion with labor. An example might be energy.

Unfortunately, Eqs. (1)–(3) cannot be estimated using standard simultaneous-equation techniques, because some of the required variables are unobservables. There are no data on the price of output from local firms. Furthermore, the value-added data are in current dollars and are only available for scattered years since 1950. The observables are l, k, w, y^*, and p^*. Solving for l in terms of the other four variables yields the reduced form equation

$$(4) \qquad l = \frac{a_1(b_2 - 1)}{\Delta} k + \frac{b_1}{\Delta} y^* - \frac{b_2}{\Delta} (w - p^*) + c_0,$$

where $\Delta = a_2 + b_2 - a_2 b_2$ and c_0 is a constant term.

This equation is the basic relation which is estimated for Boston's manufacturing sectors. In all cases, estimates of a_2 from value-added data $(\hat{a}_2)$ and the assumption that $a_1 + a_2 = 1$ are tested and used to restrict this relation. Thus the estimated relation is

$$(4') \qquad l = \frac{a_1(b_2 - 1)}{\Delta} \left[k - (w - p^*) \frac{\hat{a}_2}{1 - \hat{a}_2} \right] + \frac{b_1}{\Delta} y^* + C_0 + p^* - w.$$

The manufacturing sector was disaggregated into four industries, two nondurable and two durable industries. Nondurables one (ND1) consists of the textile, apparel, and leather industries. This used to be a major sector of the Boston economy but since the Second World War has been sharply declining in employment. In 1970 there were 34,000 employees. Nondurables two (ND2) is the balance of the nondurable sector which in Boston is primarily food processing and printing and publishing. This sector has experienced a slow but steady decline over the sample period. Its 1970 employment was 77,000.

Durables one (D1) is the high-technology sector consisting of electrical and nonelectrical machinery, instruments, and transportation equipment. Employment in this sector has moved erratically since 1950, reaching a peak in 1967 and a level of 123,000 in 1970. Durables two (D2) is the balance of the durable processors and includes primary and fabricated metal products, stone, clay and glass, and other heavy industry. This sector has also varied over the period with a peak in 1953 and a very gradual decline since. The 1970 employment was 34,000.

Equation (4') was estimated for all four manufacturing sectors using annual data on the Boston metropolitan area from 1950 to 1971. The final estimates chosen for the model are given below. As can be seen, only the textile sector (ND1) faces an elastic demand schedule; it is the most competitive industry in the sense that rising factor costs in Boston will hurt this industry more than any other manufacturing industry. Boston investment appears in MD1 because new capital expenditures include much equipment purchased from Boston firms. For further discussion of these equations and several versions, see Engle (1979a).

2. Export Service Employment

The growth of many large cities is predominantly a result of the rapid growth in several business service sectors. Boston is fortunate to have experienced a very dramatic increase in some of these nonmanufacturing sectors to offset the declines in manufacturing.

Although it is common to consider services as commodities which cannot be transported, this is not the case. Many services can be provided to consumers outside the metropolitan area; for example, insurance companies, consulting firms, and mutual fund operators all sell their wares primarily outside the area. In addition, educational establishments train students from outside the area; hospitals, lawyers, and accountants provide services to customers who come to the city for the service. Thus, it is quite plausible to consider business services, nonprofit services, and finance insurance and real estate as sectors that could be substantial exporters.

Traditional evidence on the exportability of these sectors is usually based upon location quotients, the ratio of income generated in the sector to total income, all divided by the same ratio in the nation as a whole. The argument is then made that only if a sector is a substantial export sector can it have a location quotient much greater than one. There are many qualifications to this argument, but the coefficient has some interest. For Boston, the location quotients in 1969 for finance insurance and real estate (FIR) and for services as a whole were each 1.40, which is very large. In 1950, the FIR location quotient was 1.42 but the services quotient was only 1.20. Thus, on these grounds. FIR appears always to have been an export sector, while services have become increasingly export oriented.

The model of these services must recognize that they are partially exported, and that the export share may have varied over time. It must recognize also the important role played by the office building boom which began with the Prudential Center at the end of the 1950s and continued with construction of a great number of partially subsidized office structures throughout the 1960s and 1970s. It should discuss the impact of the controversial taxes on both financial and insurance companies. Finally, it should discuss the importance of the educational and medical sectors in attracting various business services to the city.

In order to analyze all these interactions, a rather sophisticated model is required. The model developed for manufacturing employment incorporates many of these features. From estimating the elasticity of demand for service output, the impacts of subsidies and taxes can be directly inferred. Highly competitive industries with elastic demand schedules will be hurt by taxation since the tax cannot be shifted forward to the consumer but will instead be shifted backward to the factors of production. Monopolistic industries can pass on price increases and so will not be hurt by taxation but, on the other hand, will not be helped by subsidies.

The major difference between the manufacturing and service sectors is that the output from the service sector is demanded by both external and internal customers. A substantial and possibly changing component of each of these sectors is responsive to the demand by residents of Boston. This is easily modeled by including both U.S. value added in the sector and Boston disposable income as determinants of the employment in each sector. The relative sizes of the income elasticities for these variables indicate the relative importance of the export and local demand.

A second modification of the manufacturing model leads to an assessment of the importance of the nonprofit (educational–medical) sector in encouraging business services. The presence of the nonprofit sector presumably leads to a skilled professional work force, which is a basic requirement of many business services. The lagged presence of the nonprofit sector would imply somewhat lower wages or higher skill mix for an industry and therefore more employment.

The estimates are given in Table 3. Notice that the FIR sector has a positive coefficient on the capital term while the business service sector has a negative sign. This implies the rather plausible result that the FIR sector faces a more competitive demand curve than does business services. With Hartford, Providence, and Springfield as neighboring cities, it is not surprising that the insurance industry seems competitive. Similarly, New York is still the financial capital of the United States, if not the world, and thus Boston's emerging prominence in financial management, mutual funds, and international banking can only be sustained if it can be competitive in providing these services.

On the other hand, the business service industry may face different forms of competition. A substantial portion of business services are consulting firms which provide services all over the world. This business is also extremely competitive but many of the competitors for given consulting contracts are frequently other Boston firms. While the individual firms face stiff competition, the industry in Boston may very well enjoy a rather monopolistic position in part due to the skilled professional work force.

3. Local Employment

Five sectors in Boston are assumed to respond almost entirely to local demand. Although there may be some export of the goods of these local

TABLE 3

Export Service Employment[a]

LOG(SEFIR) = 0.0948 LOG(CAPCOM/(IWFIR/DEFFIR)$^{0.308}$)
(1.89)
+ 0.588 LOG(DUVAFIR) + 0.373 LOG(DBDI)
(3.19) (1.47)
+ −0.096 + LOG(DEFFIR/IWFIR)
(0.038)
RHO = 0.599, R^2 = 0.918, SER = 0.0199

LOG(SESB) = −0.1768 LOG(CAPCOM/(IWSB/DEFSR)$^{4.47}$)
(3.789)
+ 0.478 LOG(DUVASR) + 0.659 LOG(DBDI)
(0.909) (1.62)
+ 0.745 LOG((SESN(−1) + SESN(−2) + SESN(−3))/3)
(2.461)
+ −10.17 + LOG(DEFSR/IWSB)
(2.64)
RHO = 0.44, R^2 = 0.99, SER = 0.024

[a] Asymptotic t statistics are given in parentheses. Variable names are defined in the Appendix.

service sectors, the bulk is undoubtedly consumed by Bostonians. The sectors are retail and wholesale trade; personal services; contract construction; and transportation, communication, and public utilities.

In each case, the primary factor input is assumed to be labor. Therefore, the wage rate in a constant-returns-to-scale industry will define a horizontal cost curve. If there is nonzero elasticity of demand, then higher wages will mean lower sales. The decrease in output will reflect two shifts: some consumers will shift to other products, and some will shift to imported versions of the same products. For example, if Boston shopping prices become sufficiently high, residents will travel to discount stores outside the metropolitan area, or to exclusive shops in New York. Low wages and prices thus improve the competitiveness of the export industries in the world market, as well as leading to import substitution at home.

For individual sectors, somewhat different determinants may be appropriate. Most important, as new investment is demanded in the metropolitan area, there is a derived demand for the services of contract construction. This connection closes the link familiar in Keynesian national models between the demand for investment and the generation of income. The estimated equations are given in Table 4.

TABLE 4

LOCAL EMPLOYMENT[a]

$$\text{LOG(SERT)} = 0.970 \text{ LOG(DBDI)} - 1.24 \text{ LOG(IWRT/BCPI)} - 0.976$$
$$(6.77) \qquad\qquad (3.48) \qquad\qquad (0.652)$$
$$\text{RHO} = 0.37, \quad R^2 = 0.84, \quad \text{SER} = 0.033$$

$$\text{LOG(SEWT)} = 0.647 \text{ LOG(DBDI)} - 0.568 \text{ LOG(IWWT/BCPI)} + 1.87$$
$$(2.97) \qquad\qquad (1.48) \qquad\qquad (0.795)$$
$$\text{RHO} = 0.51, \quad R^2 = 0.86, \quad \text{SER} = 0.0156$$

$$\text{LOG(SECC)} = 0.163 \text{ LOG(DBDI)} + 0.030 \text{ LOG(DINVTOT)}$$
$$(1.90) \qquad\qquad (0.995)$$
$$+ 0.552 \text{ LOG(SECC}(-1)) + 1.30$$
$$(3.05) \qquad\qquad (1.29)$$
$$\text{RHO} = 0.2, \quad R^2 = 0.90, \quad \text{SER} = 0.028$$

$$\text{LOG(SETCU)} = 0.656 \text{ LOG(DBDI)} - 0.486 \text{ LOG(IWTCU/BCPI)} + 1.22$$
$$(3.07) \qquad\qquad (1.87) \qquad\qquad (0.424)$$
$$\text{RHO} = 0.73, \quad R^2 = 0.577, \quad \text{SER} = 0.02$$

$$\text{LOG(SESP)} = 0.307 \text{ LOG(DBDI)} - 0.384 \text{ LOG(IWSP/BCPI)}$$
$$(2.08) \qquad\qquad (1.67)$$
$$+ 0.498 \text{ LOG(SESP}(-1)) - 0.0168 \text{ LOG(UUS)}$$
$$(2.96) \qquad\qquad (0.782)$$
$$\text{RHO} = 0.70, \quad R^2 = 0.70, \quad \text{SER} = 0.016$$

[a] Asymptotic t statistics are given in parentheses. Variable names are defined in the Appendix.

4. Government Employment

There are three levels of government that each have an important presence in the Boston metropolitan area. These are state, federal, and local governments. Although the local government consists of many independent agencies, these are treated as a single aggregate sector in a model of the whole metropolitan region. Individual behavior is modeled in the context of the location models.

The three levels of government are each important because they extract income from residents in the form of taxes and spend this revenue on goods and services, some of which are produced in the metropolitan area. The taxes are a leakage from the region, while the expenditures are an injection. The multiplier effects of any policy will depend substantially on the elasticity of the leakages and expenditures with respect to endogenous variables in the model.

The federal government has a substantial presence in the Boston metropolitan area, and its behavior has an important effect on Boston. However, Boston has a negligible influence on the U.S. The federal income and corporate tax rates are given exogenously, and so as Boston income or corporate profits rise, the flow of tax revenues into the federal coffers will increase. The federal government also maintains many offices in Boston and pays substantial wages and salaries to Boston residents. It seems reasonable to assume that the number of federal employees in the region is independent of the economic situation in Boston. Federal expenditures for Boston products will be felt through the normal channels of industry demands already in the model.

The state behaves in many ways as the federal government, except that Boston is a much more substantial portion of the state than of the nation. Taxes are again primarily income taxes, which are responsive to economic conditions. Thus, again, a rise in Boston income will lead to increased state tax revenues. To what extent will these new tax revenues be spent in Boston? It appears plausible that state expenditures are primarily determined by the demand for services, rather than by the revenue received from the Boston region. Thus again, employment by the state will be taken as exogenous although this assumption is more questionable than for the federal level.

For the local government, the expenditures and taxes are jointly determined by the residents. Higher services necessarily mean higher taxes and thus a balance must be reached by the citizenry. Thus, a simultaneous equation is at the heart of the behavior of the local government sector. This can be written

$$(5) \qquad E = f(t, Y, RS),$$

where E is employment, t is the tax rate, Y is income, and RS is revenue sharing.

The provision of public services as measured by employment is determined in this equation jointly by the price, as measured by the tax rate, and the income of the residents. Revenue sharing (other than matching welfare grants) may be used in ways other than pure tax reductions, and therefore, it is included separately. Furthermore, if any grants are matching grants, then revenue sharing will change the relative price.

In Massachusetts, welfare programs were administered by local governments with aid from the state and federal governments until 1966. At this point, the function was transferred to the state. Thus, nonpayroll expenditures by local governments dropped drastically as did both federal and state grants in aid.

To model this transfer of function, let W be income transfers associated with welfare which will approximately be measured by nonpayroll expendi-

TABLE 5

LOCAL GOVERNMENT[a]

$$\text{SEGVL} = -59245 \text{ RTXGVL} + 7.59 \times 10^{-9} \text{ BPI/BCPI}$$
$$(-0.37) \qquad\qquad (9.88)$$
$$-0.0046 \text{ GVLOTHR/BCPI} + 0.00289 \text{ GVLRS/BCPI}$$
$$(-2.88)$$
$$+19553$$
$$(2.64)$$
$$\text{RHO} = 0.53, \quad R^2 = 0.93, \quad \text{SER} = 2230$$

$$\text{RTXGVL} = \frac{\text{GVLDS} + \text{SEGVL}*\text{IWGV} + \text{GVLOTHR} - \text{GVLRS} - \text{GVLDCT} - \text{GVLRESID}}{\text{BPI}}$$

$$\text{GVLDEBT} = \text{GVLDEBT}(-1) + \text{GVLDCT}$$

$$\text{GVLDS} = \text{MBRATE}*\text{GVLDEBT}(-1)$$

[a] Asymptotic t statistics are given in parentheses. Variable names are defined in the Appendix.

tures. The administration of the welfare program may be assumed to require $h(W)$ employees. Similarly, total revenue sharing funds can be divided into WRS, funds depending on welfare matching formulae, and $NWRS$, non-welfare revenue sharing. Equation (5) then becomes

$$E = f(t, Y, NWRS) + h(W).$$

If the welfare matching formula can be approximated by $WRS = g(W)$, then this can be substituted to obtain

(6) $\qquad E = f[t, Y, RS - g(W)] + h(W) = f'(t, Y, RS, W).$

Assuming that few personnel are required per dollar of welfare funds and that revenue sharing has a somewhat greater effect on local government employment, the new effect of W would be expected to be negative.

Equation (6) is estimated using time series data from 1952 to 1971, correcting for first-order serial correlation. The data are the aggregates of local government annual fiscal reports. The results listed in Table 5 bear out the a priori notations of sign.

Most taxes collected by local governments are property taxes; however, additional income may be due to sales taxes, licenses, and other fees. Because housing prices and assessment practices are not described in this model, local government revenues are assumed to come from a proportional income tax. As far as income and expenditure multipliers are concerned, this should be a perfectly adequate approximation. Of course it would be unreasonable if the model were asked to analyze the decision to consume housing as opposed to other goods. The local property tax rate does appear as a determinant of the housing location choice in Bradbury et al. (1977).

B. Price–Wage Sector

The price level is an important economic variable for any economy; it suggests the competitiveness of its exports in the external economy, and it measures the cost of living in the region. With substantial amounts of inflation beginning in the late 1960s, it becomes important to distinguish different rates of inflation and their separate causes in metropolitan areas.

There are several types of prices that should be separately described. Broadly speaking there are two types of goods that are produced in Boston, export goods and goods that are consumed locally. Each is associated with a price. The other goods consumed in Boston are imported. These again have a price. Finally, all production requires factor inputs. Labor is the most important factor input, but energy, land, and capital are other inputs, each of which has its own price.

Each of these prices, frequently expanded by the number of sectors, is modeled separately based upon the interaction of supply and demand for the commodity. For example, the prices of exports are determined by the interaction of the demand from the rest of the nation, and the supply originating in Boston. These are described in detail in the manufacturing and export service sectors.

In this section, the relations between factor prices, local goods prices, and the Boston consumer price index will be derived. These all interrelate in an intricate web that determines the levels and distributions of prices and wages.

The price of labor is often seen as the basic price level in macroeconomic models, and the same is reasonable for a metropolitan model. In this model, there are more than a dozen sectors, and each requires labor as an input to production. If the price of labor is high relative to their output price, each sector will hire fewer workers, either by substituting some other input or producing less. Added together, these demands for labor schedules give an aggregate (for the metropolitan area) labor demand function, which depends upon the price of labor relative to a variety of different output or substitute prices. These derived demand for labor schedules have been described by sector.

On the other side of the labor market, there is a supply of labor function. New workers come from either participation rate changes or migration. The supply of labor schedule is described in the labor migration equation and it is a positive function of the wage rate relative to the cost of living in Boston. The aggregate demand and supply schedules of labor could determine an equilibrium wage rate.

It is well known that labor markets do not clear quickly. When the demand for labor falls, the wage rate falls only very slowly. Instead, the unemployment rate rises. A portion of the clearing of the labor market occurs by quantity adjustment rather than price adjustment. The standard explanations for this stickiness in wages rest on a variety of institutional constraints, such as fixed contracts and seniority scales, lack of information, the cost of searching for a new job, or inability to retrain or move workers to the open jobs. Many of these factors are just as important in metropolitan areas as in the national economy. The solution is to estimate a function describing the trade-off between wage change and unemployment, between price and quantity adjustment. This is traditionally called a Phillips curve.

The Phillips curve is estimated using time-series data on production worker wages for the Boston metropolitan area using two-stage least squares since both the unemployment rate and the rate of change in prices are endogenous variables that are very closely linked to the wage adjustment process. The results are given in Table 6.

The wages paid by different industries may vary because they have different skill requirements. Some industries use predominantly low-skilled workers, while others employ high-skilled workers. The effective wage for any industry therefore depends upon the overall level of wages and the specific input mix required by that industry. Furthermore, the cost of a specific input mix depends upon the relative wages of different occupations which could vary because of either supply or demand factors. For each sector a value of input mix variable was constructed that adjusts for the occupational mix of the sector and the relative wages of those occupations. These mix variables were allowed to vary over the sample period but were linearly interpolated from the three census data points. For each sector an equation such as that given in Table 6 was estimated.

Once wages are determined, the price of locally produced goods that are consumed locally is almost fully determined. Most of these sectors are services such as retail and wholesale trade, personal services, or construction, or utilities such as transportation communication and public utilities. For all of these sectors, the major cost of production is labor, although for individual sectors, one might include the cost of energy or building materials as well.

If labor is the major input, and there are constant returns to scale, then the industry could be considered a constant-cost industry with a horizontal supply curve. The price of these services is therefore determined entirely by the supply price, which is in turn determined almost entirely by the cost of labor. The estimate of this relation is in Table 6.

TABLE 6

Prices and Wages[a]

$$\frac{WMY - WMY(-1)}{WMY(-1)} = 0.034 - 0.0014 UBOS + 0.600 \frac{BCPI - BCPI(-1)}{BCPI(-1)}$$
(2.13) (−0.37) (3.64)
$R^2 = 0.44$, SER = 0.012
TWO-STAGE LEAST SQUARES

$LOG(IWMD1) = 0.055 + LOG(WMY) + 0.879\ LOG(DMD1)$
(1.92) (6.29)
RHO = 0.59, $R^2 = 0.99$, SER = 0.015

$PBSV - PBSV(-1) = -0.705 + 0.015(WMY - WMY(-1))$
(−1.75) (9.10)
RHO = −0.31, $R^2 = 0.83$, SER = 0.99

$PBCM - PBCM(-1) = 0.355 + 0.968(UCM - UCM(-1))$
(3.19) (23.02)
RHO = −0.45, $R^2 = 0.97$, SER = 0.44

$BCPI = 0.488 PBCM + 0.346 PBHS + 0.168 PBSV$

[a] Asymptotic t statistics are given in parentheses. Variable names are defined in the Appendix.

The cost of imports is largely independent of the economic state of the Boston economy. It is possible that wages in retail establishment, transportation costs, and sales taxes would have some effect on the price of commodities that are sold in Boston, but the effects are probably small. The price of commodities equation is thus simply given in Table 6.

Another major factor in production and cost of living in the Boston area is the cost of land and housing. As the price of land and housing goes up, it becomes more expensive to live in Boston and to do business in Boston. These prices are determined by the demand for land and housing relative to its supply. In the separate location model, these factors are modeled specifically and with geographical detail. But for the aggregate model, this price will be taken as exogenous until the models are coupled.

Finally, the consumer price index for Boston is composed of indices for the costs of housing, services, and commodities. The aggregate index is a linear combination of these three inputs.

C. Income Accounts

The income accounts are designed to trace the flow of income through the metropolitan area. Almost all of the relations are identities with various adjustments to employment, wages and taxes to compute measures of metropolitan value added, personal and disposable income. The adjustments wherever possible are made on the basis of the Greater Boston Metropolitan Area (GBMA) which is a five-county area substantially larger than the Standard Metropolitan Statistical Area (SMSA) but for which the *Survey of Current Business* publishes a variety of income measures. Frequently however, adjustments will be made based upon national figures.

Total earned income is the sum of employment times wages in each sector corrected for the ratio of earnings to payroll in the GBMA. This corrects for fringe benefits, employment uncovered by unemployment insurance and proprietorships.

The notation $\sum_i$ means the sum over all industries and AE(i) denotes the variable with prefix AE and suffix which varies over industry. Total value added is obtained from the Kendrick–Jaycox (1965) method by using the ratio of value added to earned income in industry i in the U.S. Total federal corporate tax payments are estimated based upon average tax rates on value added nationally for industry i.

Total property income received by Boston residents includes a portion of after tax profits earned in Boston and a portion of after tax profits earned elsewhere. The proportions depend upon corporate propensities to retain earnings and the distribution of ownership of firms. This relationship was estimated for the GBMA for the few years of data available and is assumed to apply also to the SMSA. It is listed in Table 7 and implies the reasonable result that a 10% increase in after-tax profits earned in Boston will generate a 6% increase in profits received in Boston. Personal income is the sum of these components plus transfers less social security contributions. The social security contribution rate in the GBMA is used for the SMSA, and transfers are assumed to be the same per capita in the GBMA and SMSA. Income taxes are charged on personal income plus social security contributions less transfers. Both state and federal income taxes are calculated from effective average rates. Finally, disposable income is defined to be personal income less taxes, and for the purposes of regional impact analysis these taxes should include local taxes. The definition of disposable income therefore differs slightly from the conventional definition. This has the implication that higher property taxes lead to less consumption of other goods and a multiplier for regional income determination. All of these equations are given in Table 7.

TABLE 7

INCOME ACCOUNTS[a]

$$\text{EITOT} = \sum_i \text{AE}(i) * \text{SE}(i) * \text{IW}(i)$$

$$\text{VATOT} = \sum_i \text{AVA}(i) * \text{AE}(i) * \text{SE}(i) * \text{IW}(i)$$

$$\text{CORTAX} = \sum_i \text{CTX}(i) * \text{AVA}(i) * \text{AE}(i) * \text{SE}(i) * \text{IW}(i)$$

$$\text{LOG(BPROP)} = 5.259 + 0.643 \text{ LOG(VATOT} - \text{CORTAX} - \text{EITOT)} + 0.359 \text{ LOG(UPRP)}$$

$$\text{BPI} = \text{EITOT}(1 - \text{RCON}) + \text{BPROP} + \text{TRANSF}$$

$$\text{PERTAX} = (\text{RTXGVS} + \text{RTXGVF})(\text{BPI} + \text{RCON} * \text{EITOT} - \text{TRANSF})$$

$$\text{BDI} = \text{BPI} - \text{PERTAX} - \text{RTXGVL} * \text{BPI}$$

[a] Variable names are given in the Appendix. The notation $\sum$ means the sum over all industrial sectors.

D. FACTOR MIGRATION

1. Labor

The flow of population in and out of a metropolitan area is frequently given credit for a host of economic consequences from rapid growth to massive unemployment and welfare problems. In Boston, the combination of the highest cost of living in the continental U.S. and below-average wage rates indicates that Boston is able to attract workers who could get higher real wages elsewhere. Unlike much of the New England region, the population in the Boston metropolitan area has been growing over the last two decades. Nevertheless, there is presumably some wage differential at which even the amenities of Boston will be unable to attract new workers or hold the old.

The flow of working-age population in and out of a metropolitan area is postulated to depend upon economic incentives, such as real wages and unemployment rates relative to those existing elsewhere. In addition, it clearly depends upon a host of attributes that remain constant over time and therefore are extremely difficult to distinguish. Letting M be the annual flow of working age migrants, w/p the real wage, and u the unemployment rate, this can be expressed as

(7) $$M = f((w/p)^{\text{B}}, (w/p)^{\text{US}}, u^{\text{B}}, u^{\text{US}}),$$

where the superscripts refer to Boston and the U.S. Presumably there could be substantial lags between any change in economic conditions and the change in migration.

Any change in the Boston unemployment rate can be decomposed into either a change in the size of the labor force or a change in employment. The major changes in the labor force over a long period of time result from both demographic changes in the age distribution of the population and in the arrival or departure of some portion of the population. In addition, the labor force can change due to varying participation rates in appropriate age groups. Assuming for the moment that participation rates remain constant, the change in work-force age groups occurs through natural aging of the pre-existing population, as well as through migration.

To derive the migration equation, define $TPWF$ as total potential work force, which is the population between the ages of 18 and 65 in the metropolitan area that would be expected if there were no migration. It is constructed using standard demographic cohort survival methods based upon the 1950 age distribution and the 1960 Boston life table. Then approximately

$$(8) \qquad \Delta u^B = \alpha + \beta \Delta TPWF - \gamma \Delta E + \delta M$$

where Δ means first differences and the coefficients reflect participation rate effects as well as the linearization of the unemployment rate. Substituting (7) into (8) yields an estimable equation as long as u^B in (7) is moved to the left-hand side of (8), or enters with a lag into (7).

The equation as estimated becomes

$$(9) \qquad u^B = a_0 + a_1 \Delta TPWF - a_2 \Delta E + a_4(w/p)^B/(w/p)^{US} + a_5 u^{US} + a_6 u^B_{t-1}.$$

Note that although the participation rate was assumed to be constant for the derivation, it is implicitly allowed to vary in this equation, since the wage and unemployment effects in migration operate in exactly the same direction as the participation rate effects. Thus it is not possible to identify the relative strengths of labor migration and labor participation rate changes in response to economic conditions. The estimated equation is listed in Table 8.

2. Capital

Economic Development Commissions and Chambers of Commerce are continually in search of firms that wish to locate in a particular area and provide jobs for the residents. This flow is, however, best measured by the amount of capital that comes to the region. From the development point of view, it does not particularly matter whether this is a new firm or an expansion of an old one. A model of the migration of capital is therefore just a model of new investment in a region.

TABLE 8

Labor Migration[a]

$$\text{UBOS} = \underset{(-3.89)}{-1.71 \times 10^{-5}} \Delta\text{SETOT} + \underset{(4.60)}{4.28 \times 10^{-5}} \Delta\text{TPWF}$$

$$+ \underset{(2.70)}{0.022}\left[\left(\frac{\text{WMY}}{\text{BCPI}}\right)\bigg/\left(\frac{\text{WMWUS}}{\text{UCPI}}\right)\right] + \underset{(5.05)}{434\,\text{UUS}}$$

$$+ \underset{(2.26)}{0.223\,\text{UBOS}(-1)}$$

$$\text{RHO} = 0.11, \quad R^2 = 0.93, \quad \text{SER} = 0.243$$

[a] Asymptotic t statistics are given in parentheses. Variable names are defined in the Appendix.

Most national investment models are based upon a comparison of the cost of capital services and the expected rate of return to these services. Heated controversies revolve around the measurement of these variables and the functional forms of the estimates, but each can be viewed as a special case of the general supply and demand for loanable funds.

For a regional economy, as for a small country with no restrictions on foreign investment, another variation seems promising. No longer is the cost of borrowing within the region a determinant of investment because the funds as well as the entrepreneurs can be from any other region. In a long-run equilibrium this provision for external borrowing would make no difference, since each region would presumably invest until its marginal value product of capital was driven to the national cost of capital.

However, in disequilibrium, the appropriate cost is hypothesized to be the opportunity cost of investing elsewhere. That is, the level of investment in a region depends not only on the marginal rate of return in the region, but also upon the rates of return available elsewhere. This model describes entrepreneurs who survey a variety of locations and choose to invest in the one that offers the highest profit opportunities. It seems especially appropriate for explaining the pronounced regional shifts in investment toward the southeast and southwest regions of the nation.

This model, however, does not yet determine the total flow of investment. A variety of models based upon national demand, capital markets, or supply conditions in the capital goods industries could be invoked to close this gap. Whatever model is chosen, the total flow of investment is presumably determined primarily outside the region and can be taken as given in our model. Thus, investment in a region responds to relative rates of return and the total supply of investment goods.

Annual data are used to estimate regional manufacturing investment functions for Massachusetts under the presumption that equilibrium will not be restored in less than a year. Thus, capital flows should be in the direction of the higher profit rates. The basic model is

(10) $$I^M = \beta_0 + \beta_1 r^M/r^* + \beta_2 I^{US}$$

where I^M and I^{US} refer to investment in a particular industry in Massachusetts and in the U.S., r^M is the marginal value product of capital in this industry in Massachusetts, and r^* is the rate of return elsewhere. We consider r^* sometimes as the average MVP in the whole nation, and sometimes as the MVP in the single most profitable alternative location in the nation. We expect the coefficients to be positive and that a distributed lag on the relative profit rate would shortly go to zero indicating that equilibrium was restored.

The results from this estimation are reported in Engle (1974b). The fits are quite encouraging and the lag distribution appears to be three years long. The elasticities of investment with respect to profit rate are between 0.6 and 1.6 for different manufacturing sectors.

A similar model could be estimated for the Boston SMSA; however, the data on the profit rate are not as complete as for the state. In particular, the data series on value added has many missing observations that make the sample period intolerably short. An alternative solution was employed. Assuming the same relation for the SMSA as for the state, except for the share of national investment, a linearized version of the estimated equation can be used for the simulations. The level of investment for any simulation will be the same as it was historically only if the profit rates are the same as they were historically. Any deviation of profit rates will lead to a deviation in investment according to the estimated equation. This interpretation of the result has the added attraction that only the marginal changes in investment are responsive to economic motives; major changes can still be made as a policy variable.

By this analysis the investment equations take the form

(11) $$I^B = \underline{I}^B + \beta_1(r^B - \underline{r}^B)/r^*,$$

where the underlined variables are observed historical series. For all manufacturing sectors, a three-year moving average of profit rates was used with the estimated coefficient from the Massachusetts version, and the best definition of r^*. In all sectors, except MD1, r^* was the profit rate in the state which was highest in that year. For MD1, r^* was the U.S. profit rate.

Because the Cobb–Douglas assumption is inherent in the employment equations, it was also made here. In this case, the marginal value product of capital is proportional to the average return to capital, which is proportional to the ratio of payroll to capital stock. Using this information for r^B, $\underline{r}^B$, and r^*, all the factors of proportionality cancel.

For nonmanufacturing investment, a similar form was used. For these sectors $\underline{r}^*$ was the U.S. rate just as for MD1; these are rapidly growing sectors that compete for investment funds with the whole U.S. The coefficient β was chosen to give an elasticity that is slightly above that for manufacturing industry.

From these investment data and assumptions on depreciation, the capital stock series are constructed. Estimates of current investment for 25 years before the beginning of the sample period were made so that a scrapping function could be estimated. The capital stock was assumed to maintain its value until it reached a certain age at which point it was scrapped. The total value of the investment in current dollars still in service is the measure entitled gross book value, which is available from several of the Censuses of Manufacturers for the state. Assuming a constant capital output ratio in the benchmark year, it was possible to estimate the average age at which investment goods are scrapped. For the four manufacturing sectors, it varied from 16 to 21 years. For the nonmanufacturing export service sector where the capital stock is primarily in buildings, a figure of 30 years was chosen. This lifetime was then used with constant-dollar investment to construct a deflated measure of capital stock. A two-year moving average of this was used in the model to represent the time until new investment comes on-line.

IV. Simulations

A variety of simulations have been performed with this model. Tracking experiments where observed historical data are used for the exogenous variables over the sample period give reasonably small errors for the predicted endogenous variables. Out-of-sample forecasts and long-run extrapolations have also been obtained and look reasonable. These are described in Engle and Anderson (1975).

In this paper, the primary interest lies in policy experiments where one or more of the exogenous variables are changed, and the simulation calculates how much this alters the path of the endogenous variables. Several experiments that deal with taxes, incomes, and employment will be described, but others related to energy and a variety of state tax programs are presented in the above-mentioned pair. A set of simulations comparing the effects of changes in factor supply with changes in aggregate demand are given in Engle (1979a).

A. MULTIPLIERS

In the first simulation, entitled "INCOME," personal income is decreased by $100 million in 1961 and continues at this reduced level throughout the sample period until 1971. This could result from a lump-sum increase in federal taxes, a decrease in receipts of property income, or other taxable income not associated with employment.

The second simulation is entitled "TRANSFER" and represents a decrease of $100 million in federal and state transfers each year from 1961 to 1971. This would result from a decrease in welfare payments or any other income supplement that corresponds to nontaxable income.

It could also approximately represent an exogenous increase in the expenditures for an imported commodity having demands that are separable from domestic demands. For example, when the price of energy rises, greater expenditures on energy naturally occur, and therefore there is less income remaining to spend on local goods. If the demand for energy is separable from local demands, then this could be represented by a decrease in transfers, thus leaving tax liabilities constant other than through secondary effects.

The third simulation, "EMPLOYMENT," allows the state and federal government to decrease its employment by 1000 workers in 1961–1971. This exogenous decrease in employment generates declines in income but it is assumed not to lead to lower tax rates. The revenues are presumably spent in other jurisdictions. This decreased expenditure carries a price tag of $5.36 million in 1961 and $9.16 million in 1971 since wages are then higher. The simulation would be quite similar for an exogenous change in any other sector except that the income generated might differ because of different wage rates and the receipt of profits from the private sector.

The fourth simulation, "TAX RATE," raises the state personal tax rate by 20% from 1961 to 1971. Nominally the tax rate was 5% for the sample period, and this experiment corresponds to an increase to 6%. The revenues are assumed to be spent elsewhere in the state. The simulation also corresponds to an increase in the federal income tax rate. Without secondary effects, the revenues to be expected would be $15.88 million in 1961 and $59.03 million in 1971.

Summary results from these four simulations are given in Table 9. For a variety of key variables, the difference between the policy simulation and the control simulation are tabulated for 1961 and 1971. These differences, labeled Δ, are given in absolute or percentage terms, and the corresponding multipliers are calculated as the difference divided by the size of the policy change and by the price tag or value in current dollars of the policy change. These values are given in the previous paragraphs. The latter figure is probably the most appropriate way to compare different policies. These calculations will

TABLE 9
INCOME AND EMPLOYMENT POLICY MULTIPLIERS

Variable Year	Measure[a]	Income 1961	Income 1971	Transfer 1961	Transfer 1971	Employment 1961	Employment 1971	Tax Rate 1961	Tax Rate 1971
BPI	Δ[b]	−153	−155	−153	−160	−8.40	−14.7	−7.64	−31.6
	Δ/Policy	1.53	1.55	1.53	1.60	8400	14,700	—	—
	Δ/Value	1.53	1.55	1.53	1.60	1.56	1.60	0.48	0.53
BDI	Δ[b]	−129	−127	−140	−144	−7.06	−12	−22.3	−84.7
	Δ/Policy	1.29	1.27	1.40	1.44	7060	12,000	—	—
	Δ/Value	1.29	1.27	1.40	1.44	1.32	1.31	1.40	1.43
SETOT	Δ	−829	−535	−8546	−6187	−1427	−1505	−1217	−3256
	Δ/Policy	82.9[c]	53.5[c]	85.5[c]	61.9[c]	1.43	1.51	—	—
	Δ/Value[c]	82.9	53.5	85.5	61.9	26.6	164	76.6	55.1
BCPI	%Δ	−0.0043	−0.0038	−0.0028	−0.0032	−0.0005	−0.0007	−0.0004	−0.0016
	%Δ/Policy	0.43[d]	0.38[d]	0.28[d]	0.32[d]	0.5[c]	0.7[c]	—	—
	%Δ/Value[d]	0.43	0.38	0.28	0.32	0.93	0.76	0.25	0.27
WMY	%Δ	−0.025	−0.025	−0.021	−0.020	−0.0035	−0.0048	−0.0029	−0.0100
	%Δ/Policy	2.5[d]	2.5[d]	2.1[d]	2.0[d]	3.5[c]	4.8[c]	—	—
	%Δ/Value[d]	2.5	2.5	2.1	2.0	6.5	5.2	1.8	1.7

[a] Δ is algebraic and %Δ is percentage difference between policy and control simulations
[b] In millions of current $ ($\times 10^6$).
[c] Per million $ ($\times 10^{-6}$).
[d] Per $10 billion ($\times 10^{-10}$).

give long-run multipliers if the model is essentially static. As will be shown below, all of these policies have by far their major impact in the current year so this is a good approximation. This is of course a result of the simple dynamics built into the model.

A variety of interesting features appear in Table 9. Examining the changes in disposable income as a fraction of value, all range from 1.27 to 1.44. Thus a dollar extracted from the Boston economy in one of these four ways will lead to a decrease in disposable income from a quarter to a half again as large. The largest multipliers are associated with transfers or tax rates since these are not themselves taxed. Employment and income policies have smaller multipliers since these income increases are taxed directly. The value of a single additional job is seen to be $7060 in 1961 and $12,000 in 1971, both of which are well above the wage rate. The multipliers for personal income are somewhat larger than for disposable income (except for tax changes) since the measure is gross of taxes. These results are roughly similar to the range of empirical results obtained from econometric models, input–output models, or base multiplier models as long as careful account is taken of the leakages. It is important to notice, however, that the appropriate multiplier depends upon the measure employed, and thus models with only employment or gross product may misstate the effect on any of the other aggregates.

The multipliers on total employment, however, show some dramatic differences. The employment policy has a multiplier between 1.43 and 1.51, which again is reasonable. This corresponds to 270 jobs in 1961 and 160 jobs in 1971 for every million dollars of expenditure. The other three policies, however, appear to have much smaller effects on total employment. Each produces between 50 and 90 jobs per million dollars of expenditure, and so is less than half as effective in job creation as a direct employment policy. This is of course a result of the fact that a large proportion of income is spent on imported goods and thus generates no new jobs.

The four policies also have an effect on wages and prices in the SMSA. Since they are all contractionary policies, reduced pressure on employment and output markets leads to price and wage increases below those of the control solution. The percentage change in wages and prices attributable to the policy in question is given in the table. In general the effects are rather small. If the policies are imposed at a value of $10 billion then wage decreases would range from 1.8% to 6.5% and price decreases would be only 0.25%– 1%. The size of these numbers reflects the degree to which metropolitan areas are interdependent. Wage rates and price levels are strongly influenced by phenomena outside the region. The price level in particular is determined in large measure by the prices of imported commodities. Furthermore, when the unemployment rate in Boston rises, the response of migration is sufficiently rapid that no prolonged spell of unemployment is observed, and thus no drastic change in wage rates occur. Further research is being undertaken on this particular relation.

The differences between the wage and price multipliers, however, are interesting. The largest effects again result from the direct employment policy. Here the largest employment effect has the most substantial effect on unemployment, which in turn drives wages and hence prices lower.

B. Dynamic Reversal in Income Multiplier

Another simulation was undertaken to examine the subtle dynamics of the model. A simulation was calculated where the exogenous variable was changed for only one year and then returned to its initial path. In "INCOME 2," $100 million is added to personal income in 1961. The results in absolute or percent error are presented in Table 10 for several of the key variables.

The most striking feature of Table 10 is that the largest effect is in 1961, the year of the income supplement, and then after several years the sign changes. The initial sign is the effect commonly anticipated in regional models. The reversal is unusual and can be traced to the behavior of capital and new investment. The path is rather complex and depends on the particular demand elasticities estimated in Boston.

When income increases, the demand for all local sectors increases, including the sectors that are partially export and employ capital. This increased demand increases profitability and therefore generates, with a lag, new investment. A second source of increase comes through the wage rate. As the unemployment rate is decreased, the wage will rise. This will either increase or decrease profits depending on whether the price elasticity of demand is greater or less than one. In most of the sectors this elasticity is below one, especially in the large sectors. An increase in wages will therefore generate an increase in earnings, and by the Cobb–Douglas or the Kendrick–Jaycox (1965) assumption, an increase in profits and incentives to investment. These two sources of new investment further stimulate demand for durables through direct purchases, and thus further increase profits. Because of the lags in the investment equations and in the capital stock identity, these effects lead slowly to an increase in capital stocks in the sectors with inelastic demand and to a decrease in those sectors with an elastic demand. In each case, the change in the capital stock is in a direction to decrease employment. Because of the lags, this process will lead to overshooting. Furthermore, the presence of investment demand as a direct input to construction and durables demand puts an accelerator in the model, and thus it is not surprising to find

TABLE 10
INCOME 2 SIMULATION; BPI INCREASED 100 MILLION 1961

Variable Year	BPI Δ^b	BDI Δ	SETOT Δ	RTXGVL %Δ	DINVTOT %Δ	SEGVL Δ	UBOS Δ	WMY %Δ	BCPI %Δ
1959	0	0	0	0	0	0	0	0	0
1960	0	0	0	0	0	0	0	0	0
1961	147.7	124.5	7652	−0.49	0.218	1296	−0.13	0.019	0.003
1962	3.22	2.67	547	−0.006	0.340	27	0.09	0.006	0.0008
1963	1.31	1.10	156	−0.002	0.246	11	0.03	0.002	0.0003
1964	0.77	0.65	84	−0.001	0.020	6	0.007	0.0006	0.0001
1965	0.33	0.28	30	−0.001	−0.016	3	0.003	0.0002	0
1966	−0.04	−0.03	−9	0	−0.042	0	0.001	0	0
1967	−0.29	−0.25	−34	0.0004	−0.052	−2	0.0007	−0.001	0
1968	−0.39	−0.32	−43	0.0005	−0.055	−3	0.0003	−0.002	0
1969	−0.38	−0.30	−42	0	−0.048	−3	0	−0.002	0
1970	−0.42	−0.34	−38	0.006	−0.039	−3	0	−0.002	0
1971	−0.31	−0.25	−25	0.0003	−0.028	−2	−0.0002	−0.002	0

[a] Δ is algebraic difference and %Δ is percentage difference between policy and control simulations.
[b] Millions of dollars.

overadjustment. The rather short lags in the labor migration equation produce little pressure on wages to continue rising to sustain the boom.

The economics behind this scenario are rather plausible. A city may be growing very rapidly, partly on the basis of new investment in residential and industrial construction. When the demand for its products slackens, the city may find itself with excess capital. This leads to capital labor substitution and perhaps a decline of employment and income even below its preboom level. The magnitude of this effect in the Boston model is quite small, but it is present. It would probably never be a serious concern in a policy decision; however, this is only because of the particular elasticities involved. If the reversal were stronger, it might be wise to take this into account when planning economic development.

C. Deficit Financing

A final simulation was run to examine the effect of deficit financing by the local government. The deficit was assumed to be twice as great in 1960 as it was historically, and therefore tax rates could be lowered and services expanded. This is paid for, however, by an increase in debt service charges in the future, which must be met with higher tax revenues. The change in the deficit was $8.4 million. The results in change and percentage changes are presented in Table 11.

The main effect occurs initially with an increase in total employment of 719 and in government employment of 103. The tax rate was reduced by 1.6% and government services were expanded. Subsequently, however, all series show slight deterioration, turning negative after two to four years. Income and employment are below the control solution, but only slightly. For example, the increase in employment of 719 in the first year is balanced by a decrease of perhaps 25 in subsequent years. Local government services are restricted by 3 or 4 employees.

The evaluation of this policy requires at least a present-value calculation. If indeed the losses are 25 jobs per year and the discount rate is 8%, then this is a discounted value of only 300 jobs and the policy appears sensible. However, it is more likely that the series of employment losses is growing. The average growth rate over the few years available is about 10%. If this is the case into the distant future, then the cost of the program in present value terms is infinite and deficit financing would be disastrous. Furthermore, as the debt increases, the cost of service may increase, giving still higher costs as bond ratings deteriorate. The conclusion of this experiment depends upon the behavior of the model as it is simulated over a longer sample period. The experience of some of our large cities indicates that this question is of great importance and that the pessimistic view has some empirical support.

TABLE 11

DEFICIT SIMULATION: GVLDCT INCREASED 8 MILLION 1960

Year	BPI Δ^b	BDI Δ^b	SETOT Δ	RTXGVL %Δ	DINVTOT Δ^c	GVLDS Δ^b	SEGVL Δ	UBOS Δ	WMY %Δ	BCPI %Δ
Measure[a]										
1959	0	0	0	0	0	0	0	0	0	0
1960	4.36	11.7	719	−1.64	22.8	0	103	−0.012	0.0018	0.0002
1961	0.22	0.008	58	0.03	24.2	0.18	1	0.009	0.0006	0.0001
1962	0.037	−0.156	2	0.03	24.5	0.19	−1	0.003	0.0001	0
1963	−0.029	−0.23	−8	0.04	1.1	0.22	−2	0.001	0	0
1964	−0.11[d]	−0.29	−19	0.03	−3.1	0.21	−2	0	0	0
1965	−0.14	−0.36	−23	0.03	−6.1	0.25	−2	0	0	0
1966	−0.16	−0.36	−19	0.03	−8.4	0.24	−2	0	0	0
1967	−0.28	−0.55	−29	0.04	−8.2	0.32	−4	0	0	0
1968	−0.21	−0.50	−28	0.04	−7.7	0.34	−3	0	0	0
1969	−0.21	−0.54	−27	0.04	−6.1	−0.39	−3	0	0	0
1970	−0.32	−0.76	−35	0.05	−4.9	0.52	−4	0	0	0
1971	−0.34	−0.78	−33	0.04	−3.8	0.52	−4	0	0	0

[a] Δ is algebraic difference and %Δ is percentage difference between policy and control simulation.
[b] Millions of dollars.
[c] Thousands of dollars.
[d] Δ is algebraic difference; %Δ is percentage difference.

V. Conclusion

In conclusion, the model appears to behave plausibly, and sound economic arguments can be given for most of its relationships. However, the estimates are based upon few observations, and many of the relationships are very simple. This effort therefore is meant to be an exploratory approach to building an economically rich model of a metropolitan area. The particular estimates must be taken as suggestive rather than definitive.

Appendix: Variable Names

PREFIXES

AE__	Adjustment from payroll to earned income
AVA__	Adjustment from earned income to value added
CAP__	Constant dollar capital stock, two year moving average
CTX__	Corporate tax rate as a fraction of value added
D__	Wage adjustment factor based on skill mix and relative costs
DEF__	U.S. deflator
DUVA__	U.S. value added deflated by industry wholesale price index
EI__	Earned income
INV__	New capital expenditures
IW__	Industry wage rate per year
PT__	U.S. price index net of shipping charges (F.O.B. Boston)
RTX__	Average tax rate
SE__	Employment
VA__	Value added

SUFFIXES

__CC	Contract Construction (SIC 15–17)
__COM	Commercial, the sum of SB and FIR
__FIR	Finance, Insurance and Real Estate (SIC 60–69)
__GV	Government (SIC 91–98)
__GVF	Federal Government
__GVL	Local Government
__GVS	State Government
__MD1	Manufacturing, durables 1 (SIC 35–38)
__MD2	Manufacturing, durables 2 (SIC 19, 21, 24, 25, 32, 34, 39)
__MND1	Manufacturing, nondurables 1 (SIC 22, 23, 31)
__MND2	Manufacturing, nondurables 2 (SIC 20, 26–30)

AN ECONOMETRIC MODEL OF A METROPOLITAN AREA 155

__RT Retail trade (SIC 52–59)
__SB Business services (SIC 73, 74, 80–86, 89)
__SN Non-profit services (parts of SB and SP not covered by unemployment insurance)
__SP Personal Services (SIC 70–72, 75–79, 88)
__SR All services
__TCU Transportation, Communication and Public Utilities (SIC 01–14, 40–49, 99)
__TOT All sectors
__WT Wholesale trade (SIC 50, 51)

Miscellaneous

BCPI Boston Consumer Price Index
BDI Boston disposable income after state, federal, and local tax payments
BPI Boston personal income
BPROP Boston property income received
CORTAX Federal corporate tax payments from Boston
DBDI Boston disposable income deflated by BCPI
DINVTOT Total Boston investment deflated by U.S. investment deflator
GVLDEBT Outstanding debt of all local governments in Boston SMSA
GVLDS Debt service paid by local governments
GVLOTHR Expenditures by local government other than payroll
GVLRESID Statistical discrepancy in local government accounts
GVLRS State and Federal grants-in-aid to local governments
MBRATE Municipal bond rate
PBCM Commodity component of BCPI
PBSV Service component of BCPI
PBHS Housing component of BCPI
PUCM Commodity component of UCPI
PERTAX State and Federal personal income tax receipts from Boston
RCON Ratio of social insurance contributions to personal income
TPWF Total potential work force in Boston with no migration
TRANSF Transfer payments received by Boston residents
UBOS Boston unemployment rate
UCPI U.S. Consumer Price Index
UPRP U.S. property income
UUS U.S. unemployment rate
WMWUS Weekly production worker wages in manufacturing in U.S.
WMY Yearly production worker wages in manufacturing in Boston

ACKNOWLEDGMENTS

This paper was written in part while the author was at MIT and completed at the University of California, San Diego. Financial support was provided by the NSF. Particular thanks are due to Richard Anderson and Charles Pigott who carried out most of the computational chores and to Jerome Rothenberg, John Harris, and William Wheaton for helpful discussions on many aspects of this work.

REFERENCES

Adams, F. G., Brooking, C. G., and Glickman, N. J. (1975). On the specification and simulation of a regional econometric model: A model of Mississippi. *The Review of Economics and Statistics* **57**, No. 3.

Bradbury, K. L. (1976). *Housing Supply in a Metropolitan Area*. Dissertation, Massachusetts Institute of Technology, September.

Bradbury, K., Engle, R., Irvine, O., and Rothenberg, J. (1977). Simultaneous estimation of the supply and demand for household location in a multizoned metropolitan area. In *Residential Location and Urban Housing Markets* (G. K. Ingram, ed.), pp. 51–86. Ballinger, Cambridge, Massachusetts.

Engle, R. (1974a). Issues in the specification of an econometric model of metropolitan growth. *Journal of Urban Economics* **1**, 250–267.

Engle, R. (1974b). A disequilibrium model of regional investment. *Journal of Regional Science* **14**, 367–376.

Engle, R. (1979a). Estimation of the price elasticity of demand facing metropolitan producers. *Journal of Urban Economics* **6**, 42–64.

Engle, R. (1979b). The regional response to factor supplies: Estimates for the Boston SMSA. In *Interregional Movements and Regional Growth* (W. C. Wheaton, ed.). Urban Institute, Washington, D.C.

Engle, R., and Anderson, R. G. (1975). *Policy Simulations with an Econometric Model of the Boston Metropolitan Area*. Manuscript.

Engle, R., Fisher, F. M., Harris, J. R., and Rothenberg, J. (1975). An econometric simulation model of intra-metropolitan housing location: Housing, business, transportation and local government. *The American Economic Review* **62**, No. 2.

Kendrick, J. W., and Jaycox, C. M. (1965). The concept and estimation of gross state product. *Southern Economic Journal* **32**, 153–168.

Liu, T.-C. (1963). An exploratory quarterly econometric model of effective demand in the postwar U.S. economy. *Econometrica* **31**, No. 3.

Wheaton, W. C. (1976). *An Equilibrium Model of Housing and Locational Choice: The Boston Prototype*. Manuscript, MIT.

DEPARTMENT OF ECONOMICS
UNIVERSITY OF CALIFORNIA, SAN DIEGO
LA JOLLA, CALIFORNIA

The Effect of Simple Specification Error on the Coefficients of "Unaffected" Variables

FRANKLIN M. FISHER

A basic assumption of least-squares regression theory[1] is that the regressors are uncorrelated with the disturbance. When this assumption fails, so does the consistency of least squares. Such a failure can be regarded typically as a specification error, and many such errors can be cast into this form. Failure may involve, for example, the omission of regressor-correlated variables from the equation or measurement error in the regressors[2] or simply the treating of endogenous variables as exogenous through the neglect of simultaneous feedback effects.

It sometimes happens that the crucial assumption can be maintained with respect to most of the regressors but fails as regards one of them. Thus, a single variable may be measured with error or a single variable involved in a simultaneous feedback with all other variables safely exogenous. In such a circumstance, the effect of the error on the estimated coefficient of

---

[1] Although the results of this paper are stated in terms of least squares, they obviously apply to any estimator that can be put in a least-squares-like form, hence to two-stage least squares, instrumental variables, and the like. It does not seem worthwhile making such obvious generality explicit in the notation or the text.

[2] This is the case treated in Levi (1973). Levi considers the case of only one variable measured with error (which is one way of regarding the problem treated in the present paper) and obtains the result as to the direct effect given below, showing also that the signs of the indirect effects depend on the cofactors of the cross-product matrix of regressors. Another paper, closely related to the present one, although focused on a somewhat different problem, is Leamer (1975).

the affected variable would often be easy to analyze, at least as to sign, were that variable the only one in the regression. In essence, one simply examines the sources of the problem to determine the sign of the correlation between the disturbance and the variable in question. The effect of the error on the estimated coefficient will be in the same direction.

Where the affected variable is not the only regressor, however, the situation is not quite so clear. If the remaining "unaffected" variables are not all orthogonal to the affected one, will the sign of the direct effect remain as in the simple case? Moreover, it is an elementary error to suppose that the effects of the specification error are confined to the coefficient of the directly affected variable. In general, there will be indirect effects as well, and various conjectures arise as to them.

Thus, for example, one might suppose that (after adjusting for the units in which the variables are measured) the direct effect will be larger than the indirect effects. One might also suppose that a particular indirect effect will be larger, the larger the correlation between the unaffected variable in question and the directly affected variable.

In this paper, I examine these and related questions. I show that while the sign of the direct effect does indeed remain the same as in the simple case, the conjectures as to the indirect effects are wrong unless there is only one unaffected regressor (apart from the constant term) or unless all unaffected regressors are mutually orthogonal. In particular, it is possible to produce an example in which the ratio of *every* indirect effect to the direct effect can be made indefinitely large. Thus, not only is it false to suppose that the effects of simple specification error are confined to the coefficient of the directly affected variable, it is wrong to suppose that such coefficient suffers from the principal effect.

Fortunately, the signs of the indirect effects can be estimated from the data, as can the ratios of the indirect effects to the direct effect, so that the analyst need not throw up his hands. Indeed, most of the results are obtained by showing that the ratios in question are given by the negative of the vector of regression coefficients when the affected variable is regressed on the unaffected ones.

I now proceed to the formal analysis. In the usual notation, the equation to be estimated is

(1) $$Y = X\beta + \varepsilon,$$

where Y is a T vector of observations on the dependent variable, X is a $T \times k$ matrix of observations on k regressors, β is a k vector of parameters to be estimated, and ε is a T vector of disturbances. I assume that $Q \equiv \text{Plim}(X'X/T)$ exists and is nonsingular and that

(2) $$\text{Plim}(X'\varepsilon/T) = \lambda e_k,$$

SPECIFICATION ERROR AND "UNAFFECTED" VARIABLES

where λ is a nonzero scalar and e_k is the k vector with last component unity and remaining components zero. Thus the crucial assumption of least squares is violated only for X_k, the last regressor. The sign of the correlation between X_k and ε is that of λ.

In view of (2), least squares will not be consistent, and, by Theil's specification error theorem, the inconsistency, denoted by δ, will be given by[3]

(3) $\quad \delta \equiv \text{Plim}(X'X)^{-1}X'Y - \beta = \text{Plim}(X'X)^{-1}X'\varepsilon = \lambda Q^{-1}e_k.$

I have already implicitly denoted the jth column of X by X_j. Now denote by $X(j)$ the matrix formed from X by deleting the jth column. Define

(4) $\quad \gamma \equiv \text{Plim}(\{X(k)'X(k)\}^{-1}X(k)'X_k)$

so that γ is asymptotically the vector of regression coefficients when the directly affected variable X_k is regressed on the remaining variables. I now prove:

Theorem (a) $\lambda\delta_k > 0;$ (b) $\delta_j/\delta_k = -\gamma_j, j \neq k.$

Proof (a) From (3), $\delta_k = \lambda(Q^{-1})_{kk}$ and $(Q^{-1})_{kk} > 0$, since Q is positive definite.

(b) From (3), $\delta_j = \lambda(Q^{-1})_{kj}$. Hence $\delta_j/\delta_k = Q^{kj}/Q^{kk}$, where Q^{ij} denotes the cofactor of Q_{ij}. Without loss of generality suppose that $j = 1$. Then

(5) $\quad \dfrac{Q^{k1}}{Q^{kk}} = \dfrac{(-1)^{1+k}\,\text{Det Plim}\{X(k)'X(1)/T\}}{(-1)^{2k}\,\text{Det Plim}\{X(k)'X(k)/T\}}$

$= (-1)^{1+k}\,\text{Plim}\{\text{Det}(X(k)'X(k))^{-1}X(k)'X(1)\}$

$= (-1)^{1+k} \begin{vmatrix} 0 & \cdots & 0 & \gamma_1 \\ \hline & I & & \vdots \\ & & & \gamma_{k-1} \end{vmatrix},$

where the last equality follows from the fact that the first $k - 1$ columns of $X(1)$ are identical to the last $k - 1$ columns of $X(k)$. Expanding by cofactors of the first row yields

(6) $\quad \delta_1/\delta_k = (-1)^{1+k}(-1)^{1+(k-1)}\gamma_1 = -\gamma_1,$

and the theorem is proved.

---

[3] I work in terms of inconsistency rather than bias principally because the results as to indirect effects involve ratios. Some of the results would hold for bias under appropriate assumptions.

Thus the direct effect is the same as in the simple case, while the ratios of the indirect effects to the direct effect are given by the negative of the vector of regression coefficients when the affected variable is regressed on the remaining variables. We now go on to use these results in considering the conjectures raised above.

I begin by considering the relative sizes of the indirect and direct effects. Clearly such relative size depends in the first instance on the units in which the different variables are measured. This is evident either directly from the fact that δ_j/δ_k is not unit free or from the fact that γ_j is not. Hence, by choosing units in which the variance of X_k is made very small relative to the variance of any X_j, $j \neq k$, we can make the ratios of indirect to direct effects as large as we like (unless X_k is orthogonal to all the other X_j). This does not say very much.

If the conjecture that direct effects are likely to be larger than indirect effects has any content, therefore, it must involve the case in which units are chosen to take out such trivial scale effects. Accordingly, I now assume that all variables are measured from their means and divided by their standard deviations; hence, all variables now have mean zero and variance unity, and the constant term is suppressed. I shall call these "standard units." Q now becomes a matrix of correlation coefficients, with

(7) $$Q_{ij} = r_{ij},$$

the correlation between variables i and j.

It is now easy to prove.

Corollary In standard units, if either $k = 2$ or $r_{ij} = 0$ for all $i, j, k \neq i \neq j \neq k$, then $|\delta_j/\delta_k| < 1$.

Proof In either of the two cases, γ_j will be the same as the regression coefficient in the simple regression of X_k on X_j. With the units chosen as described, however, this is r_{kj}.

Unfortunately, no similar result holds in more general cases. To see this, it suffices to examine a three-variable case with $r_{12} \neq 0$. Thus, choose $r_{12} = \mu - 1$, with $\mu > 0$. Choose $r_{13} = r_{23} = r > 0$ and $r = h\sqrt{\mu/2}$, where $0 < h < 1$. Positive definiteness of Q requires $\mu < 2$ and Det $Q > 0$. Examining the latter condition, we see that

(8) $$\text{Det } Q = 1 + 2(\mu - 1)r^2 - 2r^2 - (\mu - 1)^2$$
$$= (2r^2 - \mu)(\mu - 2) = \mu(h^2 - 1)(\mu - 2) > 0$$

in view of the restrictions placed on h and μ.

From the theorem, however, we need only examine γ_1 and γ_2. In this case,

$$(9) \quad -\gamma_1 = -\gamma_2 = \frac{r(\mu - 1) - r}{1 - (\mu - 1)^2} = \frac{r(\mu - 2)}{2\mu - \mu^2} = -\frac{r}{\mu} = -\frac{h}{\sqrt{2\mu}}$$

The absolute value of which tends to infinity as μ tends to zero. Hence *every* indirect effect can be indefinitely large relative to the direct effect.

It is clear from the corollary and the above example that colinearity among the unaffected variables can produce relatively big indirect effects. However, it is wrong to conclude that such colinearity has a monotonic effect. Consider the general three variable case (still in standard units). Then

$$(10) \quad \delta_1/\delta_3 = -\gamma_1 = (r_{12}r_{23} - r_{13})/(1 - r_{12}^2).$$

If r_{13} and r_{23} have the same sign, for example, an increase in r_{12} from zero can change the sign of γ_1, and therefore, of δ_1 as well (since $\delta_3 > 0$, by the theorem).

Similarly, all the indirect effects come about because the unaffected variables are correlated with the directly affected variable. One might therefore think that the unaffected variable most correlated with the directly affected one will be the unaffected variable whose coefficient has the biggest problem. This is clearly false as a general proposition, since there is no reason that the ratios of the γ_j that are multiple regression coefficients must lie on the same side of unity as the ratios of the r_{kj}, the correlation or simple regression coefficients. Indeed, it would be odd if this conjecture were true, since the grounds for believing it are similar to, but weaker than those for believing that the direct effect must be larger than the indirect ones.

Moreover, it is not true that increasing the correlation between the directly affected variable and a particular unaffected variable necessarily worsens the inconsistency in the estimate of the latter variable's coefficient. Thus, in the three-variable case in (10), an increase in r_{13}, other things equal, can produce a sign reversal in γ_1 and hence δ_1.

What is true about an increase in such a correlation is that it has an unambiguously negative effect on the inconsistency involved (which may itself be positive or negative). To see this (still in standard units), differentiate (4) with respect to r_{kk-1}, obtaining

$$(11) \quad \partial\gamma/\partial r_{kk-1} = \text{Plim}\{(X(k)'X(k))^{-1}\bar{e}_{k-1}\},$$

where $\bar{e}_{k-1}$ is the $k - 1$ vector with last component unity and other components zero. Comparing this with (3), it is evident that the proof of the theorem shows

(12) $$\frac{\partial \gamma_{k-1}}{\partial r_{kk-1}} > 0; \quad \frac{\partial \gamma_1/\partial r_{kk-1}}{\partial \gamma_{k-1}/\partial r_{kk-1}} = -\bar{\gamma}_j, \quad j \neq k-1,$$

where $\bar{\gamma}$ is the probability limit of the vector of regression coefficients obtained when X_{k-1} is regressed on the first $k-2$ variables. (Note that this result applies to any regression and has nothing directly to do with specification error.)

Now

(13) $$\frac{\partial \delta_k}{\partial r_{kk-1}} = \frac{\partial(Q^{kk}/\text{Det } Q)}{\partial r_{kk-1}} = -\left(\frac{Q^{kk}}{(\text{Det } Q)^2}\right)(2Q^{kk-1})$$
$$= -2\delta_k \delta_{k-1} = 2\delta_k^2 \gamma_{k-1}.$$

Thus

(14) $$\partial \delta_{k-1}/\partial r_{kk-1} = \partial(-\gamma_{k-1}\delta_k)/\partial r_{kk-1}$$
$$= -2\gamma_{k-1}^2 \delta_k^2 - \delta_k(\partial \gamma_{k-1}/\partial r_{kk-1}) < 0,$$

from (12) and (13).

Thus, the larger is r_{kk-1}, other things equal, the smaller (algebraically) will be the inconsistency in the estimate of β_{k-1}. We have already observed that this may or may not correspond to an increase in the absolute value of that inconsistency. Does this ambiguity disappear as r_{kk-1}^2 approaches unity so that increased correlation is deleterious for coefficients of variables already very highly correlated with the directly affected one?

As with the conjecture that indirect effects are small relative to direct effects, this turns out to be true only for special cases. It is obviously true for $k = 2$, or for X_{k-1} orthogonal to $X_1, \ldots, X_{k-2}$. Moreover, when either $k = 3$ or the variables $1 \cdots k - 2$ are mutually orthogonal, the parallel relation to (10) shows that as r_{kk-1}^2 approaches unity, the sign of δ_{k-1} becomes that of $-r_{kk-1}$, so that, from (14), the absolute value of δ_{k-1} is also growing (and, indeed, will be maximized at either 1 or -1). For more general cases, this is not true, essentially for the same sort of reasons as lie behind the counter-example to the proposition that indirect effects are small relative to direct ones. Similarly, it is not true that an increase in r_{kk-1} has a bigger effect on δ_{k-1} than on $\delta_j, j \neq k-1$.

The failure of so many simple conjectures is not a matter for depression, however. It is clear from the theorem that the signs of the effects of simple specification error and, indeed, their relative magnitudes can be readily determined by regressing the directly affected variable on the remaining ones. What is necessary is to refrain from behaving as though such a multiple regression is equivalent to simple ones.

REFERENCES

Leamer, E. E. (1975). A result on the sign of restricted least square estimates. *Journal of Econometrics* **3**, No. 4, 387–390.

Levi, M. D. (1973). Errors in variables bias in the presence of correctly measured variables. *Econometrica* **41**, 985–986.

DEPARTMENT OF ECONOMICS
MASSACHUSETTS INSTITUTE OF TECHNOLOGY
CAMBRIDGE, MASSACHUSETTS

Temporal Aggregation and Econometric Models*

GARY FROMM

and

E. C. HWA

I. Introduction

There are numerous reasons, both theoretical and empirical, that a monthly econometric model of a nation may be justified.[1] T. C. Liu was among the first to recognize the benefits and feasibility of constructing such monthly models. His insights were pathbreaking, and his efforts remain as classical references in the field. Perhaps the most compelling reason is that important economic policy decisions of both government and business are frequently influenced by the "latest" changes in a number of key monthly economic indicators. In theory, hazards associated with using monthly data in ad hoc fashion could be reduced substantially through the use of monthly econometric models. In addition, in view of the ever increasing role played by econometric models in overall formation of economic policies, monthly

---

* This paper was prepared under the program of research on Financial Flows and Economic Activity in the United States, supported in part by the National Science Foundation. It was requested as a contribution to this volume. It was also presented at the Second U.S.-U.S.S.R. Exchange Symposium on Econometric Modeling, Scientific and Technical Exchange Program on the Application of Computers to Management, May 23-26, 1978, Skyland, Virginia.

[1] These reasons have been spelled out variously in Liu (1969), Liu and Hwa (1976).

models have potential in contributing to more timely analyses of impacts of spontaneous shifts in government economic policies and of other exogenous events on the economy.[2] Thus, such models may permit short-term forecasting not readily possible from use of quarterly or annual models.

While conceptually there may be many advantages associated with monthly econometric models of a national economy, the viability of constructing such models has frequently been challenged on the basis of four major considerations. First, movements in monthly economic series tend to be erratic. Structural equations which incorporate lagged variables and are estimated on the basis of such data would reflect mainly the autoregressiveness in the same variables rather than meaningful relationships among different variables. Second, serial correlations in disturbances in monthly relationships could be so strong that estimates of parameters in equations containing lagged variables could be highly biased and inefficient. Third, lack of monthly observations on many important economic aggregates would make it impossible to construct an econometric model of a national economy.[3] Finally, quarterly and annual data could be less "noisy" than monthly data because erratic elements or measurement errors contained in monthly data could be averaged out. Consequently, quarterly and perhaps also semiannual models could give better results than the monthly models for use in short-term forecasting.[4]

However, the research done by Liu (1969) and by Liu and Hwa (1976) on a monthly model of the U.S. economy should dispel many qualms about the first three points. These results have demonstrated the feasibility of constructing a monthly econometric model of the U.S. economy that includes all essential sectors of the economy. Also, perhaps quite surprisingly, in spite of data-measurement problems, the Liu–Hwa monthly model, while then a newcomer in the field of macroeconometric models, fared quite well in comparison with several well-known quarterly models of the U.S. economy in the comparative studies on models simulation errors reported by Fromm and Klein (1973, 1976). These studies have compared, among other things, within and outside sample multiperiod prediction errors generated from various models for a number of common variables. In forecasting certain variables, the Liu–Hwa monthly model compared quite favorably with the forecasts of quarterly models in terms of root-mean-squared error statistics. Further, there are indications that the prediction errors of this monthly model do not increase quite as quickly as those of some quarterly models

---

[2] For a recent comparison of the relative popularity of alternative methods used to forecast economic activities, see Su (1975).

[3] While interpolation and missing observation techniques could be employed to generate monthly data, use of such techniques does not necessarily add much information.

[4] This was exactly one of the basic tenets that underlay Friend and Taubman's (1964) semiannual model.

as the prediction horizon lengthens. This is true particularly in the case of the ex-post extrapolation simulations, although no clear-cut pattern emerges. Thus, the Fromm-Klein tabulations appear to indicate that model builders have been over cautious about the use of monthly data, and their failure to exploit this important information source (for other than updating quarterly and annual initial conditions for other models) might not always be justified.

The Fromm-Klein comparative analyses of dynamic simulation errors of roughly a dozen U.S. macro models, while indicative, still are not definitive on comparisons between monthly and quarterly or annual models for the following reasons. First, as one would expect, model structures vary substantially, as do estimation periods of these models. Second, the common ex-post extrapolation period adopted to test the models' forecasting capabilities is far too short to provide reliable indication about comparative accuracy. Hence, it would also appear that the Fromm-Klein analyses have not yielded conclusive evidence about the success of monthly versus quarterly models in forecasting short-term movements in an economy. Until more rigorous tests are made, the merits or even viability of a monthly model as a short-term forecasting tool remains uncertain.

The aim of this paper is to compare the short-term predictive performance of a monthly model with that of a quarterly model in a more rigorous manner. In particular, both models will be assumed to have an identical theoretical basis and to be estimated on a common sample period. In the process, it is hoped that some insights may be gained about the structure and short-term forecasting capabilities of monthly versus quarterly models.

II. Time Aggregation and Structural Specification

Theoretical and empirical examination of effects of time aggregation on specification and estimation of econometric models has received little study to date. Notable contributions have been made by Theil (1954), Mundlak (1961), Sims (1971), Montmarquette and Zellner (1971), and Geweke (1978). Also, related, relevant work has been conducted using spectral or Fourier analysis, for example, by Granger (1966), Jenkins and Watts (1968), and Hannan (1970). However, in virtually all these cases primary emphasis has been on estimation methodology.[5]

---

[5] In another closely related area, namely, the effects of aggregation over micro decision units, for instance, aggregating from the level of a firm to that of an industry, has also been variously studied in the context of both single equation and simultaneous equation models. See for example Griliches and Grunfeld (1960), Kuh (1969), Orcutt et al. (1968), and Edwards and Orcutt (1969). Also, Fromm and Schink (1973) have studied effects of aggregating variables and sectors within the context of complete-system econometric model.

Relatively limited attention has been paid therein to relationships of economic decision processes and behavior with their timing characteristics. Generally, the assumptions made are that these processes and behavior are continuous or can be approximated by discrete time averages. Adjustments between system states thereby established or sought, too, have been taken to obey similar continuous or discrete average patterns.

Depending upon the variables, this may accord neither with economic theory nor with actual institutional arrangements. For instance, the formation of expectations of future events for selected phenomena, especially those that are infrequent, need not necessarily follow any regular time pattern. The time variance of formation may be quite large. The same holds for time patterns of such actions as regulatory proceedings and rulings, so called regulatory lag, and results of other administrative mechanisms.

Stated in other terms, time patterns of effects may be discontinuous, exhibiting sawtooth, irregular oscillations. Under these circumstances, as Geweke has observed, one would certainly hesitate to interpolate behavior between time periods as if it were continuous.

The same holds true for outcomes of processes and decisions that occur periodically and regularly, but at less frequent intervals than those of other variables of interest included in a more comprehensive model. For example, government budgets generally are set annually, nonwithheld taxes and dividends are paid quarterly, and Federal Reserve open-market committee policy generally is set monthly. If an objective is to explain monthly movements in monetary aggregates within the context of a complete econometric model, it is not sensible to posit monthly equations for variables that truly are determined less frequently.

Under these circumstances, rather than interpolate behavior to a common frequency, a more sensible approach would be to specify a model using a mix of frequencies. That is, each constituent process within the model would be analyzed using its own natural frequency. Appropriate account could still be taken of interperiod and intraperiod adjustments of revisions in prior decisions and of realizations of targeted positions. Smoothness conditions that must apply to make this possible can be inferred from Geweke (1978). We shall not develop them further here.

Rather, the emphasis will be on contrasting monthly and quarterly (or lower frequencies) models under the presumption that there is sufficient justification to posit behavioral relations on a monthly basis. The focus in the following sections is on time aggregation of forecasting errors, parameter estimation bias and efficiency, and effects of data measurement errors. Then, there is an examination of empirical results with monthly and quarterly estimates of the Federal Reserve monthly money market model.

III. Time Aggregation of Forecasting Errors

In studying dynamic simulation errors of an econometric model, it is often hypothesized that forecasting errors tend to be offsetting when aggregated over calendar time. This would imply that a quarterly model may be more successful in tracking yearly rather than quarterly movements of an economy.[6] Similarly, a monthly model may prove more accurate in predicting quarterly than monthly changes of economic variables. This argument may be elaborated as follows.

Let the forecasting error of a variable, i.e., the difference between the predicted and actual values, for basic time units and for aggregated time units be expressed by u and U, respectively; u and U are therefore related by the following identity (assuming, without loss of generality, that both u and U are measured as deviations from the mean).

$$\text{(1)} \qquad U(s) = \frac{1}{n} \sum_{i=0}^{n-1} u(ns - i), \qquad s = 1, 2, \ldots, q,$$

where n is the number of basic time periods aggregated per observation of U (e.g., $n = 3$ for monthly to quarterly aggregation) and q is the number of observations for U. Hence the number of observations for u is nq. The case of independent prediction of U is treated in Section IV.

The mean-squared error (MSE) of U is $\sum_{s=1}^{q} U^2(s)/q$, which can be expressed in terms of $\text{MSE}(u) = (1/nq) \sum_{i=1}^{nq} u^2(i)$ via the following steps.

$$\text{MSE}(U) = \frac{1}{q} \sum_{s=1}^{q} U^2(s)/q = \frac{1}{q} \sum_{s=1}^{q} \left[\sum_{i=0}^{n-1} u(ns - i)/n \right]^2$$

$$= \frac{1}{n^2 q} \sum_{s=1}^{q} \left[\sum_{i=n(s-1)+1}^{ns} u^2(i) + 2 \sum_{i=0}^{n-2} u(ns - i) \sum_{j=i+1}^{n-1} u(ns - j) \right]$$

$$= \frac{1}{n^2 q} \sum_{s=1}^{q} \sum_{i=n(s-1)+1}^{ns} u^2(i)$$

$$\times \left[1 + \frac{2 \sum_{s=1}^{q} \sum_{i=0}^{n-2} u(ns - i) \sum_{j=i+1}^{n-1} u(ns - j)}{\sum_{s=1}^{q} \sum_{i=n(s-1)+1}^{ns} u^2(i)} \right]$$

$$= \frac{\text{MSE}(u)}{n} \left[1 + \frac{2 \sum_{s=1}^{q} \sum_{k=1}^{n-1} \sum_{i=n(s-1)+1}^{ns-k} u(i)u(i + k)}{\sum_{s=1}^{q} \sum_{i=n(s-1)+1}^{ns} u^2(i)} \right]$$

[6] For evidence of this sort, see Haitovsky et al. (1974) In this study, the authors have found cancellation of forecasting errors for both the OBE and Wharton quarterly econometric models.

because

$$\frac{1}{nq}\sum_{s=1}^{q}\sum_{i=n(s-1)+1}^{ns} u^2(i) = \frac{1}{nq}\sum_{i=1}^{nq} u^2(i) = \text{MSE}(u)$$

and

$$\sum_{i=0}^{n-2} u(ns-1) \sum_{j=i+1}^{ns} u(ns-j) = \sum_{k=1}^{n-1} \sum_{i=n(s-1)+1}^{ns-k} u(i)u(i+k).$$

MSE(U) can be further transformed to the expression

(2) $$\text{MSE}(U) = \frac{\text{MSE}(u)}{n}\left[1 + 2\sum_{s=1}^{q} w(s)\zeta(s)/n\right]$$

where

$$w(s) = \frac{\sum_{i=n(s-1)+1}^{ns} u^2(i)}{\sum_{s=1}^{q} \sum_{i=n(s-1)+1}^{ns} u^2(i)},$$

$$\zeta(s) = \sum_{k=1}^{n-1} \frac{n-k}{n} \gamma_k(s),$$

and

$$\gamma_k(s) = \frac{\sum_{i=n(s-1)+1}^{ns-k} u(i)u(i+k)/(n-k)}{\sum_{i=n(s-1)+1}^{ns} u^2(i)/n}.$$

In Eq. (2), $\gamma_k(s)$ is an autocorrelation function and, therefore, the absolute value of $\gamma_k(s)$ is always smaller than or equal to unity. Consequently, the absolute value of $\zeta(s)$ is always small than or equal to $(n-1)/2$ and the value of $\mu = \text{MSE}(U)/\text{MSE}(u) - 1$ is bounded by the closed interval $[2((1/n) - 1), 0]$. There are three interesting special cases of μ: (a) when $\gamma_k(s) = 1, \mu = 0$; (b) when $\gamma_k(s) = -1, \mu = 2[(1/n) - 1]$; (c) when $\gamma_k(s) = 0$, $\mu = (1/n) - 1$. From the range of μ we can conclude: (a) MSE(U) is always smaller than or equal to MSE(u); this may be viewed as the effect of error cancellation; (b) the effect of error cancellation will be larger the higher the value of negative autocorrelation $\gamma_k(s)$ and the higher the order of aggregation n.

It should be noted that the comparison being made is between temporally aggregated and disaggregated forecasts from a given model that has been estimated with temporally disaggregated data. If forecasts are made from different models on a priori grounds there is little basis for concluding that within-aggregate-period forecasting errors are smaller than those across aggregate periods. A case can be made for either position. Conditions, too, may differ within and outside periods over which models are estimated.

Cancellation of forecasting errors has been cited as one of the distinctive advantages of a monthly model in making superior quarterly forecasts.[7] While this is true, stronger arguments in favor of a model estimated with monthly data can be made if models estimated with more temporally aggregated data suffer from significant loss of information. Other things being equal, such losses may prevent quarterly estimated models from generating equally good forecasts than monthly estimated models. This can be illustrated within the context of a classical linear regression framework.[8]

IV. Time Aggregation and Linear Regression

Let the model in basic time units be written

$$Y = X\beta + u, \tag{3}$$

where Y is a $T \times 1$ vector and X is a $T \times K$ matrix of independent variables. X is assumed to be fixed in repeated samples and u is a disturbance term with $Euu' = \sigma^2 I_T$. The ordinary least-squares estimator of β for this model is $b_0 = (X'X)^{-1}XY$. Further assume that outside the sample forecasting period

$$Y_* = X_*\beta + u_* \tag{4}$$

with dimensions for Y_* of $m \times 1$, X_* of $m \times k$, and u_* of $m \times 1$. Also postulate $Eu_* = 0$, $Euu'_* = 0$, and $Eu_*u'_* = \sigma^2 I_m$.

The forecast error is

$$\hat{Y}_{*0} - Y_* = X_*(b_0 - \beta) - u_*. \tag{5}$$

Now define a $q \times m$ matrix C_* such that C_*Y_* and C_*X_* are expressed in terms of desired time aggregates. Further assume that both the dependent and the independent variables are flows such that the matrix C_* can be defined in the form

$$\underset{(q \times m)}{C_*} = \frac{1}{n}\begin{pmatrix} \overbrace{1 \; 1 \; \cdots \; 1}^{n} & \overbrace{0 \; 0 \; \cdots \; 0}^{n} & \cdots & \overbrace{0 \; 0 \; \cdots \; 0}^{n} \\ 0 \; 0 \; \cdots \; 0 & 1 \; 1 \; \cdots \; 1 & \cdots & 0 \; 0 \; \cdots \; 0 \\ \vdots \; \vdots \; \cdots \; \vdots & \vdots \; \vdots \; \cdots \; \vdots & \cdots & \vdots \; \vdots \; \cdots \; \vdots \\ 0 \; 0 \; \cdots \; 0 & 0 \; 0 \; \cdots \; 0 & \cdots & 1 \; 1 \; \cdots \; 1 \end{pmatrix}. \tag{6}$$

---

[7] See, for instance, Bodkin (1973, p. 410).

[8] Recently, there is an increasing body of literature dealing with the effect of temporal aggregation on forecasting, see Montmarquette and Zellner (1971) and Wei (1978).

where $q = m/n$ and n is the number of time periods being aggregated. Without loss of generality, assume q to be an integer. With these assumptions, the forecasting error of the aggregated dependent variable $C_* Y_*$ using $C_* \hat{Y}_{*0}$ as the predictor becomes

(7) $$\hat{e}_{*0} = C_* \hat{Y}_{*0} - C_* Y_* = C_* X_*(b_0 - \beta) - C_* u_*.$$

The mean-squared-error matrix is

(8) $$\text{MSE}(\hat{e}_{*0}) = E\hat{e}_{*0}\hat{e}'_{*0} = V(\hat{e}_{*0}) + B(\hat{e}_{*0}),$$

where $V(\hat{e}_{*0})$ and $B(\hat{e}_{*0})$ are the covariance matrix and bias matrix of $\hat{e}_{*0}$, respectively, i.e.,

(9) $$V(\hat{e}_{*0}) = E(\hat{e}_{*0} - E\hat{e}_{*0})(\hat{e}_{*0} - E\hat{e}_{*0})'$$
$$= C_* X_* V(b_0) X'_* C'_* + C_* E u_* u'_* C'_*$$

and

(10) $$B(\hat{e}_{*0}) = E\hat{e}_{*0}(E\hat{e}_{*0})' = C_* X_* B(b_0) X'_* C'_*,$$

where $V(b_0) = E(b_0 - Eb_0)(b_0 - Eb_0)'$ and $B(b_0) = (Eb_0 - \beta)(Eb_0 - \beta)'$ are, respectively, the covariance and bias matrix of estimator b_0.

After inserting (9) and (10) into (8), we obtain

(11) $$\text{MSE}(\hat{e}_{*0}) = C_* X_*(V(b_0) + B(b_0))X'_* C'_* + C_* E u_* u'_* C_*$$
$$= C_* X_*[\text{MSE}(b_0 - \beta)]X'_* C'_* + C_* E u u'_* C_*.$$

The aggregate model corresponding to (3) may be represented by

(12) $$CY = CX\beta + Cu,$$

where the matrix C, now with dimension $p \times T$, is defined as in (6) with $p = T/n$.[9]

Since $ECuu'C' = \sigma^2 CC' = \sigma^2/nI_p$, the OLS estimator of β, b_1 is still appropriate and $b_1 = (X'C'CX)^{-1} X'C'CY$. If $C_* \hat{Y}_{*1} = (C_* X_* b_1)$ is used to predict $C_* Y_*$, the forecasting error is

(13) $$\hat{e}_{*1} = C_* X_*(b_1 - \beta) - C_* u_*.$$

Similarly, the mean-square-error matrix of $\hat{e}_{*1}$ can be shown to be

(14) $$\text{MSE}(\hat{e}_{*1}) = C_* X_*[\text{MSE}(b_1 - \beta)]X'_* C'_* + C_* E u_* u'_* C_*.$$

---

[9] If (3) is taken as the monthly model, then (12) may be looked upon as a quarterly model if $n = 3$.

Therefore, after subtracting (11) from (14),

(15)
$$\text{MSE}(\hat{e}_{*1}) - \text{MSE}(\hat{e}_{*0}) = C_* X_* [\text{MSE}(b_1 - \beta) - \text{MSE}(b_0 - \beta)] X'_* C'_*$$

Equation (15) reveals that comparison of the MSEs of the respective temporally aggregated and disaggregated predictors of CY is tantamount to a comparison of the MSEs of the respective regression estimates of β.[10]

It can now be shown that temporal aggregation results in an increase in forecasting error in the MSE sense. Since by assumption both b_0 and b_1 as estimates of β are unbiased, it follows that

(16)
$$\text{MSE}(b_0 - \beta) = V(b_0) = \sigma^2 (X'X)^{-1}$$

and

(17)
$$\text{MSE}(b_1 - \beta) = V(b_1) = (\sigma^2/n)(X'C'CX)^{-1}.$$

Hence $\text{MSE}(\hat{e}_{*1}) \geq \text{MSE}(\hat{e}_{*0})$ iff $V(b_1) \geq V(b_0)$ [from (15)]. This is equivalent to

(18) $\qquad \text{MSE}(\hat{e}_{*1}) \geq \text{MSE}(\hat{e}_{*0}) \qquad$ iff $\qquad V(b_0)^{-1} \geq V(b_1)^{-1}.$

Now we see

(19)
$$V(b_0)^{-1} - V(b_1)^{-1} = \frac{1}{\sigma^2}(X'X - nX'C'CX) = \frac{1}{\sigma^2} X'(I - nC'C)X.$$

Since $(I - nC'C)$ is an idempotent matrix, $(1/\sigma^2)X'(I - nC'C)X$ would be positive definite and $V(b_0)^{-1} > V(b_1)^{-1}$, b_0 would be more efficient than b_1 (for a proof, see the Appendix).

By way of summary, the above analysis shows that forecasts derived from a temporally disaggregated estimated model are likely to be more accurate than those from its more aggregated estimated counterpart. This is because time aggregation results in loss of information in the data. However, one

---

[10] If we let X_j denote the jth column of $(C_* X_*)'$ we see that the MSE of the jth element of $\hat{e}_{*1}$ will exceed the MSE of the jth element of $\hat{e}_{*0}$ by $X'_j [\text{MSE}(b_1 - \beta) - \text{MSE}(b_0 - \beta)] X_j$. There will be a gain in efficiency in forecasting the dependent variable in aggregate time units CY by using the disaggregated model when this expression is positive. This is seen to depend on whether $\text{MSE}(b_1 - \beta)$ is large relative to $\text{MSE}(b_0 - \beta)$. Suppose, e.g., that $\text{MSE}(b - \beta) - \text{MSE}(b_0 - \beta)$ is nonnegative definite, then $X'_j [\text{MSE}(b_1 - \beta) - \text{MSE}(b_0 - \beta)] X_j \geq 0$ for all j.

might question whether more temporally disaggregated data contain greater measurement errors than aggregated data and to what extent this conclusion thereby is weakened. This subject is explored in the next section.

V. Effects of Measurement Errors

A proposition commonly advanced that favors the use of quarterly or annual data rather than monthly data is that monthly data are prone to erratic, transient changes, or measurement errors. It has been suggested that undesirable impacts of these factors on parameter estimation and forecasting presumably could be mitigated, if not completely eliminated, if quarterly, semiannual, or annual, rather than monthly, data were used.[11]

The validity of this argument relies on "ex-ante" cancellation of errors in data in much the same way as the contention that a monthly model has the capability of producing more accurate quarterly forecasts hinges upon "ex-post" cancellation of forecasting errors. But, just as there is no guarantee that forecasting errors would cancel in an "ex-post" manner, it is equally uncertain whether transient, erratic elements, or measurement errors would cancel in time aggregation. They could perhaps even accumulate as a result of averaging over time. Moreover, the chief deficiency of this argument is that it ignores implications of information losses and accompanying adverse effects on short-run forecasting accuracy as a result of time aggregation. When this is taken into account, the theoretical supremacy of using quarterly instead of monthly data (or of using semiannual data instead of quarterly data) is no longer assured even if errors of measurement in the monthly data are presumed to be exactly offsetting.

This may be conveniently illustrated with the aid of a simple classical errors-in-variable model. Let this model be represented by the relations

(20) $$y^* = \alpha x^* + u,$$

(21) $$y = y^* + v,$$

(22) $$x = x^* + w,$$

where y^*, x^* are unobservable and y, x are observed variables. Further assume that x^*, u, v, and w are independently and normally distributed with zero means and variances $\sigma_{x^*}^2$, σ_u^2, σ_v^2, and σ_w^2, respectively, and that the covariances σ_{vw}, σ_{uv}, σ_{x^*u}, σ_{y^*v}, and σ_{x^*w} are all zero.

[11] See, for instance, Friend and Taubman (1964).

Under these assumptions, the asymptotic bias of the OLS estimator for α is the familiar expression[12]:

$$\bar{B}(\alpha_0) = -\alpha(\sigma_w^2/\sigma_0^2), \tag{23}$$

where σ_0^2 is the variance of x.

After some tedious but nonessential derivations, the asymptotic variance of α_0 can also be shown as

$$\bar{V}(\alpha_0) = \frac{\sigma_u^2}{T\sigma_0^2} + \frac{1}{T}\left(\frac{\alpha^2 \sigma_w^2 \sigma_{x*}^2 + \sigma_v^2 \sigma_0^2}{\sigma_0^4}\right), \tag{24}$$

where T is the sample size. The asymptotic MSE of α_0, $\overline{\text{MSE}}(\alpha_0)$, is $\bar{B}(\alpha_0)^2 + \bar{V}(\alpha_0)$.

Clearly, if all variable were observed without measurement error, i.e., $\sigma_v^2 = \sigma_w^2 = 0$, $\overline{\text{MSE}}(\alpha_0)$ would have been $\sigma_u^2/T\sigma_0^2$. Thus, the asymptotic bias, $\bar{B}(b_0)$, and the second term of the right hand side of (24) reflect the net addition to $\overline{\text{MSE}}(\alpha_0)$ due to the presence of measurement errors.

Under the ideal but also extreme assumption that measurement errors would be completely offsetting within calendar time so that variables aggregated over time are observed without measurement error, the OLS estimator of α in the temporally aggregated model, say α_1, would then be unbiased and

$$\overline{\text{MSE}}(\alpha_1) = \sigma_u^2/np\sigma_1^2, \tag{25}$$

where σ_1^2 is the variance of the observed independent variable in this aggregated model, n is the number of time periods being aggregated, and $p = T/n$.

After subtracting $\overline{\text{MSE}}(\alpha_0)$ from $\overline{\text{MSE}}(\alpha_1)$, the total effect of temporal aggregation is

$$\left(\frac{\sigma_u^2}{np\sigma_1^2} - \frac{\sigma_u^2}{T\sigma_0^2}\right) - \left[\frac{1}{T}\left(\frac{\alpha^2 \sigma_w^2 \sigma_{x*}^2 + \sigma_v^2 \sigma_0^2}{\sigma_0^4}\right) + \alpha^2 \frac{\sigma_w^4}{\sigma_0^4}\right]. \tag{26}$$

The first term in (26) is positive as demonstrated before (see Section IV). Thus, if this term is large enough to offset the negative contribution of the second term which is attributable to measurement error, temporal aggregation would still reduce the efficiency of forecasting even if measurement errors have been completely eliminated as a result.

---

[12] In this connection, an interesting result in the literature should be noted. For the errors-in-variable model considered here, the OLS predicator of $E(y/x)$ would still be asymptotically consistent even if the OLS estimator of α is not (Johnston, 1963, Chapter 6). Nevertheless, the OLS predicator of y is still asymptotically biased because plim $\hat{y} - y =$ plim $(\alpha_0 - \alpha)x + \alpha w - u - v \neq 0$.

VI. Empirical Tests

In order to examine realistic in contrast to theoretical consequences of temporal aggregation with econometric models, empirical tests should be run in a manner that standardizes for specification, estimation techniques, sample period, data sources, and other characteristics while varying only temporal periodicity. Ideally, a large number of models should be examined within this framework so as to ascertain average effects and establish confidence bounds about them. Such extensive testing was not possible for this paper.

However, a series of tests was conducted with an econometric model that has been employed extensively for forecasting of monetary variables and policy analyses, namely, the monthly U.S. money market model estimated by the Board of Governors of the Federal Reserve System. The unpublished specification used here, which is based on an earlier, published version was kindly provided by the Board's staff.[13] The model was re-estimated using data that also were furnished (see Table 1). Estimated coefficients in most instances were nearly identical to those supplied by the Federal Reserve. Differences in parameter estimates can be accounted for by subsequent revisions of data on money stocks and reserves since the Fed's estimates were made.

The model primarily determines money stocks and several interest rates. It contains twelve stochastic equations and three identities. There are four money demand stochastic equations: demand deposits (DDMS), currency (CUR), certificate of deposits (QCD), and time and savings deposits other than large certificates of deposit (OTS). The combination of the first two assets is commonly known as M1, that of the first three as M2, and of all four assets as M4. The money demand equations are specified as log-linear functions of own rates of interest, the interest rates of alternative assets, and personal income. The commercial paper rate (RCP) is used to represent alternative rate of return in all money demand equations.

The key interest rate in the model is the federal fund rate (RFF), which is jointly determined with bank borrowings of reserve (BOR). In particular, the model is seen to have a supply equation for borrowed reserves which can be obtained by consolidating three identities: required reserves (RR), total reserves (TR), and borrowings (BOR). When this supply equation is combined with the demand equation for borrowings, both the federal fund rate

---

[13] The unpublished specification and data were made available by Helen T. Farr, who on several occasions provided helpful guidance about the information. The latest version of the Fed's models differs from that described herein and from the earlier published version described in Thomson et al. (1975).

TABLE 1
DATA[a]

	Borrowings (BOR)	Currency Component (CUR)	Demand Deposit (DDMS)	Excess Reserves (EX)	CUR + DDMS = M1	M1 + OTS = M2	M2 + QCD = M4
1972:2	109.3	53934.7	186997.0	166.0	240932.0	494376.0	529108.0
1972:3	389.0	55147.0	190739.0	197.7	245886.0	505558.0	544650.0
1972:4	737.7	56798.3	198906.0	283.0	255704.0	521226.0	564242.0
1973:1	1525.7	56998.3	200706.0	221.3	257705.0	533173.0	581987.0
1973:2	1801.7	58799.3	201573.0	192.7	260372.0	544127.0	602031.0
1973:3	1990.0	60040.3	203701.0	228.7	263741.0	552144.0	618351.0
1973:4	1389.0	61517.3	209925.0	260.3	271443.0	566962.0	631938.0
1974:1	1185.3	62052.7	210530.0	160.0	272582.0	580667.0	646847.0
1974:2	2444.0	64143.3	211065.0	180.0	275208.0	591981.0	668176.0
1974:3	3306.0	65602.0	212206.0	177.0	277808.0	598351.0	684560.0
1974:4	1264.0	67782.3	217428.0	194.3	285210.0	610352.0	699122.0
1975:1	217.0	68136.3	214367.0	180.3	282504.0	619138.0	708865.0
1975:2	134.3	70091.3	216452.0	171.3	286543.0	635497.0	719569.0
1975:3	303.0	71971.3	219319.0	191.3	291291.0	648181.0	729889.0
1975:4	126.7	73836.6	223815.0	252.0	297652.0	660897.0	744241.0
1976:1	71.0	74290.3	222126.0	227.3	296416.0	677441.0	751867.0
1976:2	95.0	77046.0	224512.0	193.0	301558.0	696434.0	765059.0
1976:3	98.3	78848.6	225740.0	214.0	304588.0	708506.0	775312.0
1976:4	73.0	80783.6	233529.0	250.0	314313.0	732721.0	796500.0
1977:1	81.0	80960.3	233052.0	226.3	314013.0	751542.0	813290.0
1977:2	180.3	83498.6	236269.0	187.0	319767.0	770220.0	831641.0

(*continued*)

TABLE 1 (continued)

	Time & Savings Deposits (OTS)	Large CDs (QCD)	Required Reserves (RR)	Total Reserves (TR)	Time Deposits Commercial Banks (TTSC)	Unborrowed Reserves (UBR)	Personal Income (PI)
1972:2	253444.0	34731.7	32488.7	32654.7	288176.0	32545.3	927233.0
1972:3	259672.0	39091.3	32866.7	33064.3	298763.0	32675.3	948000.0
1972:4	265522.0	43016.0	32047.3	32330.3	308538.0	31592.7	982600.0
1973:1	275468.0	48813.7	31940.0	32161.3	324282.0	30635.7	1011733.0
1973:2	283755.0	57903.7	32123.7	32316.3	341659.0	30514.7	1038200.0
1973:3	288403.0	66206.6	33505.0	33733.7	354609.0	31743.7	1064300.0
1973:4	295520.0	64975.3	34678.7	34939.0	360495.0	33550.0	1095500.0
1974:1	308084.0	66180.0	35420.3	35580.3	374264.0	34395.0	1110266.0
1974:2	316773.0	76194.6	36118.3	36298.3	392968.0	33854.3	1140533.0
1974:3	320543.0	86209.3	36966.7	37143.7	406753.0	33837.3	1174266.0
1974:4	325141.0	88770.6	36642.7	36837.0	413912.0	35573.0	1194633.0
1975:1	336634.0	89727.3	35799.3	35979.7	426362.0	35762.7	1205100.0
1975:2	348954.0	84071.6	34646.0	34817.3	433026.0	34683.0	1234400.0
1975:3	356890.0	81707.6	34466.0	34657.3	438598.0	34354.3	1269666.0
1975:4	363245.0	83344.0	34481.3	34733.3	446589.0	34606.7	1304066.0
1976:1	381025.0	74426.3	34276.0	34503.3	455451.0	34432.3	1338033.0
1976:2	394875.0	68625.3	33823.3	34016.3	463501.0	33921.3	1366700.0
1976:3	403918.0	66805.3	33870.7	34084.7	470723.0	33986.3	1393900.0
1976:4	418408.0	63778.7	34504.0	34754.0	482187.0	34681.0	1432166.0
1977:1	437530.0	61748.0	34634.0	34860.3	499278.0	34779.3	1476800.0
1977:2	450453.0	61421.7	34451.3	34638.3	511874.0	34458.0	1520100.0

TABLE 1 (*continued*)

	Prime 90 day CD Rate (CD3)	Secondary CD Rate (RCDS)	Commercial Paper Rate (RCP)	Federal Funds Rate (RFF)	Time Deposit Rate (ROTS)	Treasury Bill Rate (R90)	Discount Rate (RDIS)
1972:2	4.43	4.54	4.20	4.29	4.73	3.77	4.50
1972:3	4.84	4.94	4.55	4.71	4.74	4.22	4.50
1972:4	5.22	5.32	4.97	5.16	4.76	4.85	4.50
1973:1	6.26	6.52	5.99	6.49	4.79	5.69	5.11
1973:2	7.31	7.61	7.23	7.77	4.84	6.59	5.93
1973:3	10.03	10.28	9.57	10.45	5.12	8.32	7.25
1973:4	9.04	9.21	8.90	9.98	5.31	7.50	7.50
1974:1	8.45	8.67	8.25	9.34	5.35	7.58	7.50
1974:2	10.52	11.08	9.76	11.07	5.38	8.17	7.87
1974:3	11.71	11.99	10.43	12.11	5.41	8.32	8.00
1974:4	8.96	9.40	9.00	9.36	5.44	7.34	7.93
1975:1	6.58	6.62	6.47	6.34	5.47	5.82	6.84
1975:2	5.72	6.00	5.49	5.38	5.49	5.36	6.12
1975:3	6.56	6.79	6.23	6.13	5.52	6.31	6.00
1975:4	6.10	6.21	5.62	5.44	5.54	5.67	6.00
1976:1	5.10	5.23	4.83	4.81	5.54	4.94	5.60
1976:2	5.33	5.54	5.10	5.17	5.54	5.14	5.50
1976:3	5.32	5.38	5.06	5.28	5.53	5.16	5.50
1976:4	4.83	4.90	4.66	4.90	5.53	4.71	5.39
1977:1	4.70	4.83	4.57	4.68	5.52	4.62	5.25
1977:2	5.06	5.21	4.95	5.13	5.52	4.82	5.25

[a] Personal income, reserves and various measures of money supply are in millions of dollars. Interest rates are percent per annum.

and borrowings are simultaneously obtained. All other endogenous interest rates in the model are either directly or indirectly tied to the federal funds rate.

The major exogenous, financial policy variables are unborrowed reserves (UBR), discount rate (RDIS), and various required reserve ratios. They exert their influences on interest rates and money stock through the supply equation for borrowings. Personal income is also exogenous, and expenditure and other product account variables are not included. Thus, except to the extent that simultaneous equation techniques are employed in estimation or product account impacts are collinear with the specified explanatory factors, the model may be said to have a vertical IS curve. This together with the LM curve in the model determines the monetary magnitudes.

Following the Fed's procedure, the model was estimated for the most part by ordinary least squares with Cochrane–Orcutt autoregressive error adjustments. Two types of lag distribution are used in the model: polynomial and geometric. A typical stochastic equation has either one of the following two forms[14]:

$$y_t = \sum_{i=0}^{p-1} a_i x_{t-i} + \rho u_{t-1} + \varepsilon_t, \tag{27a}$$

$$y_t = a x_t + b y_{t-1} + \rho u_{t-1} + \varepsilon_t, \tag{27b}$$

where X_t represents an independent variable, u_t is a disturbance term with a first-order Markov process, and ε_t is a random error term.

The theoretical analysis provided in the previous section is only meant to be heuristic because its underlying assumptions do not satisfy real world situations. In reality, as is argued in Section II, the decision periods of various economic agents in an economy are likely to be different rather than common, which would cast doubt on the existence of a "true" underlying model. Also, economic forecasts are usually made from a dynamic simultaneous equation model rather than from a set of independent single equations and, therefore, the problem of error accumulation across time periods as well as equations must be taken into account. Thus, from a practical point of view, it may be more interesting to compare the forecasting performance of Fed's monthly model with the model which might have been estimated with quarterly data than with its "logically implied" quarterly model which can be obtained by strictly aggregating (27a) or (27b) over time. In this spirit, the

---

[14] Either equation (27a) or (27b) is not exactly the same model as (3) because of the presence of lagged variables.

following quarterly models analogous to (27a) and (27b) are estimated:

(27a')
$$Y_t = \sum_{i=0}^{q-1} A_i X_{t-i} + PU_{t-1} + E_t,$$

(27b')
$$Y_t = AX_t + BY_{t-1} + PU_{t-1} + E_t,$$

where Y_t and X_t are quarterly aggregates of $y(t)$ and $x(y)$, respectively, U_t is a disturbance term with first-order Markov process, E_t is a random error term, q is an integer and equal to $p/3$.

The symbols and estimates for the monthly and quarterly models are shown in Tables 2 and 3. The parameter estimates of the monthly model are generally more significant than those obtained from the quarterly model, judged by t and overall equation statistics. In certain cases, the quarterly estimates have incorrect signs. These results may buttress the theoretical proposition that monthly estimates are less biased and more efficient than quarterly estimates of the same model.

The estimated long-run income elasticities of demand for money from the monthly model for demand deposits, currency, certificate of deposits, and other time and savings deposits are, respectively, 0.72, 0.76, 2.77, and 0.79. The respective estimates from the quarterly model are 0.66, 0.76, 2.80, and 0.84.

The estimated long-run interest elasticities are generally statistically significant but their magnitudes are small.[15] For instance, the estimated elasticities with respect to commercial paper rates (RCP) in the monthly money demand equations are -0.03 for demand deposits, -0.01 for currency, -0.03 for CDs, and -0.24 for other time and savings deposits. The quarterly estimates are, respectively, -0.04, -0.01, 0.12, and -0.18. In general, while there are differences between the estimated long-run elasticities or propensities across the monthly and quarterly models, these are very small in many equations. The discrepancies may reflect, among other things, the limited number of sample observations used in estimation. To the extent that long-run elasticities or propensities are different in both models, this could cause divergences of long-run multipliers.

A comparison of estimated mean lags of the monthly relationships with those of the quarterly relationships is shown in Table 4. In general, mean lags are estimated to be smaller in the quarterly model than in the monthly model for the same variable. Under certain assumptions, Engle and Liu (1972) have shown that, for a geometric distributed lag model, time aggregation would increase mean lags when serial correlation is negative while it would decrease mean lags if serial correlation is positive. This is verified here

---

[15] Interest rate variables are not significant in the QCD equation.

TABLE 2

FEDERAL RESERVE MONEY MARKET MODEL: SYMBOLS

	Variables[a]
BOR	Borrowings, n.s.a.
CD3	"Most often quoted rate" for prime 90-day CD's
CUR	Currency component of M1, n.s.a.
DDMS	Demand deposit component of M1, n.s.a.
DMC^b	Ratio of Country Bank net demand posits to M1, all n.s.a.
$DMRC^b$	Ratio of Reserve City net demand deposits to M1, all n.s.a.
EX	Excess reserves, n.s.a.
$K1^b$	Required reserve ratio against Reserve City demand deposits
$K2^b$	Required reserve ratio against Country demand deposits
$K3^b$	Required reserve ratio against CD's
$K4^b$	Required reserve ratio against time deposits rather than CD's
OTS	Time and savings deposits other than CD's, n.s.a.
PI^b	Personal income, s.a.
QCD	Quantity of large negotiable CD's, n.s.a.
$Q2^b$	Regulation Q ceiling on single maturity time deposits (< $10,00; > 2 yrs.)
RCDS	Secondary CD rate, 90 days
RCP	30–59 day prime commercial paper rate
$RDIS^b$	Discount rate
RFF	Federal funds rate
ROTS	Weighted average rate on time and savings deposits of < $100,000
RR	Required reserves
$RRND^b$	Required reserves against non-deposit items
R90	90-day Treasury bill rate
SFC^b	Seasonal factor for CUR
$SFDD^b$	Seasonal factor for DDMS
$SFTD^b$	Seasonal factor for OTS
TR	Total reserves, n.s.a.
TTSC	Total time and savings at all commercial banks, n.s.a.
UBR^b	Unborrowed reserves, n.s.a.

	Statistical Parameters
ρ	First-order autoregression coefficient
SE	Standard error of estimate
$\bar{R}^2$	Coefficient of determination corrected for degrees of freedom
DW	Durbin–Watson coefficient

[a] n.s.a. denotes not seasonally adjusted. s.a. denotes seasonally adjusted.
[b] Exogenous variable.

TABLE 3

FEDERAL RESERVE MONEY MARKET MODEL: MONTHLY AND QUARTERLY ESTIMATES[a]

30–59 Day Prime Commercial Paper Rate (First Stage); Sample Period: October 1967–December 1976; $\Delta \ln RCP_t = a\, \Delta \ln PI_t + b\, \Delta \ln RFF_t + c\, \Delta \ln M1_t$, Intercept

Coefficients

Lag Distributions

		Sum	t	$t-1$	$t-2$	$t-3$	$t-4$	$t-5$	$t-6$	$t-7$	$t-8$	$t-9$	$t-10$	$t-11$
a	M	10.59	0.0679	0.4527	0.7666	1.0095	1.1814	1.2822	1.3121	1.2709	1.1587	0.9755	0.7214	0.3962
		(1.82)	(0.07)	(0.63)	(1.22)	(1.65)	(1.87)	(1.95)	(1.96)	(1.95)	(1.92)	(1.90)	(1.88)	(1.86)
	Q	12.65	1.6295	3.7958	4.2464	2.9811								
		(1.36)	(0.41)	(1.36)	(1.35)	(1.24)								

		Sum	t	$t-1$	$t-2$	$t-3$	$t-4$	$t-5$	$t-6$	$t-7$				
b	M	0.2116	0.2721	0.1536	0.0593	−0.0107	−0.0568	−0.0788	−0.0766	−0.0503				
		(1.30)	(5.56)	(4.82)	(2.33)	(0.39)	(1.93)	(2.72)	(3.17)	(3.45)				
	Q	0.0218	0.1911	−0.0528	−0.1165									
		(0.07)	(1.19)	(0.48)	(1.15)									

		Sum	t	$t-1$										
c	M	9.8438	8.2017	1.6421										
		(4.39)	(4.39)	(0.84)										
	Q		10.0204											
			(1.89)											

Intercept

		SE	$\bar{R}^2$	DW
M	−0.1254	0.0587	0.41	1.72
	(2.97)			
Q	−0.4215	0.1450	0.14	1.87
	(2.14)			

(continued)

TABLE 3 (continued)

Demand Deposits, Sample period: July 1968–December 1973; $\Delta\text{Ln}(\text{DDMS}/\text{SFDD})_t = a\,\text{LnROTS}_t + b\,\Delta\text{LnRCP}_t + c\,\Delta\text{LnPI} + \rho U_{t-1}$

Coefficients   Lag Distributions

		t	$t-1$	$t-2$	$t-3$	$t-4$	$t-5$	$t-6$	$t-7$
a	M	−0.1107							
		(2.24)							
	Q	0.0211							
		(0.31)							
b		Sum							
	M	−0.0309	−0.0044	−0.0049	−0.0046	−0.0042	−0.0034	−0.0025	−0.0013
		(2.26)	(1.86)	(2.25)	(2.15)	(1.88)	(1.65)	(1.48)	(1.35)
	Q	−0.0417	−0.1778	−0.1494	−0.0915				
		(2.81)	(2.94)	(2.49)	(1.81)				
c		Sum	t	$t-1$	$t-2$	$t-3$	$t-4$	$t-5$	$t-6$
	M	0.7235	0.1438	0.1391	0.1292	0.1139	0.0933	0.0675	0.0364
		(9.53)	(2.05)	(4.38)	(9.53)	(4.62)	(2.84)	(2.12)	(1.73)
	Q	0.6619	0.3837	0.2030	0.0751				
		(6.80)	(4.02)	(4.31)	(1.17)				
ρ	M	0.2311							
		(1.90)							
	Q	0.5504							
		(3.32)							

		SE	$\bar{R}^2$	DW
	M	0.0033	0.58	1.97
	Q	0.0042	0.71	1.69

Currency, Sample period: January 1969–December 1973; $\text{Ln}(\text{CUR}/\text{SFC})_t = a\,\text{LnPI}_t + b\,\text{RCP}_t + \rho U_{t-1}$

Coefficients

Lag Distributions

		Sum	t	$t-1$	$t-2$	$t-3$	$t-4$	$t-5$	$t-6$	$t-7$	$t-8$	$t-9$	$t-10$	$t-11$
a	M	0.7960	0.0864	0.0882	0.0884	0.0869	0.0838	0.0790	0.0726	0.0646	0.0550	0.0437	0.0307	0.0162
		(8.16)	(2.04)	(3.13)	(5.53)	(15.2)	(31.8)	(8.74)	(5.37)	(4.01)	(3.28)	(2.83)	(2.51)	(2.29)
	Q	0.7954	0.3515	0.2386	0.1423	0.0628								
		(7.29)	(3.35)	(7.29)	(2.70)	(1.19)								
b	M	−0.0089	−0.0029	−0.0026	−0.0020	−0.0011								
		(2.02)	(1.14)	(2.02)	(1.13)	(0.77)								
	Q	−0.0102	−0.0033	−0.0069										
		(1.81)	(0.73)	(1.53)										
ρ	M	0.9618						SE	$\bar{R}^2$	DW				
		(33.79)						M 0.0019	0.99	2.06				
	Q	0.8898						Q 0.0030	0.99	1.26				
		(10.1)												

Other Time and Savings Deposits, Sample period: January 1970–December 1974; $\text{Ln}(\text{OTS}/\text{SFTD})_t = a\,\text{LnROTS}_t + b\,\text{LnRCP}_t + c\,\text{LnPI}_t + d\,\text{Ln}(\text{OTS}/\text{SFTD})_{t-1} + \rho U_{t-1}$

Coefficients

	a	b	c	d	ρ
M	0.0650	−0.0117	0.0385	0.9514	0.6378
	(2.56)	(3.86)	(3.30)	(70.01)	(7.35)
Q	0.1192	−0.0238	0.1143	0.8639	0.4436
	(1.88)	(3.12)	(3.71)	(24.5)	(4.35)

	SE	$\bar{R}^2$	DW
M	0.0022	0.99	1.99
Q	0.0049	0.99	2.46

(continued)

TABLE 3 (continued)

Secondary CD Rate, Sample period: January 1969–December 1974; RCDS$_t$ = a RCP$_t$ + b R90$_t$ + ρU$_{t-1}$

Coefficients

	a	b	ρ	SE	$\bar{R}^2$	DW
M	0.8844	0.2146	0.7309	0.2424	0.98	1.94
	(11.48)	(2.44)	(9.13)			
Q	1.2489	−0.2034	0.3085	0.2773	0.99	1.59
	(7.08)	(1.00)	(1.48)			

Treasury Bill Rate, Sample period: January 1969–December 1974; R90$_t$ = a RCP$_t$ + b RCDS$_t$ + Intercept + ρU$_{t-1}$

Coefficients

	a	b	Intercept	ρ	SE	$\bar{R}^2$	DW
M	0.4570	0.2640	0.9979	0.5288	0.2952	0.87	2.03
	(2.94)	(1.89)	(4.01)	(5.29)			
Q	0.8493	−0.0938	0.9134	0.3732	0.2751	0.95	1.88
	(4.30)	(0.53)	(3.75)	(1.92)			

Excess Reserve, Sample period: January 1969–December 1974; EX$_t$ = a(DDMS + TTSC − RR)$_t$ + b EX$_{t-1}$ + ρU$_{t-}$

Coefficients

	a	b	ρ	SE	$\bar{R}^2$	DW
M	0.0009	0.7854	−0.3529	47.06	0.97	2.13
	(3.06)	(11.77)	(3.29)			
Q	0.00009	0.7746	−0.0882	36.01	0.97	1.99
	(1.66)	(6.2)	(0.43)			

Rate on Other Time and Savings Deposits, Sample period: January 1969–December 1974; ROTS = a R90 + b Q2 + Intercept + ρU_{t-1}

Coefficients					Lag Distributions					
		Sum	t	$t-1$	$t-2$	$t-3$	$t-4$	$t-5$	$t-6$	$t-7$
a	M	0.0428	0.0102	0.0095	0.0084	0.0069	0.0049	0.0026		
		(7.58)	(2.05)	(4.85)	(6.20)	(3.02)	(2.01)	(1.55)		
	Q	0.0369	0.0011	0.0358						
		(4.97)	(0.19)	(6.10)						
b	M	0.6619	0.1862	0.14828	0.1145	0.0849	0.0595	0.0383	0.0213	0.0085
		(33.13)	(9.62)	(14.2)	(27.8)	(21.6)	(9.12)	(4.98)	(3.03)	(1.91)
	Q	0.5382	0.3016	0.1686	0.0680					
		(13.7)	(13.6)	(10.3)	(4.23)					

		Intercept	ρ	SE	$\bar{R}^2$	DW
	M	0.7510	0.5456	0.0277	0.96	2.34
		(6.98)	(4.98)			
	Q	2.2635	0.9881	0.0191	0.94	2.46
		(3.92)	(1.94)			

Commercial Paper Rate, Sample period: July 1969–December 1974; RCP$_t$ = a RFF$_t$ + b R90$_t$ + c CD3$_t$ + ρU_{t-1}

Coefficients						Lag Distributions					
		Sum	t	$t-1$	$t-2$	b	c	ρ	SE	$\bar{R}^2$	DW
a	M	0.3230	0.1420	0.1141	0.0668	0.3100	0.3798	0.7316	0.2276	0.98	2.01
		(4.16)	(1.77)	(4.15)	(1.77)	(4.20)	(4.40)	(9.94)			
	Q		0.1243			0.6288	0.3207	0.6555	0.2396	0.99	2.23
			(0.71)			(4.96)	(1.98)	(4.04)			

(continued)

TABLE 3 (continued)

Primary CD Rate, Sample period: December 1970–December 1974; $\Delta CD3_t = a\,\Delta R90_t + b\,\Delta RCP_t + \rho U_{t-1}$

Coefficients

	a	b	ρ	SE	$\bar{R}^2$	DW
M	0.1179	1.0827	−0.1654	0.2462	0.87	1.86
	(1.20)	(11.65)	(1.30)			
Q	0.2751	1.3598	0.0656	0.3839	0.92	1.75
	(0.75)	(5.08)	(0.26)			

Borrowing, Sample period: July 1969–December 1974; $[BOR/(DDMS + TTSC - RR)]_t = a\,R90_t + b\,RDIS_t + c\,RFF_t + \text{Intercept} + \rho U_{t-1}$

Coefficients

Lag Distributions

		Sum	t	$t-1$	$t-2$	$t-3$	$t-4$	Intercept	ρ
a	M	0.0002	0.0001	0.00009				0.0016	0.6923
		(0.89)	(0.73)	(0.60)				(1.57)	(7.66)
	Q		0.00085					0.0015	0.3075
			(0.19)					(1.26)	(1.45)
b	M	−0.0011	−0.00055	−0.00034	−0.00019	−0.00007	−0.00001		
		(3.74)	(1.38)	(2.65)	(2.08)	(0.51)	(0.12)		
	Q	−0.0011	−0.0012	0.00007					
		(3.06)	(1.72)	(0.16)					
c	M	0.00088	0.0005	0.00034					
		(4.63)	(3.50)	(2.25)					
	Q		0.00098						
			(3.39)						

	SE	$\bar{R}^2$	DW
M	0.0004	0.59	1.92
Q	0.0005	0.78	1.82

Certificate of Deposits, Sample period: July 1970–December 1974; $\text{LnQCD}_t = a \, \text{LnRCP}_t + b \, \text{LnCD3}_t + c \, \text{LnPI}_t + d \, \text{LnQCD}_{t-1} + \text{Intercept} + \rho U_{t-1}$

Coefficients

	a	b	c	d	Intercept	ρ
M	−0.0087	0.0995	1.0029	0.6412	−10.13	0.4737
	(0.09)	(0.98)	(3.46)	(7.59)	(3.24)	(4.08)
Q	0.1240	0.0647	2.2923	0.1820	−23.18	0.1529
	(0.37)	(0.19)	(3.28)	(0.93)	(3.04)	(1.32)

	SE	$\bar{R}^2$	DW
M	0.0233	0.99	1.84
Q	0.0391	0.98	2.17

Identities

Required Reserves

$RR_t = RRND_t + K1_t \times DMRC_t \times [0.5(DDMS + CUR)_t + 0.5(DDMS + CUR)_{t-1}] + K2_t \times DMC_t \times [0.5(DDMS + CUR)_t] + K2_t \times DMC_t \times [0.5(DDMS + CUR)_t + 0.5(DDMS + CUR)_{t-1}] + K3_t \times (0.5 \times QCD_t \times QCD_{t-1}) + K4_t \times (0.5 \times OTS_t + 0.5 \times OTS_{t-1})$

Total Reserves

$TR_t = EX_t + RR_t$

Borrowings

$BOR_t = TR_t − UBR_t$

---

[a] M, monthly; Q, quarterly; t statistics in parentheses.

TABLE 4

MEAN LAGS (MONTHS)[a]

Equation	Variables		Personal Income PI		Commercial Paper Rate RCP		Treasury Bill Rate R90		Discount Rate RDIS		Federal Fund Rate RFF		Single Maturity Time Deposits Q2	
			M	Q	M	Q	M	Q	M	Q	M	Q	M	Q
1. Polynomial distribution lag distributions														
Demand Deposits	DDMS		2.30	1.59	2.85	2.40								
Currency	CUR		4.35	2.67	1.16	2.04								
Borrowings	BOR						0.45	0.00	0.87	0.18	0.39	0.00		
Time Deposit Rate	ROTS						1.88	2.85					1.88	1.71
Commercial Paper Rate											0.77	0.00		
2. Geometric lag distributions														
Time & Savings Deposits	OTS		19.57	19.05										
Excess Reserves	EX		3.66	10.32										
Large CDs	QCD		1.79	0.66										

[a] M, monthly models; Q, quarterly models.

by three equations with geometric lags: OTS, EX, QCD. However, it seems that the sign of serial correlation bears no systematic relationship with the change in mean lag as a result of time aggregation for the equations with polynomial distributed lags.

VII. Error Analysis

The theoretical propositions presented above are cast in a purely static, single-equation framework. But, in any realistic forecasting situation, models must be solved as dynamic complete systems.

In order to ascertain empirically the relative short-term forecasting performance of the monthly and quarterly models, they were solved dynamically, starting at successive initial points, from one through twelve months for the monthly model and from one through four quarters for the quarterly model. Long-run dynamic simulations with both models also were run within and outside sample periods. The quarterly forecasts derived from the monthly model were obtained by aggregating monthly forecasts into quarterly. Average absolute percentage errors of the quarterly forecasts (AAPE) for both models were calculated according to the formula

$$\text{AAPE} = 100 \sum_i \left| \frac{P - A}{A} \right|_i \Big/ \text{number of forecasts,}$$

where P and A are, respectively, the predicted and actual quarterly observations.

The AAPEs for the monthly and quarterly models are recorded, respectively, in Tables 5 and 6. With few exceptions, errors generally increase as the forecasting horizon is lengthened. This is due to the propagation of dynamic simulation errors through lagged endogenous variables in the system. As for the relative size of within-sample and outside-sample simulation errors, one would usually expect the latter to be larger than the former for an equivalent length of forecasting horizon. This, however, is not true for all variables, in part because the post-sample simulation period is much shorter than that of the within-sample.[16] Still, it can be seen that error buildup

---

[16] A method of standardizing for different lengths of within-sample and outside-sample periods would be to divide average absolute percentage errors in complete system solutions by actual coefficients of variation of respective variables over the respective sample periods. However, this technique was not applied in this paper. The within-sample simulation period is from October 1970 to December 1973, covering thirteen quarters; the post-sample simulation period is from January 1974 through September 1975, encompassing seven quarters. A longer post-sample simulation period, January 1974 to June 1977, did not yield meaningful comparison because errors in dynamic simulations of both the monthly model and quarterly models started to expand rapidly following the third-quarter of 1975.

TABLE 5

One- To Four-Quarter and Long-Run Prediction Errors Derived from the Monthly Model Average Absolute Percentage Error $(AAPE_m)^a$

Prediction Horizon (Numbers of solutions) Variables		Simulation Period									
		Within sample 1970:4–1973:4					Outside sample 1974:1–1975:3				
		1 (13)	2 (12)	3 (11)	4 (10)	Long Run (1)	1 (7)	2 (6)	3 (5)	4 (4)	Long Run (1)
Prime 90-day CD rate	CD3	9.6	12.0	14.7	17.0	32.5	6.0	8.9	12.9	15.2	7.6
Currency	CUR	0.6	0.8	0.8	1.0	1.3	0.5	0.8	1.2	1.8	1.7
Demand deposit	DDMS	0.6	1.0	1.1	0.8	1.0	0.5	1.4	2.6	3.7	2.7
Excess reserves	EX	10.0	9.9	9.0	8.8	9.8	29.1	37.6	43.4	45.8	50.1
Time & savings deposits	OTS	0.4	0.8	0.9	1.3	1.9	0.3	0.4	0.5	0.6	0.9
Large CDs	QCD	2.8	3.9	3.3	4.0	11.4	2.9	4.5	5.3	8.2	4.5
Secondary CD rate	RCDS	8.6	9.7	10.3	10.3	11.4	6.8	7.8	11.4	15.2	10.7
Commercial paper rate	RCP	8.9	10.2	11.4	11.1	12.3	9.6	9.5	12.1	14.2	12.9
Federal funds rate	RFF	7.2	13.7	11.6	7.1	7.9	6.7	9.6	14.6	19.5	17.6
Time deposit rate	ROTS	0.7	0.9	1.0	1.0	0.9	1.6	2.3	2.4	2.6	1.9
Treasury Bill rate	R90	6.8	7.4	8.6	9.3	9.6	7.7	8.5	11.2	7.5	8.6
Borrowed reserves	BOR	26.1	98.9	102.6	73.4	94.9	72.2	143.3	246.3	386.5	255.2
Require reserves	RR	0.3	0.6	0.6	0.6	0.5	0.4	0.9	1.5	2.3	1.6
Total reserves	TR	0.3	0.6	0.7	0.6	0.5	0.6	1.0	1.8	2.5	1.9
Time deposits, commercial banks	TTSC	0.6	0.8	0.7	0.9	0.6	0.6	0.5	0.5	1.2	0.4

[a] Figures in parentheses refer to the number of forecasted periods.

TABLE 6

ONE- TO FOUR-QUARTER AND LONG-RUN PREDICTION ERRORS DERIVED FROM THE QUARTERLY MODEL AVERAGE ABSOLUTE PERCENTAGE ERRORS $(AAPE_q)$[a]

Prediction Horizon (Numbers of solutions)		Simulation Period									
		Within sample 1970:4–1973:4					Outside sample 1974:1–1975:3				
Variables		1 (13)	2 (12)	3 (11)	4 (10)	Long Run (1)	1 (7)	2 (6)	3 (3)	4 (4)	Long Run (1)
Prime 90-day CD rate	CD3	9.7	9.8	15.4	18.0	53.1	6.5	9.1	16.6	19.3	6.2
Currency	CUR	0.4	0.4	0.4	0.8	1.0	0.7	1.1	1.6	2.2	2.0
Demand deposit	DDMS	1.0	1.9	1.8	1.2	1.3	0.7	1.6	2.1	3.0	1.9
Excess reserves	EX	12.1	10.9	12.1	9.6	11.7	15.9	20.5	26.0	28.9	42.6
Time & savings deposits	OTS	0.5	0.4	0.7	0.8	2.7	0.2	0.2	0.3	0.5	0.3
Large CDs	QCD	3.2	4.1	3.2	4.5	9.9	4.2	3.8	5.7	9.6	4.8
Secondary CD rate	RCDS	8.1	8.6	12.8	14.1	24.7	4.4	6.8	12.6	17.1	3.5
Commercial paper rate	RCP	8.4	8.6	12.2	15.3	23.4	3.8	4.3	11.6	17.6	4.1
Federal funds rate	RFF	11.3	16.3	16.3	7.2	8.1	3.6	3.8	5.1	11.0	5.5
Time deposit rate	ROTS	1.0	1.3	1.0	1.2	0.8	0.7	1.2	1.9	2.6	2.3
Treasury Bill rate	R90	7.0	7.7	9.3	13.6	19.0	5.9	6.4	10.1	8.0	4.9
Borrowed reserves	BOR	93.1	115.7	93.4	103.0	87.8	19.3	40.7	137.4	258.6	106.6
Required reserves	RR	0.9	1.1	1.2	0.8	0.7	0.3	0.3	0.9	1.4	0.9
Total reserves	TR	0.9	1.1	1.2	0.8	0.8	0.3	0.3	0.9	1.5	0.9
Time deposits, commercial banks	TTSC	0.6	0.6	0.7	0.6	1.1	0.6	0.6	1.0	1.4	0.8

[a] Figures in parentheses refer to numbers of forecasted periods.

Relative Monthly to Quarterly Model 1 to 4 Quarter and Long-Run Prediction Errors $[(AAPE_m/AAPE_q - 1)100]$
Percentage Ratios of Average Absolute Percentage Errors[a]

Prediction Horizon (Number of solutions)		Within sample 1970:4–1973:3				Simulation Period Long Run (1)	Outside sample 1974:1–1975:3				Long Run (1)
Variables		1 (13)	2 (12)	3 (11)	4 (10)		1 (7)	2 (6)	3 (5)	4 (4)	
Prime 90-day CD rate	CD3	−1.3	22.6	−4.5	−5.6	−38.7	−7.0	−1.6	−22.3	−21.4	21.1
Currency	CUR	34.1	66.6	92.8	40.0	22.3	−27.0	−20.4	−24.9	−20.2	−17.1
Demand deposit	DDMS	−40.0	−44.3	−38.5	−36.1	−23.0	−29.0	−8.1	24.3	24.9	43.8
Excess reserves	EX	−17.3	−8.9	−26.0	−8.5	−15.9	15.9	20.5	26.0	28.9	42.6
Time & savings deposits	OTS	−8.2	83.3	32.8	72.3	−30.4	61.5	65.4	74.5	17.1	126.4
Large CDs	QCD	−10.6	−3.4	3.8	−9.6	15.3	−31.0	17.9	−7.8	−14.7	−6.5
Secondary CD rate	RCDS	6.5	13.1	−19.5	−26.9	−53.8	53.6	14.5	−9.5	−10.9	207.2
Commercial paper rate	RCP	6.1	18.6	−6.5	−27.4	−47.4	143.9	119.5	4.4	−19.1	211.7
Federal funds rate	RFF	−36.6	−15.9	−28.8	−1.0	−2.8	87.8	147.8	186.1	76.8	216.7
Time deposit rate	ROTS	−30.0	−28.4	−3.9	−14.8	11.6	127.5	89.8	27.2	−2.1	−15.7
Treasury Bill rate	R90	−3.1	2.2	−7.4	−31.4	−49.6	30.8	32.3	10.3	−6.0	74.9
Borrowed reserves	BOR	−71.9	−14.0	10.3	−28.0	9.1	273.5	252.4	79.2	49.4	139.2
Required reserves	RR	−66.6	−44.0	−48.3	−20.0	−29.5	19.1	157.8	70.1	59.2	70.9
Total reserves	TR	−68.1	−47.7	−44.1	−19.2	−32.4	71.1	182.6	83.7	67.4	100.8
Time deposits, commercial banks	TTSC	−90.2	42.3	0.0	55.3	−41.5	−12.2	−9.3	−40.5	−12.4	−44.6

[a] Figures in parentheses refer to number of forecasted periods.

is faster for the post-sample simulations: outside-sample simulation errors are increasingly larger compared with those of the within-sample as the forecasting horizon is lengthened.

In order to make a sharper comparison of the forecasting errors, we have also computed the percentage deviations of the AAPEs derived from the monthly model $AAPE_m$ from those derived from the quarterly model $AAPE_q$, i.e., $[(AAPE_m/AAPE_q) - 1]100$, which are reported in Table 7. Therein, with only a few exceptions, the within-sample simulation results favor the monthly model over the quarterly model. However, the superior forecasting performance of the monthly model is not carried over to the post-sample period. In this case the results are mixed: in general terms, the quarterly model has smaller errors on interest rates but larger errors on various measures of money supply. Thus, the experiment conducted here has failed to yield a clearcut picture regarding the relative forecasting performance of the monthly model versus the quarterly model. While this result is not inconsistent with theoretical expectations, it does suggest that more experiments along lines pursued here are necessary to reach more definitive conclusions regarding forecasting error effects of time aggregation.

VIII. Policy Responsiveness

Aside from examining individual equation estimation results (including goodness of fit, parameter magnitudes, and lag distributions) and overall complete system solution errors within and outside sample periods, judgments about effects of time aggregation depend critically on magnitudes and patterns of responsiveness to alternatives policy and other exogenous shifts in models' variables and parameters. Unusual or unreasonable responsiveness characteristics are grounds for questioning a model's basic validity (structure specification, data, and estimation) and for rejecting conclusions based on its simulations. Unfortunately, objective criteria and standards for judging responsiveness have not yet been devised so that conclusions in this arena normally are founded on a priori agreement with theory or the general body of available simulation studies. This poses dangers in that, to paraphrase Harberger (1967), for every set of data it always is possible to find a model that will fit them and, for every model or set of simulation results, a theory can always be devised to explain them. Despite this problem, simulations still are quite instructive.

Within the scope of this paper, only a limited set of sensitivity analyses could be conducted. These included changes in two monetary policy instruments, exogenous shifts in personal income of varying magnitudes, tests of asymmetries in responses to restrictive and stimulative policies, and alterations in initial starting dates for simulations.

Specifically, the simulations are:

A. Decreases and increases of unborrowed reserves of $0.5 billion.
B. Increases and reductions in discount rates of 50 basis points.
C. Reductions and increases of personal income of $15 billion and $10 billion.[17]

All changes are shifts sustained throughout simulation periods.

The policy simulations were conducted for:

1. 63 months or the 21 quarter interval, April 1972–June 1977 or 1972:2–1977:2; and
2. 39 months or the 13 quarter interval, April 1974–June 1977 or 1974:2–1977:2.

All monthly and quarterly model solutions are complete systems and fully dynamic, with the models generating their own lagged monthly and quarterly endogenous values, respectively, beyond the initial starting period. Actual data are used for exogenous variables other than those being shifted.

The periods selected were chosen so as to examine potential partial equilibrium monetary impacts (given other real magnitudes) of restrictive policy during the economy's growth prior to the 1973–1974 peak and of expansionary policy during the 1974–1975 recession. The simulations were extended in order to track longer-run effects if the policy shifts were maintained. Ideally, of course, such simulations should be conducted within the context of a model which provides for impacts on and feedbacks from the real sectors of the economy. Still, the partial system results are instructive.

A. RESTRICTIVE POLICIES

Multipliers and point elasticities from the monthly and quarterly models for the 1972:2–1977:2 period under a more restrictive monetary and fiscal policy stance (as, say, implemented through individual income tax increases and reflected in personal income reductions) are shown in Tables 8 and 9, respectively. Multipliers and elasticities are given from M1 and M2, M4, the commercial paper rate, 90-day government bill rate, and rate on large negotiable CDs.

Turning first to the unborrowed reserves reduction, it can be seen that multiplier and elasticity responses of money stocks and interest rates

---

[17] Multipliers for $10 billion change in personal income are virtually the same as those of $15 billion change and hence are not reported here.

TABLE 8

MONTHLY AND QUARTERLY MULTIPLIERS FOR PERIOD 1972:2–1977:2 RESTRICTIVE POLICIES[a,b]

Number of Quarters of Impact	Unborrowed Reserves Reduction		Discount Rate Increase		Personal Income Reduction		Unborrowed Reserves Reduction		Discount Rate Increase		Personal Income Reduction	
	M	Q	M	Q	M	Q	M	Q	M	Q	M	Q
	ΔM1/Policy Change						ΔM2/Policy Change					
1	1.67	1.89	−0.92	−1.00	0.00	0.00	2.79	3.13	−1.54	−1.66	0.00	0.01
2	2.17	2.15	−1.21	−1.16	−0.01	0.00	5.37	4.66	−3.00	−2.51	0.00	0.02
3	2.28[p]	2.17[p]	−1.32[p]	−1.21[p]	−0.02	−0.01	7.41	5.79	−4.23	−3.19	0.01	0.03
4	1.79	1.62	−1.06	−0.93	−0.02	−0.01	8.16	5.87	−4.73	−3.28	0.02	0.05
5	1.58	1.40	−0.96	−0.82	−0.02	−0.01	8.51	6.03	−5.00	−3.42	0.03	0.06
6	1.36	1.23	−0.84	−0.74	−0.02	−0.01	8.57	6.06	−5.09	−3.48	0.05	0.08
7	1.40	1.27	−0.90	−0.79	−0.02	−0.01	8.88	6.32	−5.36	−3.69	0.05	0.09
8	1.34	1.22	−0.89	−0.78	−0.02	−0.01	9.18[p]	6.50[p]	−5.64[p]	−3.87[p]	0.06	0.10
9	1.13	1.00	−0.76	−0.66	−0.02	−0.01	9.02	6.30	−5.62	−3.80	0.07	0.11
10	1.01[t]	0.90[t]	−0.70[t]	−0.61[t]	−0.02	−0.01	8.58[t]	6.07[t]	−5.41[t]	−3.72[t]	0.08[p]	0.12[p]
11	1.31	1.15	−0.94	−0.79	−0.03	−0.02	8.84	6.41	−5.72	−4.02	0.08	0.12
12	1.58	1.39	−1.16	−0.98	−0.03	−0.02	9.70	7.04	−6.45	−4.54	0.07	0.12[t]
13	1.65[p]	1.41[p]	−1.24[p]	−1.03[p]	−0.04	−0.02	10.53	7.43	−7.20	−4.92	0.07	0.12[p]
14	1.52	1.34	−1.17	−1.00	−0.04	−0.03	10.82	7.54	−7.56	−5.09	0.06	0.12
15	1.48	1.31	−1.19	−1.00	−0.04	−0.03	11.00	7.63[p]	−7.87	−5.27	0.06[t]	0.12[t]
16	1.34	1.18	−1.11	−0.94	−0.04	−0.03	11.01[p]	7.61	−8.04	−5.37	0.06	0.12
17	1.25	1.08	−1.06	−0.88	−0.04	−0.03	10.87	7.51	−8.10[p]	−5.41[p]	0.06	0.12
18	1.19	1.04	−1.03	−0.86	−0.04	−0.03	10.53	7.33	−7.99	−5.38	0.06[p]	0.12[p]
19	1.17	1.02	−1.04	−0.87	−0.05	−0.03	10.21	7.18	−7.90	−5.39	0.06	0.12
20	1.08	0.95	−1.00	−0.84	−0.05	−0.04	9.91	7.04	−7.82	−5.40	0.06	0.12
21	1.01	0.87	−0.97	−0.80	−0.06	−0.04	9.50	6.81	−7.65	−5.34	0.06	0.13

(continued)

TABLE 8 (continued)

Number of Quarters of Impact	Unborrowed Reserves Reduction		Discount Rate Increase		Personal Income Reduction		Unborrowed Reserves Reduction		Discount Rate Increase		Personal Income Reduction	
	M	Q	M	Q	M	Q	M	Q	M	Q	M	Q
	ΔM4/Policy Change						ΔRCP/Policy Change					
1	1.58	1.49	−0.88	−0.79	0.05	0.09	−0.97	−1.05	0.52	0.54	0.00	0.00
2	2.74	2.34	−1.55	−1.27	0.11	0.14	−1.43	−1.25	0.77	0.65	0.01	0.01
3	3.96	3.15	−2.28	−1.74	0.15	0.17	−1.64	−1.31	0.93	0.71	0.01	0.01
4	4.63	3.43	−2.68	−1.90	0.18	0.20	−1.75	−1.35	1.02	0.76	0.01	0.01
5	5.15	3.71	−2.99	−2.07	0.22	0.24	−1.76ᵖ	−1.37ᵖ	1.05	0.79	0.01	0.01
6	5.37	3.84	−3.14	−2.16	0.24	0.26	−1.72	−1.34	1.05	0.79	0.01	0.01
7	5.63	3.99	−3.33	−2.26	0.27	0.28	−1.68	−1.31	1.06ᵖ	0.80ᵖ	0.02	0.01
8	5.88ᵖ	4.16ᵖ	−3.50	−2.39ᵖ	0.28	0.30	−1.60	−1.26	1.04ᵗ	0.79ᵗ	0.02	0.01
9	5.85	4.09	−3.51ᵖ	−2.37	0.31	0.33	−1.62	−1.25	1.08	0.81	0.02	0.01
10	5.57	3.90	−3.36	−2.28ᵗ	0.33	0.35	−1.58	−1.24	1.09ᵖ	0.82ᵖ	0.02	0.01
11	5.47ᵗ	3.87ᵗ	−3.35ᵗ	−2.29	0.34	0.36	−1.51	−1.20	1.08	0.82	0.02	0.02
12	5.65	4.08	−3.52	−2.46	0.34	0.36	−1.46ᵗ	−1.16	1.06ᵗ	0.81ᵗ	0.02ᵖ	0.02ᵖ
13	5.91	4.22ᵖ	−3.77	−2.60	0.34	0.37	−1.47	−1.14	1.10	0.82	0.02	0.02
14	5.98	4.22	−3.88	−2.64	0.35	0.38	−1.48ᵖ	−1.13	1.13	0.83	0.02	0.02
15	6.06	4.20	−4.00	−2.67	0.36	0.40	−1.46	−1.12	1.16	0.85	0.02	0.01
16	6.11ᵖ	4.20	−4.08ᵖ	−2.70ᵖ	0.38	0.41	−1.43	−1.09	1.17	0.86	0.02	0.01
17	6.01	4.13	−4.05	−2.68	0.40	0.43	−1.42	−1.08	1.20	0.88	0.02	0.01
18	5.70	3.94	−3.88	−2.58	0.42	0.45	−1.40	−1.07	1.21	0.88	0.02	0.01
19	5.33	3.69	−3.64	−2.43	0.43	0.46	−1.38	−1.05	1.23	0.89	0.02	0.01
20	4.97	3.48	−3.36	−2.27	0.46	0.48	−1.34	−1.02	1.24	0.90	0.02	0.01
21	4.51	3.22	−2.99	−2.08	0.49	0.51	−1.33	−1.00	1.26	0.92	0.02	0.01

Number of Quarters of Impact	Unborrowed Reserves Reduction		Discount Rate Increase		Personal Income Reduction		Unborrowed Reserves Reduction		Discount Rate Increase		Personal Income Reduction	
	M	Q	M	Q	M	Q	M	Q	M	Q	M	Q
	R90/Policy Change						CD3/Policy Change					
1	−0.71	−0.78	0.38	0.40	0.00	0.00	−1.13	−1.21	0.60	0.62	0.00	0.00
2	−1.05	−0.93	0.56	0.49	0.01	0.01	−1.67	−1.44	0.90	0.75	0.01	0.01
3	−1.20	−0.98	0.68	0.53	0.01	0.01	−1.92	−1.52	1.08	0.82	0.01	0.01
4	−1.28	−1.01	0.74	0.56	0.01	0.01	−2.05	−1.56	1.19	0.87	0.02	0.01
5	−1.29^p	−1.02^p	0.77	0.59	0.01	0.01	−2.06^p	−1.58^p	1.23^p	0.91	0.02	0.01
6	−1.26	−1.00	0.77	0.59	0.01	0.01	−2.01	−1.55	1.23	0.92	0.02	0.02
7	−1.23	−0.98	0.78^p	0.60^p	0.01	0.01	−1.96	−1.51	1.24	0.92^p	0.02	0.02
8	−1.17^t	−0.94	0.76^t	0.59^t	0.01	0.01	−1.87	−1.46	1.22^t	0.92^t	0.02^p	0.02^p
9	−1.18^p	−0.94	0.79	0.61	0.01	0.01	−1.89	−1.45	1.27	0.94	0.02^t	0.02^t
10	−1.16	−0.93	0.80^p	0.61^p	0.01	0.01	−1.85	−1.43	1.28^p	0.95^p	0.02	0.02
11	−1.11	−0.90	0.79	0.61	0.01	0.01	−1.77	−1.39	1.26	0.95	0.02	0.02
12	−1.07^t	−0.87	0.78^t	0.60^t	0.01^p	0.01^p	−1.71^t	−1.34	1.24^t	0.93^t	0.02^p	0.02^p
13	−1.07	−0.85	0.80	0.61	0.01	0.01	−1.71	−1.32	1.28	0.95	0.02	0.02
14	−1.08^p	−0.84	0.83	0.62	0.01	0.01	−1.72	−1.31	1.32	0.96	0.02	0.02
15	−1.07	−0.83	0.85	0.64	0.01	0.01	−1.71	−1.29	1.36	0.98	0.02	0.02
16	−1.05	−0.82	0.86	0.64	0.01	0.01	−1.67	−1.26	1.37	0.99	0.02	0.02
17	−1.04	−0.81	0.88	0.65	0.01	0.01	−1.66	−1.25	1.40	1.01	0.02^t	0.02^t
18	−1.03	−0.80	0.88	0.66	0.01	0.01	−1.64	−1.23	1.41	1.02	0.02^p	0.02^p
19	−1.01	−0.78	0.90	0.67	0.01	0.01	−1.61	−1.21	1.43	1.03	0.02	0.02
20	−0.98	−0.76	0.90	0.67	0.01	0.01	−1.57	−1.18	1.44	1.04	0.02	0.02
21	−0.97	−0.75	0.92	0.68	0.01	0.01	−1.55	−1.16	1.47	1.06	0.02	0.02

^{a} Decrease in unborrowed reserves of $0.5 billion; discount rate increase of 0.5% (50 basis points); or personal income reduction of $15 billion. Monetary stocks and changes are measured in billions of dollars and interest rates in percent.

^{b} p denotes peak; t denotes trough.

TABLE 9

Monthly and Quarterly Point Elasticities for Period 1972:2–1977:2 Restrictive Policies

Number of Quarters of Impact	Unborrowed Reserves Reduction		Discount Rate Increase		Personal Income Reduction		Unborrowed Reserves Reduction		Discount Rate Increase		Personal Income Reduction	
	M	Q	M	Q	M	Q	M	Q	M	Q	M	Q
			M1/Policy Change						M2/Policy Change			
1	0.23	0.26	−0.02	−0.02	−0.02	−0.01	0.18	0.21	−0.01	−0.02	0.00	0.02
2	0.29	0.29	−0.02	−0.02	−0.05	−0.04	0.35	0.31	−0.03	−0.02	0.01	0.03
3	0.28	0.28	−0.02	−0.02	−0.06	−0.05	0.45	0.36	−0.04	−0.03	0.02	0.05
4	0.22	0.20	−0.02	−0.02	−0.06	−0.03	0.47	0.34	−0.05	−0.03	0.04	0.09
5	0.19	0.17	−0.02	−0.02	−0.07	−0.03	0.49	0.35	−0.06	−0.04	0.07	0.13
6	0.17	0.15	−0.02	−0.02	−0.07	−0.04	0.50	0.36	−0.07	−0.05	0.09	0.15
7	0.18	0.16	−0.03	−0.02	−0.08	−0.05	0.53	0.38	−0.07	−0.05	0.10	0.17
8	0.17	0.16	−0.02	−0.02	−0.09	−0.05	0.56	0.40	−0.07	−0.05	0.12	0.19
9	0.14	0.13	−0.02	−0.02	−0.08	−0.04	0.53	0.37	−0.08	−0.05	0.14	0.22
10	0.12	0.11	−0.02	−0.02	−0.09	−0.05	0.49	0.35	−0.07	−0.05	0.16	0.24
11	0.16	0.15	−0.03	−0.02	−0.12	−0.08	0.52	0.38	−0.08	−0.05	0.15	0.23
12	0.20	0.18	−0.03	−0.02	−0.14	−0.10	0.56	0.41	−0.07	−0.05	0.14	0.23
13	0.20	0.17	−0.03	−0.02	−0.15	−0.10	0.58	0.41	0.07	−0.05	0.13	0.23
14	0.18	0.16	−0.02	−0.02	−0.16	−0.11	0.58	0.41	−0.07	−0.05	0.12	0.23
15	0.17	0.15	−0.02	−0.02	−0.17	−0.12	0.58	0.40	−0.07	−0.05	0.11	0.23
16	0.15	0.14	−0.02	−0.02	−0.18	−0.13	0.57	0.39	−0.07	−0.05	0.12	0.24
17	0.14	0.12	−0.02	−0.02	−0.19	−0.13	0.54	0.38	−0.07	−0.04	0.13	0.25
18	0.13	0.12	−0.02	−0.02	−0.20	−0.14	0.52	0.36	−0.06	−0.04	0.13	0.25
19	0.13	0.11	−0.02	−0.02	−0.22	−0.16	0.50	0.36	−0.06	−0.04	0.13	0.25
20	0.12	0.10	−0.02	−0.01	0.24	−0.18	0.48	0.34	−0.06	−0.04	0.13	0.26
21	0.10	0.09	−0.02	−0.01	−0.26	−0.19	0.45	0.32	−0.06	−0.04	0.14	0.26

Number of Quarters of Impact	Unborrowed Reserves Reduction		Discount Rate Increase		Personal Income Reduction		Unborrowed Reserves Reduction		Discount Rate Increase		Personal Income Reduction	
	M	Q	M	Q	M	Q	M	Q	M	Q	M	Q
			M4/Policy Change						RCP/Policy Change			
1	0.10	0.09	−0.01	−0.01	0.08	0.16	−8.50	−8.15	0.63	0.58	0.96	0.80
2	0.17	0.14	−0.01	−0.01	0.19	0.24	−11.11	−9.30	0.83	0.67	2.07	1.84
3	0.22	0.18	−0.02	−0.01	0.26	0.30	−10.55	−8.74	0.85	0.68	2.23	2.07
4	0.25	0.18	−0.02	−0.02	0.32	0.36	−7.52	−6.27	0.73	0.58	1.88	1.68
5	0.27	0.19	−0.03	−0.02	0.38	0.42	−6.48	−5.37	0.75	0.60	1.87	1.65
6	0.28	0.20	−0.04	−0.03	0.43	0.46	−5.73	−4.81	0.80	0.65	1.85	1.63
7	0.30	0.21	−0.04	−0.03	0.46	0.50	−5.99	−5.07	0.85	0.69	1.95	1.79
8	0.31	0.22	−0.04	−0.03	0.49	0.53	−5.89	−4.97	0.84	0.68	2.10	1.88
9	0.30	0.21	−0.04	−0.03	0.53	0.57	−4.60	−4.00	0.72	0.60	1.68	1.56
10	0.28	0.20	−0.04	−0.03	0.58	0.62	−3.99	−3.56	0.65	0.56	1.58	1.49
11	0.28	0.20	−0.04	−0.03	0.59	0.62	−5.49	−4.58	0.87	0.70	2.32	2.07
12	0.29	0.21	−0.03	−0.02	0.58	0.62	−6.97	−5.56	0.97	0.74	3.08	2.66
13	0.28	0.20	−0.03	−0.02	0.58	0.63	−7.00	−5.41	0.92	0.69	3.11	2.64
14	0.28	0.20	−0.03	−0.02	0.60	0.66	−6.19	−4.99	0.83	0.64	2.81	2.50
15	0.27	0.19	−0.03	−0.02	0.61	0.68	−5.82	−4.74	0.80	0.63	2.64	2.39
16	0.27	0.18	−0.03	−0.02	0.64	0.71	−5.10	−4.24	0.68	0.54	2.40	2.21
17	0.25	0.17	−0.03	−0.02	0.67	0.73	−4.60	−3.81	0.63	0.50	2.25	2.04
18	0.23	0.16	−0.03	−0.02	0.70	0.76	−4.29	−3.62	0.60	0.48	2.20	2.02
19	0.21	0.15	−0.02	−0.02	0.72	0.78	−4.10	−3.51	0.57	0.46	2.08	1.97
20	0.19	0.14	−0.02	−0.01	0.76	0.82	−3.71	−3.24	0.51	0.43	1.97	1.89
21	0.17	0.12	−0.02	−0.01	0.80	0.85	−3.34	−2.91	0.48	0.41	1.85	1.76

(*continued*)

TABLE 9 *(continued)*

Number of Quarters of Impact	Unborrowed Reserves Reduction		Discount Rate Increase		Personal Income Reduction		Unborrowed Reserves Reduction		Discount Rate Increase		Personal Income Reduction	
	M	Q	M	Q	M	Q	M	Q	M	Q	M	Q
	R90/Policy Change						CD3/Policy Change					
1	−6.05	−6.31	0.45	0.45	0.68	0.68	−8.78	−8.50	0.65	0.60	0.99	0.83
2	−8.24	−7.25	0.61	0.52	1.53	1.44	−11.45	−9.69	0.85	0.69	2.13	1.92
3	−8.15	−6.93	0.65	0.53	1.72	1.64	−10.83	−9.08	0.87	0.70	2.29	2.15
4	−6.25	−5.27	0.60	0.49	1.56	1.41	−7.65	−6.44	0.76	0.60	1.91	1.72
5	−5.52	−4.63	0.64	0.52	1.59	1.42	−6.58	−5.49	0.81	0.62	1.89	1.69
6	−4.98	−4.22	0.69	0.57	1.61	1.43	−5.81	−4.91	0.86	0.66	1.88	1.67
7	−5.19	−4.43	0.74	0.61	1.69	1.57	−6.07	−5.17	0.85	0.71	1.98	1.83
8	−5.10	−4.35	0.72	0.60	1.82	1.65	−5.97	−5.08	0.85	0.70	2.13	1.92
9	−4.10	−3.58	0.64	0.54	1.50	1.40	−4.65	−4.07	0.73	0.61	1.70	1.59
10	−3.61	−3.22	0.59	0.51	1.43	1.35	−4.03	−3.62	0.66	0.57	1.60	1.52
11	−4.78	−4.04	0.76	0.61	2.02	1.82	−5.56	−4.67	0.88	0.71	2.35	2.11
12	−5.84	−4.76	0.81	0.64	2.59	2.28	−7.08	−5.70	0.99	0.76	3.14	2.73
13	−5.84	−4.62	0.77	0.59	2.60	2.26	−7.13	−5.55	0.94	0.70	3.17	2.71
14	−5.26	−4.30	0.70	0.55	2.39	2.16	−6.28	−5.11	0.84	0.66	2.85	2.56
15	−4.99	−4.11	0.69	0.54	2.27	2.08	−5.91	−4.84	0.81	0.64	2.68	2.45
16	−4.44	−3.72	0.59	0.48	2.09	1.93	−5.17	−4.33	0.69	0.55	2.43	2.25
17	−4.04	−3.38	0.55	0.44	1.98	1.81	−4.65	−3.89	0.64	0.51	2.27	2.08
18	−3.79	−3.22	0.53	0.43	1.95	1.80	−4.34	−3.68	0.60	0.49	2.23	2.06
19	−3.65	−3.13	0.50	0.42	1.85	1.75	−4.15	−3.57	0.57	0.47	2.10	2.00
20	−3.33	−2.91	0.46	0.39	1.77	1.70	−3.75	−3.29	0.52	0.44	1.99	1.92
21	−3.02	−2.64	0.44	0.37	1.68	1.59	−3.37	−2.96	0.49	0.41	1.87	1.79

are sizable. A reduction in reserves triggers increases in short-term interest rates and declines in demand and savings deposits. Holdings of large CDs, however, increase because CD rates rise more than those for commercial paper or for government bills. There are portfolio shifts from these assets into CDs. Also, given stickiness in rates paid on savings deposits, there is disintermediation as funds are invested in bills, commercial paper, and CDs.

The largest impacts on M1 and large CDs occur within the first year, with a peak in two to three quarters. This reflects mainly direct effects on commercial banks of the reserves reduction. Interest rate impacts show a peak in four to five quarters, and M2 in about two years. The pattern of M4 reflects combined effects on demand, time, and CD deposit adjustments. Clearly, responses to interest rate movements in altering portfolio compositions involve inertial lags and there are feedbacks between asset yields and holdings.

Thus, it is not surprising that there are cycles in response multipliers and elasticities. In the case of M1, the initial peak impact is reached in the third quarter following the change in unborrowed reserves, a trough in the tenth quarter, and another, lower peak in the 13th quarter. Thereafter, a steady gradual decline in effects occurs. Interest rate multiplier impacts also exhibit cycles but, as already noted, the timing is somewhat different and, generally, impacts are delayed beyond those on M1. Response point elasticities of interest rates to unborrowed reserve shifts are quite strong and peaks and troughs normally occur slightly earlier or later than do those for interest rate multipliers.

The monthly and quarterly models reveal nearly identical timing patterns of multiplier and elasticity impacts. In the first quarter after the policy shift, responses in the quarterly model are stronger than those in the monthly model for nearly all variables. All subsequent quarters show the reverse. This phenomenon is discussed further in a later section below.

Increases in discount rates have much the same effects as do reductions in reserves. Market interest rates rise and demand and time deposits fall. Again, holdings of large CDs increase so that M4 multipliers are, in absolute value, less than those for M2. Cycles occur in impacts with peaks and troughs at about the same time as those in the unborrowed reserves simulations. Differences between impacts in the monthly and quarterly model, too, are similar as those for reserve changes.

The last set of simulations, that for personal income reductions, does not give the same kinds of results. A drop in income of $15 billion, or about 1.6%, has little effect in initial quarters and impacts only build up gradually. Cycles in impacts are very damped; practically none are observed for money stocks and those for interest rates are mild.

Multiplier impacts for personal income cuts appear very small, but to some extent this is misleading. After several years, cumulative impacts are of significant absolute magnitudes. Monetary response elasticities due to personal income changes greatly exceed those for discount rate shifts and are of the same order of magnitude as those for unborrowed reserve reductions (measured in absolute terms).

An interesting result of the personal income change simulations is that M1 and M4 multipliers have opposite signs. With a reduction in personal income, interest rates fall. The income effect on demand deposits and those needed for transactions purposes would, in the absence of declines in interest rates, cause a decline in those deposits. Nevertheless, demand deposits rise, presumably because of the decline in opportunity costs of holding assets in this form. Savings deposits fall, but CDs drop even faster. Declines in large CD rates are greater than those for commercial paper rates whose falls, in turn, exceed those for government bill rates. Savings deposit rates decline least, if at all. Substitution takes place within portfolios toward relatively higher yielding assets and against those whose yields have dropped most, CDs and commercial paper.

These effects are consistently shown by both monthly and quarterly versions of the model but are somewhat greater in the quarterly variant. Personal income impacts on interest rates are larger in the monthly than in the quarterly model but impacts on money stocks other than for large CDs have the tendency reversed. This is opposite the finding from the unborrowed reserve and discount rate restrictive policy simulations in which impacts in the monthly model almost always exceed those in the quarterly model.

B. Stimulative Policies

Multipliers and point elasticities from the monthly and quarterly models under more stimulative policies for a period for which this might have been beneficial, the interval beginning in early 1974 soon after the oil shock and lasting through the 1975 recession, are presented in Tables 10 and 11, respectively. In general, the results qualitatively are similar to those obtained under restrictive policies in the earlier period simulation. The direction of impacts, of course, is reversed, but the signs of multipliers and elasticities are identical.

Increases in unborrowed reserves cause declines in interest rates and increases in demand and time deposits. However, because of marked drops in large CD rates, holdings of these certificates fall, thereby producing a lesser rate of rise in M4 than M2. As in the case of the restrictive simulation, there are peaks in impacts on money stocks and interest rates which occur about

TABLE 10

MONTHLY AND QUARTERLY MULTIPLIERS FOR PERIOD 1974:2–1977:2 STIMULATIVE POLICIES[a,b]

Number of Quarters of Impact	Unborrowed Reserves Increase		Discount Rate Reduction		Personal Income Increase		Unborrowed Reserves Increase		Discount Rate Reduction		Personal Income Increase	
	M	Q	M	Q	M	Q	M	Q	M	Q	M	Q
			ΔM1/Policy Change						ΔM2/Policy Change			
1	0.74	0.87	−0.51	−0.57	0.00	0.00	1.14	1.41	−0.78	−0.92	0.00	0.01
2	1.00	1.01	−0.69	−0.67	−0.01	−0.01	2.04	2.08	−1.41	−1.37	0.02	0.03
3	1.52	1.41	−1.09	−0.95	−0.02	−0.01	3.55	3.24	−2.50	−2.15	0.03	0.04
4	2.03	1.79	−1.46	−1.21	−0.02	−0.01	5.71	4.63	−4.06	−3.10	0.03	0.05
5	2.16[p]	1.79[p]	−1.59[p]	−1.26[p]	−0.02	−0.01	7.78	5.56	−5.61	−3.80	0.03	0.06
6	1.95	1.66	−1.48	−1.20	−0.02	−0.01	9.00	6.10	−6.58	−4.24	0.03	0.07
7	1.86	1.60	−1.47	−1.19	−0.02	−0.02	9.90	6.56	−7.39	−4.64	0.03	0.08
8	1.63	1.41	−1.33	−1.09	−0.02	−0.02	10.40	6.78	−7.90	−4.89	0.04	0.09
9	1.49	1.28	−1.26	−1.03	−0.02	−0.02	10.64[p]	6.88	−8.23	−5.06	0.04	0.10
10	1.40	1.22	−1.21[t]	−1.00	−0.02	−0.02	10.62	6.91	−8.35	−5.17	0.05	0.10
11	1.36	1.20	−1.22[p]	−1.01[p]	−0.03	−0.02	10.53	6.93[p]	−8.44	−5.29	0.05	0.11
12	1.25	1.10	−1.16	−0.97	−0.03	−0.02	10.39	6.91	−8.49[p]	−5.39	0.05	0.11
13	1.16	1.01	−1.11	−0.92	−0.03	−0.02	10.09	6.77	−8.41	−5.40	0.06	0.12

(*continued*)

TABLE 10 (continued)

Number of Quarters of Impact	Unborrowed Reserves Increase		Discount Rate Reduction		Personal Income Increase		Unborrowed Reserves Increase		Discount Rate Reduction		Personal Income Increase	
	M	Q	M	Q	M	Q	M	Q	M	Q	M	Q
	ΔM4/Policy Change						ΔRCP/Policy Change					
1	0.14	0.03	−0.10	−0.01	0.08	0.15	−0.91	−0.88	0.63	0.59	0.00	0.00
2	−0.19	0.02ᵗ	0.13ᵗ	0.00ᵗ	0.20	0.23	−1.38	−1.13	0.97	0.77	0.01	0.01
3	−0.05ᵗ	0.42	0.00	−0.25	0.27	0.27	−1.51	−1.19ᵖ	1.09	0.83	0.02	0.01
4	0.50	1.12	−0.32	−0.70	0.29	0.29	−1.56	−1.18	1.14	0.84	0.02	0.01
5	1.40	1.76	−0.95	−1.12	0.30	0.31	−1.57ᵖ	−1.15	1.18	0.85	0.02	0.01
6	2.34	2.23	−1.60	−1.43	0.32	0.33	−1.57	−1.14	1.21	0.86	0.02	0.01
7	3.27	2.63	−2.27	−1.70	0.34	0.36	−1.53	−1.11	1.22	0.87	0.02	0.01
8	4.02	2.94	−2.80	−1.92	0.37	0.38	−1.49	−1.09	1.22	0.87	0.02	0.01
9	4.51	3.13	−3.16	−2.06	0.39	0.41	−1.46	−1.07	1.24	0.89	0.02	0.01
10	4.65ᵖ	3.16ᵖ	−3.28ᵖ	−2.10ᵖ	0.41	0.43	−1.43	−1.06	1.24	0.89	0.02ᵖ	0.01ᵖ
11	4.60	3.09	−3.25	−2.05	0.43	0.45	−1.40	−1.04	1.26	0.90	0.02	0.01
12	4.47	3.02	−3.13	−1.98	0.46	0.48	−1.37	−1.01	1.27	0.91	0.02	0.01
13	4.19	2.88	−2.89	−1.86	0.49	0.51	−1.35	−0.99	1.29	0.92	0.02	0.01

Number of Quarters of Impact	Unborrowed Reserves Increase		Discount Rate Reduction		Personal Income Increase		Unborrowed Reserves Increase		Discount Rate Reduction		Personal Income Increase	
	M	Q	M	Q	M	Q	M	Q	M	Q	M	Q
	ΔR90/Policy Change						ΔCD3/Policy Change					
1	−0.67	−0.66	0.46	0.44	0.00	0.00	−1.07	−1.02	0.74	0.68	0.01	0.00
2	−1.01	−0.84	0.71	0.58	0.01	0.01	−1.61	−1.31	1.13	0.89	0.01	0.01
3	−1.11	−0.89[p]	0.80	0.62	0.01	0.01	−1.77	−1.38[p]	1.28	0.96	0.02	0.01
4	−1.14	−0.88	0.83	0.63	0.01	0.01	−1.82	−1.36	1.33	0.97	0.02	0.02
5	−1.15[p]	−0.86	0.86	0.63	0.01	0.01	−1.84[p]	−1.33	1.38	0.98	0.02	0.02
6	−1.15	−0.85	0.88	0.64	0.01	0.01	−1.84	−1.32	1.41	0.99	0.02	0.02
7	−1.12	−0.83	0.90	0.65	0.01	0.01	−1.79	−1.29	1.43	1.00	0.02[p]	0.02[p]
8	−1.09	−0.81	0.90	0.65	0.01	0.01	−1.74	−1.26	1.43	1.01	0.02[t]	0.02[t]
9	−1.07	−0.80	0.91	0.66	0.01	0.01	−1.71	−1.24	1.45	1.02	0.02	0.02
10	−1.05	−0.79	0.91	0.67	0.01[p]	0.01[p]	−1.67	−1.22	1.45	1.03	0.02[p]	0.02[p]
11	−1.03	−0.77	0.92	0.67	0.01	0.01	−1.64	−1.20	1.47	1.04	0.02	0.02
12	−1.00	−0.75	0.93	0.68	0.01	0.01	−1.60	−1.16	1.48	1.05	0.02	0.02
13	−0.98	−0.74	0.94	0.69	0.01	0.01	−1.57	−1.14	1.51	1.06	0.02	0.02

[a] Increase in unborrowed reserves of $0.5 billion; discount rate reduction of 0.5% (50 basic points); or personal income increase of $15 billion.

[b] p denotes peak; t denotes trough.

TABLE 11

MONTHLY AND QUARTERLY POINT ELASTICITIES FOR PERIOD 1974:2–1977:2 STIMULATIVE POLICIES[a]

Number of Quarters of Impact	Unborrowed Reserves Increase		Discount Rate Reduction		Personal Income Increase		Unborrowed Reserves Increase		Discount Rate Reduction		Personal Income Increase	
	M	Q	M	Q	M	Q	M	Q	M	Q	M	Q
			M1/Policy Change						M2/Policy Change			
1	0.09	0.11	−0.01	−0.02	−0.02	−0.01	0.07	0.08	−0.01	−0.01	0.01	0.03
2	0.12	0.12	−0.02	−0.02	−0.04	−0.03	0.12	0.12	−0.02	−0.02	0.03	0.05
3	0.19	0.17	−0.03	−0.03	−0.06	−0.04	−0.21	0.19	−0.03	−0.03	0.05	0.07
4	0.25	0.22	−0.03	−0.03	−0.08	−0.06	0.33	0.26	−0.04	−0.03	0.05	0.09
5	0.25	0.21	−0.03	−0.03	−0.09	−0.06	0.42	0.30	−0.05	−0.04	0.05	0.11
6	0.22	0.19	−0.03	−0.02	−0.09	−0.06	0.47	0.32	−0.06	−0.04	0.05	0.13
7	0.21	0.18	−0.03	−0.02	−0.09	−0.07	0.51	0.34	−0.07	−0.04	0.06	0.15
8	0.18	0.16	−0.02	−0.02	−0.10	−0.07	0.53	0.34	−0.06	−0.04	0.07	0.17
9	0.16	0.14	−0.02	−0.02	−0.10	−0.07	0.52	0.34	−0.07	−0.04	0.08	0.19
10	0.15	0.13	−0.02	−0.02	−0.10	−0.07	0.52	0.34	−0.07	−0.04	0.09	0.21
11	0.14	0.13	−0.02	−0.02	−0.11	−0.08	0.51	0.34	−0.06	−0.04	0.10	0.21
12	0.13	0.12	−0.02	−0.02	−0.12	−0.09	0.50	0.33	−0.06	−0.04	0.11	0.23
13	0.12	0.10	−0.02	−0.01	−0.13	−0.10	0.47	0.31	−0.06	−0.04	0.12	0.24

Number of Quarters of Impact	Unborrowed Reserves Increase		Discount Rate Reduction		Personal Income Increase		Unborrowed Reserves Increase		Discount Rate Reduction		Personal Income Increase	
	M	Q	M	Q	M	Q	M	Q	M	Q	M	Q
			M4/Policy Change						RCP/Policy Change			
1	0.01	0.00	0.00	0.00	0.14	0.25	−2.89	−3.06	0.46	0.48	0.51	0.43
2	−0.01	0.00	0.00	0.00	0.35	0.40	−3.69	−3.49	0.61	0.56	1.13	1.01
3	0.00	0.02	0.00	0.00	0.45	0.46	−5.83	−4.82	0.94	0.75	2.17	1.74
4	0.02	0.06	0.00	−0.01	0.49	0.49	−7.98	−5.99	1.12	0.82	3.19	2.39
5	0.07	0.08	−0.01	−0.01	0.51	0.52	−8.17	−5.77	1.08	0.75	3.44	2.48
6	0.11	0.10	−0.01	−0.01	0.55	0.57	−7.14	−5.24	0.96	0.69	3.18	2.40
7	0.15	0.12	−0.02	−0.01	0.58	0.60	−6.60	−4.90	0.91	0.66	3.08	2.36
8	0.17	0.13	−0.02	−0.01	0.61	0.64	−5.69	−4.36	0.76	0.57	2.82	2.21
9	0.19	0.13	0.02	−0.01	0.65	0.68	−5.06	−3.91	0.70	0.52	2.66	2.09
10	0.19	0.13	−0.02	−0.01	0.68	0.72	−4.68	−3.70	0.66	0.51	2.61	2.08
11	0.18	0.12	−0.02	−0.01	0.72	0.75	−4.45	−3.59	0.62	0.49	2.50	2.05
12	0.17	0.12	−0.02	−0.01	0.76	0.79	−4.01	−3.31	0.56	0.45	2.37	1.99
13	0.16	−0.11	−0.02	−0.01	0.81	0.84	−3.59	−2.99	0.53	0.43	2.23	1.87

(*continued*)

TABLE 11 (continued)

Number of Quarters of Impact	Unborrowed Reserves Increase		Discount Rate Reduction		Personal Income Increase		Unborrowed Reserves Increase		Discount Rate Reduction		Personal Income Increase	
	M	Q	M	Q	M	Q	M	Q	M	Q	M	Q
	\multicolumn{6}{c}{R90/Policy Change}							
1	−2.47	−2.65	0.40	0.41	0.43	0.38	−3.18	−3.35	0.51	0.52	0.56	0.47
2	−3.30	−3.11	0.55	0.50	1.01	0.90	−4.01	−3.77	0.67	0.61	1.23	1.09
3	−5.04	−4.21	0.81	0.66	1.88	1.52	−6.54	−5.31	1.05	0.83	2.43	1.91
4	−6.61	−5.08	0.92	0.69	2.64	2.03	−9.32	−6.77	1.30	0.92	3.72	2.69
5	−6.71	−4.89	0.89	0.63	2.82	2.10	−9.60	−6.53	1.27	0.84	4.04	2.79
6	−5.99	−4.49	0.80	0.59	2.67	2.06	−8.22	−5.89	1.10	0.77	3.66	2.69
7	−5.60	−4.23	0.77	0.57	2.61	2.04	−7.54	−5.47	1.04	0.74	3.52	2.62
8	−4.90	−3.80	0.66	0.50	2.43	1.93	−6.40	−4.82	0.86	0.63	3.17	2.43
9	−4.41	−3.45	0.61	0.46	2.32	1.84	−5.64	−4.29	0.78	0.57	2.96	2.28
10	−4.11	−3.28	0.58	0.45	2.29	1.85	−5.18	−4.04	0.73	0.55	2.89	2.27
11	−3.93	−3.19	0.55	0.43	2.21	1.83	−4.90	−3.90	0.68	0.53	2.75	2.23
12	−3.57	−2.96	0.50	0.40	2.11	1.78	−4.38	−3.58	0.61	0.49	2.59	2.16
13	−3.23	−2.70	0.47	0.38	2.01	1.69	−3.90	−3.22	0.57	0.46	2.42	2.02

[a] Increase in unborrowed reserves of $0.5 billion; discount rate reduction of 0.5% (50 basic points); or personal income increase of $15 billion.

one year after initiation of the policy change. But, in the stimulative simulations, there are no pronounced secondary peaks. Again, the monthly and quarterly models display nearly identical timing patterns of multiplier and elasticity impacts. Stimulative impacts on money stocks in the quarterly model are somewhat stronger than in the monthly model in the first quarter or two. These results are the same as those in the restrictive simulation. Yet, where it comes to interest rates, this no longer is true and impacts in the monthly model always are stronger than those in the quarterly model.

In the restrictive simulation for the earlier period a discount rate policy change had much the same effects as did a shift in unborrowed reserves. This still holds true in the stimulative simulation. Multipliers for M4 are less (in absolute value) than those for M2. Also, cyclical patterns for money stocks and differences between impacts in the monthly and quarterly models are about the same for the two types of stimulative policies. The cyclical pattern similarly does not extend to interest rate impacts, however, where for unborrowed reserve increases there is a peak in impacts and then a gradual decline whereas for discount rate reductions impacts grow monotonically (that is, commercial paper and other interest rates decrease steadily throughout the simulation period).

With respect to personal income increases in the later period as contrasted to decreases in the earlier period, effects are much the same in the two simulations. Impacts grow steadily from quarter to quarter and become sizable after a few years. Monthly and quarterly model comparisons show that impacts in the latter are greater for money stocks but less for interest rates and quantities of large CDs (except in the first two quarters).

C. Interperiod Comparisons

Some of the most noticeable differences in all the policy simulations between the monthly and quarterly models in the two periods is in impacts on large CD rates and holdings. In general, for CDs multipliers and elasticities in the quarterly model not only are higher than in the monthly model but peaks in effects are significantly greater, especially in the later period (see Table 12 for a sample of results). This last difference in effects in the two time periods is probably in large measure due to the relatively limited but growing use of CDs in the early 1970s. From 1972 to 1974 there was a broadening of markets for these securities with an approximate doubling of CD rates and holdings (data are listed in Table 1).

For other money stock and interest rate variables there also are distinct differences between policy impacts in the two periods. Figures 1 and 2

TABLE 12

MONTHLY AND QUARTERLY ELASTICITIES FOR QUANTITY OF CDs

Number of Quarters of Impact	Period 1972:2–1977:2 Restrictive Policies								Period 1974:2–1077:2 Stimulative Policies						
	Unborrowed Reserves Reduction		Discount Rate Increase		Personal Income Reduction				Unborrowed Reserves Increase		Discount Rate Reduction		Personal Income Increase	
	M	Q	M	Q	M	Q			M	Q	M	Q	M	Q
1	−1.13	−1.48	0.09	0.11	1.20	2.07			−0.46	−0.61	0.07	0.09	1.17	2.03
2	−2.27	−1.96	0.17	0.14	2.61	2.93			−0.86	0.80	0.14	0.13	2.49	2.84
3	−2.55	−1.93	0.21	0.15	3.18	3.19			−1.40	−1.12	0.22	0.17	3.15	3.18
4	−2.16	−1.49	0.21	0.14	3.27	3.17			−2.10	−1.43	0.29	0.19	3.59	3.38
5	−1.77	−1.25	0.21	0.14	3.27	3.16			−2.49	−1.43	0.32	0.18	3.85	3.45
6	−1.57	−1.13	0.22	0.15	3.27	3.15			−2.36	−1.33	0.31	0.17	3.86	3.44
7	−1.54	−1.15	0.22	0.16	3.29	3.19			−2.15	−1.24	0.29	0.16	3.82	3.43
8	−1.51	−1.14	0.21	0.16	3.30	3.20			−1.86	−1.10	0.24	0.14	3.75	3.40
9	−1.30	−0.95	0.20	0.14	3.28	3.15			−1.61	−0.98	0.22	0.13	3.68	3.36
10	−1.09	−0.83	0.18	0.13	3.23	3.13			−1.45	−0.92	0.20	0.12	3.63	3.35
11	−1.25	−1.01	0.20	0.15	3.30	3.23			−1.36	−0.88	0.18	0.12	3.62	3.35
12	−1.55	−1.21	0.22	0.16	3.46	3.36			−1.23	−0.82	0.17	0.11	3.59	3.34
13	−1.69	−1.21	0.22	0.15	3.58	3.39			−1.09	−0.74	0.16	0.10	3.53	3.31
14	−1.62	−1.14	0.21	0.15	3.56	3.37								
15	−1.51	−1.09	0.21	0.14	3.51	3.34								
16	−1.36	−0.98	0.18	0.13	3.46	3.30								
17	−1.22	−0.89	0.16	0.12	3.40	3.26								
18	−1.13	−0.83	0.16	0.11	3.37	3.25								
19	−1.07	−0.81	0.15	0.11	3.36	3.24								
20	−0.99	−0.75	0.13	0.10	3.34	3.23								
21	−0.89	−0.68	0.13	0.09	3.31	3.21								

illustrate these effects for the unborrowed reserve and discount rate simulations, respectively. Multipliers shown therein often do not peak in the same quarters nor are their magnitudes in the same neighborhoods at peaks.

Differences in multiplier and elasticity impacts in the two periods might be explained by changed structural characteristics of the economy, the initial state or conditions under which policy shifts are undertaken, and other factors. It might also be hypothesized that differences are caused by introduction of restrictive policies during the first period and of opposite, stimulative policies in the second period.

D. Asymmetries in Stimulative and Restrictive Policy Responses

In order to test whether differences in policy impacts between the two periods were due to asymmetrical responses to stimulus versus restraint, additional simulations were run in which the original policy shifts were reversed. That is, during the first period a stimulative instead of a restrictive policy was introduced and during the second period restrictive policies were substituted for stimulative policies.

Results of the simulations for changes in unborrowed reserves and in discount rates are shown in Table 13. Ratios of stimulative to restrictive policy multipliers reveal very slight asymmetries for interest rate responses in the first period but none in the second period. Interest rate changes from stimulative unborrowed reserve policies are about 97–98% of those for restrictive policies from 1972–1975 while over the same interval comparable stimulative–restrictive ratios for discount rate are approximately 98–99%. In the second interval stimulative–restrictive interest rate ratios are almost identically unity.

However, ratios of stimulative to restrictive multipliers for money stocks nearly all are greater than unity in both periods (the few exceptions occur for M4 during the first three quarters of impact in the second period, when its multipliers are extremely small—near zero). For M1 the ratios are about 1.05–1.10, for M2 about 1.07–1.12, and for M4 about 1.10–1.30. In the case of M4, relative stimulative-restrictive responses to unborrowed reserve shifts are approximately 7–10% greater than those for discount rate changes.

Thus, there are asymmetries in money stock responses to stimulative versus restrictive policies, with the former's impacts being somewhat larger than those for the latter policies. Yet, the magnitudes of these asymmetries are nearly the same across the two periods. Consequently it can be concluded that the interperiod differences in responses reported in Tables 7–10 are not due to asymmetries in restrictive versus stimulative policy impacts.

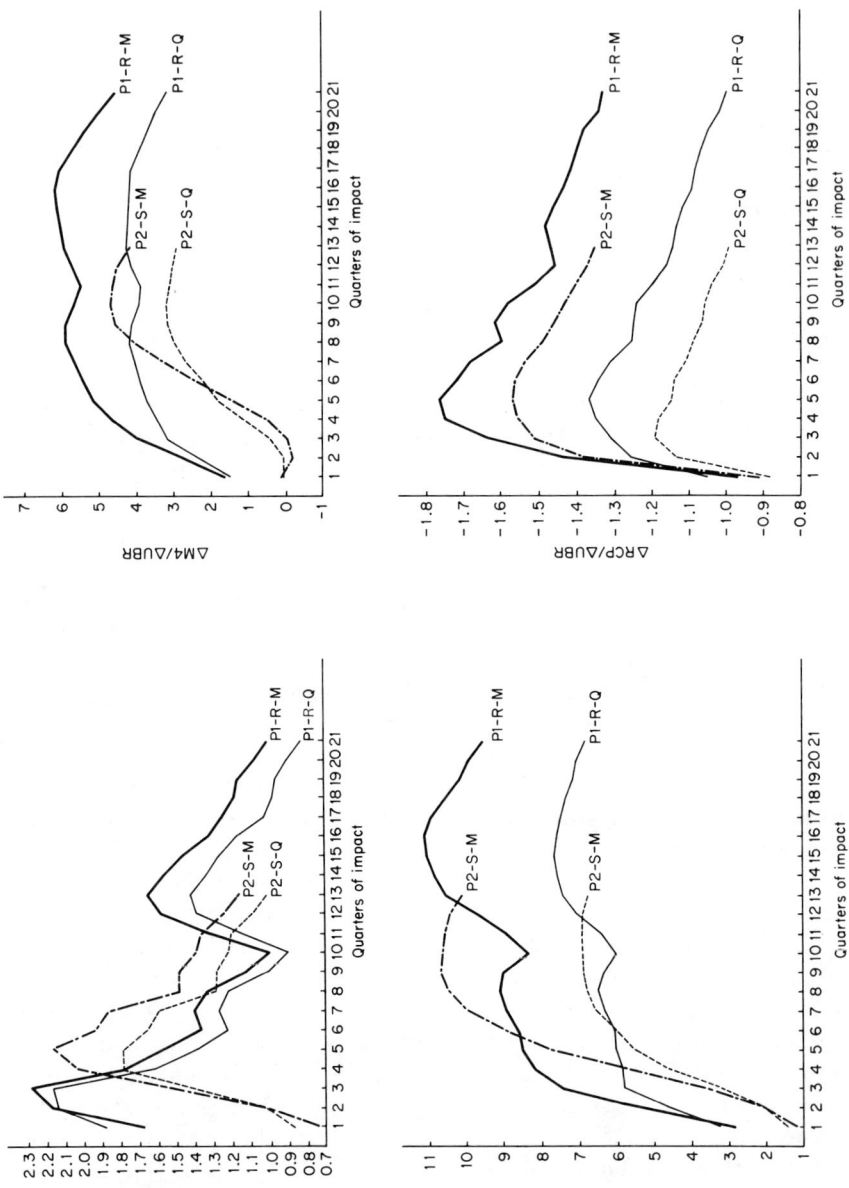

Figure 1 Multipliers: unborrowed reserves.

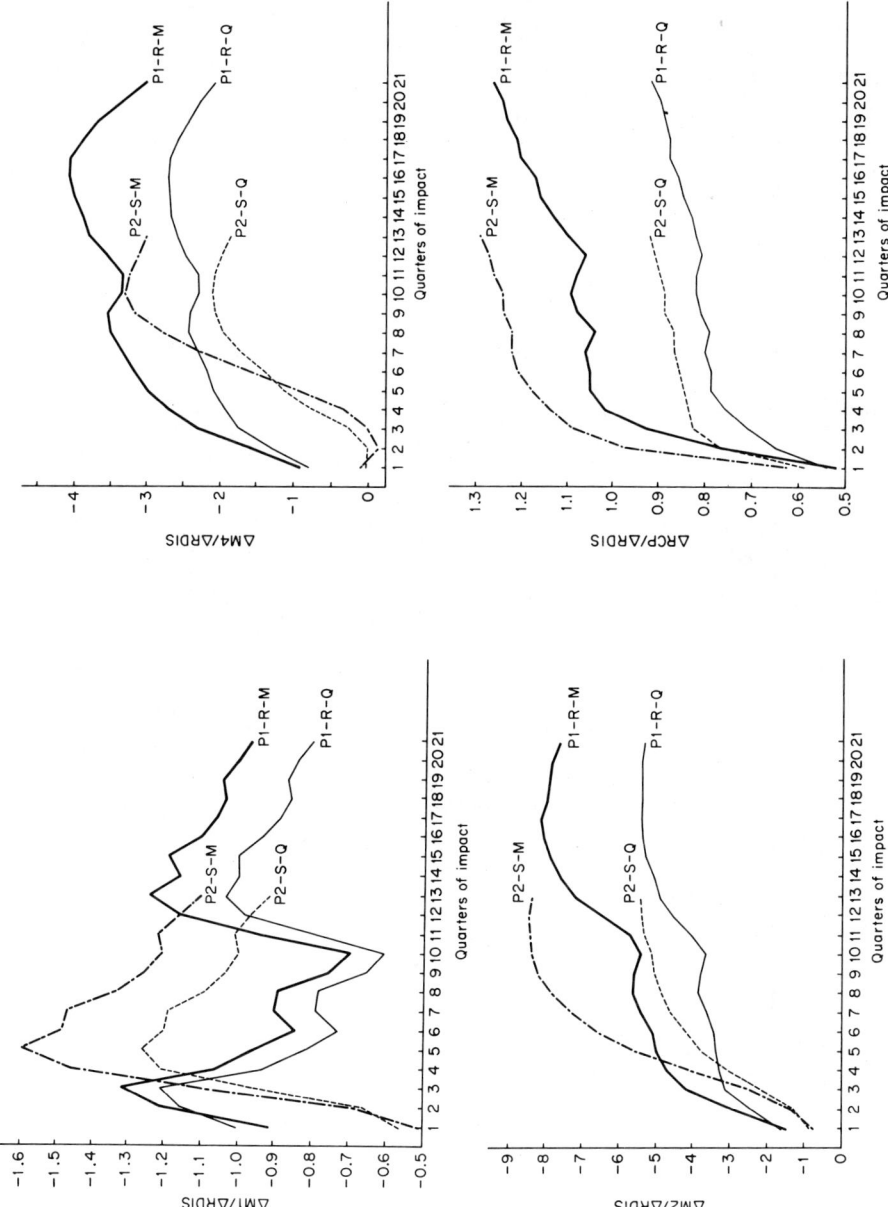

Figure 2 Multipliers: discount rate.

TABLE 13

RATIOS OF STIMULATIVE TO RESTRICTIVE POLICY MULTIPLIERS FOR THE MONTHLY AND QUARTERLY MODEL IN TWO PERIODS POLICY CHANGES IN UNBORROWED RESERVES[a]

Quarters of Impact	M1		M2		M4		RCP		R90		CD3	
	M	Q	M	Q	M	Q	M	Q	M	Q	M	Q
Period 1												
1	1.10	1.12	1.11	1.12	1.13	1.16	0.96	0.98	0.96	0.98	0.96	0.98
2	1.12	1.12	1.14	1.13	1.19	1.18	0.95	0.97	0.95	0.97	0.95	0.97
3	1.12	1.11	1.15	1.13	1.21	1.18	0.96	0.97	0.96	0.97	0.96	0.97
4	1.09	1.08	1.15	1.12	1.21	1.16	0.97	0.97	0.97	0.97	0.97	0.97
5	1.07	1.07	1.14	1.11	1.20	1.16	0.97	0.98	0.97	0.98	0.97	0.98
6	1.06	1.06	1.14	1.11	1.20	1.15	0.97	0.98	0.97	0.98	0.97	0.98
7	1.06	1.06	1.14	1.11	1.19	1.14	0.97	0.98	0.97	0.98	0.97	0.98
8	1.05	1.06	1.13	1.10	1.19	1.14	0.97	0.98	0.97	0.98	0.97	0.98
9	1.04	1.04	1.13	1.10	1.18	1.13	0.98	0.98	0.98	0.98	0.98	0.98
12	1.06	1.06	1.12	1.09	1.17	1.13	0.97	0.98	0.97	0.98	0.97	0.98
16	1.05	1.06	1.12	1.09	1.17	1.13	0.98	0.99	0.98	0.98	0.98	0.99
20	1.04	1.05	1.11	1.08	1.17	1.13	0.99	0.99	0.99	0.99	0.99	0.99
Period 2												
1	1.04	1.07	1.04	1.08	1.10	−15.13	1.00	1.00	1.00	1.00	1.00	1.00
2	1.05	1.08	1.07	1.09	0.85	−0.65	1.00	1.00	1.00	1.00	1.00	1.00
3	1.08	1.10	1.09	1.11	0.36	1.43	1.00	1.00	1.00	1.00	10.0	1.00
4	1.11	1.12	1.12	1.13	1.59	1.27	1.00	0.99	1.00	0.99	1.00	0.99
5	1.11	1.12	1.14	1.13	1.31	1.24	1.00	0.99	1.00	0.99	1.00	0.99
6	1.10	1.11	1.14	1.13	1.27	1.23	1.00	0.99	1.00	0.99	1.00	0.99
7	1.09	1.11	1.14	1.13	1.25	1.22	1.00	0.99	1.00	0.99	1.00	0.99
8	1.07	1.09	1.14	1.13	1.25	1.21	1.00	0.99	1.00	0.99	1.00	0.99
12	1.05	1.07	1.12	1.12	1.24	1.21	1.00	0.99	1.00	0.99	1.00	1.00

POLICY CHANGES IN DISCOUNT RATES

Quarters of Impact	M1		M2		M4		RCP		R90		CD3	
	M	Q	M	Q	M	Q	M	Q	M	Q	M	Q
Period 1												
1	1.06	1.06	1.06	1.06	1.07	1.08	0.98	0.99	0.98	0.99	0.98	0.99
2	1.07	1.06	1.08	1.06	1.10	1.09	0.98	0.98	0.98	0.98	0.98	0.98
3	1.07	1.07	1.09	1.07	1.12	1.09	0.98	0.99	0.98	0.99	0.98	0.99
4	1.06	1.05	1.09	1.07	1.12	1.09	0.99	0.99	0.99	0.99	0.99	0.99
5	1.05	1.05	1.09	1.07	1.12	1.09	0.99	0.99	0.99	0.99	0.99	0.99
6	1.04	1.04	1.09	1.06	1.12	1.08	0.99	0.99	0.99	0.99	0.99	0.99
7	1.04	1.04	1.08	1.06	1.11	1.08	0.99	0.99	0.99	0.99	0.99	0.99
8	1.04	1.04	1.08	1.06	1.11	1.08	0.99	0.99	0.99	0.99	0.99	0.99
9	1.03	1.04	1.08	1.06	1.11	1.08	0.99	0.99	0.99	0.99	0.99	0.99
12	1.06	1.05	1.08	1.06	1.12	1.08	0.99	0.99	0.99	0.99	0.99	0.99
16	1.05	1.05	1.09	1.07	1.13	1.10	1.00	1.00	1.00	1.00	1.00	1.00
20	1.04	1.05	1.09	1.06	1.15	1.11	1.00	1.00	1.00	1.00	1.00	1.00
Period 2												
1	1.03	1.03	1.03	1.04	1.08	21.50	1.00	1.00	1.00	1.00	1.00	1.00
2	1.03	1.04	1.05	1.04	0.89	0.08	1.00	1.00	1.00	1.00	1.00	1.00
3	1.05	1.05	1.07	1.05	0.50	1.22	1.00	1.00	1.00	1.00	1.00	1.00
4	1.08	1.06	1.09	1.06	1.42	1.14	1.00	1.00	1.00	1.00	1.00	1.00
5	1.09	1.06	1.10	1.07	1.23	1.12	1.00	1.00	1.00	1.00	1.00	1.00
6	1.08	1.06	1.11	1.07	1.20	1.12	1.00	1.00	1.00	1.00	1.00	1.00
7	1.07	1.06	1.11	1.07	1.19	1.12	1.00	1.00	1.00	1.00	1.00	1.00
8	1.07	1.05	1.11	1.07	1.19	1.12	1.00	1.00	1.00	1.00	1.00	1.00
12	1.05	1.05	1.10	1.07	1.20	1.12	1.00	1.00	1.00	1.00	1.00	1.00

Since stimulative and restrictive multipliers generally would be opposite in sign and their ratios normally would be negative, values in the table have been multiplied by −1. Positive signs are found for ratios of stimulative to restrictive multipliers for M4 in the quarterly model for the first two quarters of the second period, but multipliers are approximately zero.

E. Monthly versus Quarterly Model Multipliers

Neither are the differences in interperiod responses attributable to differences between the monthly and quarterly models. Judging from results in Table 13, monthly–quarterly interperiod differences in multipliers are quite small (other than in the few quarters in which multipliers for M4 are virtually zero).

Nevertheless, as already observed, policy multipliers in the monthly model consistently are much larger than those in the quarterly model other than in the first quarter or two following initiation of a policy change. Ratios of monthly to quarterly model multipliers are presented in Table 14 for shifts in unborrowed reserves and discount rates. As can be seen therein, after the buildups in the first year, multipliers for interest rate responses to either policy change are about 30–40% greater in the monthly model than they are in the quarterly model. Results vary more for interest rates, but after two years monthly compared to quarterly model multipliers are 10–20% greater for M1, 40–60% greater for M2, and 40–50% greater for M4.

The implications of these results potentially are quite disturbing for policy formation. If policy to achieve given targets is based on the monthly model, lesser amounts of exogenous shifts in monetary instruments would be undertaken than if based on the quarterly model. Therefore, if multipliers from the quarterly model in fact are closer to those which actually pertain in the economy, then policy changes would be insufficient to achieve targets. If the reverse situation were true and policies were predicted on quarterly model multiplier estimates, then there would be tendencies to overshoot and monetary policy could be destabilizing.

True multipliers could, of course, be somewhere between those of the monthly or quarterly models or outside the estimates from either set of equations. Evidence from other sources, including models that imbed financial sectors within more complete descriptions of the economic system, is needed before firm conclusions can be reached about the degree of reliance for policy formation which should be placed on either the Fed's monthly money market model, or its quarterly counterpart.

F. Unborrowed Reserve versus Discount Rate Impacts

Findings for use of unborrowed reserve versus discount rate policies, however, are less equivocal. Here the monthly and quarterly models present a consistent picture on the superiority of unborrowed reserve policies, at least as judged by money stock and interest rate multipliers. Ratios of multipliers for unborrowed reserve to discount rate impacts may be found in Table 15.

TABLE 14

RATIOS OF MONTHLY TO QUARTERLY MODEL MULTIPLIERS[a]

Quarters of Impact	M1 P1-R	M1 P2-S	M2 P1-R	M2 P2-S	M4 P1-R	M4 P2-S	RCP P1-R	RCP P2-S	R90 P1-R	R90 P2-S	CD3 P1-R	CD3 P2-S
					Change in Unborrowed Reserve							
1	0.88	0.85	0.89	0.81	1.06	4.91	0.92	1.04	0.91	1.02	0.94	1.05
2	1.01	0.99	1.15	0.98	1.17	−7.98	1.14	1.22	1.12	1.19	1.16	1.23
3	1.05	1.08	1.28	1.10	1.26	−0.12	1.25	1.27	1.23	1.25	1.26	1.28
4	1.11	1.14	1.39	1.23	1.35	0.45	1.30	1.32	1.28	1.30	1.31	1.34
5	1.13	1.21	1.41	1.40	1.39	0.79	1.28	1.36	1.26	1.34	1.30	1.38
6	1.11	1.18	1.41	1.48	1.40	1.05	1.28	1.38	1.26	1.36	1.30	1.39
7	1.10	1.16	1.41	1.51	1.41	1.24	1.28	1.38	1.26	1.35	1.30	1.39
8	1.10	1.15	1.41	1.53	1.41	1.37	1.27	1.37	1.24	1.34	1.28	1.38
12	1.14	1.13	1.38	1.50	1.39	1.48	1.26	1.36	1.24	1.33	1.28	1.38
16	1.14		1.45		1.45		1.31		1.28		1.33	
20	1.14		1.41		1.43		1.32		1.29		1.33	
					Change in Discount Rates							
1	0.92	0.89	0.93	0.85	1.10	8.94	0.96	1.07	0.94	1.05	0.97	1.09
2	1.05	1.04	1.20	1.03	1.22	70.53	1.18	1.25	1.16	1.23	1.20	1.27
3	1.09	1.15	1.33	1.16	1.31	−0.18	1.30	1.31	1.27	1.29	1.32	1.33
4	1.15	1.21	1.44	1.31	1.41	0.46	1.34	1.35	1.32	1.33	1.37	1.37
5	1.17	1.27	1.46	1.48	1.45	0.85	1.33	1.39	1.31	1.37	1.35	1.41
6	1.14	1.24	1.46	1.55	1.45	1.12	1.32	1.41	1.30	1.38	1.34	1.42
7	1.14	1.24	1.45	1.59	1.47	1.13	1.33	1.41	1.30	1.38	1.35	1.43
8	1.14	1.22	1.46	1.62	1.47	1.46	1.31	1.40	1.29	1.37	1.33	1.42
12	1.18	1.19	1.42	1.58	1.43	1.58	1.31	1.40	1.29	1.37	1.33	1.41
16	1.18		1.50		1.51		1.36		1.34		1.38	
20	1.18		1.45		1.48		1.37		1.34		1.38	

[a] P1, Period 1972:2–1977:2; P2, 1974:2–1977:2; R, restrictive multiplier ratios; S, stimulative multiplier ratios.

TABLE 15

Ratios of Monthly and Quarterly Model Multipliers for Unborrowed Reserve and Discount Rate Impacts[a]

Quarters of Impact	M1 M	M1 Q	M2 M	M2 Q	M4 M	M4 Q	RCP M	RCP Q	R90 M	R90 Q	CD3 M	CD3 Q
Period 1												
1	1.82	1.90	1.82	1.89	1.81	1.88	1.88	1.95	1.88	1.95	1.88	1.95
2	1.79	1.86	1.79	1.86	1.77	1.85	1.85	1.92	1.85	1.92	1.85	1.92
3	1.72	1.79	1.75	1.82	1.74	1.81	1.77	1.84	1.77	1.84	1.77	1.84
4	1.69	1.75	1.73	1.79	1.73	1.81	1.72	1.79	1.72	1.79	1.72	1.79
5	1.64	1.70	1.70	1.77	1.72	1.79	1.68	1.74	1.68	1.74	1.68	1.74
6	1.62	1.66	1.69	1.74	1.71	1.78	1.64	1.69	1.64	1.69	1.64	1.69
7	1.55	1.61	1.66	1.71	1.69	1.76	1.58	1.63	1.58	1.63	1.58	1.63
8	1.52	1.57	1.63	1.68	1.68	1.74	1.54	1.59	1.54	1.59	1.54	1.59
9	1.47	1.53	1.61	1.66	1.67	1.73	1.49	1.55	1.49	1.55	1.49	1.55
12	1.36	1.41	1.50	1.55	1.61	1.65	1.38	1.43	1.38	1.43	1.38	1.43
16	1.21	1.26	1.37	1.42	1.50	1.56	1.22	1.27	1.22	1.27	1.22	1.27
20	1.08	1.13	1.27	1.30	1.48	1.53	1.09	1.13	1.09	1.13	1.09	1.13
Period 2												
1	1.45	1.53	1.46	1.53	1.45	2.64	1.45	1.49	1.45	1.49	1.45	1.49
2	1.43	1.51	1.44	1.52	1.42	−12.53	1.43	1.47	1.43	1.47	1.43	1.47
3	1.40	1.49	1.42	1.51	1.11	1.72	1.39	1.43	1.39	1.43	1.39	1.43
4	1.39	1.47	1.41	1.49	1.55	1.60	1.37	1.40	1.37	1.40	1.37	1.41
5	1.35	1.43	1.39	1.46	1.47	1.58	1.33	1.36	1.33	1.36	1.33	1.37
6	1.32	1.39	1.37	1.44	1.46	1.56	1.30	1.33	1.30	1.33	1.30	1.33
7	1.27	1.35	1.34	1.42	1.44	1.54	1.25	1.28	1.25	1.28	1.25	1.29
8	1.22	1.29	1.32	1.39	1.44	1.54	1.21	1.24	1.21	1.24	1.21	1.25
12	1.08	1.14	1.22	1.28	1.43	1.53	1.08	1.11	1.08	1.11	1.08	1.11

[a] Restrictive policies in period 1, 1972:2–1977:2; stimulative policies in period 2, 1974:2–1977:2

In general, irrespective of the money stock or interest rate variable examined, unborrowed reserve multipliers are greater than discount rate multipliers by about the same percentage in the initial quarter or two of impact. For restrictive policies in Period 1 (1972:2–1977:2), unborrowed reserve multipliers exceed discount rate multipliers by about 80–90% in both the monthly and quarterly models. Thereafter, there is a decay in superiority and ratios of these multipliers fall. Still, after five years, unborrowed reserve interest rate multipliers are approximately 10% greater than those for discount rates. For money stocks, the comparable ratios are greater by about 10, 30, and 50% for M1, M2, and M4, respectively.

For stimulative policies in Period 2 (1974:2–1977:2), unborrowed reserve multipliers exceed those for discount rates by approximately 45–55% in the first quarter of impact. Then, over another two years, decay in superiority falls to about the same levels as that after five years in the Period 1 simulations.

During both periods degrees of superiority of unborrowed reserves to discount rate policies are slightly lower for the monthly than for the quarterly model. But the differences are small, ranging from three to five percent of the levels of the ratios of relative impacts of these policies.

IX. Conclusion

Temporal aggregation in econometric models is a subject studied little to date but one which potentially looms important for interpretation of short-term movements in the economy and for formulation of countercyclical policies. In the absence of formal techniques for integrating monthly data into analyses of longer-term paths and projections, there will continue to be ad hoc use of information on the "latest" changes in the economy. Hazards of employing such statistics in an informal manner are great.

Under the circumstances, the possible contribution of monthly econometric models for timely analyses of the evolution of the economy, of the impact of exogenous events, and of policy alternatives should be determined. In theory, in the absence of plausible bounds on measurement errors, there are efficiency gains from temporal disaggregation which should lead to better predictive performance.

An empirical test is conducted in this paper with the monthly U.S. money market model constructed by the Board of Governors of the Federal Reserve System. The monthly version of this model is more efficient (measured by average absolute percentage errors) in complete system solutions within the sample period than the quarterly version for 12 of 15 interest rate and money stock variables. However, outside the sample period, error performance is reversed, with the quarterly model being more efficient in 10 of 15 cases.

Among the policy multiplier findings are that there are asymmetries in money stock responses to stimulative versus restrictive policies, with stimulative impacts being somewhat greater (5–10%) than those for restrictive policies. This is not found for interest rate responses, where stimulative and restrictive effects are equivalent.

Another result is that unborrowed reserve multipliers on money stocks and interest rates exceed those for discount rate changes by approximately 45–90% (depending upon the period and whether policy is stimulative or restrictive) in initial quarters of impact. Thereafter, over a two- to five-year period, there is a decay in superiority to about 10% for interest rate multipliers and 10, 30, and 50% for M1, M2, and M4 multipliers, respectively.

Policy multipliers and point elasticities of the monthly and quarterly versions differ significantly; those from the monthly model are substantially greater than those from the quarterly model. Therefore, unless other evidence is brought to bear in choosing between the two versions, the implications of these results potentially are quite disturbing for U.S. policy formation. Depending on the choice of whether the monthly or quarterly model is selected and the true structure of responses of the economy, there may be a tendency to undershoot or overshoot in selecting settings for monetary policy instruments.

The above empirical findings, of course, should not be taken to be applicable generally; they are from solutions and simulations with only a single model. Further, that model has a limited money market purview and exhibits some weaknesses in specification and statistical quality. Yet the results are suggestive. More testing with additional models of the kinds conducted here is needed so that more definitive conclusions can be reached about possible gains and losses from temporal disaggregation.

Appendix

Proof First define an unity vector l with dimension $n \times 1$: $l' = (1, 1, \ldots, 1)$. Then form a matrix A_n of dimension $n \times n$:

(a) $$A_n = l(l'l)^{-1}l' = \frac{1}{n}\begin{pmatrix} 1 & 1 & \cdots & 1 \\ 1 & 1 & \cdots & 1 \\ \vdots & \vdots & & \vdots \\ 1 & 1 & \cdots & 1 \end{pmatrix}.$$

It can be seen easily that the Kronecker product of an identity matrix I_p (dimension $p \times p$) and A_n is $nC'C$, i.e.,

(b) $$I_p \otimes A_n = nC'C,$$

where C, recall, is a matrix with dimension $p \times T$ and has been defined in a similar way as in (6) in the text (also, $np = T$).

Let us further define a matrix with dimension $n \times n$ such that

(c) $$M_n = I_n - A_n,$$

where I_n is an identity matrix.

Therefore

(d) $$I_p \otimes M_n = I_n \otimes (I_n - A_n) = I_p \otimes I_n - I_p \otimes A_n = I_T - nC'C$$

because $I_p \otimes I_n = I_{np} = I_T$ (recalling $T = np$) and, from (b), $I_p \otimes A_n = nC'C$.

From (d), it is clear that in order to show $I_T - nC'C$ is an idempotent matrix, it need only be shown that M_n is an idempotent matrix. From (c), it is obvious that M_n is a symmetrix matrix because both I_n and A_n are. We now proceed to show $M_n M_n = M_n$:

$$\begin{aligned} M_n M_n &= (I_n - A_n)(I_n - A_n) \\ &= [I_n - l(l'l)^{-1}l'][I_n - l(l'l)^{-1}l'] \quad \text{(from (a))} \\ &= I_n - l(l'l)^{-1}l = I_n - A_n = M_n \quad \text{Q.E.D.} \end{aligned}$$

ACKNOWLEDGMENTS

This research was supported in part by the National Science Foundation. A significant part of the research was completed while E. C. Hwa was a member of the staff of SRI International. The views expressed herein are those of the authors and do not necessarily reflect those of the organizations with which they are associated or of the National Science Foundation. The authors are indebted to Lawrence R. Klein, Gary Smith, and Arnold Zellner for helpful comments.

REFERENCES

Bodkin, R. G. (1973). Discussion. *American Economic Review*, **43**, 410–411.
Edwards, J. B., and Orcutt, G. H. (1969). Should aggregation prior to estimation be the rule? *Review of Economics and Statistics* **51**, 409–420.
Engle, R. F., and Liu, T. C. (1972). Effects of aggregation over time on dynamic characteristics of an economic model. *In Econometric Models of Cylical Behavor* (B. G. Hickman, ed.), Studies in Income and Wealth. No. 36, Vol. 2. New York: National Bureau of Economic Research.
Friend, I., and Taubman, P. (1964). A short-term forecasting model. *The Review of Economics and Statistics* **46**, 229–236.
Fromm, G., and Klein, L. R. (1973). A comparison of eleven econometric models of the United States. *American Economic Review* **43**, 385–393.
Fromm, G., and Klein, L. R. (1976). The NBER/NSF model comparison seminar: An analysis of results. *Annals of Economic and Social Measurements* **5**, No. 1, 1–28.
Fromm, G., and Schink, G. R. (1973). Aggregation and econometric models, *International Economic Review* **14**, No. 1, 1–32.

Geweke, J. (1979). Temporal aggregation in the multiple regression model. *Econometrica* **46**, 643–662.

Granger, C. W. J. (1966). The typical spectral shape of an economic variable, *Econometrica* **34**, 150–161.

Griliches, Z., and Grunfeld, Y. (1960). Is Aggregation necessarily bad? *Review of Economics and Statistics* **42**, 1–13.

Haitovsky, Y., Treyz, G., and Su, V. (1974). *Forecasts with Quarterly Macroeconomic Models*, New York: National Bureau of Economic Research.

Hannan, E. J. (1970). *Multiple Time Series Analysis*. New York: Wiley.

Harberger, A. C. (1967). Discussion. In *Tax Incentives and Capital Spending* (G. Fromm, ed.), Chapter VII. Washington, D.C.: The Brookings Institution.

Jenkins, G. M., and Watts, D. G. (1968). *Spectral Analysis and Its Applications*. San Francisco, California: Holden-Day.

Johnston, J. (1963). *Econometric Methods*. New York: McGraw Hill.

Klein, L. R., and Burmeister, E. (1976). *Econometric Model Performance: Comparative Simulation Studies of the U.S. Economy*. Philadelphia, Pennsylvania: University of Pennsylvania Press.

Kuh, E. (1969). *An Essay of Aggregation Theory and Practice*. Working Paper No. 43, Department of Economics, Massachusetts Institute of Technology, Cambridge, Massachusetts.

Liu, T. C. (1969). A monthly recursive econometric model of the United States: A test of feasibility. *Review of Economics and Statistics* **51**, 1–13.

Liu, T. C., and Hwa, E. C. (1976). A monthly model of the U.S. economy. *In Econometric Model Performance: Comparative Simulation Studies of the U.S. Economy* (L. R. Klein and E. Burmeister, eds.). Philadelphia, Pennsylvania: University of Pennsylvania Press.

Montmarquette, C., and Zellner, A. (1971). A study of some aspects of temporal aggregation problems in econometric analyses. *Review of Economics and Statistics* **50**, 335–341.

Mundlak, Y. (1961). Aggregation over time in distributed lag models, *International Economic Review* **2**, No. 2, 154–163.

Orcutt, G. H., Watts, H. W., and Edwards, J. B. (1968). Data aggregation and information loss. *American Economic Review* **58**, 773–787.

Sims, C. A. (1971). Discrete approximations to continuous time distributed lags in econometrics. *Econometrica* **39**, 545–563.

Su, V. (1975). An evaluation of ASA/NBER business outlook survey forecasts. *Explorations in Economic Research* **2**, No. 4.

Theil, H. (1954). *Linear Aggregation of Economic Relations*. Amsterdam: North-Holland Publ.

Thomson, T. D., Pierce, J. L., and Parry, R. T. (1975). A monthly money market model. *Journal of Money Credit and Banking*, 411–431.

Wei, W. W. S. (1978). Some consequences of temporal aggregation in seasonal time series models. *In Seasonal Analysis of Economic Time Series* (A. Zellner, ed.). Washington, D.C.: U.S. Bureau of the Census.

Gary Fromm
SRI INTERNATIONAL
ARLINGTON, VIRGINIA

E. C. Hwa[*]
SRI INTERNATIONAL
SPRINGFIELD, VIRGINIA

[*] Present address: International Monetary Fund, Washington, D.C.

Recent Economic Fluctuations and Stabilization Policies: An Optimal Control Approach

LAWRENCE R. KLEIN

and

VINCENT SU

I. Introduction and Summary

Generally speaking, the U.S. economy has suffered a series of setbacks that began in the fourth quarter of 1970, when the General Motors strike brought the economy as a whole into a relapse in recovery from the 1969 recession. In that quarter, the inflation rate was at a 6.3% annual rate, while the unemployment rate rose to 5.8%. This was the first time since 1958 that we had both rapid inflation and high unemployment simultaneously. This, in turn, led to confusion over corrective policies. In early 1971, a rapid upswing in the wage rates of construction workers and a sharp rise in lumber prices combined to increase construction costs drastically. The impact of high construction costs not only substantially enhanced the price and rental cost of houses but also quickly spread into other sectors and led to another round of serious inflation. In the meantime, because of a poor harvest, the price of food was shooting up sharply during the summer of 1971. High housing expenditures and food bills forced households to reduce other types of consumption; the decline in consumption, in turn, discouraged employment. The unemployment rate therefore remained high in spite of high inflation.

The New Economic Policy aimed at curbing inflation and stimulating employment was initiated by President Nixon on August 15, 1971. The major actions were a 90-day freeze on wages, prices, and rents; the imposition of a temporary 10% surcharge on dutiable imports; and suspension of convertibility of the dollar into gold. A number of other edicts were issued at the same time. In the subsequent two and a half years, wages and prices remained subject to some sort of controls. The controls program was not completely lifted until the end of April, 1974. However, the incomes policy failed miserably to attain its target of cutting inflation. The general price level continued to climb after 1971:4. Toward the end of 1973, the annual inflation rate had already reached 8.55% a year; the unemployment level, nevertheless, had come down to 4.7%. At the same time, with the new economic policy in effect, the foreign trade balance remained unfavorable until 1973:1.

The worldwide oil embargo, starting at the end of 1973, led the U.S. into a formidable problem of inflationary recession. Real GNP suddenly plunged at an annual rate of -7% in the first quarter of 1974. Because of the energy shortage, the inflation rate jumped into double-digit figures for most of 1974. The unemployment rate rapidly climbed to a 35-year high of 9%, with real GNP falling for six consecutive quarters. Indeed, the economy was in very serious trouble. By the end of the first quarter of 1975, there was no indication of recovery in sight.

Some of these troubles were initially caused by exogenous events that were out of the government's control, such as the poor agricultural harvest and the induced energy shortage resulting from the oil embargo. In addition, the psychological effects of the Watergate incident and its subsequent consequences were clearly unanticipated. The economic disturbances of these external shocks, which were by no means completely avoidable, should have been limited to a minimum by effective and prompt macroeconomic policy actions. Therefore, it is worthwhile to evaluate the economic policies that were designed to pursue macroeconomic objectives in this period.

Of course, there are macroeconomic policies that can either reduce inflation or moderate recession. However, policies that help to ease inflation will often intensify recession. It is therefore interesting to determine whether the government can remove or at least reduce the severity of the recent inflation and recession simultaneously by exercising fiscal and monetary policies in a reasonable range. In other words, is there a set of effective policies that could have avoided the current exogenously induced inflationary recession?

In recent years, the development of macroeconometric models and the availability of computational algorithms have made optimal control theory, originally developed in electrical engineering, a possible means of economic policy evaluation. Given an econometric model that is a comprehensive representation of the economy, and given an objective function that represents the targets and objectives of economic stabilization, the optimal values of policy variables in a given period of time can be obtained through model simulation techniques. The selection of the objective function is usually subjective and often arbitrary. The number of target variables, the number of policy variables, the magnitudes of their weights, and the length of the control period reflect the subjective decision of the policymaker. For discrete-time econometric models, the optimal control problems can be looked upon as problems in choosing variables to optimize the objective function.

The problem of optimum control in the context of econometric models can be stated as follows: An economy can be described by an equation system as

(1) $$f_i(y'_t, y'_{t-1}, \ldots, y'_{t-p}, x'_t, z'_t) = e_{it}, \quad i = 1, 2, \ldots, n,$$

where

$$y_t = \begin{bmatrix} y_{1t} \\ y_{2t} \\ \vdots \\ y_{nt} \end{bmatrix}, \quad x_t = \begin{bmatrix} x_{1t} \\ x_{2t} \\ \vdots \\ x_{mt} \end{bmatrix}, \quad z_t = \begin{bmatrix} z_{1t} \\ z_{2t} \\ \vdots \\ z_{rt} \end{bmatrix}, \quad e_t = \begin{bmatrix} e_{1t} \\ e_{2t} \\ \vdots \\ e_{nt} \end{bmatrix},$$

y_t are endogenous (target) variables, x_t exogenous control (policy) variables, z_t exogenous noncontrol variables, e_t random errors. The econometric model in (1) is a stochastic, nonlinear dynamic equation system. It is a discrete-time representation of a continuous economic universe and depends on a finite number of parameters that have been estimated from sample data.

The objective, or welfare, function in general can be written

(2) $$C = -C[(y_t - y_t^*)', \ldots, (y_{t+h} - y_{t+h}^*)'; x'_t, \ldots, x'_{t+h}, w'_n; p'_m],$$

where w_n and p_m are the vectors of weights applied to the target variables and the policy variables. Total welfare, negatively measured, is a function of the deviations of endogenous variables from their targets (y_t^*) over the planning horizon h and also of the values of the controlled exogenous (policy) variables that are used to steer the system toward targets.

Since not all target variables are viewed as being of equal importance, more emphasis should be given to the variables that are more important. Therefore the deviations of different variables from their targets carry different weights in the welfare function. The values of the weights, which are subjectively determined, reflect the relative importance of target variables in the evaluator's opinion.

Of course, not all elements in x_t need be used as instruments at any point of time, nor do all elements of y_t needed be targeted. If only one endogenous variable is targeted and one instrument is to be used, an obvious solution, which would have the value of the target variable fall exactly on the target, can be sought in a deterministic simulation. The usual methods of solution of the econometric system are simply applied to a case of reclassification of variables in which the target variable, originally endogenous, changes place with the instrument variable, originally exogenous. If the number of endogenous variables to be targeted is greater than one, a problem of choice involving optimization conditions exists unless exactly two instruments are also being used. Because the econometric model is a simultaneous and single-valued system, it is not possible to have two or more target variables fall exactly on their targets, especially when two target variables are closely related or contradictory in the system. For example, there is no way to keep inflation at a low rate when the economy is at a full-employment level no matter how many instruments are used, because these two variables are related elsewhere in the model by a Phillips curve. It is therefore necessary to augment the econometric model system with additional relations derived from the maximization conditions of the welfare function. The number of additional relations must be equal to the number of instruments used, because the values of instrument variables also have to be determined in the system.

Because of the nonlinearity in econometric models, the systems are usually solved by the Gauss–Seidel iterative method. If the model is solved for more than one period, the solution values of the endogenous variables for previous periods are used as values for the lagged endogenous variables in the current period. If the planning horizon includes h periods, the optimal control problem for a deterministic model is to choose values for policy variables $x_t, x_{t+1}, \ldots, x_{t+h}$ so as to maximize C in (2) subject to the econometric model (1).

Without any constraints on policy variables, the optimal solutions for policy variables may become unrealistic and unreasonable. A set of unreasonable values of policy variables may often disturb the convergence of the solution. In other words, the model cannot be solved at the optimal level. A policymaker usually prefers to achieve the goals while maintaining a smooth movement of all policy variables. A policymaker would not be willing to have a sizable change in government spending or money supply from quarter to quarter even though the change is sometimes necessary to achieve the maximum welfare. Instead, the government would rather have a deviation from its current level that is as small as possible. Therefore the welfare function should imply a set of penalties on the policy instruments that substantially deviate from the current level or some desired level. The size of these penalties would be determined by the extent of stability desired in economic policies.

The optimal solution so obtained lies somewhere between the realization and the target. The closeness of the solution to the target depends on the specification of and the weights and penalties in the welfare function. After the specification is determined, for each set of weights and penalties there is in general only one optimal solution. This optimal solution should also fully reflect the economic priorities of target variables and the required stabilities of policy variables.

II. Experimental Design

Our objective in this paper is to find out whether there existed a set of feasible public policies that could have been pursued by the Federal Government over the period of 1971:1–1975:1 that would have avoided the inflationary recession and achieved a remarkably better economy. We are also interested in finding the extent of the improvement that could have been achieved if these optimal policies were in fact implemented. In addition, it is also interesting to know the proportions of total improvement that could be attributed to different fiscal and monetary policies.

The objectives were investigated on behalf of the Wharton model's participation in the seminar on model comparison of the Conference in Econometrics and Mathematical Economics. Overall seminar results are being presented in a paper by Hirsch, Hymans, and Shapiro (1978).

A. The Econometric Model

The model used to evaluate economic policies in this study is the Wharton MARK IV quarterly model. This version of the Wharton model is now outdated because of basic revisions in the national income and product accounts from January, 1976. It is a system of nonlinear simultaneous equations with approximately 450 equations and identities and 200 exogenous variables. The ordinary-least-squares method was used to estimate all coefficients, subject, however, to the Cochrane–Orcutt technique for adjusting those equations that had significant serial correlation of residuals. The sample period used for estimating most of the equations was from the third quarter of 1953 to the fourth quarter of 1973. The problem is to show how a large nonlinear system can be analyzed by the method of optimal control. We are able to show that this approach is entirely feasible.

B. THE WELFARE FUNCTION

In order to compute the optimal control solution for a model, it is necessary to specify the objective function in parametric form. To be realistic, economic policymakers should adopt a modest set of targets and use only a few major instruments. It is not generally possible for them to think in high dimensions simultaneously. In our study, four target variables are the growth rate of real GNP, the inflation rate, the unemployment rate, and the foreign trade balance. The policy variables are government spending, an income tax surcharge, and unborrowed reserves. The number of effective targets (4) is greater than the number of instruments (3). We did not want to have an equal or greater number of instruments. The period of evaluation is from the first quarter of 1971 to the first quarter of 1975, a total of 17 quarters.

The welfare function in our study is assumed to be a quadratic function as follows:

$$(3) \quad C = -\sum_{t=1971:1}^{1975:1} [w_1(y_{1t} - y_{1t}^*)^2 + w_2(y_{2t} - y_{2t}^*)^2 + w_3(y_{3t} - y_{3t}^*)^2$$
$$+ w_4(y_{4t} - y_{4t}^*)^2 + p_1(x_{1t} - x_{1t}^*)^2 + p_2(x_{2t} - x_{2t}^*)^2$$
$$+ p_3(x_{3t} - x_{3t}^*)^2],$$

where y_1 is the growth rate of GNP, y_2 the rate of inflation, y_3 the rate of unemployment, y_4 the ratio of foreign trade balance to GNP, x_1 government expenditures, x_2 an average income tax rate level, x_3 unborrowed reserves. An asterisk indicates the optimal goal or desired level; w_is are the subjective weights attached to target variables; and p_js are the penalties attached to the use of policy instruments. The maximum total welfare should be equal to zero when all endogenous variables fall right on their targets. Total welfare will be negative if any endogenous variable deviates from its target.

The specification of the objective function assumes that policymakers are just looking term-by-term at deviations in the square of y_{it} from y_{it}^* or x_{jt} from x_{jt}^*. They are not paying attention in a highly sophisticated way to the cross products of $(y_{it} - y_{it}^*)(y_{kt} - y_{kt}^*)$ or $(x_{jt} - x_{jt}^*)(x_{kt} - x_{kt}^*)$. They also ignore the values of z_{it}, the noncontrol exogenous variables, although they take account of the effects of these variables in the econometric model.

A quadratic objective function so specified has some mathematical convenience in implementation. A quadratic function so specified is differentiable with respect to all variables included, and none of the first derivative solutions is trivial provided these weights are positive. However, the target variables so included in the objective function indicate that the deviations of a variable from its target value are equally undesirable regardless of

RECENT ECONOMIC FLUCTUATIONS AND STABILIZATION POLICIES 231

their signs. In reality, positive deviations may be viewed as more or less undesirable than the negative deviations according to the nature of the target variable. For example, negative deviations from the target of unemployment rate and inflation rate may be much more desirable than positive deviations. On the other hand, positive deviations from the targets of foreign trade balance and economic growth are more desirable than negative deviations. We have not investigated asymmetry in this paper, but it would be possible to make optimal control simulations with asymmetric welfare functions.

The objective function in matrix notation is

(4) $$C = -[Y'WY + X'PX],$$

where

$$Y = \begin{bmatrix} y_{1,1} - y^*_{1,1} \\ y_{2,1} - y^*_{2,1} \\ y_{3,1} - y^*_{3,1} \\ y_{4,1} - y^*_{4,1} \\ \vdots \\ y_{4,17} - y^*_{4,17} \end{bmatrix}, \quad W = \begin{bmatrix} w_1 & & & & & & & & 0 \\ & w_2 & & & & & & & \\ & & w_3 & & & & & & \\ & & & w_4 & & & & & \\ & & & & \ddots & & & & \\ & & & & & w_1 & & & \\ & & & & & & w_2 & & \\ & & & & & & & w_3 & \\ 0 & & & & & & & & w_4 \end{bmatrix},$$

$$X = \begin{bmatrix} x_{1,1} - x^*_{1,1} \\ x_{2,1} - x^*_{2,1} \\ x_{3,1} - x^*_{3,1} \\ \vdots \\ x_{3,17} - x^*_{3,17} \end{bmatrix}, \quad P = \begin{bmatrix} p_1 & & & & & & 0 \\ & p_2 & & & & & \\ & & p_3 & & & & \\ & & & \ddots & & & \\ & & & & p_1 & & \\ 0 & & & & & p_2 & \\ & & & & & & p_3 \end{bmatrix}.$$

Y is a 68 × 1 column vector of target variables because there are four target variables and seventeen control periods. X is a 51 × 1 vector of policy variables because there are three policy variables and seventeen control periods. W is a 68 × 68 diagonal matrix of subjective weights whose diagonal values indicate the weights of target variables in different time periods. P is a 51 × 51 diagonal matrix of penalties whose diagonal values indicate the relative penalties on use of instrumental variables in different time periods.

C. Optimization

In order to maximize total welfare, we differentiate the welfare function with respect to all policy variables in all time periods:

$$\frac{dC}{dX} = -2\frac{dY}{dX}WY - 2PX.$$

Letting $U' = (dY/dX)$, which is a 68 × 51 matrix, and setting the above equation equal to zero, we obtain

(5) $$X = -P^{-1}U'WY.$$

This is a set of 51 equations that can be added to the econometric model in order to "endogenize" the three policy variables for 17 periods.

The matrix U' consists of the partial derivatives of each element of Y with respect to each element of X. They are, in fact, the well-known dynamic multipliers of an economic (model) system. For a linear system, the matrix U' would consist of constant entries. Dynamic multipliers vary with time, but they are invariant with respect to initial conditions and are constant for variation with respect to an element of X. The variation of the elements of X accounts for variation over time.

If the system were linear, the elements of U' would be evaluated once and for all by dynamic simulation of the system, and, except for round-off error, these multiplier values would be independent of the increments in elements of X used to obtain estimates of the consequent variation of elements of Y.

Given that the system is nonlinear, in general, we *approximate* the elements of U' by calculating the dynamic multipliers of the system from an arbitrary (historical) set of initial conditions. As will be indicated below, it is possible to iterate the calculation and recalculate the elements of U' as initial conditions change as a result of the optimization process itself.

A baseline solution with which optimal simulations are to be compared is a *tracking* solution, i.e., a historical solution in which single-equation residuals have been added back to the constant term of each stochastic equation in order that the baseline solution generates this historical dataset [see Treyz (1972)].

The solution algorithm consists of an interaction back and forth between solutions to (1) and (5). The model is solved along the baseline path by applying the usual Gauss–Seidel method to (1). Elements of Y are taken from that solution and inserted in the right-hand side of (5) to obtain a revised estimate of X. The new values for X are inserted into (1) to obtain a new solution. A second revised estimate of X is obtained from (5), and so on until the welfare function remains unchanged from iteration to iteration. It takes about seven iterations for the Wharton model to converge in such optimal control calculations but most of the alterations to the baseline solution occurs in the first two iterations.

This algorithm converges for the particular weighting systems used in this paper but is sensitive to choice of low weights for the instruments. In case it is desired to "explore" the weighting pattern and consider the possibility of large swings in instrument values, the algorithm may diverge. A simple modification turns it into a convergent algorithm for such cases (see Section VI).

The linearity of (5) results from the quadratic specification of the welfare function. This is why this quadratic is so simple to handle. The virtue of this entire algorithm is that it builds directly on all the software that is repeatedly used in general model simulation.

III. Dynamic Multiplier

In order to study the net impact of policy variables on target variables, a study of dynamic multipliers was made using the tracking solution as a baseline case. In total, 51 simulations have been computed. They were grouped into three categories to derive the dynamic multipliers of government spending, tax change and monetary action. Each category consisted of seventeen simulations and each simulation started at a different time period. from 1971:1 to 1975:1. Some target variables were transformations of endogenous variables in the model. The target variables included in the objective function are defined in terms of Wharton Model variables as follows:

$$Y_{1t} = [(GNP_t/GNP_{t-1})^4 - 1] * 100,$$
$$Y_{2t} = [(P_t/P_{t-1})^4 - 1] * 100,$$
$$Y_{3t} = UR_t,$$
$$Y_{4t} = [(EX\$_t - IM\$_t)/GNP\$_t] * 100,$$

where GNP is the gross national product in 1958 dollars, P the GNP deflator, UR the unemployment rate, EX$ total exports in current dollars, IM$ total imports in current dollars, GNP$ the gross national product in current dollars.

In the government-spending simulations, the policy change was a $5 billion sustained increase above the observed level in Federal defense expenditures. Defense expenditures were arbitrarily used because the multipliers of defense and nondefense expenditures were practically the same in the Wharton MARK IV model. The macroeconomic impact of policy actions in this particular nonlinear model has proved to be approximately symmetric; therefore, it did not matter whether the initial change was positive or negative. We used a $5 billion change as a unit instead of $1 billion in order to amplify the final impact on target variables. The simulation paths of the four target variables were then compared with their time paths in the baseline solution. The differences showed the net effects of a $5 billion sustained increase in government spending.

Federal defense expenditures were measured in current dollars, and the real strength of a $5 billion increase declined due to the rapid inflation during the period of this study. For example, $5 billion in government spending in the first quarter of 1975 was equivalent to $3.55 billion in the first quarter of 1971, after deflation.

Nine different income tax rates, one for each tax bracket, were included in the Wharton model to calculate the tax base. A flat 5% sustained decrease of the tax rates of all brackets was assumed in the tax multiplier simulations. Total income tax revenue is closely related to cyclical fluctuation of income. A 5% tax decrease in a prosperous year is substantially more stimulative than in a recession year. Therefore, we expected the influence of a sustained 5% change in tax rates to be very responsive over the course of the business cycle.

The money supply (M1) in the Wharton model is an endogenous variable and could not be directly controlled. The most effective control variable that would directly influence money supply and interest rates was unborrowed reserves. In the monetary policy simulations, the only change made in exogenous variables was a $0.5 billion sustained increase in unborrowed reserves. A $0.5 billion increase in unborrowed reserves causes approximately a $2.0 billion increase in money supply in the Wharton model. Since unborrowed reserves are measured in current dollars, the net impacts on target variables measured in real terms or ratios diminish due to the rapid inflation.

The distribution of net effects of different types of policy actions on various target variables over time is worth some discussion. A simple comparison of the time path of a target variable of a policy simulation with that of the baseline solution indicates the effectiveness of the policy action. The differences between the time paths of different policy simulations beginning in the first quarter of 1971 and that of the baseline solution are plotted in Figures 1–4 as examples because this set of simulations covers all 17 quarters. The effectiveness of macroeconomic policies in the first simulation can be summarized as follows:

A. REAL GNP

The initial impact of a $5 billion sustained increase in government spending on real GNP was $4.3 billion in 1958 dollars in the first quarter of 1971; it

RECENT ECONOMIC FLUCTUATIONS AND STABILIZATION POLICIES

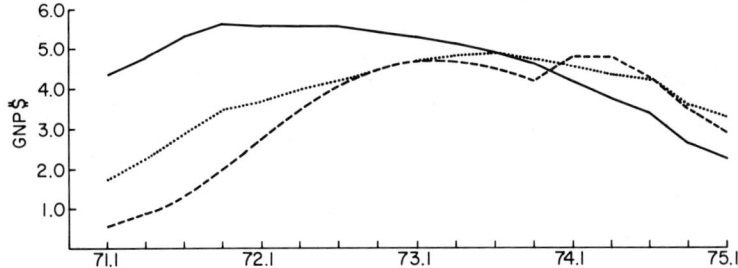

Figure 1 The time paths of the differences between various policy simulations and actual data of GNP in simulation initialized 1971:1. Solid line: government-spending simulation; dotted line: tax-cut simulation; dashed line: monetary simulation.

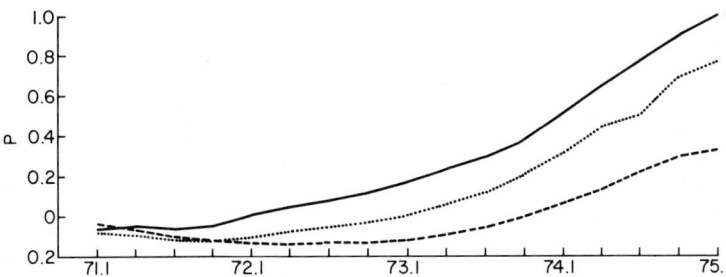

Figure 2 The time paths of the differences between various policy simulations and actual data of price deflator in simulation initialized 1971:1. Solid line: government-spending simulation; dotted line: tax-cut simulation; dashed line: monetary simulation.

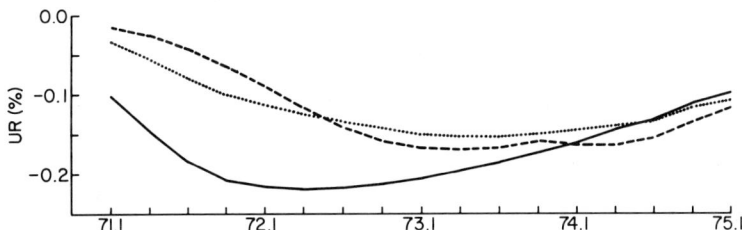

Figure 3 The time paths of the differences between various policy simulations and actual data of unemployment rate in simulations initialized 1971:1. Solid line: government-spending simulation; dotted line: tax-cut simulation; dashed line: monetary simulation.

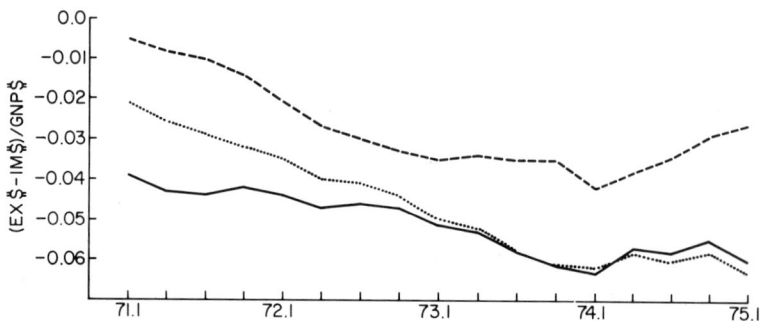

Figure 4 The time paths of the differences between various policy simulations and actual data of trade-balance–GNP ratio in simulation initialized 1971:1. Solid line: government-spending simulation; dotted line: tax-cut simulation; dashed line: monetary simulation.

is equivalent to $6.02 billion in current dollars. The first-quarter (short-run) multiplier is about 1.2. The impact reached its peak after four or five quarters. The peak effect was usually 25–30% stronger than the initial impact, the multiplier at the peak quarter is approximately 1.6. The effect remained strong for four of five quarters and then began to decline gradually. At the end of the fourth year, the total impact dropped to a level of $2.23 billion in 1958 dollars, or $4.07 billion in current dollars. The multiplier of the last quarter is less than one.

It seems that the reaction of GNP to a cut in tax rates is less responsive than to a change in government spending in the first several quarters. The initial effect on real GNP in the first quarter of 1971 was only $1.71 billion if there were a 5% tax cut, whereas added government expenditures of equal amount induce a rise in GNP of $4.3 billion. The total impact of a tax cut takes a much longer time, roughly nine or ten quarters, to reach its peak. At the peak, the impact is about three times greater than the initial impact. Net effects start to decline gradually after the peak has been reached. At the end of four years, the impact drops to $3.248 billion.

The level of real GNP responds to monetary actions very slowly in the first several quarters. The initial increase in real GNP resulting from a sustained increase of $0.5 billion in unborrowed reserves is only $0.514 billion. The effect builds up rapidly to a peak after eight or nine quarters and remains at a high level. However, there was a dip in the fourth quarter of 1973 when the Fed had actually tightened up money supply. The net effect at the peak is about nine to ten times greater than the initial effect. The total effect drops rapidly after 1974:2, it was only $2.89 billion in the last quarter of our control period.

B. THE PRICE LEVEL

It seems that none of the policy actions would have a very effective impact on the general price level in this period. Among the three different types of policy actions, government spending has a slightly stronger impact. The GNP price deflator decreases slightly in the first four simulated quarters and then becomes monotonically increasing as the federal defense spending is increased by $5 billion per year. At the end of fourth year, the price deflator rises approximately one index point.

In a static analysis, the tax cut would stimulate aggregate demand and push up prices. However, in our dynamic simulation, the impact of a sustained 5% tax cut on the level of prices is negative in the first two years. It turns positive and accumulates to three-quarters of an index point at the end of the simulation period. There are some minor cyclical movements in the time path of the tax simulation because the amount of tax revenue fluctuates with the business cycle.

The impact of the changes in money supply on the price level is not significant. The level of price would be consistently lower for eleven quarters if the money supply had a sustained increase of $2 billion a quarter. This was quite contrary to the argument of the Federal Reserve Board during this period. However, the price level starts to climb moderately in the third year after the initial increase in the money supply. At the end of the simulation period, the level of price is only 0.335 index points higher than the actual level.

C. THE RATE OF UNEMPLOYMENT

It was apparent that the rate of unemployment should decline when the government spending increases. In the 1971:1 government spending simulation, the unemployment rate is only 0.1% lower than the actual level in the first quarter. The impact of government spending on the rate of unemployment reaches its peak after six quarters. At the peak the rate of unemployment is 0.22% lower than the actual. The effect declines gradually as the real value of a 5 billion increase in government spending decreases. The last-quarter impact is reduced to 0.1%.

Obviously, tax policy has weaker initial effect on the unemployment rate than the public expenditure policy. The first-year impact on the unemployment rate due to a 5% tax cut is only one-half of that due to a $5 billion increase in government spending. The first-quarter impact is only a 0.03–0.04% reduction in the rate of unemployment. It takes about ten quarters for the impact to accumulate to a peak. At the peak, the rate of unemployment is only 0.15–0.16% lower than the actual. It is declining at a much slower pace after the peak has been reached. At the end, its effect is slightly higher than that due to spending policies.

The first year impact on the unemployment rate due to a $2 billion increase in money supply is the least significant. For example, it is only -0.014% in the first quarter. The peak impact is found in the tenth quarter, and its strength is more than ten times greater than the first quarter impact. The declining path after the peak is smoother. The last-quarter impact is slightly stronger than that of the other two policy actions.

D. The Trade-Balance–GNP Ratio

The influences of different policy actions on the trade-balance–GNP ratio are all cyclical and rather weak. The influences of both fiscal policies indicate similar time paths, but expenditure policy has a stronger impact on the trade balance ratio than tax policy in the first several quarters. In the first several quarters, the effect of tax actions is approximately one-half that of expenditure action. However, both paths reach their peaks in the first quarter of 1974. Both paths also show a pattern of fluctuations in the period right after the oil embargo.

The impact of monetary action is the least significant for trade effects. Its time path indicates that the effect is very small in the beginning quarters and accumulates to a peak in the first quarter of 1974. However, the strength of the effect diminishes after the peak is reached. The impact of monetary policy is only one-half that of fiscal policies in the last quarter.

The lag distribution of the effects of policy actions on target variables in other simulations, which are initialized at later quarters, are quite similar to the first one. However, the magnitudes of the initial effect and the peak effect are affected by business cycles. Generally speaking, we can draw the following conclusions according to our experiments:

1. The expenditure policy action has stronger effect on all four target variables than other policies. The effect of monetary policy action seems to be the weakest among them all.

2. Since there is no simple way to compare the implementation difficulty of a $5 billion rise in federal defense expenditures with that of a 5% cut in income tax rates or with that of a $0.5 billion increase in unborrowed reserves, it is difficult to draw clearcut conclusions of the relative effectiveness of these three policy actions.

3. In general, the influence of expenditure policy on target variables is quicker and very strong in the beginning quarters. The influence of tax

policy is not very strong in beginning quarters and takes a longer period of time to reach its peak. The influence of monetary policy is insignificant in the short run and usually takes more than two years to reach its peak. However, the influence also declines at a slower rate after the peak is reached.

4. A comparison of Figs. 1 and 3 indicates that the distributions of policy impacts on these two variables are similar if one graph is inverted. This denotes the close relationship between GNP and the rate of unemployment.

IV. The Optimal Control Solutions

A. A Simple Optimal Solution

In the first experiment, we tried a straightforward optimal solution. The goals and weights of target variables were arbitrarily assigned as

$$Y^*_{1t} = 4.0, \quad Y^*_{2t} = 4.0, \quad Y^*_{3t} = 4.0, \quad Y^*_{4t} = 0.0,$$
$$W_1 = 1, \quad W_2 = 1, \quad W_3 = 1, \quad W_4 = \tfrac{1}{3}.$$

It indicated that the targets of the growth rate, the inflation rate, and the unemployment rate were all set at an annual rate of 4% in the 17-quarter period. The desirable foreign trade balance was set at the level that made imports equal to exports. The weights of target variables were all equal to unity except the weight of trade balance, which was one-third. It implied that the goal of economic growth, price stability, and full employment were equally important, but the goal of maintaining a zero trade balance was considered as only a third as important as the other three goals.

The desired level of all three policy variables was the actual level observed in the 17-quarter period. Hence, the desired level changed from quarter to quarter. The penalties on three policy variables were set as

$$P_1 = 1.0, \quad P_2 = 1.0 \quad P_3 = 0.05.$$

It assumed that the implementation difficulty of a $5 billion change in government spending was equal to that of a 5% change in income tax rates. Nevertheless, a change in unborrowed reserves, which would not require legislative actions, was considered to be implemented more easily. The penalty on monetary policy is therefore only one-twentieth of the penalties on fiscal policies.

In this solution, we do not stress the importance of any particular quarter or quarters so that the weights and penalties are the same in all quarters. If it is desirable to treat any particular quarter of quarters differently for whatever reasons, the weights or the penalties or both could be assigned different numerical values.

After all parameters in the welfare function are defined, we should then be able to obtain a set of optimum policies by using the algorithm discussed in the previous section. This set of policies would maximize total welfare in the welfare function. The actual and optimal levels of both target and policy variables are reported in Table 1.

Table 1 indicates that the optimal solution is not much different from reality. Generally speaking, the optimal solution has slightly smoothed the cyclical movements in the target variables. The optimal solution pushes more growth in real GNP in 1971 and in early 1972 and 1973. Therefore, the level of real optimal GNP at the peak of 1973:4 is $3.0 billion lower than the actual. As the economy slips into the recession after the oil embargo, it declines at a slower rate. The real GNP is $3.0 higher than the actual in the first quarter of 1975.

The optimal solution raises the inflation rate in 1972 and early 1973, when inflation is relatively moderate, in order to bring down the high inflation after the oil embargo. However, the double-digit inflation in late 1974 and early 1975 was not avoidable. At the end of the simulation period, the price level is about 0.18 of an index point higher than the actual data.

The impact of optimal policies on unemployment rates has been confusing. It reduces the unemployment rate in the period from the third quarter of 1971 to the last quarter of 1972, when the problem of unemployment was not serious. However, the optimal policies push up the rates of unemployment in the last quarter of 1974 and the first quarter of 1975, when the problem of unemployment was serious.

There is no significant influence on the ratio of foreign trade balance to GNP in the optimal solution because policy actions affect both imports and GNP in the same direction. In the 17-quarter period, the trade balance ratio is pushed closer to zero in only six quarters. There are but trivial effects on the levels of total imports and total exports, except in the first quarter of 1975. In that particular quarter, total imports are pushed up by more than $11 billion and exports by $6.2 billion. It reduces the favorable trade balance of $8.8 billion in that quarter to $3.9 billion in the optimal solution.

This optimal solution indicates that there are no substantial differences between the optimal solution and reality. In other words, macroeconomic policies implemented during this period have already been optimized given the economic conditions in this period and the assumptions made in the welfare function. Since it is hard to believe that the economy has been near the optimal level, our assumptions of targets, desired policies and weights and penalties, which were all used to derive the optimal solution, should be reexamined.

TABLE 1

THE ACTUAL AND OPTIMAL LEVELS OF TARGET AND POLICY VARIABLES IN THE SIMPLE OPTIMAL SOLUTIONS

	Y_1		Y_2		Y_3		Y_4		X_1		X_2		X_3	
	Actual	Optimal	Actual	Optimal	Actual	Optimal	Actual	Optimal	Actual	Optimal	Actual	Optimal	Actual	Optimal
1971:1	10.282	9.088	4.618	4.630	5.946	6.020	0.281	0.299	71.8	69.1	1.000	1.009854	29.68	30.33
2	2.731	3.677	4.906	4.696	5.910	5.938	−0.009	0.005	70.8	69.7	1.000	1.000141	29.80	30.37
3	2.796	3.169	2.608	2.551	5.958	5.945	0.009	0.007	70.0	69.4	1.000	0.997474	29.89	30.16
4	6.608	10.747	1.842	1.446	5.957	5.754	−0.315	−0.375	72.1	78.1	1.000	0.975875	30.76	30.99
1972:1	6.359	7.455	5.434	5.399	5.820	5.584	−0.628	−0.709	75.9	83.0	1.000	0.975160	32.19	32.31
2	8.385	5.537	2.071	2.526	5.674	5.461	−0.606	−0.644	75.9	77.3	1.000	1.000843	32.53	32.18
3	6.046	4.886	3.209	3.534	5.560	5.383	−0.413	−0.430	72.6	72.4	1.000	1.008140	32.67	32.32
4	8.240	6.744	4.086	4.371	5.301	5.190	−0.441	−0.433	74.7	72.8	1.000	1.012998	31.57	31.27
1973:1	9.496	7.516	5.549	5.806	4.987	5.078	−0.058	−0.015	75.0	71.0	1.000	1.021494	30.69	30.35
2	2.145	2.937	7.187	7.116	4.905	4.969	0.039	0.065	74.0	73.3	1.000	1.004199	30.45	30.33
3	1.599	1.373	8.364	8.318	4.757	4.826	0.519	0.546	73.3	72.9	1.000	1.002049	31.78	31.73
4	2.339	2.259	8.546	8.565	4.749	4.827	0.693	0.716	75.3	75.1	1.000	1.000685	33.51	33.49
1974:1	−7.033	−7.020	12.415	12.334	5.146	5.316	0.832	0.851	75.8	75.1	1.000	1.000440	34.43	34.40
2	−1.585	−1.243	9.329	9.227	5.151	5.256	−0.108	−0.102	76.6	76.6	1.000	0.999513	33.85	33.86
3	−1.895	−1.534	11.867	11.716	5.514	5.573	−0.220	−0.224	78.4	78.6	1.000	0.998645	33.83	33.85
4	−8.916	−9.022	14.402	13.787	6.596	6.610	0.124	0.070	84.0	83.5	1.000	0.999653	35.60	35.65
1975:1	−11.433	−9.740	8.508	9.281	8.340	8.486	0.619	0.276	84.7	84.5	1.000	0.999929	35.73	36.20

B. A Revised Optimal Solution

In this experiment, we still use a quadratic welfare function with four target variables and three policy variables. However, there were some modifications in the welfare function. First, instead of treating the rate of economic growth as a goal, we emphasize the full utilization of capacity, because the idling of capacity has been considered a serious problem in a recession. Therefore, the definition of Y_{1t} has been changed to

$$Y_{1t} = \text{GNP}_t/\text{GNPCEA}_t,$$

where GNPCEA_t is the potential GNP (estimated by the Council of Economic Advisors) in the tth quarter. This modification requires additional calculations to derive dynamic multipliers of the rate of capacity utilization with respect to different types of policy actions. The goal of Y_{1t}, Y_{1t}^*, is of course set equal to unity.

Second, it is not realistic to set a unique goal of 4% inflation for the whole period, as we did in the previous experiment. The high inflation in 1974 and 1975 was a consequence of the exogenous and unavoidable events of the oil embargo and the energy shortage. Therefore we have two sets of goals for price inflation. The goal of inflation Y_{2t}^* is set equal to 3% for 1971:1–1973:4 and 7% afterwards.

Third, in this experiment, a favorable deviation from the targets would not generate any loss to total welfare. The favorable deviations imply that actual GNP is greater than the potential GNP, that the rate of inflation is less than 4%, or that the rate of unemployment is less than 4%. However, the favorable trade balance would generate losses in the welfare function.

Fourth, since the rate of capacity utilization and the rate of unemployment are highly related in the Wharton model, when one is pushed to the target the other one has to approach the target. If the full weights were assigned to both of them, it would overemphasize the importance of these two goals. The weights of these two variables are therefore reduced to 0.75, the weights of inflation rate and ratio of trade balance to GNP are arbitrarily set equal to 1.0. The new welfare function appears as follows:

$$C = -\sum_{t=1971.1}^{1975:1} \left[0.75\left(\frac{\text{GNP}_t}{\text{GNPCEA}_t} - 1.0\right)^2 + 1.00\left[\left(\frac{P_t}{P_{t-1}}\right)^4 - 1 - g\right]^2 \right.$$
$$+ 0.75(\text{UN}_t - 0.04)^2 + 1.00\left(\frac{\text{EX}_t - \text{IM}_t}{\text{GNP\$}_t} - 0.0\right)^2 + 1.0(X_{1t} - X_{1t}^*)^2$$
$$\left. + 1.0(X_{2t} - X_{2t}^*)^2 + 0.05(X_{3t} - X_{3t}^*)^2 \right].$$

If $(GNP_t/GNPCEA_t) > 1.0$, loss $= 0.0$;
if $(P_t/P_{t-1})^4 - 1 < 0.04$, loss $= 0.0$;
if $UN_t < 0.04$, loss $= 0.0$;
for 1971:1–1973:4, $g = 0.03$;
for 1974:1–1975:1, $g = 0.07$.

In order to maximize total welfare, the welfare function was differentiated with respect to all three policy variables and all first derivatives were set equal to zero. A set of optimal policies were obtained by using the dynamic multipliers for approximation. An optimal solution was created by a dynamic simulation of the Wharton model with all optimal policies incorporated in the simulation. The actual and optimal levels of both target and policy variables are reported in Table 2. Since this part of the simulation was done at a later date, there were some small discrepancies between the actuals in Table 1 and Table 2 due to the subsequent revisions.

In this exercise, the optimal solution deviated more from the actual than in the previous case. In general, the optimal solution still has a tendency to smooth the cyclical movements in the target variables over the simulation period. The average capacity utilization rate is raised by less than 1% over the 17-quarter period, but it substantially increases in the late-1974 and early-1975 period. However, the capacity utilization rate in the years before the oil embargo was slightly reduced, i.e., the optimal solution does not push the economy into its full strength in that period.

The level of real GNP is $818.7 billion, which is $38.7 billion higher than the actual, in the last quarter of the optimal solution. It averaged at about $8 billion a year in the 17-quarter period. The level of real GNP in the optimal solution shows that the fast expansion of the economy between 1972:3 and 1973:3 was curbed. The real GNP has declined only in 1974:1, 1974:4, and 1975:1. In other words the severity of this recession was substantially reduced.

The optimal solution also shows that the sharp inflation in 1974 is slightly reduced, but far above the target of 7%. It indicates that macroeconomic policies fail to subdue the rapid inflation caused by exogenous factors. However, the high unemployment rates in 1974 and 1975 are significantly lower. When the rate of capacity utilization was pushed up in the recession, employment of labor, of course, increases. The ratios of trade balance to GNP were not very significantly affected. The only significant improvement was found in the first quarter of 1975 when this ratio dropped from 0.621 to 0.224.

The more detailed results of the target variables in the control solution and in the optimal solution are presented in Tables 3 and 4. The value, goal, absolute loss, and percentage loss of each target variable in different quarters are reported. The absolute loss of a particular variable in a quarter is the

TABLE 2

THE ACTUAL AND OPTIMAL LEVELS OF TARGET AND POLICY VARIABLES IN THE COMPLICATED OPTIMAL SOLUTION

		Y_1	Y_2		Y_3		Y_4		X_1		X_2		X_3	
	Actual	Optimal	Actual	Optimal	Actual	Optimal	Actual	Optimal	Actual	Optimal	Actual	Optimal	Actual	Optimal
1971:1	0.9499	0.9614	4.693	4.118	5.948	5.880	0.282	0.198	71.8	80.1	1.000	0.956	29.7	29.9
2	0.9473	0.9599	4.846	4.797	5.911	5.779	−0.010	−0.105	70.8	78.8	1.000	0.948	29.8	29.8
3	0.9445	0.9542	2.575	2.806	5.960	5.799	0.009	−0.057	70.0	75.5	1.000	0.985	29.9	29.5
4	0.9512	0.9543	1.900	2.318	5.961	5.815	−0.314	−0.336	72.1	73.5	1.000	1.019	30.8	30.4
1972:1	0.9555	0.9649	5.491	5.323	5.823	5.662	−0.628	−0.687	75.9	82.0	1.000	0.980	32.2	32.0
2	0.9655	0.9687	1.922	2.492	5.678	5.543	−0.604	−0.621	75.9	78.7	1.000	1.027	32.5	32.1
3	0.9700	0.9684	3.316	3.607	5.565	5.485	−0.411	−0.394	72.6	73.2	1.000	1.048	32.7	32.3
4	0.9800	0.9729	4.046	4.485	5.306	5.303	−0.440	−0.384	74.7	72.7	1.000	1.065	31.6	31.4
1973:1	0.9925	0.9813	5.489	5.816	4.992	5.075	−0.056	0.031	75.0	70.6	1.000	1.068	30.7	30.9
2	0.9883	0.9791	7.286	6.979	4.908	5.046	0.039	0.105	74.0	71.5	1.000	1.039	30.4	31.1
3	0.9826	0.9782	8.265	7.810	4.757	4.904	0.520	0.539	73.3	72.6	1.000	0.991	31.8	32.7
4	0.9787	0.9809	8.643	7.795	4.747	4.852	0.692	0.647	75.3	75.2	1.000	0.946	33.5	34.7
1974:1	0.9518	0.9640	12.309	11.475	5.143	5.141	0.832	0.686	75.8	78.4	1.000	0.912	34.4	36.6
2	0.9386	0.9548	9.357	9.227	5.147	5.031	−0.108	−0.275	76.6	81.0	1.000	0.943	33.8	34.7
3	0.9249	0.9505	11.875	11.290	5.510	5.248	−0.219	−0.474	78.4	86.8	1.000	0.878	33.8	34.5
4	0.8946	0.9354	14.437	12.924	6.595	6.123	0.126	−0.286	84.0	99.2	1.000	0.714	35.6	36.5
1975:1	0.8594	0.9020	8.459	8.550	8.348	7.695	0.621	0.224	84.7	103.6	1.000	0.802	35.7	36.2

squared deviation from its target multiplied by the appropriate weight. The percentage loss is the absolute loss divided by the sum of absolute losses in four target variables.

Total loss over the 17-quarter period is 7.0163 in the baseline solution and drops to 4.4506 in the optimal solution. Although total loss was not meaningful in an absolute sense, the relative comparison indicates that the welfare of the economy would have been improved by 36.5% if the optimal policies were implemented. This calculation excluded the reduction in welfare due to the policy implementation difficulties.

In the baseline solution, 62.94% of the loss can be attributable to idle capacity, 30.3% to high inflation, 6.3% to high unemployment, and 0.46% to the nonzero trade balance. The importance of the unemployment rate seems to be understated. In fact, a part of loss due to idle capacity was contributed by the low employment level in the economy. This was why the weights of these two target variables in the welfare function were reduced. In the optimal solution, the combination is slightly changed. There was 54.63% of total loss attributable to unutilized capacity, 36.6% to high inflation, 8.11% to high unemployment, and 0.66% to the nonzero trade balance. This change indicates that the optimal policies could more efficiently push the economy towards full capacity rather than reduce high unemployment and high inflation.

It is also interesting to point out in Table 3 that 65.35% of the total loss in the 17-quarter period was accumulated in the last five quarters after the oil embargo. The recent inflation recession, caused by the energy shortage, has really done damage to the economy. The optimal solution in Table 4 has smoothed the economy and reduced the loss in the last five quarters to 55.06%. Total loss in numerical terms in the last five quarters is 4.5849 in the baseline solution and 2.4504 in the optimal solution. The main improvement is in the area of capacity utilization. The loss in this variable has been cut down from 3.195 to 1.467. On the other hand, the loss due to inflation was reduced only from 1.149 to 0.8089. Total welfare in the period after the oil embargo has been substantially improved.

V. A Final Correction

The matrix of multipliers U, introduced in Eq. (5), is invariant with respect to initial values from which the multipliers are (dynamically) computed if the system is linear. In nonlinear systems, it is well known that the dynamic multipliers depend on the initial points from which they are evaluated. The question with regard to any particular nonlinear model being used is, How strong are the nonlinearities?

TABLE 3

THE ACTUAL LEVEL, TARGET LEVEL, ABSOLUTE LOSS, AND PERCENTAGE LOSS OF TARGET VARIABLES IN THE CONTROL SOLUTION

	Y_1	Y_1^*	Absolute loss	Percentage loss	Y_2	Y_2^*	Absolute loss	Percentage loss
197101	0.94986	1.0000	0.18856	2.6875	0.46927E−01	0.30000E−01	0.28654E−01	0.40839
197102	0.94728	1.0000	0.20845	2.9709	0.48464E−01	0.30000E−01	0.34091E−01	0.48589
197103	0.94451	1.0000	0.23095	3.2917	0.25750E−01	0.30000E−01	0.0	0.0
197104	0.95018	1.0000	0.18614	2.6530	0.19001E−01	0.30000E−01	0.0	0.0
197201	0.95550	1.0000	0.14850	2.1165	0.54914E−01	0.30000E−01	0.62068E−01	0.88463
197202	0.96551	1.0000	0.89224E−01	1.2717	0.19218E−01	0.30000E−01	0.0	0.0
197203	0.96998	1.0000	0.67587E−01	0.96329	0.33161E−01	0.30000E−01	0.0	0.0
197204	0.97990	1.0000	0.30297E−01	0.43181	0.40460E−01	0.30000E−01	0.10940E−01	0.15593
197301	0.99249	1.0000	0.42279E−02	0.60259E−01	0.54890E−01	0.30000E−01	0.61950E−01	0.88294
197302	0.98832	1.0000	0.10239E−01	0.14593	0.72864E−01	0.30000E−01	0.18373	2.6186
197303	0.98259	1.0000	0.22741E−01	0.32411	0.82648E−01	0.30000E−01	0.27718	3.9506
197304	0.97871	1.0000	0.34007E−01	0.48468	0.86432E−01	0.30000E−01	0.31845	4.5387
197401	0.95175	1.0000	0.17458	2.4882	0.12309	0.70000E−01	0.28187	4.0174
197402	0.93861	1.0000	0.28269	4.0290	0.93573E−01	0.70000E−01	0.55567E−01	0.79197
197403	0.92494	1.0000	0.42260	6.0231	0.11875	0.70000E−01	0.23765	3.3872
197404	0.89463	1.0000	0.83278	11.869	0.14437	0.70000E−01	0.55303	7.8821
197501	0.85941	1.0000	1.4824	21.128	0.84594E−01	0.70000E−01	0.21298E−01	0.30355
			4.4161	62.94			2.1259	30.30

	Y_3	Y_3^*	Absolute loss	Percentage loss	Y_4	Y_4^*	Absolute loss	Percentage loss
197101	0.59476E−01	0.40000E−01	0.28448E−01	0.40545	0.28216E−02	0.0	0.79613E−03	0.11347E−01
197102	0.59107E−01	0.40000E−01	0.27380E−01	0.39023	−0.95475E−04	0.0	0.91155E−06	0.12992E−04
197103	0.59595E−01	0.40000E−01	0.28797E−01	0.41044	0.94230E−04	0.0	0.88794E−06	0.12655E−04
197104	0.59605E−01	0.40000E−01	0.28826E−01	0.41084	−0.31388E−02	0.0	0.98523E−03	0.14042E−01
197201	0.58228E−01	0.40000E−01	0.24919E−01	0.35516	−0.62780E−02	0.0	0.39414E−02	0.56174E−01
197202	0.56780E−01	0.40000E−01	0.21118E−01	0.30098	−0.60368E−02	0.0	0.36442E−02	0.51940E−01
197203	0.55650E−01	0.40000E−01	0.18370E−01	0.26182	−0.41050E−02	0.0	0.16851E−02	0.24017E−01
197204	0.53056E−01	0.40000E−01	0.12784E−01	0.18220	−0.43994E−02	0.0	0.19355E−02	0.27586E−01
197301	0.49922E−01	0.40000E−01	0.73836E−02	0.10523	−0.56050E−03	0.0	0.31416E−04	0.44776E−03
197302	0.49082E−01	0.40000E−01	0.61860E−02	0.88166E−01	0.39127E−03	0.0	0.15309E−04	0.21819E−03
197303	0.47565E−01	0.40000E−01	0.42920E−02	0.61172E−01	0.51952E−02	0.0	0.26990E−02	0.38468E−01
197304	0.47474E−01	0.40000E−01	0.41901E−02	0.59720E−01	0.69196E−02	0.0	0.47881E−02	0.68243E−01
197401	0.51426E−01	0.40000E−01	0.97913E−02	0.13955	0.83162E−02	0.0	0.69159E−02	0.98568E−01
197402	0.51472E−01	0.40000E−01	0.98701E−02	0.14067	−0.10840E−02	0.0	0.11750E−03	0.16747E−01
197403	0.55101E−01	0.40000E−01	0.17102E−01	0.24375	−0.21888E−02	0.0	0.47908E−03	0.68281E−02
197404	0.65951E−01	0.40000E−01	0.50507E−01	0.71986	0.12580E−02	0.0	0.15824E−03	0.22554E−02
197501	0.83480E−01	0.40000E−01	0.14179	2.0208	0.62121E−02	0.0	0.38590E−02	0.55000E−01
			0.4420	6.30			0.0323	0.46

247

TABLE 4

THE OPTIMAL LEVEL, TARGET LEVEL, ABSOLUTE LOSS, AND PERCENTAGE LOSS OF TARGET VARIABLES IN THE REVISED OPTIMAL SOLUTION

	Y_1	Y_1^*	Absolute loss	Percentage loss	Y_2	Y_2^*	Absolute loss	Percentage loss
197101	0.96143	1.000	0.11157	2.5068	0.41184E−01	0.30000E−01	0.12509E−01	0.28106
197102	0.95994	1.0000	0.12033	2.7038	0.47969E−01	0.30000E−01	0.32288E−01	0.72547
197103	0.95420	1.0000	0.15732	3.5348	0.28060E−01	0.30000E−01	0.0	0.0
197104	0.95427	1.0000	0.15682	3.5236	0.23177E−01	0.30000E−01	0.0	0.0
197201	0.96486	1.0000	0.92590E−01	2.0804	0.53233E−01	0.30000E−01	0.53978E−01	1.2128
197202	0.96866	1.0000	0.73651E−01	1.6548	0.24923E−01	0.30000E−01	0.0	0.0
197203	0.96843	1.0000	0.74733E−01	1.6792	0.36069E−01	0.30000E−01	0.0	0.0
197204	0.97287	1.0000	0.55190E−01	1.2401	0.44850E−01	0.30000E−01	0.22053E−01	1.49551
197301	0.98127	1.0000	0.26316E−01	0.59128	0.58156E−01	0.30000E−01	0.79276E−01	1.7812
197302	0.97909	1.0000	0.32781E−01	0.73655	0.69794E−01	0.30000E−01	0.15835	3.5580
197303	0.97817	1.0000	0.35740E−01	0.80303	0.78103E−01	0.30000E−01	0.23139	5.1990
197304	0.98090	1.0000	0.27372E−01	0.61502	0.77947E−01	0.30000E−01	0.22989	5.1653
197401	0.96400	1.0000	0.97179E−01	2.1835	0.11475	0.70000E−01	0.20028	4.5000
197402	0.95477	1.0000	0.15345	3.4479	0.92270E−01	0.70000E−01	0.49595E−01	1.1143
197403	0.95054	1.0000	0.18347	4.1224	0.11290	0.70000E−01	0.18405	4.1353
197404	0.93540	1.0000	0.31298	7.0321	0.12924	0.70000E−01	0.35092	7.8846
197501	0.90202	1.0000	0.71994	16.176	0.85501E−01	0.70000E−01	0.24027E−01	0.53986
			2.4314	54.63			1.6286	36.60

248

	Y_3	Y_3^*	Absolute loss	Percentage loss	Y_4	Y_4^*	Absolute loss	Percentage loss
197101	0.58798E−01	0.40000E−01	0.26503E−01	0.59549	0.19805E−02	0.0	0.39223E−03	0.88128E−02
197102	0.57792E−01	0.40000E−01	0.23743E−01	0.53347	−0.10487E−02	0.0	0.10998E−03	0.24710E−02
197103	0.57988E−01	0.40000E−01	0.24268E−01	0.54527	−0.57387E−03	0.0	0.32933E−04	0.73996E−03
197104	0.58149E−01	0.40000E−01	0.24703E−01	0.55505	−0.33621E−02	0.0	0.11303E−02	0.25397E−01
197201	0.56616E−01	0.40000E−01	0.20708E−01	0.46527	−0.68711E−02	0.0	0.47211E−02	0.10608
197202	0.55429E−01	0.40000E−01	0.17853E−01	0.40113	−0.62102E−02	0.0	0.38567E−02	0.86654E−01
197203	0.54847E−01	0.40000E−01	0.16533E−01	0.37148	−0.39383E−02	0.0	0.15510E−02	0.34849E−01
197204	0.53032E−01	0.40000E−01	0.12738E−01	0.28621	−0.38376E−02	0.0	0.14727E−02	0.33090E−01
197301	0.50749E−01	0.40000E−01	0.86662E−02	0.19472	0.30533E−03	0.0	0.93225E−05	0.20946E−03
197302	0.50457E−01	0.40000E−01	0.82010E−02	0.18427	0.10538E−02	0.0	0.11106E−03	0.24953E−02
197303	0.49035E−01	0.40000E−01	0.61220E−02	0.13755	0.53927E−02	0.0	0.29082E−02	0.65342E−01
197304	0.48522E−01	0.40000E−01	0.54464E−02	0.12237	0.64742E−02	0.0	0.41915E−02	0.94178E−01
197401	0.51405E−01	0.40000E−01	0.97557E−02	0.21920	0.68600E−02	0.0	0.47060E−02	0.10574
197402	0.50311E−01	0.40000E−01	0.79746E−02	0.17918	−0.27475E−02	0.0	0.75486E−03	0.16961E−01
197403	0.52480E−01	0.40000E−01	0.11682E−01	0.26247	−0.47383E−02	0.0	0.22452E−02	0.50446E−01
197404	0.61234E−01	0.40000E−01	0.33816E−01	0.75980	−0.28564E−02	0.0	0.81592E−03	0.18333E−01
197501	0.76947E−01	0.40000E−01	0.10238	2.3004	0.22419E−02	0.0	0.50262E−03	0.11293E−01
			0.3611	8.11			0.0295	0.66

For most econometric models in use today, but perhaps not for all, it does not matter very much where the calculations are initialized. Just to be doubly sure and also to investigate the properties of the Wharton model with respect to nonlinearity, we reinitialized the calculation of U along the "optimal" path and reevaluated the solution to the optimization problem.

There are two contributing factors that may affect the solution obtained in this iteration:

1. the distance of the "optimal" path from the observed path of the target variable; and
2. the degree of nonlinearity of the system.

Since we constrained the movement of the instruments by penalizing their use in the loss function, we effectively did not allow the "optimal" path to get too far from the actual path.

Some interesting statistics of the recalculation are shown in the following comparative analysis of two solutions—the first iteration, using the original estimates of U and reported in the previous section (this is called OPTIMALPATH), and the second iteration, using the previous solution as initial conditions for recalculating U [this is called OPTIMALPATH (PRIME)]. It is evident that the calculation converges faster to the solution values in the latter case. The reduction of the loss function values from 4.4506 to 4.2080 (four terms) or 5.4769 to 5.4063 (seven terms) is not very great, although it is noticeable.

We could, of course, iterate again, but it hardly seems to be worth while. Repeated iteration would bring the process to a definite conclusion soon. For all practical purposes, this exercise tells us that we can, in fact, treat U as approximately invariant with respect to initial conditions, as though the system were linear, while it really is not.

The main advantage of the algorithm we used is its great simplicity and cheapness—especially because it operates as an augmentation of standard simulation programs that are all set up in any case. The extra iterations involving the recomputation of U are not expensive, but if they can be dispensed with, that is an added advantage.

Comparisons of the target variables for OPTIMALPATH and OPTIMALPATH (PRIME) shows that they differ only in the third significant digit in most cases.

I. When recalculating the derivatives using the previously determined optimal path as the baseline, the model took significantly fewer iterations for the period 197101 to 197501. The total number of iterations for all 17 periods was

$$\text{OPTIMALPATH} = 86$$

$$\text{OPTIMALPATH(PRIME)} = 69$$

II. After the new derivatives were calculated, the control algorithm was used to recalculate new policy instruments, using the same weights that were used when arriving at the original optimal path. The values for the four-term (targets) and the seven-term (targets and instruments) loss functions were

	OPTIMALPATH	OPTIMALPATH(PRIME)
4 term	4.4506	4.2080
7 term	5.4769	5.4063

III. The distribution of the loss among the four targets was

	OPTIMALPATH	OPTIMALPATH(PRIME)
GNP target	54.63%	53.18%
Price target	36.60	37.80
Unemployment rate target	8.11	8.34
Trade target	0.66	0.68
	100.00%	100.00%

IV. The distribution of the loss among the seven targets and instruments was

	OPTIMALPATH	OPTIMALPATH(PRIME)
GNP target	44.39%	41.39%
Price target	29.74	29.42
Unemployment rate target	6.59	6.49
Trade target	0.54	0.53
Government spending instrument	5.27	5.82
Nonborrowed reserves instrument	5.77	6.14
Personal tax rate instrument	7.70	10.21
	100.00%	100.00%

V. In the OPTIMALPATH(PRIME) solution, the model approaches the neighborhood of the final value of the loss function more quickly than in the OPTIMALPATH solution. The values for the seven-term loss function per each iteration were

Iteration	OPTIMALPATH	OPTIMALPATH(PRIME)
1	6.996	5.479
2	6.369	5.604
3	5.645	5.414
4	5.916	5.561
5	5.525	5.408
6	5.788	5.549
7	5.477	5.406

VI. An Algorithmic Variation

The failure of the basic algorithm of Section II to converge for some combinations of weights between instruments and targets can be readily illustrated by a simple example, which is both instructive and indicative of what can be done to alter the algorithm so that it does, in fact, converge.

Consider first the simplest possible optimization problem consisting of a linear model, one time period, one target, one instrument, and no other variables in the system. This case has an evident solution and algorithm dynamic. Let the estimated structural model be

$$y = bx$$

and associated loss function be

$$L = w(y - y^*)^2 + px^2.$$

Loss is minimized, subject to the model, when

$$\frac{dL}{dx} = 0 = 2w(y - y^*)b + 2px.$$

The iteration procedure then is to solve the model for y, given x, put the solution value for y into the optimization equation, solve for x, obtain a new iterate for y, etc.

The iteration equations can be written

$$y^{(s)} = bx^{(s-1)},$$

$$x^{(s)} = \frac{-wb}{p}(y^{(s)} - y^*).$$

These steps give rise to the finite difference equation

$$x^{(s)} = \frac{-wb^2}{p} x^{(s-1)} + \frac{wb}{p} y^*.$$

For this equation to converge we must have

$$|-wb^2/p| < 1.$$

It is evident that there exist values of p sufficiently small that this condition will be violated. That is to say the algorithm is "conservative" because if the penalty on use of instrument x is small, allowing wide swings in policy, the algorithm will not converge. If we were to explore the possibility of weight variation to make w relatively large and p relatively small, convergence criteria could be violated.

It is easy to correct this procedure in the optimization conditions by writing

$$px + \lambda x = -wb(y - y^*) + \lambda x.$$

We have simply added λx to both sides. The new algorithmic procedure is to be

$$y^{(s)} = bx^{(s-1)},$$
$$(p + \lambda)x^{(s)} = -wb(y^{(s)} - y^*) + \lambda x^{(s-1)}.$$

The finite difference equation

$$x^{(s)} = \frac{-wb^2 + \lambda}{p + \lambda} x^{(s-1)} + \frac{wby^*}{p + \lambda}$$

has the convergence criterion

$$\left|\frac{-wb^2 + \lambda}{p + \lambda}\right| < 1.$$

For any choice of p we can find a value for λ such that convergence will be obtained.

Let us now consider Eq. (5), written $PX = -U'WY$. We should add $U'WUX$ to each side to obtain

$$[U'WU + P]X = -U'WY + U'WUX.$$

Since we assume invariant dynamic multipliers on the first round, we can write $Y = UX$ and obtain

$$[U'WU + P]X = -U'WY + PX,$$
$$X = [U'WU + P]^{-1}[-U'WY + PX].$$

In this form, our algorithm is the same as that of Holbrook (1974). In this form, convergence has been readily obtained for wide variation in W and P, particularly those variations making elements of P small. Of course, U is not invariant with respect to initial conditions and must be recomputed in successive steps as illustrated in Section V.

The whole point in introducing the class of algorithms considered in this paper has been to make use of standard simulation packages that are being used, in any case, for model analysis. This method whether in the original or amended form does just that.

REFERENCES

Hirsch, A. A., Hymans, S. H., and Shapiro, H. T. (1978). Econometric review of alternative fiscal and monetary policy, 1971–75, *Review of Economics and Statistics* **60**, 334–345.

Holbrook, R. S. (1974). A practical method for controlling a large non-linear stochastic model, *Annals of Economic and Social Measurement* **3**, 155–175.

Treyz, G. (1972). An econometric procedure for ex post policy evaluation, *International Economic Review* **13**, 212–222.

Lawrence R. Klein
DEPARTMENT OF ECONOMICS
UNIVERSITY OF PENNSYLVANIA
PHILADELPHIA, PENNSYLVANIA

Vincent Su
BARUCH COLLEGE
CITY UNIVERSITY OF NEW YORK
NEW YORK, NEW YORK

QUANTITATIVE ECONOMICS AND DEVELOPMENT

Notes on Income Distribution in Taiwan

SIMON KUZNETS

I. Introduction

This paper was written in an attempt to exploit the rich data that are available on distribution of income among households in Taiwan since the mid-1960s. If acceptable findings on trends or other changes in income inequality could be established, they would be of particular interest because during most of that period—viz, up to 1973—the country's economy experienced an unusually high rate of growth and of structural change; and because the last two years examined, 1974 and 1975, were marked by a slowdown associated with the worldwide inflation-marred depression that began in late 1973.

As should have been expected, the effort to secure firm findings on changes in distribution of incomes that approximate long-term levels and are related to proper recipient units, encountered various difficulties—some of which are noted below. But it seemed worthwhile to persist, if only in the hope that both the difficulties and the limited results would be of interest to scholars in the field.

Table 1 provides selected data on the official sample surveys of household income and expenditures for Taiwan. The numbers in lines 1a–1c refer to households covered for distribution of income; the schedules dealing in detail with household expenditures were collected from a much smaller number of units. The published volumes contain a wealth of information

TABLE 1

SELECTED DATA ON THE FAMILY HOUSEHOLD SURVEYS OF INCOME, TAIWAN, 1964–1975

		1964 (1)	1966 (2)	1968 (3)	Year Covered by Survey 1971 (4)	1972 (5)	1973 (6)	1974 (7)	1975 (8)
(1a)	Total[a] sample households	3,000	3,000	3,000	5,730	5,760	5,830	5,870	9,460
(1b)	Taipei City[a]	na	na	na	1,230	1,260	1,300	1,400	1,356
(1c)	Taiwan Province[a]	na	na	na	4,500	4,500	4,530	4,470	8,104
(2)	Total income (current receipts) of households, bill (NT$)[b]	64.4	76.5	96.4	141.6	167.7	213.1	294.5	337.7
(3)	Total households (thousands)[b]	2152	2281	2373	2688	2772	2859	2916	3039
(4)	Number of persons (millions)[b]	12.61[c]	13.36	13.84	15.20	15.47	15.64	15.55	16.03
(5)	Income per person (thousands of NT$)[d]	5.10	5.72	6.96	9.32	10.84	13.63	18.94	21.07
(6)	Consumer price index (1971 = 100)[e]	78.6	80.2	89.4	100.0	103.0	111.4	164.3	172.9
(7)	Income per person, 1971 prices (thousands of NT$)	6.49	7.13	7.79	9.32	10.52	12.24	11.53	12.19
(8)	Line 7, index (1971 = 100)	69.6	76.5	83.6	100.0	112.9	131.3	123.7	130.8
(9)	Index, income and transfer receipts of HHs, per person, in 1971 consumer prices[f]	62.9	71.0	78.9	100.0	109.9	128.0	112.8	110.9

[a] For years through 1972 from Kuo (1975). For 1973–1975 from the two volumes of surveys of family income and expenditures for each year, one for Taipei City by the municipal government, and the other for Taiwan Province by the provincial government.

[b] From the single or double reports for each year. The number of persons reported appears to be for the end of the year, whereas income is for the year; but we made no adjustment for this slight discrepancy. For 1964, the number of persons given by occupational groups and by the distribution of households by classes of number of persons, yielded a per household average of close to 6.4 persons—far higher than that yielded by basic data and leading to a total population significantly in excess of the comprehensive total for the country. We assumed here that the population covered in 1964 was such as to yield a 6% growth to the total shown in the source for 1966.

[c] Estimated.   [d] By divisor of totals in line 2 by those in line 4.   [e] From DGBAS (1977a).

[f] The underlying data on income and transfer receipts of households (including private nonprofit associations) are from DGBAS (1977b). Mid-year population was derived from the same source, dividing national income by per capita income (both in current factor prices [see DGBAS (1977b, Table 7, p. 21, and Table 10, p. 25)]). The per capita income and transfer receipts in current prices were then adjusted for price changes by the consumer price index in line 6; and the results converted to an index, 1971 = 100.

also on the size of households, age of head, occupation of head, area groupings, types of income; and only a few of these variables are noted in the discussion here.

As is usually the case, the income totals derived from the household sample surveys fall short of the comparable totals in the national accounts by margins that are difficult to approximate firmly, but range at about 20% of the larger totals. An adjustment for this discrepancy, and the needed correction of both the sample totals and their distribution, are not feasible for an individual scholar. For this reason, all findings suggested below are tentative, pending a much desired scrutiny and reconciliation of the data by scholars with access to the basic data and full familiarity with them.[1]

The two per capita income series, in 1971 prices, shown in Table 1, (lines 8 and 9) are of interest in documenting the high growth rate over the decade to 1973, and the slowdown thereafter; and compare the movements (but not the levels) of per capita income in the household surveys and in the national accounts (also referring to households). Both series show high rates of growth from 1964 to 1973, a span of nine years, the per capita income almost doubling or more than doubling (lines 8 and 9, columns 1–6); and both show a decline after 1973, sharper in line 9 than in line 8.

Given the broad similarity of movements in lines 8 and 9, the differences may arise from elements of incomparability in the scope of income covered. The household surveys include in family income not only the factor incomes of households and such customary transfer receipts as those flowing from government and from abroad, but also those from other households (covering, under outlays, transfers *to* other households). This comprehensive concept of household incomes, referred to below (and in the source) as current receipts, had to be retained since the size-of-income classification in the source is based on it. The national accounts totals include income not only to households, but also to nonprofit associations; and, with the difficulty in separating income of self-employed and unincorporated entrepreneurs from private corporate savings, the latter item is included under household income. It may well be that the sharper upward trend from 1964 to 1973 and the sharper decline to 1975 in line 9 than in line 8, are due, at least partly, to the inclusion of savings of private corporations in the total in line 9.

Whatever the qualifications, one can reasonably argue that the major

---

[1] I have omitted from discussion several published earlier distributions, based on a few hundred households, and showing changes, compared with those in the later, wider, and better-organized sample surveys, that are not acceptable without much further testing [on these earlier distributions see Kuo (1975)]. Thus, these earlier distributions show Gini coefficients of 0.56, 0.44, and 0.46 for 1953, 1959–1960, and 1961, respectively; the later official surveys show Gini coefficients at a stable level of 0.33 for 1964, 1966, and 1968 [see Kuo (1975, Table 5, p. 94)]. The drop shown from 1961 to 1964, in just three years, is neither plausible, nor explicable.

movements in real per capita income of households, as revealed by the family surveys, are in rough consonance with the per capita household incomes as shown in the national accounts; that the period covered included a long segment of high growth rates in per capita income, associated, as they always are, with rapid structural changes; and that the last two years are characterized by a decline and slowdown, a marked contrast to the earlier years. One may thus ask what changes occurred in the distribution of income, that might be found as expected corrollaries of the changing growth trends.

II. Changes in Income Distribution, 1964–1975

The distributions summarized in the top panel (lines 1–6) of Table 2 are of the conventional type, in which households are grouped by the size of current total income per household; and then the array, in increasing order of per household income, is examined for the overall or partial magnitude of inequality revealed. The shares of quintiles in such an array, in columns 1–5 were taken directly from the source cited in the notes to the table. The measures of aggregate inequality in columns 6 and 7 are simple. The TDM, in column 6, is the sum of differences in percentage shares in number of households and total income, signs disregarded. It is a simplified version of the Gini coefficient, with the advantage that it retains the original classes in the two distributions and makes it easy to identify the major sources of inequality in any comparison of two distributions.[2] The range in column 7 reflects the extreme span, and can, obviously, change in ways different from an average like the TDM or the Gini coefficient.

The measures, as they stand in lines 1–6, suggest a reduction in income inequality, occurring largely between 1964–1968 and the 1970s[3]; and reveal no perceptible effect of the shift from the high growth rates to decline and slowdown after 1973. How are we to interpret these movements in the con-

---

[2] For a more detailed discussion of the TDM and numerous illustrations which reveal that the TDM and the Gini coefficients change in a closely similar fashion see my paper Kuznets (1976a). This paper, in turn, is a substantial revision of an earlier paper, cited in the notes to line 9 of Table 2. Both contain a variety of evidence on income distribution in Taiwan in 1972, and comparisons with size distributions of income for several other countries.

[3] The source shows the quintile shares also for 1970, with the shares ranging from 8.4 to 39.7 percent, a TDM of 42.4, and a range of 4.61. This suggests that the break in the level of the TDMs and ranges occurred between 1968 and 1970, which is also confirmed by the Gini coefficients in Table 5 of Kuo's paper: these change from a level of 0.33 in 1964, 1966 and 1968, to 0.31 in 1970. But the only published volume for 1970 households' income relates to Taiwan province alone; and as Kuo's paper indicates, there was a special adjustment to cover Taipei City. For our purposes it was not essential to include the estimates for that year.

ventional size distribution of income, in the light of our goal of dealing with long-term levels of income flowing to properly defined recipient units?

At least two major problems arise in such an interpretation. First, even assuming no serious qualifications arising from the shortage of the survey income totals relative to those in the national accounts (noted above), we must recognize that the households are classified on the basis of the income of the *current* year, with whatever transient deviations from long-term levels may have occurred. But such transient components of a single year's income may differ over time; and one can easily envisage changes associated with economic growth. Thus, reduction in the proportion of households engaged in agriculture (assuming the latter to be subject to particular short-term disturbances) and the reduction in the proportions of other small-scale entrepreneurs (in favor of increasing proportions of employees), may both reduce the amplitude of transient changes and thus also their effects on the measured inequality in the distribution of annual incomes. To illustrate: if we assume that in both 1964–1968 and in the 1970s, the underlying, long-term income levels were a 10% share for the lowest quintile and a 35% share for the top quintile, we could derive the present entries in Table 2 (lines 2–6) by assuming that the transient elements *depressed* the shares of the lowest quintile by 22% in 1964–1968 and by only 12% in the 1970s, which would lead to average income shares of 7.8% in 1964–1968 and of 8.8% in 1972–1975. A parallel assumption would be that the transient component *raised* the share of the top quintile by 18% in 1964–1968, yielding an average of somewhat over 41%; and by about 10% in 1972–1975, which would yield an average of over 38%. These are purely conjectural illustrations. They are intended only to suggest that the transient components in annual income may well be subject to trends associated with economic growth; and that specific assumptions as to their magnitude and changes are required if one is to shift from distributions by annual income to the desired distributions by the long-term levels of income.

The second problem, related to the recipient unit, is of possibly greater magnitude, and lends itself to some realistic measurement. The immediate aspect of this problem is that households differ substantially in the number of persons, and thus in the numbers of both possible income producers and of consumers dependent upon that income. A further aspect is that, regardless of size, households go through a life cycle associated with the active lifespan of the household head, and differences in household income may reflect the phase of the life cycle, not disparities in the levels of lifetime incomes.

It is the first aspect of the problem that is reflected in the entries in lines 7–11. The association between the size of household, as revealed by the number of persons, and the income of the household, is usually positive; and the variables involved are correlated over a substantial range. It will

TABLE 2

Income Shares of Quintiles, Households by Total Income (Current Receipts) per Household, Unadjusted and Adjusted for Number of Persons per Household, Selected Years, 1964–1975

		Quintiles					Inequality Measures	
		I (1)	II (2)	III (3)	IV (4)	V (5)	TDM (6)[a]	Range (7)[b]
Percentages Shares of Quintiles in Total Income								
(1)	1964[c]	7.7	12.6	16.6	22.0	41.1	46.2	5.34
(2)	1966[c]	7.9	12.5	16.2	22.0	41.4	46.8	5.24
(3)	1968[c]	7.8	12.2	16.3	22.3	41.4	47.4	5.31
(4)	1972[c]	8.6	13.2	17.1	22.5	38.6	42.2	4.49
(5)	1974[c]	8.8	13.5	17.0	22.1	38.6	41.4	4.39
(6)	1975[c]	8.9	13.6	17.3	22.3	37.9	40.4	4.26
Percentage Shares of Quintiles in Total Persons								
(7)	1966[d]	12.1	17.5	19.2	23.4	27.8	22.4	2.30
(8)	1968[d]	13.5	18.4	20.5	22.4	25.2	16.2	1.87
(9)	1972[e]	15.0	18.7	20.3	21.9	24.1	12.6	1.61
(10)	1974[f]	15.0	18.8	20.4	21.9	23.9	12.2	1.59
(11)	1975[f]	15.2	19.2	20.1	21.7	23.8	11.2	1.57
Income Relatives per Person								
(12)	1966[g]	0.65	0.71	0.84	0.94	1.49	27.2	2.29
(13)	1968[g]	0.58	0.66	0.80	1.00	1.64	23.4	2.83
(14)	1972[g]	0.57	0.71	0.84	1.03	1.60	30.2	2.81
(15)	1974[g]	0.59	0.72	0.83	1.01	1.62	29.8	2.75
(16)	1975[g]	0.59	0.71	0.86	1.03	1.59	29.4	2.70

[a] TDM (total disparity measure) is the sum of differences, signs disregarded, between percentage shares in two distributions that are being compared. For lines 1–6 the differences are between the shares in income and in households (the latter being 20.0 for each quintile). For lines 7–11, the differences are between the shares of quintiles in total persons and in the total of households (i.e., 20.0 each). For lines 12–16, the differences are between the shares of quintiles in income (lines 2–5) and in total of persons (lines 7–11).

[b] The range is the ratio of entry in the top quintile to that in the bottom quintile (i.e., column 5 to column 1).

[c] Columns 1–5: From DGBAS (1977c, Table 5, p. 52).

[d] Columns 1–5: Estimated from the distributions of households by classes of income per household, which show also the numbers of persons in the households. The interpolation of the partition values for the quintiles (by income per household) is based on logarithms of shares in numbers (of both households and hence also of persons).

(continued)

e Columns 1–5: The estimation here is based on the tables relating to the 1972 income distribution in Taiwan in Kuznets (1975). I used the series for the total of Taiwan in Table 14, pp. 444–45. The interpolation of the partition values was by the procedure referred to in the note *d*.

f Columns 1–5: We took the average numbers of persons for each decile, in the distribution of households by distributed factor income per household, on the reasonable assumption that such numbers would be close to those in the distribution of households by total income. The data are given, for 1974, in DGBAS (1976a), pp. 64–5; for 1975, in DGBAS (1977c), pp. 102–3.

g Columns 1–5: By division of the shares in income (lines 2–6) by shares in total numbers (lines 7–11).

thus be seen that in the first quintile, by income per household, the average size of the household is as low as 0.6 of the average in 1966 (i.e., 12.1 in line 7, column 1, divided by 20); whereas in the top quintile in that year, it is as large as 1.39 of the average household (line 7, column 5). Similar disparities in size of household in quintiles set by total income per household are observed in other years. But what is to be noted is that the differences in size among households, grouped in the quintiles by income per household, decline markedly. Thus the TDM in lines 7–11, column 6, drops from 22.4 to 11.2; and the range from 2.30 to 1.57.[4]

The evidence of lines 7–11 is that differences in size among households made a *declining* contribution to income inequality among households by income per household. It follows that when we adjust the distribution among households, in lines 2–6, for differences in size of household, the distribution so adjusted is marked by substantially reduced income disparities, the TDMs dropping to an average of about 30, from one well above 40 (see column 6, lines 2–6 and 12–16); and the ranges declining from an average somewhat below 5 to one well below 3 (see column 7, lines 2–6 and 12–16). What is even more significant, the apparent trend toward reduction in inequality shown in the conventional distribution in lines 2–6 disappears. The average TDM for 1966 and 1968 of slightly below 30 is about the same as for the three years, 1972, 1974, and 1975 that follow; and the ranges, in column 7, lines 12–16, show, if anything, a slight rise from the average of 1966 and 1968 to that of the three years in the 1970s. Yet in terms of relation of income to persons as producers and consumers, the adjusted distribution in lines 12–16 is far more meaningful than the conventional distribution in lines 2–6.

The factors that would explain the diminished contribution of size differentials among households to income inequality among the latter when classified by income per household cannot be fully explored within the scope of this paper. But Table 3, prepared in another connection, is of interest

[4] This relevant item on number of persons per household could not be secured properly for 1964, because of the inconsistency between the size of household data shown for that year and the estimate of total population (see note in Table 1).

TABLE 3

Distribution of Income among Households, and among Persons in Households, by Size of Household (Comparison of 1966 and 1972)

Household Size Classes	Total Income (%) (1)	HHS (%) (2)	Income Relative per HH (3)[a]	Persons (%) (4)	Income Relative per Person (5)[a]	Ratio, Columns 4–2 (6)
			1966			
(1) 1 person	2.6	6.6	0.39	1.1	2.36	0.17
(2) 2 persons	4.2	5.4	0.78	1.8	2.22	0.33
(3) 3 persons	5.9	7.7	0.77	4.0	1.47	0.52
(4) 4 persons	9.7	11.5	0.84	7.9	1.23	0.69
(5) 5 persons	14.0	15.3	0.92	13.0	1.08	0.85
(6) 6 persons	14.5	14.8	0.98	15.1	0.96	1.02
(7) 7 persons	16.2	14.9	1.09	17.8	0.91	1.19
(8) 8 persons and over	32.9	23.8	1.38	39.3	0.84	1.65
(9) Totals and TDMs[d]	96.4	2,281	20.8[e]	13.36	17.2[f]	37.4[b]
			1972[c]			
(10) 1 person	1.4	3.3	0.45	0.6	2.23	0.18
(11) 2 persons	2.8	4.1	0.68	1.5	1.87	0.37
(12) 3 persons	7.7	9.3	0.83	5.0	1.54	0.54
(13) 4 persons	12.5	13.8	0.91	9.8	1.26	0.71
(14) 5 persons	20.9	21.2	0.99	18.9	1.09	0.89
(15) 6 persons	19.6	19.3	1.02	20.7	0.94	1.07
(16) 7 persons	13.7	12.6	1.09	15.8	0.87	1.25
(17) 8 persons and over	21.4	16.4	1.30	27.7	0.78	1.69
(18) Totals and TDMs[d]	167.7	2,772	12.8[e]	15.47	19.0[f]	31.8[b]

[a] The income relatives in columns 3 and 5 are derived as ratios of shares in income to those in households or in persons.

[b] Measures disparities between the shares in numbers of households and those in the number of persons.

[c] The entries for 1966 are from the BAS report for that year, Table 16, pp. 310ff. The entries for 1972 are from the table in Kuznets (1975, Table 13, pp. 440–442). In the source the classification by size is given through 10 persons, then for 11–15, and for 16 and over. We used the detailed classification through 10, and assigned a mean of 12 and 17 respectively to the two upper size classes. The resulting discrepancy from the total of persons is insignificantly small.

[d] Totals for income are in bill, NT$; for households—in thousands; for persons—in million. The TDMs are in columns 3, 5, and 6, lines 9 and 18.

[e] Measures disparities between shares in income and shares in numbers of households.

[f] Measures disparities between shares in income and shares in total number of persons.

in summarizing the changes, from 1966 to 1972, in income inequality among households associated with different sizes of households; and in revealing the different nature of the association when household income is reduced to a per person basis.

Column 3, the income relative per household, shows clearly that the larger the household, the larger its total income—the range in the relative being from 0.4 for one-person households to 1.3 or 1.4 for the largest class of households with eight or more persons each. But from 1966 to 1972, the disparity among households in per household income associated with size classes declined appreciably. The TDM drops from 20.8 to 12.8; and even the range declines from well over 3 in 1966 (see column 3, lines 1 and 8) to below 3 in 1972 (column 3, lines 10 and 17). Thus, the declining contribution of size differences to income inequality among households was true not only within quintiles distinguished by income per household (see Table 2), but also for a classification that stresses the size differences among households regardless of their position in the income array.

Of even greater interest are the comparisons in Table 3 between the shares in income in column 1 and the shares in persons in columns 4 and 5. These show that while *per household* income is the greater the larger the household, the *per person* income is negatively associated with size of household—the income relatives per person declining continuously and markedly as we move from the smaller to the larger households in lines 1–8 and 10–17. This strongly suggests that on a per person basis, it is the smaller households that are at higher income levels than the larger; and, indeed, the laborious calculations involved in shifting the arrays from per household to per person income basis confirms this suggestion—not only for Taiwan, but also for other countries, in the two papers cited in footnote 2 above. If per capita income rather than per household income is the proper basis for size-of-income classification of households, the identity of the upper and lower income groups will differ substantially from that of upper and lower income groups in the conventional size-distribution—since it will be the smaller households at the top and the larger households at the bottom in the *per capita* income arrays and the opposite in the *per household* income arrays. But even per capita income arrays are not a safe guide to long-term, life-cycle income levels—since even they are affected by the phases of the life cycle.

It is of interest to note that while the TDM in column 3 shows a marked decline from 1966 to 1972, reflecting a reduced contribution of size differences among households to inequality in distribution of income *per household*, the TDM in column 5 shows a perceptible rise from the earlier to the later year. This suggests greater contribution of size differences among households to income inequality in an array by *per capita* per household. And it should also be noted that the disparities in the distribution among size classes of households and of persons (see the ratios in column 6) decline from 1966 to 1972. This can also be observed in column 2. The 1966 distribution is marked by greater shares of the extremes, with 6.6% for one-person households and 23.8% for the largest households, compared with 3.3 and 16.4%, respectively, in 1972. These changes in structure of households by size is intriguing, particularly the decline in the share of smaller households (one and two persons), whereas in the course of economic growth one would expect the share of such small household units to *decline*. But the exploration of this finding would take us well beyond the limits of this paper.

The upshot of this discussion is that the evidence for significant reduction in income inequality in Taiwan over the decade preceding 1975 does not stand up under scrutiny. The crude adjustments for size of households remove the trend suggested by the conventional distributions; and leave us with apparent constancy over the period. But perhaps a more important conclusion of the discussion is the difficulty of deriving meaningful movements in income distribution from annual distributions of income among households, whether on a per household income or even a per person income basis. It is because of the difficulties, discussed in the earlier papers, that I suggested, as a possibly effective alternative, dealing with distributions among occupational or other economic groups, meaningfully associated with the process of economic growth in its differential impact on such groups. We shift now to an attempt to deal with data for these groups, again for the period from the mid-1960s to 1975.

III. Distribution among Groups by Occupation of Household Head, 1964–1975

Grouping by economically distinct occupational attachment of household heads minimizes some of the difficulties noted above in the conventional size distribution of income among households by income per household. First, averages for occupational groups, each covering a larger number of households, would tend to reduce the short-term variance of nearly stochastic character; and if deviations from long-term trends still remain in the year's data (affecting, e.g., farmers more than industrial worker families), there is the possibility of identifying and evaluating such deviations. Second, an occupational group, unless narrowly limited to young family heads (in transitional occupations) or to old (at peak types of occupation requiring long personal experience), would have a wide mix of households at different stages of their life cycle; and the effect of such stages on the income average would be greatly reduced. At the same time, the differences in average size of households among various occupational groups can be established; and the disparities in occupational incomes can then be shifted from per household to per person (or other unit) basis. Third, and most relevant, an effective occupational grouping distinguishes sectors within the active economic population that are associated with the basic production sectors in the economy—and the changes in their relative weights and contributions should be familiar to us from whatever we learned about them in the study of economic growth. To be sure, limiting our view to averages for occupational groups excludes *intra* occupational income inequalities; but distributions of income among households or persons *within* the occupational group are most subject to distortion by short-term elements in income, and by the demographic components reflected in the size of households and age of head in the life cycle. At any rate, it seemed of interest to review the distributions among the groups of occupations for the period covered in the preceding section.

In turning to the survey data, we find, as usual, some difficulties. To begin with, the source reports use two different classifications by occupation of head of household, one for 1964 and 1966, and the other for 1968 and later years. These are presented in Table 4, with some attempt to reduce them to a smaller number of more comparable groups; and while there is some continuity, differences persist. Then, the 1964 data, with their inconsistently large levels of numbers of persons per household, could be used only if we made the qualifying assumption that the proportional overstatement was the same for the several occupation-of-head groups distinguished. Yet, with some limitations, a continuous view from 1964 to 1975 can be obtained.

A glance at the two occupational classifications in Table 4 suggests five major groups—some of them not fully matchable. The large group of households whose heads are identified as farmers (or in such related occupations as fishing, forestry, or hunting) is the same in the two classifications, and accounts for about three-tenths of all households and over a third of the total population in households. Among the nonfarm households, three major groups are easily discernible—the higher level white-collar occupations—represented by managers and professionals and probably by most, but not all of the large group of government employees etc. in 1966 and by professionals-technicians and administrators-managers in the 1968 classification. It is followed by a middle-type nonfarm group—in lines 4 and 5 of Panel A and lines 18 and 19 in Panel B, comprising in 1966 white-collar employees in private firms and a high proportion of owners of small firms (comparable to the sales workers category of 1968). We then have a fourth group of manual labor and lower levels of other workers, a group that, taken together, is almost as large as that of farm households. The fifth and final group is the retired, not employed, an unclassified category, which, in the

TABLE 4

DISTRIBUTION OF INCOME AMONG GROUPS BY OCCUPATION OF HOUSEHOLD HEAD, TWO OCCUPATIONAL CLASSIFICATIONS

		% Shares in			Disparities		
		Households (1)	Persons (2)	Total Income (3)	Columns 3 and 1 (4)	Columns 3 and 2 (5)	Columns 2 and 1 (6)
	A. Classification for 1966 (and 1964)[a]						
(1)	Managers and professional	1.6	1.4	3.2	1.6	1.8	−0.2
(2)	Government employees, including teachers and servicemen	11.6	10.1	12.7	1.1	2.6	−1.5
(3)	Total, 1 and 2	13.2	11.5	15.9	2.7	4.4	−1.7
(4)	Employees, private, public, nonprofit enterprises	7.8	7.2	11.4	3.6	4.2	−0.6
(5)	Owners of small firms	11.9	12.5	14.5	2.6	2.0	0.6
(6)	Total, 4 and 5	19.7	19.7	25.9	6.2	6.2	0
(7)	Farmers and related occupations	30.9	37.8	29.8	−1.1	−8.0	6.9
(8)	Industrial laborers	15.2	13.7	11.7	−3.5	−2.0	−1.5
(9)	General laborers	11.6	9.7	9.7	−1.9	0	−1.9
(10)	Total, 8 and 9	26.8	23.4	21.4	−5.4	−2.0	−3.4
(11)	Personal service and repair workers	6.9	6.4	5.2	−1.7	−1.2	−0.5
(12)	Unclassified industries, unemployed and retired	2.5	1.2	1.8	−0.7	0.6	−1.3
(13)	TDM, full classification (9 branches)	100.0	100.0	100.0	17.8	22.4	15.0
(14)	TDM, reduced classification (6 branches)	100.0	100.0	100.0	17.8	22.4	13.8
	B. Classification for 1968 and all later years[b]						
(15)	Professionals and technicians	5.3	4.8	8.4	3.1	3.6	−0.5
(16)	Administrators and managers	2.5	2.7	4.7	2.2	2.0	0.2
(17)	Total, 15 and 16	7.8	7.5	13.1	5.3	5.6	−0.3
(18)	Clerical workers	8.9	8.1	10.9	2.0	2.8	−0.8
(19)	Sales workers	14.2	14.0	17.2	3.0	3.2	−0.2
(20)	Total, 18 and 19	23.1	22.1	28.1	5.0	6.0	−1.0

(*continued*)

		% Shares in			Disparities		
		Households (1)	Persons (2)	Total Income (3)	Columns 3 and 1 (4)	Columns 3 and 2 (5)	Columns 2 and 1 (6)
(21)	Farmers and related occupations	31.6	36.3	24.8	−6.8	−11.5	4.7
(22)	Craftsmen and workers, including miners	18.5	18.1	16.7	−1.8	−1.4	−0.4
(23)	Transport workers	6.4	6.7	7.5	1.1	0.8	0.3
(24)	Total, 22 and 23	24.9	24.8	24.2	−0.7	−0.6	−0.1
(25)	Service, sports, and recreational workers	6.0	5.0	5.1	−0.9	0.1	−1.0
(26)	Unclassified industries, military, nonworkers	6.6	4.3	4.7	−1.9	0.4	−2.3
(27)	TDM, full classification (9 branches)	100.0	100.0	100.0	22.8	25.8	10.4
(28)	TDM, reduced classification (6 branches)	100.0	100.0	100.0	20.6	24.2	9.4

[a] Calculated from Bureau of Accounting and Statistics (1968).
[b] Calculated from Bureau of Accounting and Statistics (1970).

later classification, includes households with heads in military service. We shall have occasion to revert to this broad grouping in observing the interoccupational differentials in selected years from 1964 through 1975.

Two further comments on the classifications in Table 4 can be made. First, there are substantial differences among the household grouped by occupation of head in average *size* of the household, it being largest among farm households, smallest among the retired and similar groups, and relatively small in the high-level white-collar occupations. There is, on the whole, negative association between average size of household in the occupational group and the per *household* average income in that occupation. As a result, the shift from per household to per person income basis *widens* the magnitude of the income differentials among the occupational groups, as is shown by the larger TDMs in column 5 than in those in column 4 (see lines 13–14 for Panel A classification, and lines 27 and 28 for the Panel B classification).

Second, the assignment of a household to, say, the farm classification because its head is engaged in farming does not mean that the total income of the household is secured from farming; nor even that the dominant proportion of the household's income is from that source. It is quite possible for the head of the household to be identified as farmer (or owner of a small firm with a nonfarm industry attachment) and most of the income to originate in the wages or salary earning activities of other employed members of the household or even of the head himself, let alone some actual and imputed (rent) property types of income. This mixed-source character of a household's total income is an important factor in the function of the family household as an equalizing mechanism, offsetting wider *single* source income inequalities possibly generated in economic growth. In particular, a decline in the weight of an occupation, the relative demand for which may be reduced by economic growth, would tend to be offset, in the affected household, by shift of available labor supply into other, more favored pursuits, thus diversifying the sources of a household's total income. The occupational classification that we are using, and any that would be based on a single occupation of the head of household alone, overstates the concentration of the household's income in the occupational source indicated; and this would be even more the case were the classification more detailed.

In Table 5, Panel A provides an overall review of aggregate disparities in income, either per household or per person, among the nine groups by occupation of household head. If we allow for some incomparability between the earlier and later occupational classifications, several tentative findings may be suggested.

TABLE 5

MEASURES OF INCOME DIFFERENCES AMONG HOUSEHOLDS GROUPED BY OCCUPATION OF HEAD, SELECTED YEARS, 1966–1975

A. Total Disparity Measures, 9 Occupational Groups[a]

		Income per Household (1)	Persons per HH (2)	Income per Person (3)	Income per Person, Excluding Farm Households (4)
(1)	1964[b]	17.0	(15.8)	(23.0)	(23.2)
(2)	1966	17.8	15.0	23.9	19.6
(3)	1968	22.8	10.4	25.8	16.8
(4)	1971	23.0	8.8	25.8	20.6
(5)	1972	21.4	9.0	23.8	19.2
(7)	1973	24.4	8.6	28.2	21.0
(7)	Average, 1971–1973	22.9	8.8	25.5	20.3
(8)	1974	21.0	8.8	24.2	20.4
(9)	1975	22.4	8.6	25.6	21.4
(10)	Average, 1974–1975	21.7	8.7	24.9	20.9

(*continued*)

B. Distribution Among Four Broad Occupational Groups, Income per Person[c]

		Nonfarm Groups			Farm HHs (4)	Measures of Inequality	
		Top (1)	Middle (2)	Lower (3)		Total (5)	Excluding Farm (6)
	1964 (estimated)						
(11)	Percent shares in persons	10.6	18.0	23.9	47.5	22.4	21.6
(12)	Income relatives	1.44	1.36	0.89	0.82	1.76	1.62
	1966						
(13)	Percent shares in persons	11.5	19.7	31.0	37.8	21.2	18.6
(14)	Income relatives	1.38	1.31	0.92	0.79	1.75	1.50
	1968						
(15)	Percent shares in persons	7.5	22.1	34.1	36.3	23.2	16.6
(16)	Income relatives	1.75	1.27	1.00	0.68	2.57	1.75
	1971						
(17)	Percent shares in persons	10.9	26.4	35.1	27.6	25.4	19.8
(18)	Income relatives	1.69	1.20	0.90	0.67	2.52	1.88
	1972						
(19)	Percent shares in persons	10.6	26.7	32.6	30.1	23.8	17.8
(20)	Income relatives	1.63	1.19	0.94	0.70	2.33	1.74
	1973						
(21)	Percent shares in persons	10.7	25.2	34.5	29.6	27.4	19.8
(22)	Income relatives	1.83	1.19	0.92	0.63	2.90	1.99
	Average, 1971–73						
(23)	Percent shares in persons	10.7	26.1	34.1	29.1	25.5	19.0
(24)	Income relatives	1.72	1.19	0.91	0.67	2.57	1.89
	1974						
(25)	Percent shares in persons	10.3	28.4	34.2	27.1	24.2	19.0
(26)	Income relatives	1.70	1.17	0.89	0.70	2.43	1.91
	1975						
(27)	Percent shares in persons	9.9	25.4	24.8	29.9	25.4	19.8
(28)	Income relatives	1.76	1.20	0.91	0.68	2.59	1.93

(*continued*)

TABLE 5 (*continued*)

B. Distribution Among Four Broad Occupational Groups, Income per Person

	Nonfarm Groups			Farm HHs (4)	Measures of Inequality	
	Top (1)	Middle (2)	Lower (3)		Total (5)	Excluding Farm (6)
Average, 1974–75						
(29) Percent shares in persons	10.1	26.9	34.5	28.5	24.8	19.4
(30) Income relatives	1.73	1.19	0.90	0.69	2.51	1.92

[a] The entries here are the TDMs for the distributions by nine occupational groups shown for 1966 and 1968 in Table 4. The occupational grouping of 1968 is continued through the later years, separately for Taipei City and Taiwan Province, which are combined into a total for Taiwan. The reports for Taipei City are by the Bureau of Budget, Accounting and Statistics of the Taipei City Government; those for Taiwan province is by a similarly titled Bureau of the Taiwan Provincial Government. The TDMs in column 4 are for the disparities between the % shares of occupational groups in the total of income and of persons, but for only eight groups, excluding the major group of farm and related occupation households.

[b] The entries for 1964, relating to persons and per person parameters, were estimated on the assumption that the overstatement of persons per household was proportionately the same for all groups by occupation of head of household. The occupational grouping for 1964 is the same as that for 1966 shown in Table 4.

[c] The eight nonfarm occupational groups are combined into three, of which the top is that formed in Table 4 by groups 1 and 2 (for years beginning with 1968, professional and administrators); the middle one is formed of the next two nonfarm groups (for 1968 and later years, clerical and sales workers); and the lower one comprises all other nonfarm occupational groups (dominated in the 1968 and later grouping by craftsmen and other industrial workers, but including also transport, service, and miscellaneous workers and retired).

The entries in columns 1–4 are taken from the nine group distributions.

The entries in lines 10, 12, 14 and other even-numbered lines are the TDMs, either for the four-group distribution (including farm households) in column 5, or for the three-group distribution (excluding farm HHs) in col. 6. The entries in lines 11, 13 etc., are the ranges in the income relatives, either between the top nonfarm group in col. 1 and the farm group in col. 4 (for col. 5); or between the former and the lower nonfarm group in col. 3 (for column 6).

In averaging for 1971–73 and 1974–75, we first averaged the shares in numbers and the shares in income, and then derived the TDMs and ranges from these averages.

To begin with the disparities in income per household (column 1), there is an apparent *widening* of interoccupational differentials between 1964 and 1966 and later years, a change opposite to that suggested above by the conventional size distribution among households in the top panel of Table 2. Beginning with 1968, the aggregate disparity as measured by TDM fluctuates, with a peak in the terminal growth year of 1973; but the annual changes are minor about an average level of approximately 22.

Second, it is clear that whatever change can be discerned toward widening of the interoccupational disparities between 1964–1966 and later years is due almost wholly to the greater size differentials among households in the different occupational groupings. This is shown by the much larger TDMs for the earlier two years than in the later years (in column 2); and it is a movement from the mid-1960s to the 1970s similar to that observed by us in the changes of a household size within the conventional size distribution in the second panel of Table 2. But whereas in the preceding section, reduction of size differentials among households contributed to a *downward* trend in the TDMs in distributions by income per household, a similar reduction of size differentials among households in the different occupational groupings, contributed to a semblance of an *upward* trend in the TDMs in column 1, at least between 1964–1966 and later years.

Third, it follows that with the adjustment for differing numbers of persons per household among the occupational groups, the result is not only a wider disparity as measured by an invariably larger TDM in column 3 than in column 1; but also much less of an upward movement from 1964–1966 to the later years. The average for 1964–1966 at a TDM of 22.7, is still lower than those in 1968 and later years; but the difference, at about 1 or 2 points, can hardly be assigned much weight, given also the elements of discontinuity between the two occupational classifications.

Finally, one should note that it is the large farm household group, with its low per capita income, that contributes greatly to the overall disparity in per capita income among occupations. The exclusion of the farm group and the limitation of the classification to the eight nonfarm groups, reduces the TDM by varying proportions but averaging about a fifth (see column 4, compared with col. 3). The appearance of a relatively stable trend is, however, preserved and there is again little reflection of the change in the economy from high growth rates and much structural change in the years before 1973, contrasted with the slowdown in 1974–1975.

The purpose of Panel B is to reveal the identity of the major occupational groups with substantially different per person income levels; and, assuming comparability of these groups over time, to observe the changes in the shares and income relative of these groups. Only four rather than five major groups distinguished in earlier discussion (in connection with Table 4) are used here: the small and rather variable group of unclassified, not employed, retired, etc., was merged with the large group of lower levels of nonfarm workers (industrial, general, and service workers).

The findings may suggest that the distribution shown for 1964 is suspect, with the high proportion of persons in farm households of 47.5% (line 11, column 4), which drops, over the next two years, to 37.8% and yet, there is a similarly large proportional drop, from 1968 to 1971. What we can safely infer is that there was a substantial decline in the relative share of persons attached to farm households to the early 1970s but not much thereafter. This, incidentally, is quite compatible with a greater, and more persistent downward trend, in the proportion of employed workers in the agricultural sector (of which latter below). This decline in the share of persons in the farm households group is offset by rises in the shares of persons in the middle and lower nonfarm occupations, but not so clearly in the share of the upper nonfarm groups, although the trend may be obscured by inconsistency between the two classifications.

The disparities in income per person among the four large occupational groups are fairly sizeable—the range averaging about 2.5 beginning in 1968, with the inclusion of farm households; and close to 2.0, excluding the farm households group. But the income relatives for the wide occupational groups tend to hover about the same levels, particularly if we deal with the identical occupational classification beginning in 1968. Thus, the income relative for the farm households group ranges between 0.63 (in 1973, column 4, line 22) to 0.70 (in 1974), but averages 0.67 in 1971–1973, 0.69 in 1974–1975, and 0.68 in 1968. There is similar persistence, with minor deviations around a constant level, in the income relatives for the three wide nonfarm occupational groups, with averages for 1968, 1971–1973 and 1974–1975, at 1.75, 1.72, and 1.73 for the top group; 1.27, 1.19, and 1.19 for the middle group; and 1.00, 0.91, and 0.90 for the lower group. The only hint of a trend is the declining share of the lower nonfarm group; but this is produced by a high value for the single year, 1968.

The TDMs and ranges in columns 5 and 6 of Panel B are based on the entries in columns 1–4 for the large occupational groups. When relating to the same year and per person income basis as in Panel A, based on all nine or eight groups, these TDMs in Panel B are smaller, if smaller, by tiny margins, indicating that it is the differences among the four or three large occupational groups that dominate the overall measures of disparities.

By and large, the limited findings in Table 5, for interoccupational differences in income per person, and the limited findings in Table 2, for the conventional size distribution among households adjusted for differences among size-of-income groups in the average size of households, are similar. They are to the effect that there are no clear discernible time trends in the magnitude of income inequalities in the distributions, over a period that extends from the mid-1960s to 1975; and that there are no clear reflections of the contrast between the two last years and the preceding decade in the growth rate and other overall aspects of the economy.

IV. Differences in Per Worker Product between A and Non-A Sectors, and Disparities in Per Person Income between Farmer and Nonfarmer Households

The failure to observe well-defined trends or responses to the recent slow-down in the income distributions discussed so far may be due either to inadequacy and resulting insensitivity of the data or to the slowness with which aggregate income distributions respond to even marked trends in rates of growth of product per capita and to changes in such rates; or to the failure on our part to distinguish the relevant subgroups within the population. No judgment can be passed here on the first two possibilities, except to argue that, given the rich data available annually since 1971, and the series back to 1964, it would be surprising if *marked* trends or changes in the income distribution would be so dominated by limitations of the data as to be completely obscured by them; and that, if a long lag between income distribution and the underlying growth rates of income and their changes is to be assumed, it is not easy to provide a testable rationale for such a lag. The argument concerning the subgroups within the income producing and receiving population is clearly relevant, considering the problems discussed above in using the household as a recipient unit, in groups formed by income per household. One would have to be able to adjust such groups for both size and age of head, the two basic demographic components associated with the lifecycle; and the needed cross classification by these two variables is not available, except for Taiwan Province for 1975.

Of course, the possibility should not be ruled out that under certain conditions, properly measured inequalities in per person (or per some other relevant unit) income of households need not display long-term trends in response to underlying trends in aggregate growth of the economy and to the rates of structural change, particularly among the production sectors, that may be associated with growth. We tend to assume that rapid structural shifts are likely to contribute to widening income inequalities because the forced declines in the shares of some sectors in aggregate employment and income opportunities do not find a sufficiently prompt response in the movement of labor out of these sectors to others with widening employment opportunities. But, obviously, it is possible that, allowing for short-term lags in such an adjustment, there would be sufficient mobility out of the sectors with lower growth rates to those with higher growth rates, to limit the widening of disparities in long-term income levels. And such mobility would have to be looked for in terms of a *household* income unit, where it would apply, as already suggested, to some potentially employed members of the household if not to others, with a resulting diversification of sources of income that would add newly growing to older and less expansive sources.

These obvious arguments suggest the rationale for a comparison, in Table 6, of the differentials in product [net domestic product (NDP), at factor costs] per worker (employees, self-employed, and unincorporated active entrepreneurs) in the A sector (agriculture, and related branches of hunting, fishery, and forestry) and the non-A sector; and the disparities in per person income between farmer households (so classified by occupation of head) and the nonfarmer households. Of course, net domestic product includes pure property incomes, not necessarily flowing to active workers in the sector; but much of it is imputed rent on owned housing, and the overall share of pure property income (excluding that on entrepreneurial equity) is small enough to limit the incomparability element.

The striking feature of the top panel of Table 6, which relates to intersectoral differences in product per worker, is the clear pattern of movement of the inequalities, as reflected in both the TDM in line 4 and in the range in line 7. There is a rise from 1964 to 1971, and a marked decline from 1971 to 1975. The reduction in the 1970s, marked particularly after 1972, is due to the maintenance of the share of the A sector in total NDP in line 3 (indeed a slight rise in 1974 and 1975), combined with a decline in the share of the A sector in total active labor force, which ceased only after 1973. The product being in current prices, the constancy and slight rise of the share of the A sector in total product from 1973 onwards was due partly to the higher rise in prices of agricultural products, which began in 1973 and was in much fuller force in the next two years.[5]

The corresponding measures for per person income differences between farmer and nonfarmer households reveal much narrower magnitudes of overall inequality, the TDMs in line 10 averaging below 20 and the ranges in line 13 about 1.7, compared with averages of well over 25 and of over 2.0 in lines 4 and 7, respectively. More significant, there is only a faint indication in the lower panel of Table 6 of the conspicuous swing in the measures of inequality observed in the top panel. To be sure, if we calculate a simple, three-item moving average of the entries in line 10 we shall find the TDM moving from an average of 18.7 in the three year period centered in 1966 to a peak of 19.8 centered in the early 1970s and down to about 19 towards the end. But this movement is attenuated; and not much emphasis can be put on it.

Clearly, the lower amplitude of the per person income differences between

---

[5] The consumer price index for foods (1971 = 100) was 117 in 1973, 185 in 1974, and 199 in 1975, compared with 111, 164, and 173 for the total index. The wholesale price index for agriculture and fishery products was 132, 182, and 200 for the three years, respectively, compared with the total index of 128, 180, and 171. [See DGBAS (1976b, Tables 178 and 179, pp. 324–325).]

farmer and nonfarmer households must be associated, in good part, with the inclusion in the income of farmer households of significant income components other than net income from agriculture, to the diversification of sources of the total income of households that would not be reflected in the estimation of sectoral income per worker. This is brought out in Table 7, the main feature of which is the series on the structure of factor incomes received by the farmer households, in lines 4–7.

The finding is that even in the earlier years, net income from agriculture (corresponding to total entrepreneurial income from it) accounted for only about two-thirds of all factor incomes of farmer households, a ratio that declined to less than 50% by 1972, and hovered between 45 and 50% for the years that followed. The other major income component was wages and salaries. And the significant aspect is that, as lines 9–11 demonstrate, only a small fraction of this wage–salary component in the total income of farmer households could have come from employment in the A sector. The national accounts show that, in that sector, the ratio of wages and salaries to net operating surplus (which corresponds to net income from agriculture and related branches in the family survey reports) was varying between 6 and 10%; whereas the ratio of wages and salaries from all sources to the properly adjusted net income from agriculture received by farmer households varied between 30 to close to 90% (see lines 11 and 10). It follows that no more than a fifth, and in most years, between a seventh and a tenth, of wages and salaries received by farmer households were earned within the A sector; the dominant proportion, ranging from four-fifths to nine-tenths was earned in the non-A sector.

One should also note that farmer households did not account for all of the net income from agriculture: the nonfarm households accounted, according to the family survey reports, for between 8 and 10% of it (see line 8). But clearly diversification of income sources among the nonfarm households was far more significant than that. Households that were classified under occupation of the head of the household, say manual workers in a given range of industries, could easily be assumed to include workers in a different range, so long as the availability of employment different from that of the household head was not completely barred by space obstacles or lack of employment opportunities. A greater disaggregation of the occupation-of-head categories, combined with greater detail on the sectoral sources of household incomes other than those of the occupation of the head, would most likely reveal the prevalence of such diversification, which can now be illustrated with the present data for the farmer households alone. But the limited evidence in Table 7, added to that of Table 6, is sufficient to illustrate the role of the household as an equalizer, as one of the various mechanisms by which adjustment could be made in the distribution of income to the strains that rapid shifts in

TABLE 6

Comparison of Differences in Net Domestic Product (NDP) per Worker, A and non-A Sectors, with Differences in Per Person Income Farm and Nonfarm Households, 1964–1975

	1964 (1)	1966 (2)	1968 (3)	1971 (4)	1972 (5)	1973 (6)	1974 (7)	1975 (8)
Intersectoral Differences in NDP per Worker (Current Prices)								
(1) Percent share of workers in A, in total civilian workers[a]	44.6	43.4	39.7	35.1	33.0	30.5	31.0	30.0
(2) Line 1, adjusted for inclusion of military in LF[b]	40.1	39.9	36.5	32.6	31.0	28.7	29.1	28.2
(3) Percent share, NDP in A related to total NDP[c]	27.6	25.5	21.5	15.1	14.9	15.1	15.7	15.9
Measures of Inequality								
(4) TDM[d]	25.0	28.8	30.0	35.0	32.2	27.2	26.8	24.6
(5) Income relative, per worker, A[d]	0.69	0.64	0.59	0.46	0.48	0.53	0.54	0.56
(6) Income relat., non-A[d]	1.21	1.24	1.24	1.26	1.23	1.19	1.19	1.17
(7) Intersectoral ratio (line 6/5)[d]	1.75	1.94	2.10	2.74	2.56	2.25	2.20	2.09
Differences in Per Person Income, Farm, and Nonfarm Households								
(8) Percent shares in total persons, persons in farm households[e]	47.5	37.8	36.3	27.6	30.1	29.6	27.1	29.9
(9) Percent shares, income of farm households in income of all households[f]	39.0	29.8	24.8	18.5	21.0	18.6	18.9	20.3
Measures of Inequality								
(10) TDM[g]	17.0	16.0	23.0	18.2	18.2	22.0	16.4	19.2
(11) Income relative, farm[g]	0.82	0.79	0.68	0.67	0.70	0.63	0.70	0.68
(12) Income relative, nonfarm[g]	1.16	1.13	1.18	1.13	1.13	1.16	1.11	1.14
(13) Intersectoral ratio, line 12/11[g]	1.41	1.43	1.74	1.69	1.61	1.84	1.59	1.68

[a] Calculated from series related to all civilian employed workers from 1966 through 1975, with allocation by industrial attachment, in DGBAS (1976b). The ratio was extrapolated back from 1966 to 1964, by a similar distribution, for gainfully occupied population (end of year) (DGBAS, 1976c).

[b] The adjustment is by a crude allowance for military service personnel, all assigned to active labor force (for the estimate see Kuznets, 1976b).

(*continued*)

[c] Calculated from DGBAS, *National Income*, Dec. 1976, Table III: pp. 112–113, on industrial orgin of net domestic product at current factor costs. The A sector here, and throughout, includes agriculture, hunting, forestry, and fishing.
[d] Calculated from lines 2 and 3.
[e] Taken directly from Panel B of Table 5 above.
[f] From the entries underlying the income relatives in the same panel of Table 5.
[g] Calculated from lines 8 and 9.

TABLE 7

STRUCTURE OF TOTAL INCOME (CURRENT RECEIPTS), FARMER HOUSEHOLDS, ALL (1964–1968) AND EXCLUDING TAIPEI CITY (1971–1975)[a]

		1964 (1)	1966 (2)	1968 (3)	1971 (4)	1972 (5)	1973 (6)	1974 (7)	1975 (8)
(1)	Current Receipts (billions NT$)	25.1	22.8	23.9	25.6	35.1	39.2	54.7	68.2
(2)	Percent of transfer and unclassified receipts	2.8	3.9	5.2	6.8	4.7	4.3	4.3	4.5
(3)	Factor incomes (billions NT$)	24.4	21.9	22.7	23.8	37.5	37.6	52.4	65.2
	Percent Shares in Line 3								
(4)	Net income from agriculture, etc.	66.6	68.6	55.5	48.5	44.4	47.6	50.3	48.4
(5)	Wages and salaries	21.8	20.9	34.0	38.1	44.3	42.5	38.9	40.7
(6)	Net income from non-agriculture entrepreneurship	5.3	3.0	2.6	3.4	3.2	2.1	3.7	3.0
(7)	Property incomes (including imputed)	6.3	7.5	7.9	10.0	8.1	7.8	7.1	7.9
	Related Ratios								
(8)	Ratio of net income from agriculture in line 4 to all net income from agriculture	0.92	0.93	0.86	0.84	0.86	0.87	0.89	0.89
(9)	Ratio of wages and salaries, line 5 to net income from agriculture line 4	0.33	0.31	0.61	0.79	1.00	0.95	0.77	0.84
(10)	Line 9 times line 8	0.30	0.29	0.52	0.66	0.86	0.87	0.69	0.75
(11)	Ratio of wages and salaries in agriculture to net operating surplus (national accts)	0.06	0.06	0.07	0.08	0.08	0.09	0.08	0.09

[a] All except line 11 are taken or calculated from the reports on surveys of family income and expenditures, for the relevant years. Line 11 from DGBAS (1976d). The items are shown for *private* agriculture and livestock production, in current prices; and are parts of breakdown of national income by type of organization.

production structure generate in their unequal impact on incomes as they originate in that structure.

V. Concluding Comments

The discussion above leaves untouched a number of aspects of the income distribution in Taiwan, some of which could be explored, even with the data now available. Thus, the data distinguish various areas within the country (counties, or Taipei City and Taiwan Province since 1971); and area differences in the income distribution associated with the differing economic characteristics of the areas, could provide a basis for further analysis. We did not touch on the differentials in purchasing power between the farm and nonfarm households, which would have an obvious bearing on evaluating the real meaning of the disparities in per person nominal income as they are now measured; and the same observation would apply to disparities in nominal income among households living in conditions that affect the purchasing power of the Taiwan dollar. We did not consider the conversion of persons to equivalent consumer units in allowing for the differing size of households. We did not explore the possibility of using the distributions among households by size of consumer outlays per unit, which might reduce the incidence of transient components associated with use of annual income as basis for classification. And, most important, we did not dwell on the magnitude of income inequality in Taiwan in comparison with other countries—a task that requires far more effort and data than are available here for repairing the effects of shortages in the reported income totals relative to the comparable and comprehensive totals in the national accounts, and a task that would have to be carried through for every country in the comparison.

This brief list is cited to indicate that the findings explored and stated are subject to a variety of qualifications, the full import of which would become clear only with extension of the analysis along the lines suggested. And yet even the limited findings are perhaps sufficiently intriguing to warrant recapitulation under two brief headings.

First, as the discussion in Section II indicated, the conventional size distribution of income among households by the size of the year's income per household, can easily convey wrong notions about the identity of the top income recipients and of trends over time. Adjustments for differing and changing size of the households can change the identity of the units at the upper and lower levels, and modify time trends in per person income. And, one should add, such adjustments would be particularly crucial in any international comparisons, particularly among developed and less developed countries. At the same time, the use of annual income implies effects of transient components on the income distribution, widening inequality particularly at the extreme ends. The modifications of the conventional size distribution needed to convert it into a reliable guide to levels and trends in long-term income disparities related to the properly defined receivings units, require data and experimental analysis scarcely available as yet.

Second, it follows that other groupings of households have to be used that would reduce the difficulties just touched upon; and we used groups by occupation of head of household, with allowance for differences in the average size of household among these occupational groups. Here the important finding was the difference between the income disparities generated in the production system by sectoral inequalities in product or income per worker (including, in theory, all active participants, whether by labor, enterprise, of capital) and the disparities as they are found in household income per capita when households are grouped by occupation or industry attachment of the head. Even if the shifts in industrial structure associated with rapid economic growth, with their implicit rapid changes in demand for additional labor (or capital), cannot but affect inequality in sectoral income per worker or participant (due to lags in adjustment by mobility), the effects on household income may be greatly reduced by diversification, by shifts of some of the active members of the household away from slowly growing and toward the more rapidly growing sectors. Clearly, in Taiwan, a major factor in the relative stability of income disparities among households by occupation of head was the capacity of these households, which, interestingly enough, did *not* shift toward increasing proportion of small units (of one or two persons each), to sustain income levels through greater diversification of sectoral sources of income.

The most general implication of the brief discussion above is that the family household, in its complexity and variability through the life cycle, and in its capacity to diversify its productive activity in response to undesirable shifts in income earning opportunities induced by economic growth, is the key unit in the analysis of the income distribution. And such complexity and variability over a long span of the life cycle means also large demands for long-term data on income, which would link the changing production structure of the economy in the process of its economic growth with changing structure of family households as decision units on the earning and use of income. Further study may qualify even this general statement, particularly by revealing interrelations among households, differing among societies and over time in the extent to which larger groupings, often blood related, may set the norms for member households. But we can only speculate on what such further study might reveal.

REFERENCES

Bureau of Accounting and Statistics (1968). *Report on the Survey of Family Income and Expenditures in Taiwan, 1966*, Table 5, pp. 144ff. Taiwan Provincial Government.

Bureau of Accounting and Statistics (1970). *Report on the Survey of Family Income and Expenditures in Taiwan, 1968*, Table 2, pp. 256ff. Taiwan Provincial Government.

Directorate General of Budgets, Accounts, and Statistics (DGBAS) (1976a). *Report on the Survey of Personal Income Distribution in Taiwan Area, 1974, Taipei*, Summary Table 4, pp. 64–65; for 1975, Summary Table 4, pp. 102–103.

Directorate General of Budgets, Accounts, and Statistics (DGBAS) (1976b). *Statistical Yearbook, 1976*, Manpower, Supplement Table 1, p. 46.

Directorate General of Budgets, Accounts, and Statistics (DGBAS) (1976c). *Statistical Yearbook, 1976*, Population, Supplement Table 1, p. 20.

Directorate General of Budgets, Accounts, and Statistics (DGBAS) (1976d). *The National Income of the Republic of China*, Table IV, pp. 114–115.

Directorate General of Budgets, Accounts, and Statistics (DGBAS) (1977a). *Statistical Yearbook of the Republic of China, 1976, Taipei*, Table 179, p. 325.

Directorate General of Budgets, Accounts, and Statistics (DGBAS) (1977b). *National Accounts, 1976, Taipei*, Table VIII, pp. 124–125.

Directorate General of Budgets, Accounts, and Statistics (DGBAS) (1977c). *Report on the Survey of Personal Income Distribution in Taiwan Area, 1975, Taipei*, Table 5, p. 52.

Kuo, Wan-yong (1975). Income distribution by size in Taiwan area—Changes and Causes. In *Seminar on Income Distribution, Employment, and Economic Development in South-east and East Asia, JERC, Tokyo, and CAMS, Manila*, Vol. I, pp. 83–84.

Kuznets, S. (1975). Demographic components in size distributions of income. In *Seminar on Income Distribution, Employment, and Economic Development in South-east and East Asia, JERC, Tokyo, and CAMS, Manila*, Vol. II, pp. 389–472.

Kuznets, S. (1976). Demographic aspects of the size distribution of income. *Economic Development and Cultural Change* **25** (1), 1–94.

Kuznets, S. (1979). In *The Economic Development of Taiwan* (W. Galenson, ed.), Table 1.13. Ithaca, New York: Cornell Univ. Press, pp. 74–75.

DEPARTMENT OF ECONOMICS
HARVARD UNIVERSITY
CAMBRIDGE, MASSACHUSETTS

On the Uniqueness of the Representation of Commodity-Augmenting Technical Change

LAWRENCE J. LAU

I. Introduction

Let $y_{n+1} = F(y_1, \ldots, y_n, t)$ be a production function satisfying the following assumptions:

(1) $F(y, t)$ is a real-valued function defined on $\bar{R}_+^n \times R$.
(2) $F(y, t)$ is strictly increasing in y for every $t \in R$.
(3) $F(y, t)$ is concave in y for every $t \in R$.
(4) $F(y, t)$ is non-negative on $\bar{R}_+^n$ for every $t \in R$.
(5) $F(0, t) = 0$ for every $t \in R$.
(6) $F(y, t)$ is continuous in t for every $y \in \bar{R}_+^n$.

One possible specialization of this production function is to restrict technical change to be the commodity-augmenting type, that is, to a production function which can be written in the form

(1.1) $$A_{n+1}(t)y_{n+1} = F(A_1(t)y_1, \ldots, A_n(t)y_n),$$

where without loss of generality we take $A_i(0) = 1$, $\forall i$. Commodity-augmenting technical change is a very common assumption in the analysis of production.[1] Equation (1.1) may be rewritten in the more conventional form

(1.2) $$y_{n+1} = A_{n+1}^{-1}(t)F(A_1(t)y_1, \ldots, A_n(t)y_n).$$

If technical change is purely output-augmenting, so that $A_i(t) = 1$, $i = 1, \ldots, n$, Eq. (1.2) becomes

(1.3) $$y_{n+1} = A_{n+1}^{-1}(t)F(y_1, \ldots, y_n).$$

If technical change is purely input-augmenting, Eq. (1.2) becomes

(1.4) $$y_{n+1} = F(A_1(t)y_1, \ldots, A_n(t)y_n).$$

Let y_1 be the input corresponding to labor, then if technical change is purely labor-augmenting, Eq. (1.4) becomes

(1.5) $$y_{n+1} = F(A_1(t)y_1, \ldots, y_n).$$

However, the representation of commodity-augmenting technical change is not necessarily unique. For example, if the production function is homogeneous of degree one, then Eq. (1.3) may be rewritten

(1.6) $$y_{n+1} = F(A_{n+1}^{-1}(t)y_1, \ldots, A_{n+1}^{-1}(t)y_n)$$

so that technical change now appears to be input-augmenting rather than output-augmenting. Similarly, Eq. (1.4) may be rewritten

(1.7) $$y_{n+1} = A_1^{-1}(t)F\left(y_1, \frac{A_2(t)y_2}{A_1(t)}, \ldots, \frac{A_n(t)y_n}{A_1(t)}\right)$$

so that technical change now appears to augment every commodity with the exception of the labor input.

Thus under constant returns to scale, a production function with commodity-augmenting technical change can be represented in terms of *more than one* set of augmentation factors, each of which is associated with a specific commodity. The purpose of this article is to characterize the class of production functions with commodity-augmenting technical change which can be equivalently represented by *more than one* set of augmentation factors. The complement of this class of production functions is of course the class of production functions with commodity-augmenting technical change, each of which can be represented by a *unique* set of augmentation factors. In the latter case, and only in the latter case, one can speak unambiguously of the rate of augmentation of a specific commodity.

---

[1] See the discussion in Solow (1967).

II. Statement of the Problem

The problem that we consider may be formally stated as follows: Given a production function with commodity-augmenting technical change, and a set of augmentation factors $A_1(t), \ldots, A_{n+1}(t)$, $A_i(t) \geq 0$, $\forall t$, $A_i(0) = 1$, $\forall i$, so that

$$y_{n+1} = A_{n+1}^{-1}(t)F(A_1(t)y_1, \ldots, A_n(t)y_n),$$

what are the necessary and sufficient conditions on $F(\cdot)$ such that there exists another set of augmentation factors, $B_1(t), \ldots, B_{n+1}(t)$, $B_i(t) \geq 0$, $\forall t$, $B_i(0) = 1$, $\forall i$, where $A_i(t) \neq B_i(t)$ for at least one i such that

(2.1) $\quad y_{n+1} = A_{n+1}^{-1}(t)F(A_1(t)y_1, \ldots, A_n(t)y_n)$
$\qquad\quad = B_{n+1}^{-1}(t)F(B_1(t)y_1, \ldots, B_n(t)y_n), \qquad \forall y \in \bar{R}_+^n, \qquad \forall t \in R.$[2]

We first consider the case of two commodities, so that

(2.2) $\qquad A_2^{-1}(t)F(A_1(t)y_1) = B_2^{-1}(t)F(B_1(t)y_1).$

If $A_1(t) = B_1(t)$, then $F(A_1(t)y_1) = F(B_1(t)y_1)$, which implies $A_2^{-1}(t) = B_2^{-1}(t)$. Likewise, if $A_2^{-1}(t) = B_2^{-1}(t)$, then by monotonicity, $A_1(t)y_1 = B_1(t)y_1$, which implies $A_1(t) = B_1(t)$. We conclude that if $A(t) \neq B(t)$,[3] then $A_i(t) \neq B_i(t)$, $i = 1, 2$.

Let $y_1 = B_1(t)^{-1}y_1^*$, so that

(2.3) $\qquad A_2^{-1}(t)F(A_1(t)B_1(t)^{-1}y_1^*) = B_2^{-1}(t)F(y_1^*).$

Let $y_1^* = 1$, and

(2.4) $\qquad A_2^{-1}(t)F(A_1(t)B_1(t)^{-1}) = B_2^{-1}(t)F(1).$

Substituting Eqs. (2.4) into Eq. (2.3), we obtain

(2.5) $\qquad F(A_1(t)B_1(t)^{-1}y_1^*) = [F(A_1(t)B_1(t)^{-1})/F(1)]F(y_1^*).$

We note that Eq. (2.5) has the form

(2.6) $\qquad F(\lambda y_1^*) = g(\lambda)F(y_1^*), \qquad \lambda \geq 0, \qquad y_1^* \geq 0.$

Since $A_1(0) = B_1(0) = 1$, if $A_1(t)$ is proportional to $B_1(t)$, so that $A_1(t)B_1(t)^{-1} = k$, a constant, it implies $A_1(t) = B_1(t)$, a case which we rule out.

Since $F(\cdot)$ is non-negative and strictly increasing in its argument, $F(\cdot) > 0$ for all $y_1 > 0$. Likewise, $g(\cdot)$ must be greater than zero for all positive values

---
[2] The scale of measurement of y is taken as given and fixed.
[3] $A(t)$ and $B(t)$ are n-dimensional vectors with elements $A_i(t)$s and $B_i(t)$s respectively.

of its argument. One may therefore take natural logarithms of both sides of Eq. (2.6), so that

(2.7) $$\ln F(\lambda y_1^*) = \ln g(\lambda) + \ln F(y_1^*),$$

which may be further transformed into

(2.8) $$\ln F^*(\ln \lambda + \ln y_1^*) = \ln g^*(\ln \lambda) + \ln F^*(\ln y_1^*).$$

Equation (2.8) may be recognized as a special case of the Pexider (1903) equation. ln $F^*(\cdot)$ is continuous on its domain by virtue of concavity of $F(\cdot)$ on y. The only solution to Eq. (2.8) is therefore

(2.9) $$\ln F^*(z_1) = k_0 + k_1 z_1,$$

where k_1, k_0 are arbitrary constants.[4] This implies that the production function must have the form

(2.10) $$F(A_1(t)y_1) = e^{k_0}[A_1(t)y_1]^{k_1}.$$

In other words, $F(y_1)$ must be a homogeneous of degree k_1 function. Since $F(0) = 0$ by assumption, $k_1 > 0$. We conclude that in the two-commodity case the production function must be homogeneous of degree k_1, $k_1 > 0$.

Given $F(\cdot)$, one can now derive an explicit relationship between $A(t)$ and $B(t)$:

$$A_2^{-1}(t)F(A_1(t)y_1) = A_2^{-1}(t)A_1(t)^{k_1}F(y_1) = B_2^{-1}(t)B_1(t)^{k_1}F(y_1)$$

so that any pair $[B_1(t), B_2(t)]$ that satisfies

$$A_2^{-1}(t)A_1(t)^{k_1} = B_2^{-1}(t)B_1(t)^{k_1}$$

provides an equivalent description of the technology. There are infinitely many such pairs. Hence the representation is not unique. In the next section we shall study the general case.

III. The Main Theorem

We next consider the case of three commodities, so that

(3.1) $$A_3^{-1}(t)F(A_1(t)y_1, A_2(t)y_2) = B_3^{-1}(t)F(B_1(t)y_1, B_2(t)y_2).$$

If $A_3^{-1}(t) = B_3^{-1}(t)$, then

(3.2) $$F(A_1(t)y_1, A_2(t)y_2) = F(B_1(t)y_1, B_2(t)y_2).$$

---

[4] See Aczel (1966, pp. 141–145).

If in addition, $A_1(t) = B_1(t)$, then by monotonicity, $A_2(t) = B_2(t)$ and vice versa. Thus, we assume that $A_1(t) \neq B_1(t)$ and $A_2(t) \neq B_2(t)$.

Let $y_1 = B_1(t)^{-1} y_1^*$, $y_2 = B_2(t)^{-1} y_2^*$, so that

(3.3) $$F(A_1(t)B_1(t)^{-1} y_1^*, A_2(t)B_2(t)^{-1} y_2^*) = F(y_1^*, y_2^*).$$

Let $y_1^* = y_2^* = 1$, and

(3.4) $$F(A_1(t)B_1(t)^{-1}, A_2(t)B_2(t)^{-1}) = F(1, 1).$$

Equation (3.4), given monotonicity of $F(\cdot)$, implies that $A_2(t)B_2(t)^{-1}$ may be expressed as a function of $A_1(t)B_1(t)^{-1}$. Thus, Eq. (3.3) may be recognized to have the form

(3.5) $$F(\lambda y_1^*, g(\lambda) y_2^*) = F(y_1^*, y_2^*),$$

where $g(1) = 1$. If we make the additional assumption of once differentiability, then we can differentiate Eq. (3.5) with respect to λ and then set $\lambda = 1$:

(3.6) $$\frac{\partial F}{\partial y_1^*} y_1^* + \frac{\partial F}{\partial y_2^*} y_2^* \cdot g'(1) = 0.$$

Equation (3.6) is the generalized Euler equation for almost-homogeneous functions.[5] It implies

(3.7) $$F(\lambda y_1^*, \lambda^k y_2^*) = F(y_1^*, y_2^*),$$

where $k \equiv g'(1)$. Because of monotonicity of $F(\cdot)$, $k < 0$. Equation (3.7) implies that $F(\cdot)$ may be written in the form

(3.8) $$F(y_1^*, y_2^*) = G(y_1^* / y_2^{*1/k}) = G(y_1^* y_2^{*-1/k}).$$

It is clear that any monotonic transformation which takes the value zero at zero of $G(\cdot)$ and hence of $F(\cdot)$ still satisfies Eq. (3.6).

Equation (3.8) implies that the two alternative sets of augmentation factors must satisfy

(3.9) $$A_1(t) A_2(t)^{-1/k} = B_1(t) B_2(t)^{-1/k}.$$

Again there are infinitely many such sets.

One particular question of interest is whether the relative bias of the augmentation factors, defined as $A_1(t)/A_2(t)$ or $B_1(t)/B_2(t)$, is invariant with respect to the set of augmentation factors chosen. We note that invariance requires

(3.10) $$A_1(t)/A_2(t) = B_1(t)/B_2(t) = k^*(t).$$

[5] See Aczel (1966, pp. 231–232) and Lau (1972).

In order that Eqs. (3.9) and (3.10) hold simultaneously, we need

$$A_2(t)^{1-k} = B_2(t)^{1-k}, \quad \forall t.$$

Since $A_2(t) \neq B_2(t)$, we must have: $1 - k = 0$ or $k = 1$, but this contradicts the requirement that $k < 0$; we conclude that the bias cannot be invariant in this case.

Now suppose $A_3^{-1}(t) \neq B_3^{-1}(t)$, so that with the substitution $y_1 = B_1(t)^{-1} y_1^*$, $y_2 = B_2(t)^{-1} y_2^*$, Eq. (3.1) becomes

(3.11) $\quad A_3^{-1}(t) F(A_1(t) B_1(t)^{-1} y_1^*, A_2(t) B_2(t)^{-1} y_2^*) = B_3^{-1}(t) F(y_1^*, y_2^*).$

Let $y_1^* = y_2^* = 1$, and

(3.12) $\quad A_3^{-1}(t) F(A_1(t) B_1(t)^{-1}, A_2(t) B_2(t)^{-1}) = B_3^{-1}(t) F(1, 1).$

Substituting Eq. (3.12) into Eq. (3.11), we obtain

(3.13) $\quad F(A_1(t) B_1(t)^{-1} y_1^*, A_2(t) B_2(t)^{-1} y_2^*)$
$\qquad = [F(A_1(t) B_1(t)^{-1}, A_2(t) B_2(t)^{-1})/F(1, 1)] F(y_1^*, y_2^*).$

If $A_1(t) = B_1(t)$, then

(3.14) $\qquad\qquad F(y_1^*, \lambda y_2^*) = g(\lambda) F(y_1^*, y_2^*)$

so that $F(y_1^*, y_2^*)$ is homogeneous of degree k_1 in y_2^*, $k_1 > 0$, for every $y_1^* \in \bar{R}_+$. Similarly, if $A_2(t) = B_2(t)$, then

(3.15) $\qquad\qquad F(\lambda y_1^*, y_2^*) = g(\lambda) F(y_1^*, y_2^*)$

so that $F(y_1^*, y_2^*)$ is homogeneous of degree k_1 in y_1^*, $k_1 > 0$, for every $y_2^* \in \bar{R}_+$. It is, however, not possible for $A_1(t) = B_1(t)$ and $A_2(t) = B_2(t)$, because together they imply $A_3(t) = B_3(t)$ contrary to our supposition.

For the general case we rewrite Eq. (3.13)

(3.16) $\quad F(A_1^*(t) y_1^*, A_2^*(t) y_2^*) = [F(A_1^*(t), A_2^*(t))/F(1, 1)] F(y_1^*, y_2^*).$

Differentiating Eq. (3.16) with respect to t, and setting $t = 0$, we obtain

(3.17) $\quad \dfrac{\partial F}{\partial y_1^*}(y_1^*, y_2^*) \dot{A}_1^*(0) y_1^* + \dfrac{\partial F}{\partial y_2^*}(y_1^*, y_2^*) \dot{A}_2^*(0) y_2^*$

$\qquad = \dfrac{1}{F(1, 1)} \left[\dfrac{\partial F}{\partial y_1^*}(1, 1) \dot{A}_1^*(0) + \dfrac{\partial F}{\partial y_2^*}(1, 1) \dot{A}_2^*(0) \right] F(y_1^*, y_2^*).$

Equation (3.17) is the generalized Euler equation for almost-homogeneous functions. The general solution is a function $F(\cdot)$ such that

(3.18) $\qquad\qquad F(\lambda^{k_1} y_1, \lambda^{k_2} y_2) = \lambda^{k_3} F(y_1, y_2).$

It is easy to verify that for such a production function there exist more than one equivalent sets of augmentation factors.

The above analysis can be generalized to n dimensions in a straightforward manner. Thus, we have proved:

Theorem *Under the standard assumptions on the production function (1)–(6) and once continuous differentiability, a production function with commodity-augmenting technical change can be equivalently represented by more than one set of augmentation factors if and only if it is an almost-homogeneous function.*

A related question is invariance of the bias. Under almost homogeneity,

(3.19) $\quad A_3^{-1}(t)F(A_1(t)y_1, A_2(t)y_2)$
$\qquad = F(A_3^{-1}(t)^{k_1/k_3}A_1(t)y_1, A_3^{-1}(t)^{k_2/k_3}A_2(t)y_2).$

For invariance, we need, first

(3.20) $\quad A_1(t)/A_2(t) = A_3^{-1}(t)^{k_1/k_3}A_1(t)/A_3^{-1}(t)^{k_2/k_3}A_2(t),$

which implies $k_1 = k_2$. Thus, the bias is not invariant unless $k_1 = k_2$. But $k_1 = k_2 = k$ is precisely the condition for homogeneity of degree k of the production function. We thus conclude that if there exist more than one equivalent set of augmentation factors, a necessary condition for invariance of the biases is that the production function be homogeneous of degree k. In addition, we need

(3.21) $\qquad \dfrac{A_1(t)}{A_3 t)} = A_3^{-1}(t)^{k_1/k_3}A_1(t),$

(3.22) $\qquad \dfrac{A_2(t)}{A_3(t)} = A_3^{-1}(t)^{k_2/k_3}A_2(t).$

These equations can hold simultaneously if and only if $k_1 = k_2 = k_3 = 1$, that is, if and only if the production function is homogeneous of degree one. We conclude that homogeneity of degree one is a necessary condition for invariance of the bias.

We shall now show that in the three-commodity case, homogeneity of degree one is sufficient except for the Cobb–Douglas case. Under homogeneity of degree one, a production function with commodity-augmenting technical change

$$y_3 = A_3^{-1}(t)F_1(t)y_1, A_2(t)y_2)$$

may be rewritten

$$y_3 = F(A_3^{-1}(t)A_1(t)y_1, A_3^{-1}(t)A_2(t)y_2),$$

where $A_3^{-1}(t)A_1(t)$ and $A_3^{-1}(t)A_2(t)$ may be recognized as the biases. Suppose now there exists another set of biases $B_3^{-1}(t)B_1(t)$ and $B_3^{-1}(t)B_2(t)$ such that $y_3 = F(B_3^{-1}(t)B_1(t)y_1, B_3^{-1}(t)B_2(t)y_1)$ and at least one of the $A_3^{-1}(t)A_1(t)$'s is not equal to the corresponding $B_3^{-1}(t)B_1(t)$. By homogeneity of degree one, the production function may be rewritten

$$y_3/y_1 = A_3^{-1}(t)A_1(t)F(1, A_1^{-1}(t)A_2(t)y_2/y_1)$$

and

$$y_3/y_1 = B_3^{-1}(t)B_1(t)F(1, B_1^{-1}(t)B_2(t)y_2/y_1).$$

Then by the application of the result in Section 2, $F(1, \cdot)$ must be a homogeneous of degree k function in the second augment. Thus $y_3/y_1 = C(y_2^k/y_1)$. It then follows that $y_3 = Cy_1^{(1-k)}y_2^k$ or the production function is Cobb–Douglas. It is verified immediately that if the production function is Cobb–Douglas, the biases are not invariant to the choice of alternative but equivalent sets of augmentation factors.

For the four-or-more-commodity case, there is *lack of invariance* if the production function written in the normalized form

$$y_{n+1}/y_1 = F(1, y_2/y_1, \ldots, y_n/y_1)$$

is almost homogeneous in $\{y_2/y_1, \ldots, y_n/y_1\}$.

The main theorem shows that for all production functions that are *not* almost homogeneous, the representations of commodity-augmenting technical change is unique—there can be one and only one set of augmentation factors corresponding to each commodity-augmenting technology. Obviously, the relative biases are also uniquely and unambiguously identified.

IV. Conclusion

The conclusion of our line of reasoning is that under the assumption of almost homogeneity (which includes homogeneity) it is not possible to assign augmentation factors uniquely and unambiguously to the various commodities. An infinite number of possibilities exist. Thus, under almost homogeneity one must be cautious in interpreting such statements as "the improvement in technology comes primarily from labor augmentation" or "the rate of augmentation of labor is so many percentage points higher than that of capital." Such statements may be useful in providing a summary description of the technology *given* the choice of a particular representation. They do not have any intrinsic technological significance in themselves.

In particular, they do not necessarily reflect "improvements in the quality" of specific outputs and inputs.

Moreover, under the assumption of almost homogeneity but not constant returns, it is not possible to identify even the relative biases of the augmentation factors uniquely and unambiguously. Under the assumption of constant returns, however, it is possible to identify the relative biases of the augmentation factors uniquely and unambiguously if and only if the production function does not satisfy any other generalized Euler equation for an almost homogeneous function. In the three-commodity case, this implies that the production function must be homogeneous of degree one but not Cobb–Douglas. The nonuniqueness in the Cobb–Douglas case is well known.

In all non-almost-homogeneous cases, the representation of commodity-augmenting technical change in terms of augmentation factors is unique and unambiguous. The results presented here may be extended in a straightforward manner to the case of multiple outputs and inputs.

Finally, we note that in the derivation of the results for the two-commodity case, the differentiability assumption is not necessary. In the derivation for the general case we assume once continuous differentiability. It appears plausible that the differentiability assumption may be dispensed with even in the general case. However, the latter question remains open at present.

ACKNOWLEDGMENTS

This work was supported by National Science Foundation Grant SOC75-21820 at the Institute for Mathematical Studies in the Social Sciences, Stanford University. This note was completed while the author was a National Fellow at the Hoover Institution on War, Revolution and Peace, Stanford University. Financial support from the National Fellows Program is gratefully acknowledged. The author wishes to thank Theodore Bergstrom for helpful discussion.

REFERENCES

Aczel, J. (1966). *Lectures on Functional Equations and Their Applications.* New York: Academic Press.
Hildenbrand, G. H., and Liu, T. C. (1966). *Manufacturing Production Functions in the United States, 1957: An Interindustry and Interstate Comparison of Productivity.* Ithaca: New York State School of Industrial and Labor Relations, Cornell Univ.
Lau, L. J. (1972). Profit functions of technologies with multiple inputs and outputs, *Review of Economics and Statistics* **54**, 281–289.
Lau, L. J. (1977). Applications of profit functions, in *Production Economics: A Dual Approach to Theory and Applications* (M. A. Fuss and D. L. McFadden, eds.), pp. 133–216. Amsterdam: North-Holland Publ.

McFadden, D. L. (1967). Review of G. H. Hildenbrand and T. C. Liu, *Manufacturing Production Functions in the United States, 1957: An Interindustry and Interstate Comparison of Productivity*, Journal of the American Statistical Association **62**, 295–300.

Pexider, J. V. (1903). Notiz über Funktionaltheoreme, *Monatshefte für Mathematik und Physik* **14**, 293–301.

Solow, R. M. (1967). Some recent developments in the theory of production, in *The Theory and Empirical Analysis of Production* (M. Brown, ed.), pp. 25–50. New York: Columbia Univ. Press.

DEPARTMENT OF ECONOMICS
STANFORD UNIVERSITY
STANFORD, CALIFORNIA

Technological Change and Growth Performance in Taiwan Agriculture, 1946–1975

ERIK THORBECKE

and

JACKSON KARUNASEKERA

I. Introduction[1]

The economic progress of the Nationalist Republic of China (hereinafter, Taiwan) during the past few decades has been phenomenal. The country emerged from the Second World War with a devastated economy. The production levels were reduced to that of 1920. From an uncomfortable position and without the benefit of significant natural resources, Taiwan embarked on a course of economic development that moved the agriculture-based economy to a semi-industrial one in two decades.

At the outset of the post–World War II period, Taiwan was predominantly agricultural with a rapidly increasing population. Over half of Taiwan's labor force was employed in the agricultural sector, and about 44% of the net domestic product was generated in that sector. These shares fell to 30 and 14%, respectively, in 1975. Gross domestic product measured in real terms grew at an annual rate of 7.7% during the period 1952–1967 and thereafter by 10%. Per capita income increased from $137 in 1951 to $845 in 1975.

[1] The authors benefited greatly from comments by Henry Wan.

The agricultural sector contributed in a major way to the overall economic development of Taiwan—particularly until the mid-1960s. Because of the tremendous scarcity of land and extremely small farms, the agricultural development process in Taiwan has depended heavily upon the improvement in land productivity. Crop production per hectare has been raised to a very high level, which averages about six times higher than in the U.S.[2] In fact, gains in agricultural productivity have made possible the net transfer of large amounts of capital to the nonagricultural sector and thereby have contributed to the economic growth in the rest of the economy.[3]

Until the mid-1960s the technological changes that took place in agriculture tended to be extremely labor absorbing. Subsequently, a labor shortage appeared, which pushed up the agricultural wage rate and led to widespread mechanization.

The rapid growth of agricultural output achieved by Taiwan has clearly been the result of a number of interacting economic, political, and social factors that are not easy to quantify. More specifically, this study attempts, first, to review briefly the postwar growth performance of the agricultural sector by subperiods (Section 2). Second, the technological changes that were crucial to the rapid transformation of the agricultural sector are analyzed in Section 3. A recursive model is specified and estimated to examine the determinants of demand for mechanical energy, and to evaluate those variables which influenced absorption of labor. Third, in Section 4 the implications of technological change on relative factor shares are examined. The final section of this paper is devoted to a summary and conclusions.

II. Growth Performance of the Agricultural Sector

Some discrete changes occurred in the growth performance of the agricultural sector during the period 1946–1975, which suggest that this performance can best be analyzed in terms of a number of subperiods, i.e., (i) the recovery period (1946–1953); (ii) the growth period (1954–1967); and (iii) slow down or stagnation (1968–1975).[4] The delineation of phases of growth contains some arbitrary elements. Nevertheless, it will be seen subsequently that the above-mentioned phases correspond to and are correlated with important technological changes that occurred in the agricultural development process in Taiwan.

A concise picture of the differential growth performance for the whole

---

[2] See Christensen (1968, p. 2).
[3] This is one of the major findings of Lee (1968).
[4] For a detailed discussion of these phases see Thorbecke (1979).

TABLE 1

TAIWAN: GROWTH RATES OF AGRICULTURAL OUTPUT IN DIFFERENT PHASES OF AGRICULTURAL DEVELOPMENT, 1946–1974 (ANNUAL PERCENTAGE RATES)[a]

Phases[b]	Agricultural Production (Crop and Livestock	Common Crops		Special Crops	Fruits	Vegetables	Livestock
		Total	Rice Only				
I 1947–53 Recovery	10.3	8.1	8.8	17.4	1.2	5.7	17.0
II 1954–67 Growth	4.4	3.2	3.0	2.9	14.2	5.9	6.3
III 1968–74 Slowdown	2.3	−0.6	−0.1	−0.8	6.1	9.7	5.9
IV 1947–74	5.1	3.2	3.3	4.9	8.7	6.9	8.7

[a] Source: Thorbecke (1979), Table 2.5. Reprinted from W. Galenson (ed.): *Economic Growth and Structural Change in Taiwan*. Copyright © 1979 by Cornell University. Used by permission of the publisher, Cornell University Press.

[b] The annual growth rates in each phase have been computed on the basis of three-year averages centered on the first and last year of each period, i.e., 1947 average 1946–48, 1953 average 1952–54, etc.

of agricultural output and among groups of products during these three phases emerges from Table 1. Likewise, Table 2 reveals clearly that different inputs (and combinations of inputs) contributed to the growth of agricultural output in each one of these phases.

A. RECOVERY, 1946–1953

Table 1 shows that during the recovery period the annual growth rate of agricultural production amounted to 10.3% with common crops, special crops, and livestock registering remarkable growth rates of 8.8, 17.4, and 17.0%, respectively. Agricultural output increased mainly because of a more intensive use of labor and land. As Table 2 indicates, the former is reflected by the high growth rate of total man-days of agricultural labor (amounting to 6.4% annually), while the actual number of workers rose by only 1.6% per annum. Likewise, the increase in the intensity of land cultivation is reflected by a relatively high annual rate of growth of crop area of 3.8% in contrast with the cultivated land area which increased only marginally.[5]

[5] The substantial jump in labor- and land-intensive use can be illustrated by, respectively, the average number of man-days of labor per agricultural worker, which rose from 111 in 1946 to 168 in 1953, and the multiple cropping index, which went up from 117 to 170 over the same period.

TABLE 2

TAIWAN: GROWTH RATES OF INPUTS IN DIFFERENT PHASES OF AGRICULTURAL DEVELOPMENT, 1946–74 (ANNUAL PERCENTAGE RATES)[a]

Phases[b]	Labor			Land		Fixed Capital		Current Inputs		
	Total Man-days	Number of Workers	Man-days per Worker	Culti-vated Area	Crop Area	Total Value	Machinery Horse-power	Total Value	Fertilizer in Nutrient Equivalent	
									Chemical	Organic
	(1)	(2)	(3)	(4)	(5)	(6)	(7)	(8)	(9)	(10)
I 1947–53 Recovery	6.4	1.6	4.7	0.6	3.8	4.7	—	26.7	n.a.	n.a.
II 1954–67 Growth	1.7	0.4	1.3	0.2	0.9	3.5	77.0	7.3	5.7	3.3
III 1968–74 Slowdown	−0.9	−0.7	−0.2	0.1	−0.7	5.9[c]	17.3	16.2[c]	3.7	1.2
IV 1947–74	2.0	0.4	1.6	0.3	1.1	4.0[d]	49.9[e]	13.0[d]	2.5[f]	−1.0[c]

[a] Source: Thorbecke (1979). Table 2.8. Reprinted from W. Galenson (ed.): *Economic Growth and Structural Change in Taiwan*. Copyright © 1979 by Cornell University. Used by permission of the publisher, Cornell University Press.
[b] The annual growth rates prevailing in each phase have been computed on the basis of three-year averages centered on the first and last year of each period, i.e., 1947 = average 1946–1948, 1953 = average 1952–1954, etc.
[c] Average of 1968–1972.
[d] Average of 1947–1972.
[e] Average of 1954–1974.
[f] Average of 1954–1974.

Furthermore, during the recovery period, use of current inputs grew substantially from an abnormally low base prevailing in 1946.

The extremely high rate of growth of agricultural output over this period reflects the fact that resources were not used anywhere near full capacity. The substitution of chemical fertilizer for farm-made fertilizer and the introduction of biological innovations form the main instruments of technological change associated with this phase. Human and animal energy were the major source of power.

B. SUSTAINED GROWTH, 1954–1967

During this phase, the annual growth rate of agricultural production amounted to 4.4%, with common crops, special crops, and livestock registering growth rates of 3.2, 2.9, and 6.9%, respectively (see Table 1). Since the agricultural sector was working closer to full capacity, the extremely high growth rates of the previous period could not be maintained. However, high-valued commodity groups such as vegetables and fruits grew rapidly, with fruits acting as the most dynamic commodity group.

On the input side, labor input in terms of total man-days continued to rise, but at the low rate of 1.7% per annum mainly through the continuing but small increase in the average number of man-days per worker. The growth of current inputs was also high in this period and contributed to continued gains in labor and land productivities. By the end of this phase the labor constraint became superimposed upon the land constraint, which had already become binding by the mid-1950s. Consequently, the last part of this period is marked by mechanization.

The most interesting changes that characterize this period from a technological standpoint were the continued substitution of chemical fertilizer for farm fertilizer, the substitution of human labor for animal labor, and the beginning of mechanization, particularly through the adoption of power tillers. Following the land reform that was completed in the early part of this phase, Taiwan's agriculture was transformed from an essentially tenant-operated tenure system to one predominated by small owner cultivators. The average farm size was about 1.05 ha, and land distribution tended to be unimodal.

With regard to commodity composition, this period is characterized by a trend toward product diversification, particularly toward higher-valued crops requiring more labor per unit of output.

The momentum of industrial development, which coincided with the outset of the export substitution phase at the beginning of the 1960s, provided expanding working opportunities outside of agriculture. The regionally

TABLE 3

Taiwan: Sources of Human, Animal, and Mechanical Energy in Crop Production in Horsepower-Day Equivalent Units and Percentages of Total, 1952–1975[a]

Year	(1) Human Labor in Equivalent Horsepower Days (Millions)	(2) Percent of Total Energy	(3) Animal Labor in Equivalent Horsepower Days (Millions)	(4) Percent of Total Energy	(5) Mechanical Labor in Equivalent Horsepower Days (Millions)	(6) Percent of Total Energy	(7) Total Energy in Horsepower Days (Millions)
1952	24.20	67	11.94	33	—	—	36.14
1953	24.70	67	12.15	33	—	—	36.85
1954	24.60	66	12.64	34	0.01	0	37.25
1955	24.30	65	12.82	35	0.01	0	37.13
1956	25.20	66	12.89	34	0.02	0	38.11
1957	26.90	67	12.89	32	0.07	1	39.86
1958	27.60	67	13.32	32	0.25	1	41.17
1959	27.50	66	13.04	31	0.98	3	41.52
1960	27.00	65	13.04	31	1.76	4	41.80
1961	26.70	63	12.94	30	2.92	7	42.56
1962	26.80	60	12.66	28	5.21	12	44.67
1963	27.50	59	12.17	26	6.58	15	46.25
1964	28.30	59	11.85	25	8.13	16	48.28
1965	30.10	60	11.57	23	8.55	17	50.22
1966	30.80	54	11.26	20	14.84	26	56.90
1967	30.40	56	10.56	19	13.21	25	54.17
1968	30.50	53	10.13	18	17.12	29	57.75
1969	29.90	50	9.57	16	20.35	34	59.82
1970	29.60	47	8.59	14	24.19	39	62.38
1971	29.90	45	7.66	11	29.23	44	66.79
1972	28.80	42	7.10	10	32.45	48	68.35
1973	28.80	39	6.39	9	38.86	52	74.05
1974	28.50	35	6.09	8	46.02	56	80.61
1975	28.20	35	6.12	7	47.37	58	81.69

[a] Source: Thorbecke (1979), Table 2.11. Reprinted from W. Galenson (ed.): *Economic Growth and Structural Change in Taiwan*. Copyright © 1979 by Cornell University. Used by permission of the publisher, Cornell University Press.

decentralized nature of industrial development was an important element in achieving a full utilization of available labor resources and in equalizing income distribution among farm households.

C. Agricultural Slowdown, 1968–1975

It is apparent from Table 1 that this period was marked by a sharp drop in the growth rate of agricultural output. The same table also shows that common crops and special crops displayed negative growth rates during this phase. Rice production remained essentially constant, while the growth performance of vegetables, fruits, and livestock products continued to be remarkable.

From a technological standpoint, the binding constant to further agricultural growth in this phase was clearly labor. There is some evidence that, as a result of the labor shortage, the agricultural wage rate rose significantly compared to that of factory workers.

As is evident from Table 2, the negative growth rates of labor and crop area during this phase could only be relaxed through mechanization. Increasingly, capital was being substituted for labor, and to some extent for land. Substantial mechanization and the increasing use of chemical fertilizer made possible the continuation of the postwar trend of increasing yields per hectare. The dramatic move away from an agricultural technology that relied mainly on human and animal labor as major sources of energy until the mid-1960s to one based increasingly on mechanical power in the third phase is evident in Table 3. The tremendous shift in the relative importance of the three types of energy during the postwar period is clearly revealed in Table 3. Hence, whereas in the recovery period roughly two-thirds of the total energy used in agricultural crop production came from human labor and one-third from animal labor, by 1975 human labor represented only about 35% of total energy and animal energy 7%. On the other hand, mechanical energy, which was practically nonexistent at the outset, appeared to contribute 58% of total energy in crop production in 1975.

In the following sections an attempt is made to analyze more rigorously the technological changes that have been identified in the preceding brief review.

III. Choice of Techniques in Taiwan's Agriculture

It is fashionable to dichotomize production techniques into "labor intensive" or "capital intensive" categories. However, it could be argued that technical choice is not only dualistic but pluralistic. Hence, what is appropriate is an optimal degree of total factor intensity determined by relative factor prices and the state of technical know-how.[6] In Taiwan, the production techniques have undergone changes during the past three decades with the increasing use of modern inputs (biochemicals and mechanical). In particular, the dramatic rise in the use of mechanical power in more recent years has accelerated this process of technological change.[7] Hence, this section is devoted to a quantitative analysis of (a) the determinants of technological change and (b) the implications of technological changes with regard to labor absorption.

The quantitative analysis is based on cross-sectional observations of a sample of farms broken down by farm size and regions for the year 1974.[8]

A. Determinants of Technological Change

There are a number of factors that influence technological change and the combinations of capital, labor, land, and other inputs to be used in the production process. The main question to be asked within the Taiwan context is what were the major determinants of mechanization that characterized the recent phase, essentially from 1968 onward. The major factors that appear to have affected mechanization are increasing labor costs, cropping intensity, diversity of the cropping pattern, and farm size.

The effectiveness of mechanical energy is estimated on the basis of the following recursive model:

(1) $\ln y_1 = \alpha_{10} + \alpha_{11} \ln x_1 + \alpha_{12} \ln x_2 + \alpha_{13} \ln x_3 + \alpha_{14} \ln x_4 + \varepsilon_1$,

(2) $\ln y_2 = \alpha_{20} + \alpha_{25} \ln x_5 + \alpha_{26} \ln x_6 + \varepsilon_2$,

(3) $\ln y_3 = \alpha_{30} + \alpha_{34} \ln x_4 + \alpha_{35} \ln x_5 + \alpha_{36} \ln x_6 + \beta_{31} \ln y_1 + \beta_{32} \ln y_2 + \varepsilon_3$,

(4) $\ln y_4 = \alpha_{40} + \alpha_{43} \ln x_3 + \beta_{42} \ln y_2 + \beta_{43} \ln y_3 + \varepsilon_4$,

where y_1 is the wage–rental ratio, y_2 expenditure on biochemicals per unit of crop area (New Taiwan Yuan per hectare), y_3 mechanical energy per unit of labor (horsepowers used per man-day), y_4 crop area per unit of labor (hectares per man-day), x_1 family labor per unit of crop area (man-day per hectare), x_2 hired labor per unit of crop area (man-day per hectare),

---

[6] For a lucid discussion see Bhalla (1975).

[7] However, in Taiwan, mechanization was applied selectively, first to plowing, harrowing, and levelling activities followed by reaping and transplanting. The power tiller is the symbol of technological change in Taiwan as it is the most preponderant form of mechanical energy in use.

[8] The sample covers eight regions and five average farm sizes for a total of 40 observations.

x_3 animal labor per unit of crop area (man-day per hectare), x_4 multiple cropping index (MCI), x_5 irrigation charges per hectare of crop area (New Taiwan Yuan per hectare), x_6 farm size (hectare) and ε_i an error term. The causal arrow diagram of this recursive system is shown in Fig. 1 and the OLS estimates of the parameter of this model are given in Table 4.

The first three equations of the recursive model explain jointly the determination of mechanical energy used per hectare. The complete system, in turn, helps explain through Eq. (4) the extent of labor absorption in terms of the land–man ratio. In this section we concentrate on the determinants of mechanical energy on the basis of the subset of three equations above while Section 3.2 is devoted to explaining the variables affecting the land–man ratio on the basis of the complete recursive system.

The effective use of mechanical energy in Eq. (3) is regressed on (a) the wage–rental ratio y_1, which is used to reflect high labor costs; (b) expenditures on biochemicals per hectare y_2, a variable that is used as a proxy for cropping intensity; (c) the multiple cropping index[9] x_4, which is supposed to reflect the diversity of the cropping pattern; (d) irrigation charges per hectare x_5, and (e) farm size x_6. Before analyzing the results of the statistical estimation of the model, it is important to describe and justify briefly the logic underlying the recursive model and the measures used to represent the various variables in the system.

The first issue to resolve concerns the best way to measure mechanical energy. In Taiwan, the mechanization trend implies the expansion of power tillers, tractors, sprayers, and thrashers, and more recently, rice combines and reapers. Since this equipment comes in different capacities and is used unevenly during the year, the number of machines, or corresponding number of horsepowers, do not reflect the actual effective degree of mechanization. Therefore, in this analysis mechanical energy input is measured in terms of total horsepower-hours of machine use per year.[10]

The wage–rental ratio captures the relative cost of labor. One would expect this ratio to be positively correlated with the multiple cropping index and the use of hired labor and negatively correlated with the availability of family and animal labor at the farm level. [See Eq. (1) and, for the statistical results, Eq. (1a)].

The second equation yields the determination of expenditures on biochemical inputs. This variable is used here as a proxy for cropping intensity. The application of biochemical inputs combined with irrigation shortens the

---

[9] The ratio of the crop area to the cultivated area.

[10] The process of estimating the actual number of horsepower-hours used on the farm per year is cumbersome but possible, given the data available in Taiwan. For methodology see Thorbecke (1979).

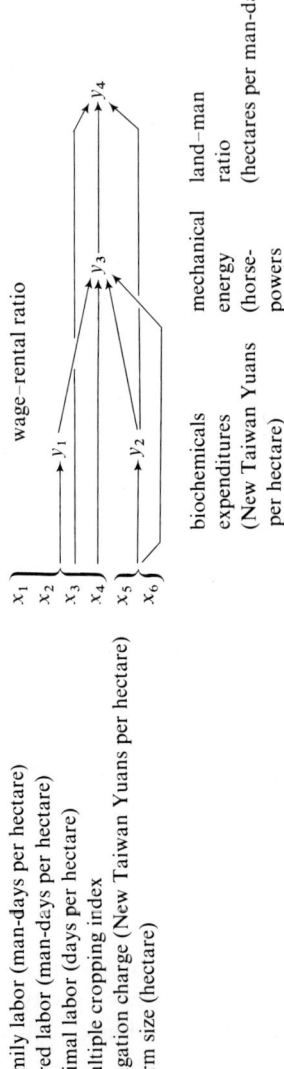

Figure 1 Causal arrow diagram of recursive model. See Eqs. (1)–(4) in text and Table 4 for empirical results.

TABLE 4

OLS Estimates of the Recursive System

Dependent Variable	Equation Number	Constant[a]	Family Labor/ Unit of Crop Area[a] $\ln x_1$	Hired Labor/ Unit of Crop Area[a] $\ln x_2$	Animal Labor/ Unit of Crop Area[a] $\ln x_3$	MC 1[a] $\ln x_4$	Irrigation Charge/Unit of Crop Area[a] $\ln x_5$	Farm Size[a] $\ln x_6$	Wage Rental Ratio[a] $\ln y_1$	Bio-chemicals Unit of Crop Area[a] $\ln y_2$	Mechanical Energy per Unit of Labor[a] $\ln y_3$	R^2
wage/rental ratio $\ln y_1$	(1)	1.3125 (0.59)	−0.3562 (−1.62)	0.6012 (4.12)	−0.5844 (−3.92)	0.8835 (2.08)						0.53
Biochemical expenditures per ha $\ln y_2$	(2)	6.6144 (9.83)					0.2899 (4.29)	0.0374 (0.44)				0.31
Mechanical energy per man-day $\ln y_3$	(3)	−16.4769 (−5.97)				1.3945 (2.73)	0.0460 (0.39)	0.5661 (5.00)	0.6665 (5.56)	0.2457 (1.15)		0.61
Crop Land per man-day ratio $\ln y_4$	(4)	0.9692 (0.89)			−0.1602 (−1.84)					−0.6116 (−4.98)	0.1633 (2.41)	0.58

[a] t-values are given in parentheses.

maturity of varieties, permitting a larger output of a given crop or more different crops to be grown in a year. On a priori grounds it would be expected that biochemical inputs are positively correlated with irrigation (the two variables are complementary) and negatively correlated with farm size (a small farm is likely to be more intensively cultivated than a larger one). When yields are low and the application of biochemical inputs small, the opportunity cost of crop failure is accordingly low. Conversely, large scale application of biochemicals, because of its yield effect, increases substantially this opportunity cost. In such a situation it is imperative that the critical operations should be completed rapidly to reduce the risk associated with inclement weather and possible shortage of labor. One way of reducing the risk involved is to mechanize the critical operations, which is why expenditures on biochemicals appear as an explanatory variable affecting mechanical power in Eq. (3).

A more diversified cropping pattern is also likely to affect the factor proportion choice, i.e., the increased use of mechanical energy. Thus, for example, the appearance of new products such as vegetables and fruits that have marked seasonal production characteristics will probably accentuate the demand for mechanical power. A large number of products and crops cultivated per year requires a tight scheduling of activities such as land clearance, planting, and harvesting. As previously mentioned, the multiple cropping index was used as a proxy for the cropping diversity effect.

The recursive model was estimated, by ordinary least squares, on the basis of cross-sectional data covering eight regions and five farm sizes (for a total of 40 observations) from the Report of the Farm Record-Keeping Families in Taiwan for the year 1974.[11] The summarized results are presented in Table 4. The estimated parameters in Eq. (3) in Table 4 reveal clearly the significance of the wage–rental ratio, of the multiple cropping index, and of farm size as explanatory variables. Of the remaining variables, expenditures on biochemical inputs (the proxy for cropping intensity) carries the expected sign but is significant only at the 10% probability level and irrigation charges are not significantly different from zero. Furthermore, the results emerging from Eq. (1) conform closely with theoretical expectations, i.e., the wage–rental ratio is positively influenced by the greater use of hired labor and higher values of the multiple cropping index and negatively affected by higher amounts of animal and family labor. Finally, Eq. (2) reveals that irrigation charges are positively and significantly correlated with the use of biochemicals, while the effect of farm size is not significant.

[11] Provincial Government of Taiwan, Department of Agriculture and Forestry, *Report of Farm Record-Keeping Families in Taiwan*, 1974, Taipei (July 1975).

B. Labor Absorption Potential Entailed in Technological Change

It is useful to examine next the effects of modern inputs on labor absorption since these inputs largely embody technological change. The labor absorption potential of agricultural inputs can perhaps best be analyzed by dichotomizing the inputs into labor-using and labor-saving categories. It is customary in the literature to define biochemical inputs such as seed, fertilizers, and chemicals other than weed killers as land saving but labor using (Johnston and Cownie, 1969; Sen, 1968; Yudelman et al., 1971), in contrast with mechanical energy which is considered as labor saving.

The impact of mechanization on productivity could rise in two ways, i.e., the effect it has on yield and the expansionary effect on the land–man ratio. This could be illustrated by way of a simple identity:

(5) $$Y/L = Y/A \times A/L.$$

Here Y represents agricultural output, L the number of workers (in man-years of man-days of adult labor), and A the area of cultivated land. This identity expresses output per worker as being equal to the product of output per hectare of cultivated land (i.e., the productivity of land) and the amount of cultivated land per worker (i.e., the land–man ratio). Mechanization has its impact primarily on the third term of the above expression. The expansionary effect of mechanization is due to the rise in cultivated area per worker. In contrast, the primary effect of biochemicals falls on the second term of the above expression, i.e., the yield effect.

Thus it can be seen from Eq. (4) of Table 4 that mechanization (i.e., a rise in K/L) is associated with a rise in the land-man ratio (A/L) as one would have expected. Conversely, an increased use of biochemicals and intermediate inputs is negatively correlated with the land-man ratio, as is empirically confirmed by the sign of the regression coefficient in Eq. (4), Table 4. The adoption of high-yielding varieties and the increased application of fertilizer augments plant density and the number of crops and products that can be grown during the year. In turn, the larger resulting output per hectare (i.e., Y/A) requires more labor inputs and a consequent fall in the land–man ratio.[12] The parameter of the third independent variable appearing in Eq. (4), i.e., animal labor, carries an unexpected negative sign.[13]

---

[12] There is evidence to support this view. See M. Yudelman et al. (1971, p. 74), Gotsch and Willis (1972).

[13] On a priori grounds one would have expected that the more animal labor per hectare, the greater the crop area per unit of labor (the land–man ratio) since animal labor is a substitute for human labor.

In short, the empirical results reveal clearly that the biochemical–intermediate-input variable and mechanical energy had the expected opposite effect on labor requirements per unit of land or the land–man ratio. Hence, the introduction of modern inputs was complementary to the local resource structure. Mechanization relieved a shortage of labor during the peak period, and biochemicals were useful in providing an additional demand for labor particularly during the slack season. The former was instrumental in increasing the land–man ratio and the latter the productivity of land. The net result was rising incomes in the rural sector.

IV. Relative Income Shares and Technological Change in the Agricultural Sector

The next question, which follows logically from the preceding analysis, is, What are the elements that affect the factorial income distribution? In the present analysis three major elements are identified: (a) non-neutral or factor-biased technological change; (b) the factor-prices ratios and, more specifically, the rental–wage ratio; and (c) changes in the elasticity of substitution.

In this section the focal point of analysis (i.e., the dependent variable) is the changes in relative factor shares accruing to labor and capital. It was assumed—consistent with the underlying structure of Taiwan's agriculture—that the agricultural sector is composed of a mass of small-scale producers so that the product market can be approximated by perfect competition. In this case, the distributional impact of the three elements (a), (b), and (c) can be estimated within a CES-type model.

The estimable form of the model[14] can be specified as follows:

(6) $$\ln(L/K) = \sigma \ln[(1 - \delta)/\delta] + \sigma \ln(q/w) + u,$$

where L is human labor (adult man-days), K the value of fixed assets on the farm in Taiwanese dollars deflated by the wholesale price index, w the wage rate per man-day in Taiwanese dollars derived from dividing the total wage bill by the total number of man-days deflated by the consumer price index, q the rental rate of capital per unit in Taiwanese dollars derived by dividing the share of capital in value added on each farm by the total amount of capital on the farm[15]; $(1 - \delta)/\delta$ the labor intensity index, and σ the measure of the substitution elasticity.

---

[14] This model follows closely Brown and DeCani (1963) and Srivastava and Heady (1973).

[15] The share of capital in value added per observation was derived by subtracting the wage bill of hired labor and expenditures on seed, fertilizer, irrigation charges, taxes and fees, feeds, miscellaneous farm expenses and nonfarm expenses from the value of total output.

A variant of the above model can be expressed as

(7) $\qquad \ln(S) = \sigma \ln[(1 - \delta)/\delta] + (\sigma - 1) \ln(q/w) + u,$

where S is the ratio of labor's share to capital's share of total value added. Equation (7) is derived from expression (6) by subtracting from it the logarithm of q/w.

The model given in (6) was estimated using cross-sectional cost-accounting data obtained from the Report of Farm Record-Keeping Families in Taiwan for the years 1964, 1968, and 1974, respectively. In this model the labor intensity index $(1 - \delta)/\delta$ is designed to capture the effect of non-neutral technological change. For simplicity, if we assume constant factor price ratios and a constant elasticity of substitution, a movement in the labor intensity index must be compensated by a movement in the opposite direction in the optimal ratio of capital to labor. A positive movement [increase in $(1 - \delta)/\delta$] means a labor using technological change. A negative movement [decrease in $(1 - \delta)/\delta$] means a labor saving (capital using) technological change.

The estimated parameters of the model specified in equation (6) are presented in Table 5. All the parameters of the model are significant at the 1% probability level. There is evidence to suggest that the parameters have changed over time.

According to the results given in Table 5, it is apparent that there have been significant changes in all three forces affecting relative shares of incomes. The decline in the factor price ratio q/w over time indicates a rapid rise in the wage rates relative to rental rates. This is reflected in the labor intensity index $(1 - \delta)/\delta$, which has declined over time indicating a reduction in the use of labor relative to capital. It should be noted that such a decline in $(1 - \delta)/\delta$ would adversely affect the relative share of labor S *ceteris paribus*. However, the net effect on S depends also on the magnitudes of σ and q/w.

TABLE 5

TAIWAN: REGRESSION RESULTS OF THE PARAMETERS OF THE DISTRIBUTIVE SHARES MODEL[a]

Year	$\ln(1 - \delta/\delta)$	σ	$\bar{R}^2$	$\ln(q/w)$	actual $\ln(S)$	(S)
1964	−2.8101 (0.4832)	0.7536 (0.0993)	0.59	−4.8569 (0.3282)	−0.9210	0.40
1968	−3.9889 (0.8375)	0.6444 (0.1512)	0.32	−5.5157 (0.5117)	−0.6089	0.54
1974	−7.3112 (0.6798)	0.4898 (0.1082)	0.33	−6.0779 (0.5869)	−0.4801	0.62

[a] Standard errors are given in parentheses.

Since the factor price ratio q/w and the elasticity of substitution σ both fell over time, the joint effect of these two forces more than compensated for the decline in $(1 - \delta)/\delta$ in leading to a substantial rise in the labor share of value added. Two main conclusions emerge from this empirical study. First, the technological change has been labor saving (capital using); and second, the labor share has improved throughout the period 1964–1974 in spite of greater capital intensity.

To recapitulate: (a) the non-neutral technological change that transformed the agricultural sector of Taiwan was of a labor-saving character; (b) agricultural wage rates rose—particularly in the third phase—relative to rental rates; and (c) the elasticity of factor substitution σ was relatively low (less than unity) and declined over time. The interaction of these forces brought about an increase in the relative share of labor. The implication of these results for the agricultural workers is most encouraging as they tend to be correlated with a more equal income distribution among farm households.

V. Conclusions

This study attempted to provide a systematic examination of the growth performance of the agricultural sector of Taiwan during the post–World War II period with particular reference to the nature of technological change. Three distinct agricultural development phases were identified. It was shown that significant differences in growth performance and in technology characterize these phases. During the first subperiod a more intensive use of labor and land, triggered largely by greater reliance on a biochemical technology, was instrumental in leading to a recovery of the economy. The growth momentum was sustained during the second subperiod. However, with the continued rapid increase in the use of biochemicals, labor shortages appeared towards the end of this subperiod. This paved the way for a labor-saving mechanical technology to be introduced. The final subperiod reveals the emergence of mechanical-*cum*-biological technology and a much diminished role for agriculture in the economic development of Taiwan.

In order to establish the major determinant of technological choice in the process of agricultural development, a recursive model was specified and estimated. The results indicate that the wage rate, timeliness of operation, greater cropping intensity, and farm size are the foremost factors in the mechanization decision.

Since the modern inputs were the main instruments of technological change, the labor absorption potential of these inputs was evaluated by dichotomizing them into labor-absorbing and labor-saving categories with biochemical inputs in the former category and mechanical inputs in the latter. The empirical results have clearly demonstrated that biochemical inputs and mechanical energy had the expected results on labor requirements per unit of land or the land–man ratio.

Perhaps the major conclusion that emerges from the empirical analysis on distributive shares of income is that the relative share of income accruing to labor rose during the post war period (mainly because of higher wage rates) in spite of a technological change of a labor-saving (capital-using) nature.

REFERENCES

Bhalla, A. S. (1975). The concept and measurement of labor intensity, *In Technology and Employment in Industry* (A. S. Bhalla, ed.). Geneva: ILO.
Brown, M. (1966). *On the Theory and Measurement of Technological Change*. London and New York: Cambridge Univ. Press.
Brown, M., and DeCani, J. S. (1963). Technological change and distribution of income, *International Economic Review* **4**.
Christensen, R. P. (1968). Taiwan's Agricultural Development: Its Relevance to Developing Countries Today. United States Department of Agriculture, Economic Research Service, Foreign Agricultural Economic Report, No. 39.
Gotsch, C. H. (1972). Technological change and distribution of income in rural areas, *American Journal of Agricultural Economics* **54**.
Johnston, B. F., and Cownie, J. (1969). Seed fertilizer revolution and labor absorption, *American Economic Review* **49**.
Karunasekera, J. (1978). Productivity, Technological Choice and Distribution of Income in Taiwan's Agricultural Sector, 1946–1975. Unpublished Ph.D. dissertation, Cornell Univ.
Lee, T. H. (1968). Intersectoral Capital Flow in the Economic Development of Taiwan, 1850–1960. Unpublished Ph.D. dissertation, Cornell Univ.
Sen, A. K. (1968). *Choice of Techniques*. Oxford: Blackwell.
Srivastara, U. K., and Heady, E. O. (1973). Technological change and relative factor shares in Indian Agriculture: An empirical analysis, *American Journal of Agricultural Economics* **55**, No. 3.
Thorbecke, E. (1979). Agricultural development. *Economic Growth and Structural Change in Taiwan* (W. Galenson, ed.), Chapter 2. Ithaca, New York: Cornell Univ. Press.
Willis, I. R. (1972). Projections of effects of modern inputs in agricultural income and employment in a community development block, U.P., India. *American Journal of Agricultural Economics* **54**, August.
Yudelman, M., Butler, G., and Banerji, R. (1971). Technological Change in Agriculture and Employment. OECD.

Erik Thorbecke
DEPARTMENT OF ECONOMICS
CORNELL UNIVERSITY
ITHACA, NEW YORK

*Jackson Karunasekera**
COMMONWEALTH SECRETARIAT
LONDON, ENGLAND

* Present address: Department of Economics, Cornell University, Ithaca, New York.

Exchange Rate, Interest Rate, and Economic Development

The Experience of Taiwan

S. C. TSIANG

I. Introduction

T. C. Liu was a man with many talents. He is best known in the U.S. for his contributions to econometrics and as a highly effective teacher. Not as well known perhaps are the facts that he was also an accomplished Chinese opera performer with a great deal of stage experience,[1] and that, as an economic adviser to the government of the Nationalist Republic of China in Taiwan (hereinafter, Taiwan), he contributed in no small measure to the remarkable economic development of Taiwan during the 20 years before his tragic death.

It may not be inappropriate, therefore, for me, who had nearly always worked with him in our economic advisory work, to put on record in this memorial volume some of the basic recommendations we made that set Taiwan onto its rapid growth path. These recommendations, or rather the

---

[1] His last stage performance was in the summer of 1974, the year before his death, in Taipei, when he played the leading role of Admiral Chou Yu, the Commander-in-Chief of the Kingdom of Wu, in the opera based upon the romanticized story of a naval battle on the Yangtze River (A.D. 208) in the Three-Kingdom Period of the Chinese history, with many first-rate professional actors in the supporting roles. It was a great success in front of a packed house. A few days later, it was televised in full. This turned out to be his swan song. It demonstrated amply, however, the zest he had for life until he was worn down by the incurable disease.

principles underlying them, are of certain theoretical interest, and they are made even more significant by the fact that they were later adopted by South Korea and were at least partially responsible for its equally spectacular economic growth after 1964.

T. C. and I were first invited to Taiwan for advisory work in the summer of 1954, when we were both working at the International Monetary Fund. At that time Taiwan was still recovering from the ravages of World War II, and had at the same time to accommodate and provide for the large influx of over a million soldiers and civilian refugees from mainland China. With the resumption of U.S. aid to the Nationalist government after the outbreak of the Korean War in 1950, and the introduction of a special system of time deposits paying extraordinary high nominal rates of interest in March of the same year, runaway inflation had gradually been brought under control. By the first half of 1954, prices had finally been brought to some sort of stability.

However, from July 1949, the month following an unsuccessful monetary reform that introduced the New Taiwan Yuan (NT$), prices had already risen by 616% by the end of 1953. The exchange rate between the New Taiwan yuan and the U.S. dollar was at first fixed at five of the former to one of the latter at the time of the monetary reform, i.e., June 1949. In 1953, the exchange rate was readjusted to NT$15.55 to one U.S. dollar and had been maintained at that rate into 1954. Since the wholesale prices in Taiwan had since then gone up more than sixfold by the end of 1953, there was no question but that in 1954 the New Taiwan yuan had already become very much overvalued at the official exchange rate.

The balance of payments of Taiwan, however, was kept in a sort of tolerable balance by strict quota restrictions on imports and controls on other exchange transactions, since Taiwan had already run through practically all its exchange reserves by the spring of 1951. Under such artificially supported exchange rates, export industries simply could not be developed, even those in which Taiwan with its relatively cheap and abundant supply of labor, should obviously have had a comparative advantage.

The rampant inflation was gradually brought under control essentially by two measures. The first was the resumption of U.S. aid to Taiwan after the outbreak of the Korean War. By agreement between the two governments, the sales proceeds of aid commodities in Taiwan were partly used to finance the budget deficits of the Taiwan government, which used to be financed by borrowing from the Bank of Taiwan, and partly were impounded in the Bank of Taiwan as Counterpart Fund Deposits, which gradually accumulated to a total of NT$724 millions at the end of July 1954, or 40% of the money supply (currency plus demand deposits) then in circulation. Thus, the proceeds of U.S. aid had contributed enormously to the contraction, or rather the prevention of more rapid increase, of the money supply, and at the same time relieved the scarcity of essential imported goods.

The other measure was a determined effort to curb the expansion of money supply by a high-interest policy and strict credit restrictions. In March 1950, a special system of time deposits, called the Preferential Interst Rate Deposits (PIR Deposits), was introduced by the Bank of Taiwan, which offered an extraordinary nominal interest rate of 7% per month for one-month savings deposits. When compounded monthly, this came to 125% per annum, as compared with merely 20% per annum on traditional one-year time deposits offered by the same bank since September of the preceding year. The new high rate was expected to be attractive enough to savers even in the face of a price inflation of 82% in the second half of 1949 after the unsuccessful monetary reform of the same year, followed by another 34% in the first three months of 1950.

This measure was a sort of compromise response to the urging by some economists, including the present author,[2] to introduce a system of price-index-escalated savings certificates to attract private savings (and excess money supply) into banks to provide the finance for vital investments which hitherto the banks had to supply out of monetary expansion. Unlike the price-index-escalated savings certificates, however, this high-nominal-interest deposit scheme obviously carried the risk of turning its own interest rate unbearable by its very success.[3] This explained why at first

---

[2] This author had as early as April, 1947 (before the fall of mainland China to the Communist regime) put forward a proposal for a kind of price-index-escalated savings certificates, the capital value as well as interest payments of which are to be increased in terms of money in proportion to the wholesale price index, so that the effective real interest rate on such certificates would never become negative even during rapid inflation. This proposal was put forward in two articles in the Chinese language journal *Ching-Chi Ping Ruen* (*Economic Review*), published in Shanghai, April 6 and May 19, 1947.

This proposal was completely ignored by the Nationalist government in their final years of control on the mainland, but was quite unexpectedly adopted in the second half of 1949 by the new Communist regime in a modified form, viz, in the form of a scheme called "real goods savings deposits" (Tsiang, 1967).

[3] The Communist experiment with their "real goods savings deposits" and "real unit bonds" had apparently also achieved remarkable success. The new savings deposits were introduced in the second half of 1949 and the issue of "real unit bonds" was started in December that year. By March 1950, the rapidly rising price level was already brought to a halt. From March 1950 onward, the official wholesale price index showed a substantial decline.

The drop in prices, though an evidence of the success of the scheme, apparently became a deterrent to the further attraction of savings into banks, as by the original arrangement the capital values of savings in money terms would also be reduced in proportion to prices. Thus, in May 1950, a new scheme of savings deposits, which would increase in money value when prices rise, but retain their original cash values when prices fall, were introduced. These deposit schemes, however, were phased out after 1951, when the banking system in the Peoples Republic of China (PRC) was completely overhauled on the basis of the Russian pattern and price stability was already quite well established. It should be interesting to compare the Communist Chinese experiment of the "real goods deposits scheme" with the Nationalist Chinese experience with the "preferential interest deposits scheme."

this preferential interest rate was offered only on one-month savings deposits. Obviously, the Bank felt the need to keep its freedom to alter the nominal interest rate from month to month as the rate of inflation slowed down.

The impact of the introduction of these savings deposits was indeed very prompt and successful. Total time and savings deposits including the new PIR deposits in the whole banking system quickly rose from a meager NT$6 millions, or barely 1.7% of the contemporary money supply (currency plus demand deposits), at the end of March 1950 to NH$28 millions at the end of June, which was approximately 7% of the money supply at that time. What is even more remarkable is the fact that price inflation was rapidly brought to a halt. From March to July 1950, the cumulative rise in prices was hardly 1%, and indeed starting from May, prices were actually declining a little. This surprising result happened before the turn of fortune in favor of Taiwan, viz, the resumption of U.S. aid to Taiwan.

Partly encouraged by the immediate success and partly fearing that the 125% per annum interest rate would be intolerable with stable prices, the government sharply cut the interest rate payable on one-month deposits in July by half to 3.5% per month and again in October to only 3.0%.

The public, taken quite aback by the abrupt reversal of the government's high-interest policy so soon after its inauguration, reacted by stopping the flow of their savings into the banks and even started to withdraw their deposits. By the end of December the same year, total savings and time deposits had fallen to only NT$26 millions, or 4.5% of the current money supply. Prices resumed their rapid rise from August, until in February 1951 they were 65% higher than in July 1950, when the cut in interest rate was announced.

Thus, in March 1951, the monthly rate on one-month deposits was raised again to 4.2% (equivalent to a yearly rate of 64%). The flow of savings into the banking system then resumed at such a spectacular pace that by the end of March of the next year, total savings and time deposits had already reached NT$271 million, or 31.2% of the contemporary money supply, and prices were once more stabilized.

The monetary authorities then gingerly lowered the interest rate whenever they felt that the stability of prices warranted it, until at the end of June 1954, when total savings and time deposits had reached NT$747 million or 41.3% of the current money supply and prices had remained almost completely stable since October 1953, the monthly rate of interest on one-month savings deposits was brought down to 1% per month. This move proved later to be too precipitate, and sent prices on the upward climb again.

These successive downward adjustments were guided only by the feelings of the monetary authorities with respect to the general expectation of future price inflation. They did not and could not accurately reflect the true supply and demand conditions for loanable funds of the economy. For instance, in July 1954, when the rate on one-month deposits was cut to 1% per month and the rate on loans at the banks to 1.95% per month, the rates on the unorganized money market outside the banking system were still 3.5% per month for secured loans and 4.5% per month for unsecured loans.

Such enormous gaps between the loan rates inside and outside the banking system implied a stringent credit rationing on the part of banks, which was bound to lead to rather inefficient (nonoptimal) allocation of the available loanable funds. Furthermore, as the banking system was not permitted to raise their interest rates to the competitive levels as indicated by the market, part of the supply of loanable funds would inevitably be diverted to the unorganized market where the risk was necessarily higher, and hence the interest rate there must include a high risk premium, which could be avoided if this part of the supply of loanable funds was also absorbed into the banking system with banks performing the function of the intermediation and risk spreading.

Against this background of facts, our recommendations were basically the following:

(1) Adopt an exchange surrender certificate system and let the certificates be traded freely on the market between exporters and importers under no quantitative restrictions so as to establish an equilibrium and flexible rate of exchange for the available export earnings of foreign exchange.

(2) Remove the government controls of the interest rates on deposits and loans at all banks and let them follow the competitive interest rates on the market, and at the same time repeal the legal ceiling on the rate of interest on the money market outside in the banking system.

(3) Let the monetary authorities concentrate on keeping the money supply from increasing too fast in comparison with the increase in real national product and the volume of trade, while leaving the interest rates to be determined by the demand for and supply of loanable funds.

These recommendations were quite against the mainstream of economic thinking in those days, although lately they would probably be more widely supported. Nevertheless, even though academic opinion appears to have changed in our direction, thanks mostly to the increasing popularity of Professor Friedman's writing, it seems to be useful for me to give my own explanation of why we thought the then-prevailing views about trade and monetary policies, which accounted for the strong inhibitions against devaluation and raising interest rates, were either invalid or irrelevant when applied to a developing country in Taiwan's economic situation. It could be a useful lesson to other developing countries that have difficulties in achieving satisfactory rate of growth.

II. Objections to Our Proposals and the Invalidity or Irrelevance of Their Arguments

A. The Alleged Harmful Effects of a Devaluation

In those early postwar years, it was widely believed that a devaluation would be very harmful to the real welfare of a developing country, since the world demand for their products was assumed to be highly inelastic. Furthermore, according to the prevailing cost-push theory of inflation, a devaluation was supposed to pour fuel on the fire of inflation, as it would raise the costs of imports and hence push up prices at home. Fortunately, the essence of this type of argument had been formalized in many precise models, so that it would be easy for us to point out exactly where they went wrong.

The alleged harmful effect on welfare of a devaluation was most elegantly demonstrated by the late Professor Warren L. Smith (1954) of Michigan. A quick review of his arguments may be in order here so that we can point out where his model disagrees with the actual situation, in which Taiwan as well as many other countries with inflation and trade balance difficulties in those years found themselves.

Smith used the following simple model to discuss the problem. First he gives the transformation function between domestic goods in physical units E' and exports X

(1) $$E' = F(X).$$

Then he gave

(2) $$-F'(X) = p,$$

where p may be regarded as the supply price of exports in terms of domestic goods E'.

The demand for imports was assumed to be a function of the price of imports in terms of domestic goods E', i.e., q, viz,

(3) $$M = \phi_1(q).$$

The supply of imports by foreign countries was assumed to be a function of the foreign price of M, i.e.,

(4) $$M = f(q').$$

The foreign demand for exports was also assumed to be a function of the foreign price of exports,

(5) $$X = \phi_2(p').$$

The balance of trade was defined as

(6) $$B = p'X - q'M,$$

and the relations between domestic and foreign prices of exports and imports are

(7) $$p = \pi p',$$

where π is the exchange rate, expressed as the price of foreign currency in terms of domestic currency, and

(8) $$q = \pi q'(1 + t),$$

where t is the domestic tariff rate. This model obviously assumed that there were no import restrictions or export subsidies.

Smith proposed to measure total welfare as total goods and services available for domestic use expressed in terms of domestic goods, i.e.,

(9) $$E = E' + qM = E' + \pi q'(1 + t)M.$$

Then, by total differentiation and substitution, it may be worked out that the effects of an adjustment in exchange rate on the welfare of the country is represented by the equation

(10) $$\frac{dE}{d\pi} = -\frac{s_x d_x}{d_x + s_x} - (1 + t)M \frac{s_m d_m}{d_m + s_m},$$

where s_x and s_m are, respectively, the supply elasticities of exports and imports, and d_x and d_m are, respectively, the demand elasticities of exports and imports. These two demand elasticities are defined as positive magnitudes, according to Marshall. Thus, the right-hand side of Eq. (10) is practically always negative. In other words, the effects of a devaluation (i.e., an increase in π) is always harmful.

The meaning of this equation can be made clearer by the following rearrangement. Noting that the effect of an exchange rate adjustment on the balance of trade ($B = p'X - q'M$) and on the terms of trade ($T = p'/q'$) are, respectively,

(11) $$\frac{dB}{d\pi} = X\frac{s_x(d_x - 1)}{d_x + s_x} + M\frac{d_m(s_m + 1)}{d_m + s_m}$$

and

(12) $$\frac{dT}{d\pi} = \frac{d_m}{d_m + S_m} - \frac{s_x}{d_x + s_x} = \frac{d_m d_x - s_m s_x}{(d_m + s_m)(d_x + s_x)},$$

we may rewrite Eq. (10)

(10′) $$\frac{dE}{d\pi} = -\frac{dB}{d\pi} + X\frac{dT}{d\pi} - B\frac{d_m}{d_m + s_m} - M\frac{td_m s_m}{d_m + s_m}.$$

Equation (10′) splits the effect of a devaluation into four components. (1) The first term on the right-hand side is the improvement in the trade balance, which takes a negative sign since it implies a decrease in goods and services available for domestic uses. (2) The second term represents the adverse effect of the induced change in the terms of trade. This component can be either positive or negative, depending upon whether the terms of trade improve or deteriorate after devaluation. In the early postwar years, however, most economists, with a few prominent exceptions, believed that the terms of trade would be likely to worsen rather than improve as it was generally believed that the two demand elasticities (d_m and d_x) were likely to be smaller than the two supply elasticities (s_m and s_x). (3) The third term depends on the original trade balance. If the latter is orginally positive, then this term will be negative; and vice versa. (4) The fourth term depends on the original import tariff, and will always be negative so long as the tariff is above zero.

This model of course failed to take into consideration monetary influences that modern monetarists are wont to emphasize. However, as a framework for analyzing the direct effects of a devaluation in a country with unrestricted trade (apart from tariffs), it is fairly adequate. Nevertheless, when applied to the countries that were considering whether to devalue or not in those postwar years, this model was so far amiss as to be hopelessly misleading, for most countries with exchange rate overvaluation and implicit balance of payments difficulties do not maintain unrestricted trade as Smith assumed but generally impose stringent quantitative restrictions on trade and exchange.

The disagreement between the model used by Smith and the actual situation confronted by Taiwan, for instance, can best be shown with a

EXCHANGE RATE, INTEREST RATE, AND ECONOMIC DEVELOPMENT

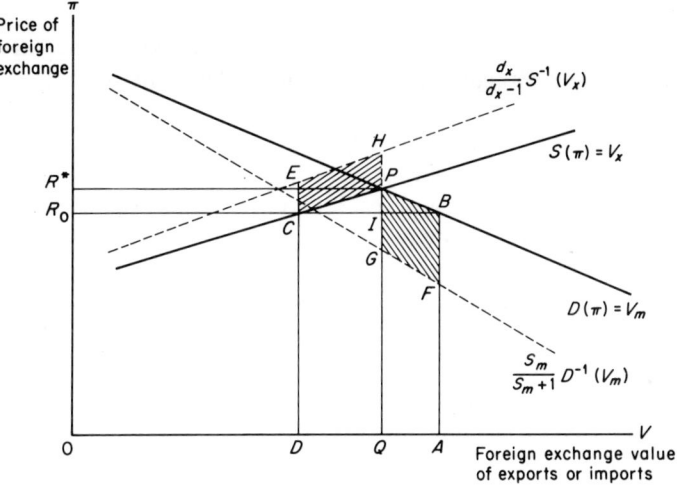

Figure 1 Diagrammatic representation of Smith's analysis of the effects of devaluation.

simple diagrammatic device. Smith's argument is shown in Fig. 1. On the horizontal axis we measure the supply of foreign exchanges earned by exports $V = S(\pi)$, or the demand for foreign exchanges for imports $V = D(\pi)$. On the vertical axis we measure the price of foreign exchange in domestic currency π.

The $D(\pi)$ curve represents the demand for foreign exchanges for import purposes as a monotonic decreasing function of the exchange rate π. The $S(\pi)$ curve represents the supply of foreign exchange proceeds from exports as a monotonic increasing function of π. The latter implies an assumption that the foreign elasticity of demand for domestic exports is greater than unity throughout the range that we are interested in, which is certainly the case for most small countries.

The height of the declining $D(\pi)$ curve measures the marginal utility of each dollar's worth of imports in terms of domestic currency. However, unless the elasticity of supply of imports is infinitely large (i.e., unless the foreign prices of imports are constant) it does not represent the true marginal revenue in utility of each additional dollar of foreign exchange available for imports. For if the country is confronted with a finite elasticity of supply of imports, each additional unity of expenditure on imports would tend to push the prices of imports up so that each additional dollar would bring back less and less in imports, not only because the prices of the additional imports are going up, but also because the country would have to pay more for the previous amount of imports too. Thus, by a well-known formula, the marginal utility of an additional dollar available for imports would be only $s_m/(s_m + 1)$ times the marginal utility of a dollar's worth of imports. The curve of the marginal utility of foreign exchange earnings, therefore, lies below the $D(\pi)$ curve.

When the exporters of the country are competitive, the height of the rising supply curve $S(\pi)$ may be regarded as the marginal cost curve of each dollar's worth of export goods, because each exporter would sell abroad until his marginal cost is equal to the price of exports. However, the marginal cost of each additional dollar earned is higher, unless the foreign demand for exports is infinitely elastic. Otherwise, each additional physical unit of exports would bring in smaller and smaller dollar proceeds, according to the well-known formula for marginal revenue. Therefore, the true marginal cost of foreign exchange earned by exports is higher than the supply curve of foreign exchange $S(\pi)$ as indicated by the $[d_x/(d_x - 1)]S^{-1}(V)$ curve.

Smith's argument about the harmful effect of a devaluation can now be explained with the help of this diagram. Suppose the country concerned originally had an exchange rate equal to OR_0 and then devalued to OR^*, the equilibrium rate. The original deficit AD is thus eliminated. According to Smith, the country's welfare is first of all reduced by $-dB/d\pi$, which on our diagram is represented by the area $ADCB$, which, upon setting the original exchange rate OR_0 equal to one as Smith did, is simply equal to AD the improvement in the balance of trade. Apparently this is based on the assumption that the original amount of import surplus was enjoyed by the domestic population without any quid pro quo, which of course is a highly questionable assumption. Because of the noninfinite elasticity of foreign supply of imports, however, the actual loss of utility from the decrease in imports in dollar value of AQ is not the column $BAQI$, but only $FAQG$. On the other hand, the incremental costs of increasing export proceeds by DQ is not merely the column $DCIQ$, but $DEHQ$. Therefore, the area $BFGI$ must be deducted from, and the area $CEHI$ must be added to, the first estimate of welfare loss by the trade balance improvement. Assuming that the triangles BPI and CPI are both of second order of smalls and therefore can both be neglected, we might say that $CEHI - BFGI \cong CEHP - BFGP$, and this difference should be added to the first estimate of the so-called loss from the devaluation, i.e., $(dB/d\pi) \Delta\pi$.

Furthermore, since, setting $OR_0 = 1$,

$$CEHP \cong \left(\frac{d_x}{d_x - 1} - 1\right)DQ = \left(\frac{d_x}{d_x - 1} - 1\right)\frac{d(p'X)}{d\pi}\Delta\pi$$

$$= \frac{1}{d_x - 1} \cdot \frac{s_x(d_x - 1)}{d_x + s_x} X \Delta\pi = \frac{Xs_x}{d_x + s_x}\Delta\pi$$

and similarly

(13) $$BFGP = \left(1 - \frac{s_m}{s_m + 1}\right) AQ = \frac{1}{s_m + 1} \cdot \frac{d(q'M)}{d\pi} \Delta\pi$$
$$= \frac{1}{s_m + 1} \cdot \frac{d_m(s_m + 1)}{d_m + s_m} M \Delta\pi = \frac{M d_m}{d_m + s_m} \Delta\pi.$$

Therefore,

$$CEHP - BFGP = \left[\frac{X s_x}{d_x + s_x} - \frac{M d_m}{d_m + s_m}\right] \Delta\pi$$
$$= \left[X \frac{(s_x s_m - d_x d_m)}{(d_x + s_x)(d_m + s_m)} + B \frac{d_m}{d_m + s_m}\right] \Delta\pi$$
$$= \left[-X \frac{dT}{d\pi} + B \frac{d_m}{d_m + s_m}\right] \Delta\pi.$$

Comparing (13) with Eq. (10′) above, we can readily see that the second and third terms of that equation merely indicate that $(dB/d\pi) \Delta\pi$, or the area $ABCD$, understates (or overstates) the loss of welfare from a devaluation and, hence, the area $(CEHP - BFGP)$, if positive, should be added to the estimated loss (if negative, the absolute difference should be deducted from the estimated loss). The fourth term presumes the presence of tariff on imports, which we have omitted from our diagram for the sakes of simplicity.

Thus, presented diagrammatically, it is easy to see why Smith's argument, apart from its questionable way of treating the trade balance as having no quid pro quo, does not fit the actual situation, with which countries like Taiwan were confronted. As we pointed out in the introduction, the actual situation in Taiwan in 1954 was that, although the exchange rate was no doubt overvalued, the trade balance was not allowed to go into a deficit by the quota restrictions of imports. In fact, since 1951, the government managed to squeeze out a small balance of payments surplus every year to replenish the exhausted exchange reserves.

In 1954, Taiwan certainly did not allow imports to enter in accordance with the domestic demand function, nor would the domestic prices of imports be determined by their foreign prices multiplied by the exchange rate plus the tariff rate, as assumed in Smith's model. The effects of a devaluation on a country in such a situation are quite different from those depicted by Smith's model. They should be illustrated with a different diagram such as that of Fig. 2.

In Fig. 2, the $D(\pi)$ and $S(\pi)$ are drawn as in Fig. 1. The initial official exchange rate OR_0 is far below the equilibrium rate KL. Imports, however,

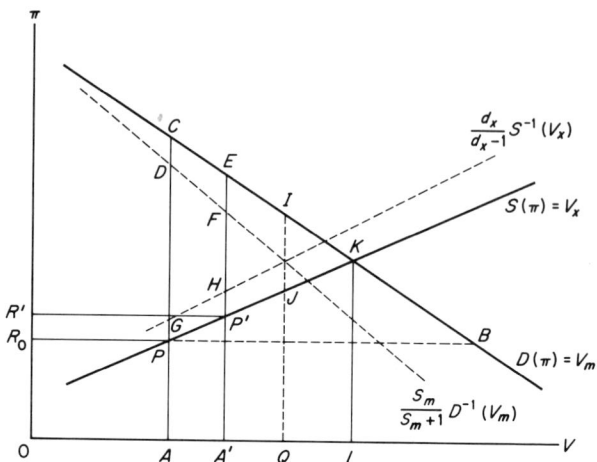

Figure 2 Actual effects of devaluation in countries with exchange control.

are not permitted to expand according to the domestic demand curve for imports to point B as in Fig. 1, but are held back by restrictions to equal exports proceeds OA (plus whatever foreign aid or borrowing the government can count on, or minus any amount of foreign exchange the government wants to hold back and add to its reserves). The domestic market price of imports (per dollar's worth) will not be OR_0 or AP but will be AC. Smith's model is therefore wrong in assuming that imports are determined by the import demand function and that the domestic price of imports is equal to its foreign supply price times $(1 + t)\pi$. Furthermore, when the country devalues, imports should not be assumed to decrease according to the demand function, but should instead increase with the increase in export proceeds. In other words, neglecting the complications of foreign aid and reserve replenishment, we may say that quantitative import restrictions should see to it that $p'X = q'M$ and, therefore, $dM = dX + Xdp' - Mdq'$.

In this case, if the country devalues, say, from OR_0 to OR', the effect on the trade balance is obviously zero. The effect on the terms of trade is, however, unambiguously adverse if not zero, as both exports and imports would increase, in contrast to the previous case of an increase in exports coupled with a decrease in imports. Nevertheless, the welfare of the country will generally improve so long as the initial percentage gap between the domestic market price of imports and the domestic currency equivalent of foreign exchange cost of imports, i.e., $(AC - AP)/AP$, which we may call the implicit tariff rate on imports, is greater than the so-called "optimum tariff rate," i.e., the tariff rate which if it were imposed, instead of trade restrictions, would make the marginal utility of an incremental dollar's worth of imports equal to the marginal cost of earning an additional dollar from exports, which in Fig. 2 is shown to be $(QI - QJ)/QJ$. For instance, if the country devalues from OR_0 to OR', the gain in welfare can be roughly represented by the trapezoid $DFHG$. For a small country this is most likely to be the case, since a small country usually enjoys a very elastic foreign demand for its exports as well as a very elastic foreign supply of its imports; hence the optimum tariff rate for it is usually very close to zero.

In mathematical terms, this may be demonstrated in the following way to facilitate comparison with Smith's result. Let us continue to use Smith's measurement of real income as the criterion for welfare change, i.e.,

$$dE/d\pi = dE'/d\pi + q'_0(1 + \tau_0)\, dM/d\pi \gtreqless 0, \qquad (14)$$

where τ_0 is now not the explicit tariff rate imposed upon imports, but the implicit tariff rate contained in the initial gap between the domestic market price of imports and the domestic currency equivalent of the foreign exchange cost of imports, viz, $(AC - AP)/AP = [D^{-1}(V_0) - \pi_0]/\pi_0$. This implicit tariff rate is normally not constant but would change with the amount of imports permitted by quota restrictions. For the measurement of changes in real income, however, we shall treat τ as well as q' in (14) as fixed at their initial values, respectively, i.e., we shall be comparing $\sum Q_1 p_0$ with $\sum Q_0 p_0$.

Since the purpose of restrictions is to ensure $p'X = q'M$, we may assume that $dM = dX + X\,dp' - M\,dq'$. Substituting into (14), we get

$$\frac{dE}{d\pi} = -p_0 \frac{dX}{d\pi} + q'_0(1 + \tau_0)\left(\frac{dX}{d\pi} + X\frac{dp'}{d\pi} - M\frac{dq'}{d\pi}\right)$$

$$= -X\frac{d_x s_x}{d_x + s_x} + (1 + \tau_0)\left[X_d \frac{d_x s_x}{d_x + s_x} - X\frac{s_x}{d_x + s_x}\right.$$

$$\left. - \frac{X(d_x - 1)s_x}{(1 + s_m)(d_x + s_x)}\right] = X\frac{s_x}{d_x + s_x}\left[\frac{\tau_0 s_m(d_x - 1) - (s_m + d_x)}{1 + s_m}\right]$$

$$\gtreqless 0 \quad \text{according as} \quad \tau_0 \gtreqless \frac{d_x + s_m}{s_m(d_x - 1)} = \tau^* \quad \text{(provided } d_x > 1\text{),}$$

where τ^* is the usual optimum tariff rate, which would approach zero as d_x and s_m both approach infinity.

For a small country with an obviously overvalued exchange rate where the balance of trade is kept in balance by stringent restrictions on imports, therefore, a devaluation of the exchange rate toward the probable equilibrium rate will most likely improve the country's welfare. This kind of beneficial effect of a devaluation of an overvalued currency is what Professor Machlup calls "the resources reallocation effect" (Machlup, 1956).

The above argument is of course dependent on the assumption that foreign demand for the devaluing country's exports has an elasticity greater than unity (i.e., $d_x > 1$). In the early postwar year, when elasticity pessimism used to prevail, this assumption was very likely to elicit criticism. In fact, when we made the recommendation of letting the exchange rate devalue to its equilibrium level, one well-informed cabinet minister actually admonished us that foreign demand for Taiwan's chief exports are highly inelastic; for the two major items in Taiwan's exports during that period were sugar and rice, which together accounted for nearly 80% of the total value of exports in the early fifties. Taiwan's sugar export was practically fixed for her by the international sugar agreement that allotted world market share annually for each participating sugar producing country. Its rice export went exclusively to Japan, and the quantity and price (in terms of U.S. dollars) were fixed each year by direct negotiation between the two governments. Thus, these two major items of exports were literally independent of the exchange rate of Taiwan's currency.

Nevertheless, we believed that even if the traditional major exports were confronted with foreign demands of little elasticity, there must be hundreds of new products that can be produced with the cheap labor supply and readily sold in the world market, provided that the relative cheapness of Taiwan's labor was not covered up by the overvaluation of her currency. Later development of the foreign trade of Taiwan has certainly borne out our prediction.

Another prevalent view of that time that contributed strongly to the inhibition against devaluation was the belief that a devaluation would surely add fuel to inflation. According to the then-prevalent cost-push theory of inflation, a devaluation would raise the prices of imported finished products as well as raw materials, and, hence, would give a big boost to the inflation of prices and wages. This view may be right for the situation discussed by Smith as depicted in Fig. 1, but is totally wrong in the situation shown in developing countries with overvalued currency and quantitatively controlled foreign trade.

It is well known that cost alone cannot determine price except when the supply curve is infinitely elastic. At the other extreme, when the supply curve has zero elasticity then cost would have no effect at all on price, which will be determined entirely be demand and the available supply. In Fig. 1, when the exchange rate is raised from OR_0 to OR', the price of a dollar's worth of imports will increase by the same amount, as it is tacitly assumed there that foreign exchanges are supplied to importers at the official exchange rate without limit.

In Fig. 2, however, the supply of foreign exchange is limited by quantitative restrictions to total export proceeds (plus aid if any). That is, at the exchange rate OR_0, the supply curve of foreign exchanges to importers is the right-angled curve $R_0 PC$, that turns vertical at P. When the exchange rate is devalued to OR', the supply curve is shifted to $R'P'E$, which is also vertical at its relevant marginal section $P'E$. Thus, although the cost of foreign exchange is raised from OR_0 to OR', the price of a dollar's worth of imports is likely to fall from AC to $A'E$ instead of rising with the exchange rate (unless imports had always been rationed by the government strictly at landed costs). In Taiwan, as in most developing countries, no such effective rationing system existed. Imported goods had always been sold at what the market would pay for them. It is therefore totally wrong to say that because the cost of foreign exchange to importers will be raised by a devaluation, the prices of imports and the goods made with imported materials must rise in prices.

If any prices are to rise after a devaluation, they would be those of exportable goods, because their prices in the world market would become higher in domestic currency and their production would expand until their marginal costs rise enough to match their prices. Whether the general price level on balance would rise or not cannot be determined by cost-push theory alone, but should be determined in terms of the aggregate effective demand for and the aggregate supply of all goods and services. If an increase in exports leads automatically a relaxation of import restrictions so that trade continues to balance, there will be no expansion of aggregate effective demand in money terms directly attributable to the devaluation. On the other hand, so long as the tariff on imports implied by the initial import restrictions is higher than the optimum rate, there will no doubt be an increase in real income due to more efficient reallocation of resources. Thus, provided that no monetary expansion is inadvertently permitted to occur during the process of resources reallocation, the general price level is more likely to fall than to rise as claimed by the cost-push theorists. An essentially similar argument has been expounded by the late Professor E. Sohmen (1958, 1961). However, in 1954, Liu and myself had already used the argument to dispel the fear that a devaluation would spur inflation.

It is most unfortunate that so prevalent were the views that devaluation tends to be harmful to the welfare of the country and that it is an inflationary factor that together they cast a strong inhibition on many countries with a clearly overvalued currency against making the necessary adjustment.

B. Inhibition against Raising Interest Rates and the Invalidity of Its Theoretical Underpinning

Similar inhibition existed against raising interest rates in the postwar years. Before the introduction of the Preferential Interest Rate Deposits scheme in March 1959, Taiwan actually had been enforcing a low-interest policy that let the real rate of interest drop to a negative level during the rapid inflation. The virtual drying up of the inflow of private savings into the banking system, however, forced the Bank of Taiwan to introduce the PIR Deposits that paid a nominal interest rate of 7% per month (equivalent to 125% per year), as described in Section I.

It appeared that the authorities had realized through painful experience that an adequate non-negative real interest rate was a necessary inducement for savers and depositors, but the function of the interest rate as a necessary criterion for the efficient allocation of scarce investible funds was still not quite understood. The fear of cost-push inflation was still so deeply rooted that, when the interest rate on one-month savings deposits was raised to 7% per month, the rate on term loans at the Bank of Taiwan was still kept down at only 2.10% per month, while, on the free money market, the rate of interest on loans with collateral stayed at the fantastic level of 14% per month. This amounted to a heavy subsidy to investors who were favored with relatively cheap loans from government-controlled banks, and it implied that such cheap loans must be strictly rationed (in fact, practically restricted to public enterprises only). When, in July 1954, the rate on one-month savings deposits was brought down to 1% per month and the lending rate of the Bank of Taiwan down to 0.99% per month, the free money market rate for loans with collateral was still as high as 3.50% per month.

Against this background, our recommendation for interest policy was (1) to legalize the free money market by removing the legal ceiling on interest rates, so as not to add to the risks of lending and borrowing there; (2) to discontinue the government control of interest rates on deposits and loans at all banks and let them raise the rates according to the supply and demand for loanable funds in keeping with the free money market; (3) that the Bank of Taiwan (which was acting as the Central Bank at that time) should watch only the money supply and keep it from increasing by more than a moderate percentage every year so as to keep the price level more or less constant.

To rebut the prevailing view that such a general upshift of the structure of bank rates would impart a strong boost to the cost-push inflation, and to demonstrate that the controlled low-interest-rate policy would not only result in a reduction of the total supply of noninflationary investible funds but also in less efficient allocation of such funds, we had used the diagrammatic device shown in Fig. 3 to present our argument.

Let DD' be the demand curve for the loanable funds and SS' be the supply curve of ex ante (planned) savings of the public to the banking system, which we shall assume to be fairly adequately represented by the increment to the savings and time deposits at all banks. These savings are assumed to provide the noninflationary financing for prospective investments. Here economists who are brought up to think in terms of the Keynesian liquidity preference

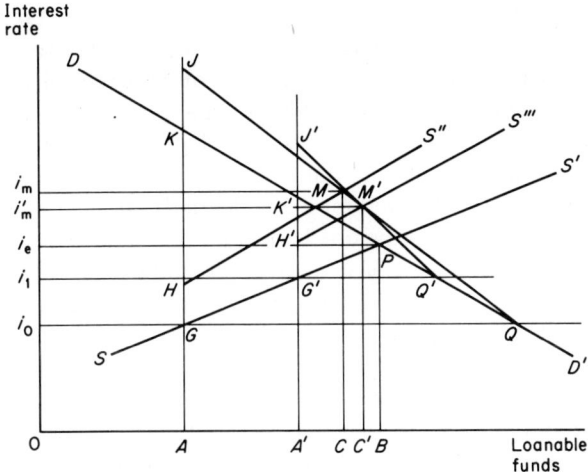

Figure 3 Demands and supplies of loanable funds and curb money-market interest rate under government control of interest rates charged by banks.

interest theory would probably immediately object why these two curves should be singled out for the analysis of the money market instead of the usual demand and supply for money. It would be a long argument to settle the issues between loanable funds and liquidity preference theories. Here I shall merely refer the interested or skeptical readers to a previous article of mine, in which it was shown that the two theories really come to the same thing if Keynes's "finance demand for liquidity" is understood to be the proper transactions demand for money as it should be (Tsiang, 1956, 1977). The loanable-funds approach, however, has a definite advantage over the liquidity preference theory in that the former can better portray the social function of the banking system as the intermediary between the suppliers of savings and the demanders for finance for investments.

We have not, however, shown all possible components of demands and supplies of loanable funds in our Fig. 3. According to Robertson's formulation of the loanable-funds theory, apart from planned savings and planned investments, increases in money supply and hoarding (or dishoarding) of money should also be included as components of the supply of or demand for loanable funds. We shall, however, exclude the increase in money supply as an additional source of supply of financing for investment because of its undesirable inflationary effects, which rule that it should be consciously avoided. As to hoardings or dishoardings (i.e., increases or decreases of idle or speculative cash balances), we regard them as to be of negligible importance in a country with a lengthy recent experience of rampant inflation, where the interest on savings deposits currently stood at 1% per month, and where in the unorganized money market beyond the control of monetary authorities the rate of loans with collateral remained at 3.50% per month. Thus we shall operate with the two curves in Fig. 3 alone and observe the policy implications of the control of interest rates by the banking authorities.

Suppose that the rate of interest on deposits is controlled by the authorities at i_0, which is substantially below the equilibrium rate of interest that would equated the demand for loanable funds on the part of investment and business operations on the one hand, and the supply of ex ante savings, on the other hand. The flow of savings per period of time into the banking system, which, we have reason to believe, can be fairly adequately measured by the net increase in the total time and savings deposits at the banks, would be only OA. There is thus a huge excess demand for loanable funds at the banks, if the banks lending rates are not much higher than i_0, as was in fact the case in Taiwan. If expansion of money supply is to be excluded, strict credit rationing must be imposed to hold demand to the available supply. There is thus a large amount of unsatisfied demand spilling over to the unorganized money market. If credit rationing is conducted in a perfectly efficient way so that only those investment demands that yield the highest returns (i.e., only those with a marginal yield higher than AK) are offset by the supply, then the spill-over demand to the money market outside the banking system will simply be the portion of the demand curve below K. With discretionary allocation by bureaucrats, however, this is rather unlikely to happen. Inevitably, some investment demands with an expected marginal yield little higher than i_0, or AG, might get allotted their full or partial requests for funds, whereas some demands with expected yields higher even than AK may be denied satisfaction. In this case, the spill-over demand curve for loanable funds on the money market outside the banking system, with the vertical line through AK as its zero axis, will be a partially tilted version of the original demand curve below K, viz, something like JQ, which, however, must coincide with the original demand curve at Q, since when the curb money market rate coincides with the interest rate charged at the banks, the combined demands for funds in the two markets must be what the aggregate demand curve indicates.

The spill-over supply of loanable funds to the unorganized money market will not be just the untapped portion of the original supply curve either, because the unorganized money market does not have big intermediaries with established reputation to help the lenders spread risks, and, furthermore, in countries where the authorities impose a legal ceiling on interest rates on the basis of the antiusury law, loan contracts made at the uncontrolled money market rates are denied legal enforcement. Therefore, a considerable risk premium must be added to the original supply curve of loanable funds to the banking system, so that the supply curve of loanable funds to the unorganized money market will be a curve like HS'', higher than the original supply curve. The risk premium required is presumably an increasing function of the supply to the unorganized money market, as marginal risk aversion generally tends to rise with the amount of risk taken. Thus, the rate of interest there will be determined at M, the intersection of the spill-over demand and supply curves, which obviously can be very much higher than i_0, and even higher than the equilibrium rate i_e also.

This depicts fairly accurately the actual situation of the banking system and the curb money market in Taiwan around 1954. Under such circumstances, the marginal cost of investible funds to most producers is not i_0 (or rather the lending rates of banks based upon it), but the curb money market rate i_m or CM. For with strict credit rationing on the part of banks to make the insufficient supply of loanable funds go around, no borrowers, except a few privileged public enterprises, were likely to have their full demands satisfied at the banks' lending rate. Most borrowers would have to resort to the uncontrolled money market for their marginal credit requirements for credit and pay the ruling market rate.

Confronted with such a situation, if the monetary authorities should raise the controlled rate on deposits from i_0 to i_1, which we presume to be still lower than the equilibrium rate i_e, the flow of savings attracted into the banking system could be increased from OA to OA'. Again if the banking system devotes the increased inflow of savings to finance the most productive of the demands for funds, the new spill-over demand curve for funds on the curb money market will simply be the demand curve below K', i.e., the portion of aggregate demand curve to the right of the vertical line through A'. If, as is more likely to happen, the banking system should fail to lend the increased supply of loanable funds to the most productive investment demands, then again the spill-over demand curve would be tilted upward from the original demand curve, say, to start from a point J' above K', but must converge to the original demand curve at Q' where the latter cuts the horizontal line drawn from i_1, the new rate charged by banks.

The new spill-over supply curve in the curb money market would start from H' above G' on the original supply curve of loanable funds and run toward S'''. It would lie throughout its whole length below HS'', the spill-over supply curve of funds on the curb market before the rise of the banks' rate, because of the principle of increasing risk premium.

Thus, barring very extreme and unlikely happenings, e.g., that the second spill-over demand curve for funds $J'Q'$ should be tilted upward from the original demand curve DD' to a much greater extent than the first one, i.e., JQ, the new rate of interest on the curb market will generally be lower than the original one, i.e., $C'M'$ or $i'_m < CM$ or i_m, and the aggregate supply of non-inflationary investible funds is likely to be increased, i.e., $OC' > OC$.

The scale of operations of the curb money market would indeed be reduced from AC to $A'C'$, but nevertheless the total amount of investments that can be financed with noninflationary funds is likely to be increased (from OC to OC'). Furthermore, since the gap between the interest rates of the banking system and of the outside money market is bound to be reduced, the allocation of investible funds would be more efficient, as the higher lending rate of the banks would rule out many low yield projects, that were only marginally profitable at the former low rate, and would force investors to seek faster rate of turnover for their investment.

It is quite wrong to say, as a large number of economists seemed to believe at that time, that such a rise in the controlled interest rate of the banking system would contribute to cost-push inflation.[4] For the true relevant marginal cost of investable funds to most entrepreneurs would be more likely to fall, from CM to $C'M'$, than to rise. Besides, there would be the beneficial effects on total output of larger aggregate supply of noninflationary investable funds available for the expansion of productive capacity, and the more efficient allocation of available investable funds.

Many Keynesian economists were brought up to think that any increase in investment, however financed, is inflationary. We are of the opinion, however, that an increase in investment financed by genuine increase in savings (i.e., a reduction in planned consumption), or by a switching from hoardings of commodities, precious metals, or foreign currencies, will not inflate the effective demand to any significant extent. On the contrary the increase in productive capacity resulting from the increased investment activities, particularly when the latter are confined to those with very high returns and quick turnover by the high real rate of interest, would instead be an anti-inflationary force in the longer run (Tsiang, 1949).

It is a great pity that under the prevailing influence of Keynesian economics so many developing countries, in spite of their great shortage of capital and savings, would indulge in the wrong policy of keeping the interest rate of their domestic banking system down at the conventional level of developed countries with more stable prices, under the mistaken idea that this is necessary for checking cost-push inflation or for stimulating real investment. Actually, such an enforced low interest rate policy would either add fuel to domestic inflation by creating an enormous excess demand for bank credits, or would slow down real capital formation at home by discouraging the inflow of savings into organized financial intermediaries, or both at the same time.

---

[4] Unless it can be shown that the controlled interest rate somehow directly enters the official cost of living index (e.g., as mortgage interest cost) and such cost of living index forms the basis for wage determination. This, however, has not been the case in Taiwan.

IV. The Effects of Our Proposals on the Economic Development of Taiwan

Our recommendations were by no means accepted immediately nor were they ever in full. On exchange policy, our recommendations were adopted fairly fully for some length of time although after considerable lags. The basic exchange rate of NT$15.55 to one U.S. dollar that had been in force since 1953 was kept unchanged until April 1958. However, private exporters were awarded on top of the basic buying rate, exchange surrender certificates for 50% or 80% (according to types of goods they exported) of their exchange proceeds surrendered to the exchange authorities. These certificates could be sold freely on the market for a price which varied from NT$6.10 in 1955 to NT$16.80 in 1957. Thus the effective rate for most private exporters were in effect devalued in 1955 from NT$15.55 to either NT$18.60 to NT$20.43, according to whether they received the 50% or 80% award of exchange surrender certificates for their export earnings. On the other hand, most private importers had to pay the basic selling rate of $15.55 + $3.13 plus the price of exchange certificates, which they must obtain from the market before they could apply for foreign exchange at the Bank of Taiwan.

Furthermore, in July 1955, the government passed regulations that stipulated for the rebate of commodity tax, import duty, and defense tax on exported products or raw materials embodied therein. This was a great boost to the exports of manufactured products, as Taiwan is a small island with very limited natural resources, but very dense population, and, hence, her manufactured exports must rely largely on imported raw materials. This opened the way for Taiwan to develop her export-oriented manufacturing industries, which, in effect, export the value added by the abundant local supply of labor above the cost of imported materials.

Quota restrictions on imports, however, were not abolished at that time, in spite of our recommendation. Importers were still allotted licenses to import different types of goods, within fixed quotas, on the basis of their performance records in the preceding years. These licenses, however, were permitted to be traded on the market, where licenses for different categories of imports naturally fetched quite different prices. If any importer wished to import more of any foreign goods than stipulated in his own allotted license for that type of goods, he would have to purchase the license for the additional import from the market on top of the exchange certificates necessary for acquiring the foreign exchange. The market price for exchange certificates, therefore, could not reflect correctly the gap between the basic exchange rate and the equilibrium exchange rate, nor could the allocation of total available foreign exchanges to different categories of imports conform to the rational choice of the public.

It was only since April 1958, when K. Y. Yin, whom we had convinced of the validity of our argument, became the Chairman of the Foreign Exchange and Trade Control Commission, that the principle of devaluation coupled with liberalization of trade was adopted as a conscious policy goal. On April 14 of that year, the basic exchange rate was devalued from NT$15.55 to NT$24.58 buying and NY$24.78 selling. What was more significant was that thenceforth exporters (except those of sugar, rice, and salt) would be awarded exchange surrender certificates representing the full amount (instead of only 50% or 80%) of their exchange proceeds surrendered to the Bank of Taiwan. They could sell these certificates on the market to importers, who had to present these certificates in the amount of foreign exchanges they wish to purchase from the Bank of Taiwan for their imports (with the exemption of importers of certain specified goods, viz, important machinery, fertilizer, crude oil, cotton, soy bean, and wheat for domestic consumption only). At the same time, to make the market demand for exchange certificates correctly reflect the market demand for imports, the quota restrictions on all types of permissible imports were boldly removed, although what were classified as luxury goods were still forbidden to be imported. In general, the existing high import tariffs were still maintained, but the 20% defense surcharge, which used to be assessed on the basis of the value of imports, was thenceforth assessed on the basis of the duty payable. Thus the market-determined price of the certificates would constitute a flexible margin to be added to the fixed basic rate, and would enable the resulting effective rate to approach the equilibrium exchange rate under the existing system of tariffs and to adjust automatically in accordance to changes in supply and demand conditions.

A few months later (in November 1958) it was decreed that the three special export products, sugar, rice, and salt, were also to be treated in the same way as all other exports, and that the excemption from the obligation to present corresponding amounts of exchange certificates in applying for foreign exchanges that was extended to certain specified groups of "essential" imports, viz, certain types of machinery, fertilizer, crude oil, cotton, soy bean, and wheat, was abolished. It was also announced that the same effective rate would be applicable to most remittances and transfers. This spelled the end of the complicated multiple exchange rate system, and the rate of exchange was to all intents and purposes unified. The effective rate for the closing months of 1958 ranged from NT$36.38 to NT$37.88 for exporters, implying a devaluation of 28–30% as compared with the effective rate for most private exporters of NT$26.35 in the second half of 1957.

In August of the following year (1959), in order to comply with the regulations of the International Monetary Fund, the Bank of Taiwan discontinued the practice of separating the effective exchange rate into the two components of the basic rate and the price of exchange certificates, and declared that henceforth the exchange rate of the new Taiwan yuan was to be NT$38.08 to one U.S. dollar buying, and NT$38.38 selling. Exporters would still get exchange certificates for the full amount of the foreign exchange proceeds of their exports. They were free either to sell these certificates on the market or directly to the Bank of Taiwan at the price of NT$38.08.

The market price of the certificates, which was no doubt to some extent stabilized but not pegged by the Bank of Taiwan, was allowed to creep up to NT$40.00 to one U.S. dollar in 1960, where it was pegged until February 1973, when the U.S. shocked the world by announcing the devaluation of the dollar by 20%. As Taiwan was at that time enjoying a big trade surplus (which amounted to as much as US$647 million during 1972, and the foreign exchange assets of the Central Bank increased by US$598 million during that year) it was decided that it was not necessary for Taiwan to devalue to the full extent together with the United States *vis-à-vis* the rest of the world; therefore the exchange rate with the dollar was raised to NT$38.00 to one U.S. dollar. Up to this date, the New Taiwan yuan is still linked with the U.S. dollar at this rate.[5]

The effect upon the foreign trade of Taiwan of this policy devaluation coupled with liberalization had been truly remarkable, as can be seen from Table 1. The devaluations and the tax rebate on exports started in 1955 were certainly effective in reviving export trade from its low point of 1954 and set it on an upward trend, but it was only in the 1960s, after the exchange rate was linked with the liberalized demand for imports, that expansion of the exports really took off. By 1977, 23 years after our first advisory mission in 1954, export value in U.S. dollars had increased nearly a hundredfold, i.e., from US$95.9 million to US$9,494 million. The structure of the economy has been thoroughly changed to an export-oriented country as the following figures would amply reveal. In 1954, total exports constituted only 5.4% of the GNP of Taiwan; in 1977 total exports constituted 48.4% of the GNP of the year. In 1976, Taiwan with a population of only 16 million was already exporting more in dollar value than India and Pakistan combined, which had a combined population of 724 million, or 45 times that of Taiwan.

The gross domestic product in real terms also increased spectacularly. From 1954 to 1960, GDP at constant prices increased by 44.8% averaging 6.4% per annum. For the decade 1961–1970, the increase in GDP was

---

[5] Since the submission of this manuscript for publication, the New Taiwan yuan has been revalued again on July 10, 1978, to NT$36 to one U.S. dollar, with a further announcement by the Central Bank that, after certain necessary legislative changes in exchange control regulations, the exchange rate of New Taiwan yuan would be allowed to float.

TABLE 1
MERCHANDISE TRADE OF TAIWAN[a]

	Exports (Millions of U.S. Dollars)	Average Annual Rate of Growth	Quantum Index[b]	Imports (Millions of U.S. Dollars)	Average Annual Rate of Growth	Quantum Index[b]	Trade Balance (Millions of U.S. Dollars)
1950	93.1		—	123.9		—	−30.8
1951	93.1		—	142.5		—	−49.5
1952	119.5		100.0	208.3		100.0	−88.8
1953	128.6		150.0	192.9		123.5	−62.3
1954	95.9		103.0	204.9		129.8	−109.0
1955	127.1		129.0	184.7		120.7	−57.6
1956	124.1		124.7	222.1		116.1	−98.0
1957	148.3	9.4%	145.1	244.7	5.7%	125.4	−96.4
1958	155.8		177.0	273.5		140.0	−117.7
1959	156.9		166.9	263.9		154.7	−107.0
1960	164.0		163.8	286.5		171.3	−122.5
1961	195.2		168.7	330.3		186.4	−135.1
1962	218.2		192.1	328.0		187.0	−109.8
1963	333.7		237.9	373.3		216.0	−39.6
1964	434.5		312.8	395.4		246.4	39.1
1965	450.8	24.5%	356.4	517.2	16.9%	312.7	−66.4
1966	542.7		428.3	545.6		330.9	−2.9
1967	653.7		497.2	728.1		425.4	−74.4
1968	816.3		609.9	888.8		479.4	−72.5
1969	1081.4		777.9	1093.0		643.4	−11.6
1970	1468.6		1024.9	1363.4		793.1	105.2
1971	2047.2		1392.8	1754.6		903.3	292.6
1972	2979.3		1870.3	2331.9		1098.5	647.4
1973	4475.9		2260.2	3709.9		1283.9	766.0
1974	5592.0	30.6%	2160.9	6403.9	29.4%	1589.8	−811.9
1975	5304.1		2137.2	5558.6		1412.8	−24.5
1976	7805.5		3312.4	7105.6		1875.0	699.9
1977	9493.9		3566.7	8279.2		1873.8	1214.7

[a] Source: *Taiwan Financial Statistics Monthly*, The Central Bank of China.

[b] These quantum indices are taken from *Taiwan Statistical Data Book 1978*, the Council for Economic Planning & Development (formerly known as the Economic Planning Council), Republic of China. These indices must be used with caution as many new commodities have entered trade during this period and the compositions of both exports and imports have changed drastically.

138.1% averaging 9.1% per annum. For the seven years 1971–1977 the increase was 74.8%, averaging 8.3% per annum. Over the entire 23-year period 1954–1977 real GDP increased six times. Compared with the performances of those countries that had stuck to the strategy of developing import substitutes under heavy protection and stringent exchange controls, such sustained high rates of growth in real GDP were truly remarkable.[6] (See Table 2.)

As to the question of whether devaluations provided boosts to the inflationary forces, the evidence was on the whole in our favor, even though in the 1950s it might appear to casual observers as leaning towards the opposite side. First of all, the devaluation of 1955 was not accompanied by the removal of quota restrictions on imports, as we recommended. In fact, although exports were stimulated to US$127 million in 1955 from a low of US$96 million in 1954, imports were cut back from US$205 million to US$185 million. At the same time, the money supply was allowed to increase by 20.1% in 1955 and by another 23.7% in 1956. It is not surprising that wholesale prices should have risen in 1955 by 14.1% over the preceding year, and by another 12.7% in 1956.

The devaluation of March 1958, however, was accompanied by the abolition of import quotas. Prices during that year hardly increased at all (the increase in the price index amounting to only 1.4%), even though the monetary authorities were very uncooperative in letting the money supply increase by 39% during that year. Yet prices remained fairly stable until August 1959, when there was a disastrous flood in the chief agricultural area of the island, causing a heavy loss in the rice crop and an estimated loss in properties of NT$3.4 billion. This was followed by a drought in the first half of 1960 and then by a bad typhoon in August 1960. These natural calamities combined with the increases in government expenditures for the relief of the disaster areas, rather than the exchange reform of 1958, appeared to be the factors that contributed to the rises of prices of 10.3% and 14.2% in 1959 and 1960, respectively.

After 1960, both exports and imports were expanding at tremendous rates, but prices remained fairly stable until 1972. With the sole exception of 1963, the annual increase in wholesale prices never exceeded 4% during the 11-year span 1961–1971. The average rate of increase of prices for this whole period was less than 2% per year.

In 1972, the world-wide inflationary market gave Taiwan an unprecedented export surplus of US$647 million, which was chiefly responsible for the

---

[6] U.S. General Economic Aid to Taiwan had terminated in 1964, which fact had little effect on the growth trend of the economy of Taiwan.

TABLE 2

Gross Domestic Product of Taiwan at Current Prices and at Constant 1971 Prices (in Millions of New Taiwan Yuan)[a]

	At Current Prices	Chain Index	At Constant 1971 Prices	Chain Index
1951	12,322		52,146	
1952	17,251	140.00	57,809	110.86
1953	22,992	133.28	62,593	108.28
1954	25,229	109,73	68,032	108.69
1955	30,091	119.27	73,277	107.71
1956	34,550	114.82	77,162	105.30
1957	40,346	116.78	82,561	107.00
1958	45,006	111.55	87,221	105.64
1959	51,967	115.47	93,302	106.97
1960	62.814	120.87	98,528	105.60
1961	70,363	112.02	105,048	106.62
1962	77,578	110.25	112,744	107.33
1963	87,853	113.24	122,387	108.55
1964	102,872	117.10	136,354	111.41
1965	113,732	110.56	150,696	110.52
1966	126,667	111.37	162,348	107.73
1967	146,091	115.33	179,003	110.26
1968	171,375	117.31	195,106	109.00
1969	195,819	114.26	211,588	108.45
1970	226,840	115.84	234,573	110.86
1971	261,558	115.31	261,558	111.50
1972	307,293	117.49	292,625	111.88
1973	388,699	126.49	327,698	111.99
1974	524,655	134.98	329,697	100.61
1975	560,027	106.74	339,863	103.08
1976	655,813	117.10	379,856	111.77
1977	745,640[b]	113.70	410,118[b]	107.97

[a] *National Income of the Republic of China*, Directorate-General of Budgets, Accounts and Statistics, Executive Yuan.
[b] Preliminary.

34.6% expansion of the money supply during that year. By then, the principle of flexible exchange rates was abandoned already, and the New Taiwan yuan was rigidly pegged to the U.S. dollar at the rate of 40 to 1. The monetary authorities were unwilling to go back to the flexible certificate rate system and were too slow in reducing tariffs and removing the ban on import of so-called luxury goods. As a result of the huge trade surplus, the foreign exchange assets of all banks increased by NT$24.398 million (equivalent to US$642 million) and domestic money supply increased by NT$14,152 million. In 1973, even though the New Taiwan yuan was appreciated with respect to U.S. dollar in February (from 40 to 1, to 38 to 1), it was actually devalued with respect to the currencies of Japan and most European currencies. The export surplus grew further to the level of US$766 million, and domestic money supply increased by another NT$25,872 million, or 47% of that of the preceding year. Small wonder that price inflation was resumed in 1972 and became much worse in 1973, during which year the index of wholesale prices registered an increase of 40.3%.

Thus, over the whole period of trade expansion after devaluation and trade liberalization, the evidence appears to bear out our argument that if devaluation is coupled with trade liberalization, such that the trade balance remains constant, it would not by itself constitute an inflationary factor.

Our suggestion on interest policy fell upon much less receptive ears. That the interest rate of time and savings deposits is a necessary inducement to attract the public's savings into the banking system, and that the increased inflow of savings into the banking system constituted a significant antiinflationary force was repeatedly and convincingly demonstrated by experience. For instance, when Preferential Interest Deposits were first started in March 1950, at a monthly interest rate of 7%, by June the same year, the total of time and savings deposits including the new PIR deposits quickly increased from a mere 1.7% of the contemporary money supply to 7.0% of the money supply, and the rate of price inflation that had been as high as 10.3% per month in the first quarter of 1950 dropped dramatically to only 0.4% per month in the second quarter. But when the monetary authorities, in the first flush of the unexpectedly quick success, cut the interest rate by one-half to 3.5% per month on July 1, and then further reduced it to 3.0% on October 1, total savings and time deposits not only stopped increasing after September, but dropped absolutely by NT$10 million from September to December to a level that was merely 4.5% of the contemporary money supply at the end of 1950. Prices quickly resumed their upward trend and rose by 39.3% during the second half of 1950 and continued to rise at a rate of 4.8% per month in the first quarter of 1951.

Only after the interest rate was raised again to 4.2% per month on March 26, 1951, and kept there until the end of April 1952, was the upward trend of the savings and time deposits resumed. These deposits then rose spectacularly from NT$30 million (or 4.1% of the contemporary money supply) at the end of March 1951, to NT$541 million (or 56.4% of the contemporary money supply) at the end of September 1952. During 1951, the rate of inflation was already visibly reduced by the raise in interest rate, and in 1952, prices were completely stabilized. (See Table 3.)

If I appear to overemphasize the deflationary effect of the interest rate of bank deposits to the neglect of the interest rate on bank loans, the reason is to be found in my theoretical argument in the previous section. With stringent credit rationing in force, the lending rates of banks are no longer a significant factor. What is more significant is the question, From what sources do the funds that banks ration out originate? If the funds come from monetary expansion, then the lending operation is inflationary. The more we can substitute the inflow of voluntary savings into banks for monetary expansion as the source of funds for lending, the less inflationary the lending operations of banks will be.

Monetary theorists steeped in the Keynesian monetary theory would no doubt point out that savings and time deposits are also liquid assets created by banks. According to them, therefore, whether banks finance their loans by creating one kind of liquid assets (currency and demand deposits) or the other (savings and time deposits) should not make that much difference. In fact, savings and time deposits have frequently been called "quasi-money" and lumped together with currency and demand deposits as M2, the money supply in a broader sense, an alternative monetary aggregate to be used in substitution for M1, the money in the strict sense.

This is, however, an unfortunate consequence of overemphasizing the function of money as a store of value and exaggerating the substitutability of savings and time deposits for money in the strict sense even in the latter's primary function as means of payments. In fact, in countries like Taiwan with a painful and very recent experience of rampant inflation, M1 has long ceased to be regarded as an effective store of value. With respect to this function, it is completely dominated by other high-interest-yielding assets with little risk of nominal capital depreciation. M1 is practically kept solely for its means-of-payments function, i.e., for transactions purposes only. If the public submit their cash holdings to the banks to exchange them into savings or time deposits, it implies fairly accurately that they are planning to refrain from expending that amount until they convert it back into cash.

Anyway, the Taiwanese monetary authorities have learned by experience to treat the increment of savings and time deposits as an anti-inflationary factor and the reduction of such deposits as an inflationary factor, and thus watch their movements closely over the years. As the economy of Taiwan took off into a spectacular growth in the 1960s, savings and time deposits at the banks also went into a steep climb (see Tables 3 and 4.) From a start in 1950 of a mere NT$6 million, or 1.7% of the contemporary money supply M1, they increased to NT$50.2 billion or 145.4% of the contemporary money supply in 1970. In the 1970s, they continued their rapid increase and reached

TABLE 3

Money Supply; Savings, Time, and PIR Deposits; Interest Rates; and Wholesale Prices 1950–1954[a]

End of Period	Money Supply (Millions of New Taiwan Yuan)	Savings, Time, and PIR Deposits (Millions of New Taiwan Yuan)	Column 2 as Percent of Column 1	Monthly Interest Rate on One-Month PIR Deposits	Monthly Rate of Price Inflation During the Quarter Just Ended
1950 March	348	6	1.7	7.00 (effective	10.3%
June	401	28	7.0	7.00 (from March 25)	0.4
September	595	36	6.1	3.50 (from July 1)	6.0
December	584	26	4.5	3.00 (from October 1)	5.4
1951 March	732	30	4.1	4.20 (from March 26)	4.8
June	942	59	6.3	4.20	3.9
September	687	164	23.9	4.20	1.8
December	940	163	17.3	4.20	3.9
1952 March	867	271	31.2	4.20	2.6
June	942	494	52.4	3.80 (from April 29)	−1.0
				3.30 (from June 2)	
September	959	541	56.4	3.00 (from July 7)	−0.4
				2.40 (from September 8)	
December	1336	467	34.9	2.00 (from November 30)	0
1953 March	1074	499	46.5	2.00	1.5
June	1198	640	53.4	2.00	1.4
September	1292	671	51.9	1.50 (from July 16)	1.6
December	1683	599	35.6	1.20 (from October 10)	0.5
1954 March	1622	667	41.1	1.20	0
June	1809	747	41.3	1.20	−1.4
September	1923	782	40.6	1.00 (from July 1)	−0.6
December	2128	765	35.9	1.00	1.3
1955 March	2300	816	35.5	1.00	2.7

[a] *Taiwan Financial Statistics Monthly*, The Central Bank of China; and *Taiwan Commodity Prices Statistics Monthly*, Bureau of Accounting and Statistics, Taiwan Provincial Government.

TABLE 4

MONEY SUPPLY, SAVINGS, AND TIME DEPOSITS, INTEREST RATE AND WHOLESALE PRICES 1955–1978[a]

End of Period	Money Supply (Millions of New Taiwan Yuan)	Savings and Time Deposits	Column 2 as Percent of Column 1	Interest Rate on One-Year Time Deposits (Percent per Annum)	Average Rate of Price Increase Over the Preceding Year (Percent)
1955	2,555	993	38.9	20.98	14.08
1956	3,161	1,006	31.8	23.87	12.71
1957	3,740	1,399	37.4	21.70	7.22
1958	5,041	2,464	48.9	21.70	1.39
1959	5,486	3,290	60.0	18.43	10.27
1960	6,037	4,536	75.1	18.43	14.51
1961	7,231	7,478	103.4	15.39	3.23
1962	7,832	9,368	119.6	14.19	3.04
1963	10,060	12,228	121.6	12.68	6.46
1964	13,259	15,480	116.8	11.35	2.48
1965	14,695	18,161	123.6	11.35	−4.66
1966	17,004	23,629	139.0	10.56	1.47
1967	21,875	28,559	130.6	10.16	2.52
1968	24,649	32,166	130.5	10.16	1.99
1969	28,584	40,046	140.1	10.16	−0.24
1970	34,508	50,169	145.4	9.72	2.72
1971	40,914	70,241	171.7	9.25	0.02
1972	55,066	94,307	171.3	8.75	7.25
1973	80,938	114,543	141.5	11.00[b]	40.34
1974	86,617	157,638	182.0	13.50[b]	14.87
1975	109,303	201,808	184.6	12.00[b]	−0.60
1976	130,568	254,610	195.0	10.75	4.50
1977	171,170	342,047	199.8	9.50	2.64
1978 (April)	172,972	366,862	212.1	9.50	2.01[c]

[a] Sources: *Taiwan Financial Statistics Monthly*, The Central Bank of China, and *Monthly Statistics of the Republic of China*, Directorate-General of Budget, Accounting and Statistics.
[b] The interest rate was first raised to 9.50% on July 26, 1973, then to 11.00% on October 24, 1973, and finally to 15.00% on January 27, 1974. On September 19, 1974, however, it was lowered to 14.00%; on December 13, 1974, to 13.50%; on February 22, 1975, to 12.75%; and on April 21, 1975, to 12.00%.
[c] Percentage price increase over April 1977.

NT$366.9 billion or 212.1% of the contemporary money supply in April 1978.

This phenomenon appears to defy explanation by the modern wealth approach to the demand for money and other assets. For the interest rates on savings and time deposits were being reduced steadily since 1950 with only a few short interruptions, yet the ratio of time and savings deposits to the money supply increased on a steep rising trend from less than 2% to 212%. This long-run phenomenon is to be sharply distinguished from the short-run relationship we have noted above that a change in the interest rate on savings and time deposits by the monetary authorities would generally tend to change the rate of increase in these deposits in the same direction. This long-run trend seems to indicate that the money supply, in the strict sense, and savings and time deposits are two quite different types of assets. The former is essentially a medium of exchange, the demand for which is determined chiefly by the volume of transactions to be carried out with its service as such. The latter, in the case of Taiwan at least, is essentially an instrument of savings or store of value, for which the demand increases cumulatively with the annual savings of the public. There is no reason whatever that the two should increase in the same proportion even when the nominal or real interest rates remain absolutely constant.[7]

Even though the structure of these deposits has changed significantly towards longer term deposits (with one- and two-year time deposits becoming the dominant components instead of the one or three months deposits as in the early years), they impose a potential threat to the monetary authorities. For if the monetary authorities should upset the public's confidence in the stability of the purchasing power of the currency, or cut the interest rate to too low a level with the mistaken idea of thereby cheapening the supply of credit, a mass withdrawal from these deposits could be induced, which would either create a banking crisis, if the Central Bank does not print

---

[7] It is for the difficulty of separating this long-run phenomenon form the short-run effects of policy adjustments in the deposit rates of interest that we did not resort to the usual regression analysis for the whole period under investigation (i.e., 1950–1977) to determine the causal relationship between the amount, or the rate of increase, of total savings and time deposits and the rates of interest on them. The long-run trend of the steep climb of total savings and time deposits in spite of the fairly steady decline in the nominal interest rate on them, due to the slowing down of inflation and the increasing propensity to save of the public, would surely dominate the scene and result in a misleading negative regression coefficient for the interest rate as a determining variable for savings and time deposits.

We have therefore chosen rather to examine each major adjustment in the deposit rates of interest, specifically adopted by the monetary authorities to cope with a specific crisis of sharply reduced inflow of savings into banks and excessive price inflation, and to trace out whether its effects had not been in the desired directions.

currency notes fast enough to meet the withdrawal, or a major inflation if the Central Bank does print enough currency to meet it. This has, however, turned out to be a salutary constraint on the monetary authorities. It has so far impelled them to hold the rate of price inflation well within the one-digit limit (usually around 4% per annum) in normal times and to take fairly prompt actions if exogenous disturbances should bring about a spurt of inflation.

For instance, in 1972 and 1973, two successive big trade surpluses amounting to US$647 million and US$766 million, respectively, caused the money supply M1 to increase by 34.6% and 47.0%, respectively, in those two years. As a result, prices started to rise by 7.3% in 1972 and in 1973 shot up by a further 40.3%. This of course evoked the specter of inflation, which was still fresh in the memory of the public in Taiwan. The annual rate of increase of savings and time deposits dropped from 40.0% in 1971 to 21.5% in 1973. If no quick action was taken, the rate of increase could quickly turn into a rate of decrease. The monetary authorities reacted by raising interest rates on time and savings deposits, e.g., the rate on one-year savings deposits from 8.75% to 9.50% in July 1973, then to 11.00% in October, and finally to 15.00% in January 1974, in the hope of arresting the decreasing tendency of the rate of increase of such deposits. These efforts proved quite successful, for during 1974 savings and time deposits increased by NT$43,095 million or 37.6% as compared with the increase during 1973 of only NT$20,236 million or 21.5%. This increment of NT$43,095 million in savings and time deposits was equal to 49.8% of the total money supply M1 of the year 1974, out of which this sum would have to be transferred unless the banks restored the latter with their lending and investment operations.

This anti-inflationary force was to be added to the huge trade deficit of US$811.9 million (equivalent to NT$30,852 million) during 1974, which the government partly deliberately created by relaxing the restrictions on imports of luxury products, including foreign automobiles, and by encouraging the imports of raw materials and machinery. These two hefty anti-inflationary forces were powerful enough to curb the increase in money supply and to bring it down to only 7% during 1974. Price inflation was promptly reduced to 14.9% during 1974, in spite of the big oil price increases, and in 1975 the price level was completely stabilized.

As to the target for the control of the rate of growth of the money supply, the monetary authorities have found out by experience that if the rate of growth of the money supply is kept within 25% per annum, the increase in money supply could be absorbed by the increase in demand for the medium of exchange on the part of the 9% annual increase in real GDP and the more than 30% annual increase in the volume of foreign trade without causing more price inflation than 2%–4%, which is considered acceptable in the current world of inflation.[8] Although they may not have always succeeded in adhering to this guideline, this is at least what I understand the Taiwanese monetary authorities to be aiming at. Apparently, they are more successful in maintaining fairly stable prices than their counterparts in many developed countries who boast of more sophisticated methods.[9]

Although the function of interest rate on deposits as a necessary inducement to attract savings into the banking system appears to be well understood and to have frequently been put to good use, the function of the interest rate as a necessary criterion for efficient allocation of scarce investable funds seems not yet to have been recognized. To most planning authorities, the most efficient allocation is usually the one in accordance with their own discretion. They are generally interested in keeping the interest rate for loans as low as feasible so that they may have more options in allocating funds, even to projects which have relatively low yields but which might rank high in their own scale of priority. There is therefore great reluctance to raise interest rates on loans and deposits toward the highest marginal rate of return obtainable for the available investable funds at the disposal of the banking system.

That the loan rates of the banks are not near the highest obtainable marginal rate of return of the available investible funds is obvious from Table 5. For example, the lending rate for unsecured loans at commercial banks in 1976 was 14% per annum. At the same time, the rate on loans against post-dated checks (a credit instrument which has come to be very widely used in Taiwan) was as high as 29% per annum on the curb money market. It is sometimes vehemently argued that the rate on loans from the curb money market should by no means be taken as any indication of the

---

[8] In a recently published article (Tsiang, 1977b), I have presented a simple estimate of the demand function for real money balances in Taiwan as below:

$$\ln m = 0.1037 + 0.8313 \ln y + 0.6965 \ln T/Y - 0.3219 \ln r$$
$$(2.8882) \quad (0.2493) \quad (0.2216) \quad (0.1780)$$
$$(3.3349) \quad (3.1430) \quad (-1.8080)$$

$R^2 = 0.9950$, $S^2 = 0.0036$, $DW = 1.8925$, where m is the real money balances, y is the GDP in real terms, T/Y is the ratio of the volume of trade to GDP both in their current nominal values, and r is the average market rate of interest. The first row of bracketed numbers under the estimated coefficients gives their respective standard errors, and the second row of such numbers gives their respective t values. Thus with a 9% annual rate of growth of y, and a 30% plus rate of growth of the volume of trade (which together would imply roughly 20% of growth in T/Y), the rate of growth of the demand for real money balances might indeed be estimated to be roughly 21.4%.

[9] The big trade surplus of US$791 million in 1976, which had already resulted in a 19.5% increase in the money supply, and the continued trade surplus of similar dimensions during 1977, however, may spell a repetition of the inflationary price rise of 1973-1974, unless something is done quickly.

TABLE 5

INTEREST RATES OF THE BANKING SYSTEM AND ON THE CURB MONEY MARKET (PER ANNUM)[a]

	Interest Rates of Banks			Interest Rates on the Curb Money Market in Taipei[b]	
	Unsecured Loans	Secured Loans	One-Year Loans	Loans Against Post-Dated Checks	Rate on Deposits with Firms
	(Effective in December)			Average for the Year	Average for the Year
1970	13.20	12.00	9.72	22.85	20.98
1971	12.50	12.00	9.25	22.70	20.27
1972	11.75	11.25	8.75	23.73	20.27
1973	13.75	13.25	11.00	25.63	22.71
1974	15.50	14.75	13.50	32.61	25.49
1975	14.00	13.25	12.00	28.93	23.29
1976	14.00	13.25	12.00	29.66	24.02
1977 (July)	14.00	13.25	12.00	28.48	22.13

[a] Source: *Taiwan Financial Statistics Monthly*, The Central Bank of China.

[b] Taken rates are given in the source book as monthly rates. They were compounded into annual rates for comparison with the interest rates of banks.

marginal rate of returns of investible funds, as allegedly only distressed borrowers with no credit standing would ever have recourse to this kind of loan. This argument, however, is easily refuted by referring to the last column of Table 5. The fact is that the credit rationing by banks is so stringent that even firms with good reputations cannot obtain all their regular credit requirements from banks. They frequently had to resort to taking in deposits from the public as a private bank themselves. The rates of interest that they are willing to pay are frequently twice as high as the rate paid by banks to their depositors. Since these firms, which must have well-established reputations at attract depositors, are doing this on a regular basis, it cannot be argued that they are borrowing constantly at distress. There is no question, therefore, that banks in Taiwan do not offer a competitive rate of interest on their deposits nor do they charge the competitive interest rate on their loans. If both the deposit and loan rates of interest at banks were allowed to be raised towards the competitive market rates, the banking system could surely expand its share of mediation services at the expense of the less efficient curb money market. Not only would there be a net increase in total available investible funds, but the available funds would be allocated more efficiently and productively, as we have demonstrated above.

By keeping the interest rates on savings and time deposits at fairly attractive levels and by other tax measures to encourage savings, e.g., exempting from personal income tax the interest income from savings and time deposits with maturity terms of two years or longer, exempting from corporation income tax profits that are plowed back for investment etc., the authorities have succeeded very rapidly in turning Taiwan from a country with a very low propensity to save into a country with a remarkably high saving propensity. The enlarged inflow of voluntary savings into the banking system provided exactly the needed noninflationary financing for the domestic investment stimulated by the concurrent exchange devaluation and trade liberalization, which opened up vast investment opportunities in the new export industries. On the other hand, as the economy of Taiwan took off into a spectacular growth in the 1960s, voluntary savings in turn got a big boost;

TABLE 6

Taiwan's Savings as Percentage of National Income (Compared with Several Other Selected Countries)[a]

Period	Republic of China (Taiwan)	Japan	Belgium	Canada	Netherland	U.K.	U.S.
1952	5.2	24.1	8.6	15.9	18.2	6.4	10.4
1953	5.0	17.3	8.8	14.9	19.9	8.0	10.0
1954	3.2	18.2	8.1	10.6	20.5	8.0	8.9
1955	4.8	20.4	11.4	13.8	22.3	9.8	12.2
1956	4.7	25.5	13.4	16.8	19.3	10.4	12.8
1957	5.9	27.4	12.5	14.2	20.8	10.5	11.1
1958	5.0	24.2	12.4	11.5	20.8	9.9	8.2
1959	4.9	26.5	10.2	12.5	23.1	10.2	10.4
1960	7.5	27.7	10.2	7.8	22.6	10.9	8.1
1961	7.9	29.9	12.2	7.1	20.9	11.0	8.4
1962	7.5	28.4	13.1	10.1	19.0	9.4	9.0
1963	13.2	26.6	11.6	10.5	17.2	9.8	8.4
1964	15.7	25.2	15.5	11.8	19.8	11.2	9.8
1965	16.2	24.3	15.4	12.9	19.7	12.3	10.9
1966	19.6	24.7	15.1	14.2	19.0	11.5	10.3
1967	20.8	27.5	15.7	12.8	19.4	10.5	8.8
1968	21.3	29.4	14.7	12.4	20.7	11.3	9.0
1969	22.6	29.8	16.1	13.4	20.2	12.8	9.2
1970	24.1	31.3	18.7	11.4	19.8	12.9	6.9
1971	26.9	30.6	17.4	12.1	19.6	11.2	7.1
1972	29.1	30.4	17.5	13.1	20.1	9.6	8.0
1973	32.3	31.1	17.5	14.5	21.2	9.4	9.7
1974	29.3	27.3	18.0	15.2	19.3	7.4	6.8
1975	23.6	25.6	13.9	11.0	14.4	5.4	3.5

[a] For Taiwan, the source is *Taiwan Statistical Data Book*, 1978; for other countries, the source is *Yearbook of National Accounts Statistics*, 1976, United Nations.

TABLE 7

Gross Capital Formation as Percentage of Gross National Expenditure in Taiwan and Several Other Selected Countries[a]

Period	Republic of China (Taiwan)	Japan	Belgium	Canada	F.R.G.	Netherland	U.K.	U.S.
1952	14.4	27.8	14.9	23.7	23.8	18.6	13.2	17.1
1953	13.3	23.7	16.4	24.3	21.9	21.0	14.3	21.0
1954	14.8	26.4	15.9	21.3	24.0	24.9	13.7	16.6
1955	12.7	24.9	17.2	23.0	26.3	25.1	15.8	23.7
1956	15.0	28.4	19.1	27.8	25.4	26.6	15.7	23.2
1957	15.0	33.9	19.0	26.4	25.0	27.6	16.3	21.4
1958	16.3	28.1	17.1	23.5	24.3	23.6	15.6	20.1
1959	17.3	31.0	18.1	24.1	25.7	25.0	15.9	22.0
1960	18.6	34.2	18.9	21.2	29.4	27.7	17.3	17.7
1961	18.5	39.8	20.7	21.3	27.8	27.3	18.1	16.7
1962	17.6	35.8	20.9	22.2	27.4	25.8	16.8	17.8
1963	17.5	35.4	20.5	22.2	26.7	24.5	17.1	17.7
1964	19.2	36.1	23.4	23.3	28.5	27.6	20.0	17.8
1965	22.1	33.4	22.6	25.6	28.7	26.6	19.6	19.9
1966	23.0	34.1	23.3	26.4	26.8	26.8	29.2	19.9
1967	24.8	37.3	23.1	23.9	23.6	26.6	19.5	18.7
1968	25.7	38.3	22.2	22.8	26.1	27.4	19.9	18.8
1969	25.0	38.3	23.1	23.4	27.5	26.8	19.7	19.0
1970	26.0	39.8	24.6	21.5	29.1	27.7	19.7	17.5
1971	26.5	37.7	23.6	22.3	27.8	27.1	18.9	18.2
1972	25.3	37.5	22.5	22.4	27.1	25.1	18.5	18.9
1973	29.0	39.9	23.1	23.3	26.4	25.5	20.3	19.5
1974	35.4	37.8	24.9	25.1	23.6	24.6	20.7	19.3
1975	28.5	32.3	21.4	23.5	21.3	21.2	18.3	16.0

[a] For Taiwan, the source is *Taiwan Statistical Data Book*, 1978; for other countries, the source is *Yearbook of National Accounts Statistics*, 1976, United Nations.

for with a rapid growing gross national product and per capita income, savings become relatively effortless because of the ratchet effect in consumption, which enables domestic savings to grow like a snowball. In 1952, the percentage of national income saved in Taiwan was only 5.2%, which further declined to 3.2% in 1954. In 1963, the percentage of national income saved had already risen to 13.2%, surpassing the corresponding percentages of both the United Kingdom (9.8%) and the United States (8.4%). By 1973, the percentage saved had climbed to the outstanding level of 32.3%, commensurate to that of Japan (31.1%), and leaving most developed as well as developing countries far behind (see Table 6).

This kind of high domestic propensity to save, supplemented by a moderate amount of capital import, enabled the country to invest a very high percentage of the national product on productive capital formation without creating undue inflation. Thus gross capital formation as a percentage of gross national expenditure in Taiwan increased from 14.4% in 1952 and 14.8% in 1954, to 17.5% in 1963, which was already abreast with the United Kingdom and the United States. In 1974, the percentage for Taiwan had further risen to 35.4%, again comparable to that of Japan (37.9%) but surpassing all other countries, including West Germany (26.4 in 1973 and 23.6 in 1974). (See Table 7.) It is this kind of high level of domestic savings and investment, rather than any government stimulus to effective demand, that constituted the real forces making for the high rate of growth of real income in Taiwan.

On the whole, Taiwan, by following a trade policy and a monetary policy that were not so popular at the time, was able to achieve a remarkable success in developing export industries and promoting a rapid growth of her real national income. Nowadays it seems that more academic economists are coming around to favor this type of policy. For instance, Professor R. McKinnon of Stanford, in his book *Money and Capital in Economic Growth* (1973), now declares that devaluation towards the free trade equilibrium rate of exchange and lifting the interest rate above the rate of inflation are the sine qua non for successful economic development. The success story of Taiwan, therefore, offers us many lessons in development, trade, and monetary policies that should stand other developing countries in good stead. In particular, it points out a more humane and tested path of rapid economic development as an alternative to the harsh, yet by no means demonstrably successful, way of totalitarian regimentation enforced by the Communist countries.

REFERENCES

Keynes, J. M. (1937). The exante theory of the rate of interest, *Economic Journal* **47**, 663–669.

Machlup, F. (1956). The terms-of-trade effects of devaluation upon real income and the balance of trade. *Kyklos* X 4. Reprinted as *International Payments, Debts and Gold*, Chapter IX, pp. 195–222. New York: Scribners.

McKinnon, R. (1973). *Money and Capital in Economic Growth*. Washington, D.C.: Brookings Institute.

Smith, W. L. (1954). The effects of exchange rate adjustments on the standard of living. *American Economic Review* **44**, 808–825.

Sohmen, E. (1958). The effect of devaluation on the price level. *Quarterly Journal of Economics* **72**, 273–283.

Sohmen, E. (1961). *Flexible Exchange Rates Theory and Controversy*, Chapter VI. Chicago, Illinois: Univ. of Chicago Press.

Tsiang, S. C. (1949). Rehabilitation of time dimension of investment in macrodynamic analysis. *Economica N.S.* **16**, 204–217.

Tsiang, S. C. (1956). Liquidity preference and loanable funds theories of interest, multiplier and velocity analysis: A synthesis. *American Economic Review* **46**, 539–564.

Tsiang, S. C. (1967). Money and banking in Communist China. *In An Economic Profile of Mainland China*, pp. 323–339. Studies prepared for the Joint Economic Committee, Congress of the United States, Washington, D.C.

Tsiang, S. C. (1977a). *Keynes's Finance Demand for Liquidity, Robertson's Loanable Funds Theory and Friedman's Monetarism*. Discussion Paper No. 142, Department of Economics, Cornell University. [*Quarterly Journal of Economics* (to be published).]

Tsiang, S. C. (1977b). The monetary theoretic foundation of the modern monetary approach to the balance of payments. *Oxford Economic Papers* **30**, 312–338.

DEPARTMENT OF ECONOMICS
CORNELL UNIVERSITY
ITHACA, NEW YORK

ECONOMIC THEORY, ECONOMETRICS, AND MATHEMATICAL ECONOMICS

Consulting Editor: Karl Shell

UNIVERSITY OF PENNSYLVANIA
PHILADELPHIA, PENNSYLVANIA

Franklin M. Fisher and Karl Shell. **The Economic Theory of Price Indices:** *Two Essays on the Effects of Taste, Quality, and Technological Change*

Luis Eugenio Di Marco (Ed.). **International Economics and Development:** *Essays in Honor of Raúl Presbisch*

Erwin Klein. **Mathematical Methods in Theoretical Economics:** *Topological and Vector Space Foundations of Equilibrium Analysis*

Paul Zarembka (Ed.). **Frontiers in Econometrics**

George Horwich and Paul A. Samuelson (Eds.). **Trade, Stability, and Macroeconomics:** *Essays in Honor of Lloyd A. Metzler*

W. T. Ziemba and R. G. Vickson (Eds.). **Stochastic Optimization Models in Finance**

Steven A. Y. Lin (Ed.). **Theory and Measurement of Economic Externalities**

David Cass and Karl Shell (Eds.). **The Hamiltonian Approach to Dynamic Economics**

R. Shone. **Microeconomics:** *A Modern Treatment*

C. W. J. Granger and Paul Newbold. **Forecasting Economic Time Series**

Michael Szenberg, John W. Lombardi, and Eric Y. Lee. **Welfare Effects of Trade Restrictions:** *A Case Study of the U.S. Footwear Industry*

Haim Levy and Marshall Sarnat (Eds.). **Financial Decision Making under Uncertainty**

Yasuo Murata. **Mathematics for Stability and Optimization of Economic Systems**

Alan S. Blinder and Philip Friedman (Eds.). **Natural Resources, Uncertainty, and General Equilibrium Systems:** *Essays in Memory of Rafael Lusky*

Jerry S. Kelly. **Arrow Impossibility Theorems**

Peter Diamond and Michael Rothschild (Eds.). **Uncertainty in Economics:** *Readings and Exercises*

Fritz Machlup. **Methodology of Economics and Other Social Sciences**

Robert H. Frank and Richard T. Freeman. **Distributional Consequences of Direct Foreign Investment**

Elhanan Helpman and Assaf Razin. **A Theory of International Trade under Uncertainty**

Edmund S. Phelps. **Studies in Macroeconomic Theory, Volume 1:** *Employment and Inflation.* **Volume 2:** *Redistribution and Growth.*

Marc Nerlove, David M. Grether, and José L. Carvalho. **Analysis of Economic Time Series:** *A Synthesis*

Thomas J. Sargent. **Macroeconomic Theory**

Jerry Green and José Alexander Scheinkman (Eds.). **General Equilibrium, Growth and Trade:** *Essays in Honor of Lionel McKenzie*

Michael J. Boskin (Ed.). **Economics and Human Welfare:** *Essays in Honor of Tibor Scitovsky*

Carlos Daganzo. **Multinomial Probit:** *The Theory and Its Application to Demand Forecasting*

L. R. Klein, M. Nerlove, and S. C. Tsiang (Eds.). **Quantitative Economics and Development:** *Essays in Memory of Ta-Chung Liu*

In preparation

Giorgio P. Szegö. **Portfolio Theory with Application to Bank Asset Management**

M. June Flanders and Assaf Razin. **Development in an Inflationary World**